Shojo Beat

Kaze
HIKARU

20

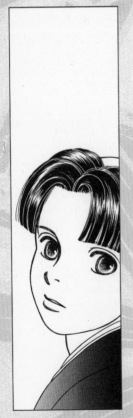

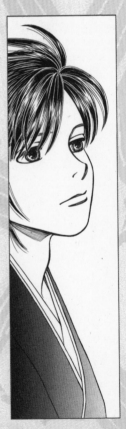

Story & Art by
Taeko Watanabe

Contents

Story Thus Far

It is the end of the Bakufu era, the third year of Bunkyu (1863) in Kyoto. The Shinsengumi is a band of warriors formed to protect the shogun.

Tominaga Sei, the daughter of a former Bakufu *bushi*, joined the Shinsengumi disguised as a boy by the name of Kamiya Seizaburo to avenge her father and brother. She has continued her training under the only person in the Shinsengumi who knows her true identity, Okita Soji, and she aspires to become a true *bushi*.

Foreign forces have come to the offshore of Hyogo. While scouting the city of Osaka, which has been thrown into chaos, Sei and Okita meet a pleasure-seeker named Ukinosuke. Unknown to them, he is Hitotsubashi Yoshinobu, who would later become the last shogun of the Tokugawa Bakufu. Yoshinobu demonstrates his skills by neutralizing rising tensions between the Bakufu and the Imperial Court.

Kondo and Ito have traveled to Osaka to examine the Choshu forces. Sei and Okita meet a photographer who talks them into taking their picture together. But this simple act results in dramatic, unforeseen consequences!

Characters

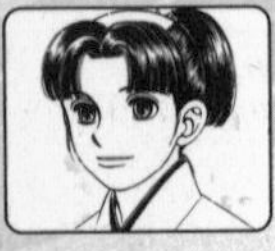

Tominaga Sei

She disguises herself as a boy to enter the Mibu-Roshi. She trains under Soji, aspiring to become a true *bushi*. But secretly, she is in love with Soji.

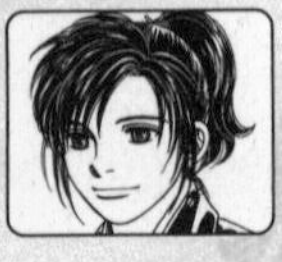

Okita Soji

Assistant vice captain of the Shinsengumi and licensed master of the Ten'nen Rishin-Ryu. He supports the troop alongside Kondo and Hijikata and guides Seizaburo with a kind yet firm hand.

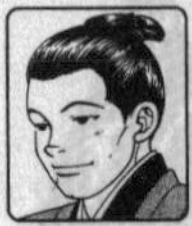

Kondo Isami

Captain of the Shinsengumi and fourth grandmaster of the Ten'nen Rishin-ryu. A passionate, warm and well-respected leader.

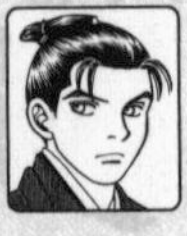

Hijikata Toshizo

Vice captain of the Shinsengumi. He commands both the group and himself with a rigid strictness. He is also known as the "Oni vice captain."

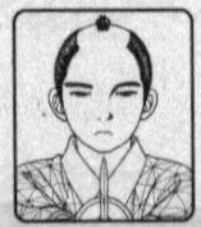

Saito Hajime

Assistant Vice Captain. He was a friend of Sei's older brother. Sei is attached to him in place of her lost brother.

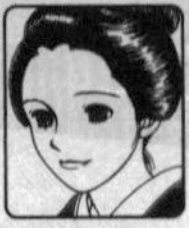

Sato

Formerly known as the Shimabara geisha, Akesato. After the death of her love, Yamanami, she has supported Sei as "Seizaburo's lover."

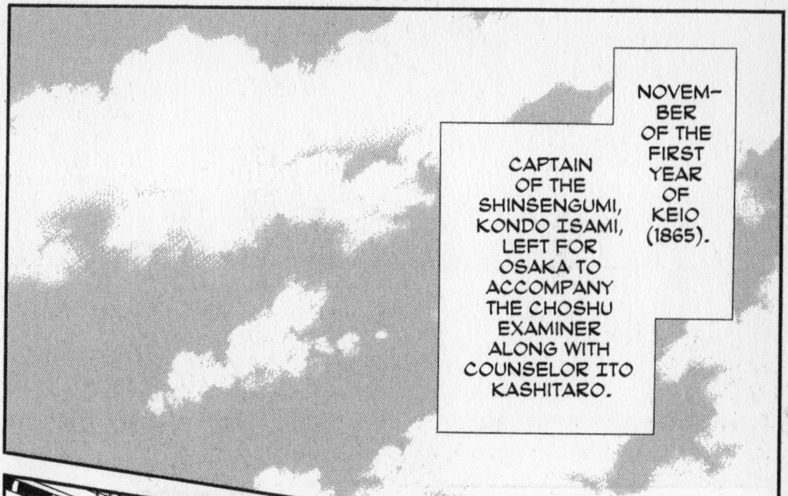
NOVEMBER OF THE FIRST YEAR OF KEIO (1865).
CAPTAIN OF THE SHINSENGUMI, KONDO ISAMI, LEFT FOR OSAKA TO ACCOMPANY THE CHOSHU EXAMINER ALONG WITH COUNSELOR ITO KASHITARO.
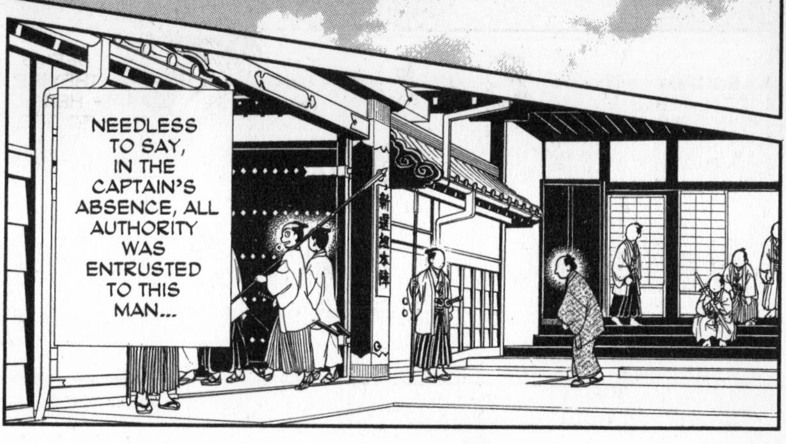
NEEDLESS TO SAY, IN THE CAPTAIN'S ABSENCE, ALL AUTHORITY WAS ENTRUSTED TO THIS MAN...
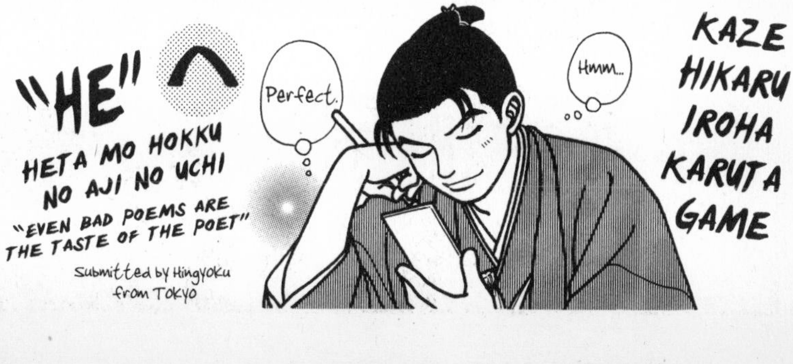
KAZE HIKARU IROHA KARUTA GAME
"HE" へ
HETA MO HOKKU NO AJI NO UCHI
"EVEN BAD POEMS ARE THE TASTE OF THE POET"
Submitted by Hingyoku from Tokyo
Hmm...
Perfect.

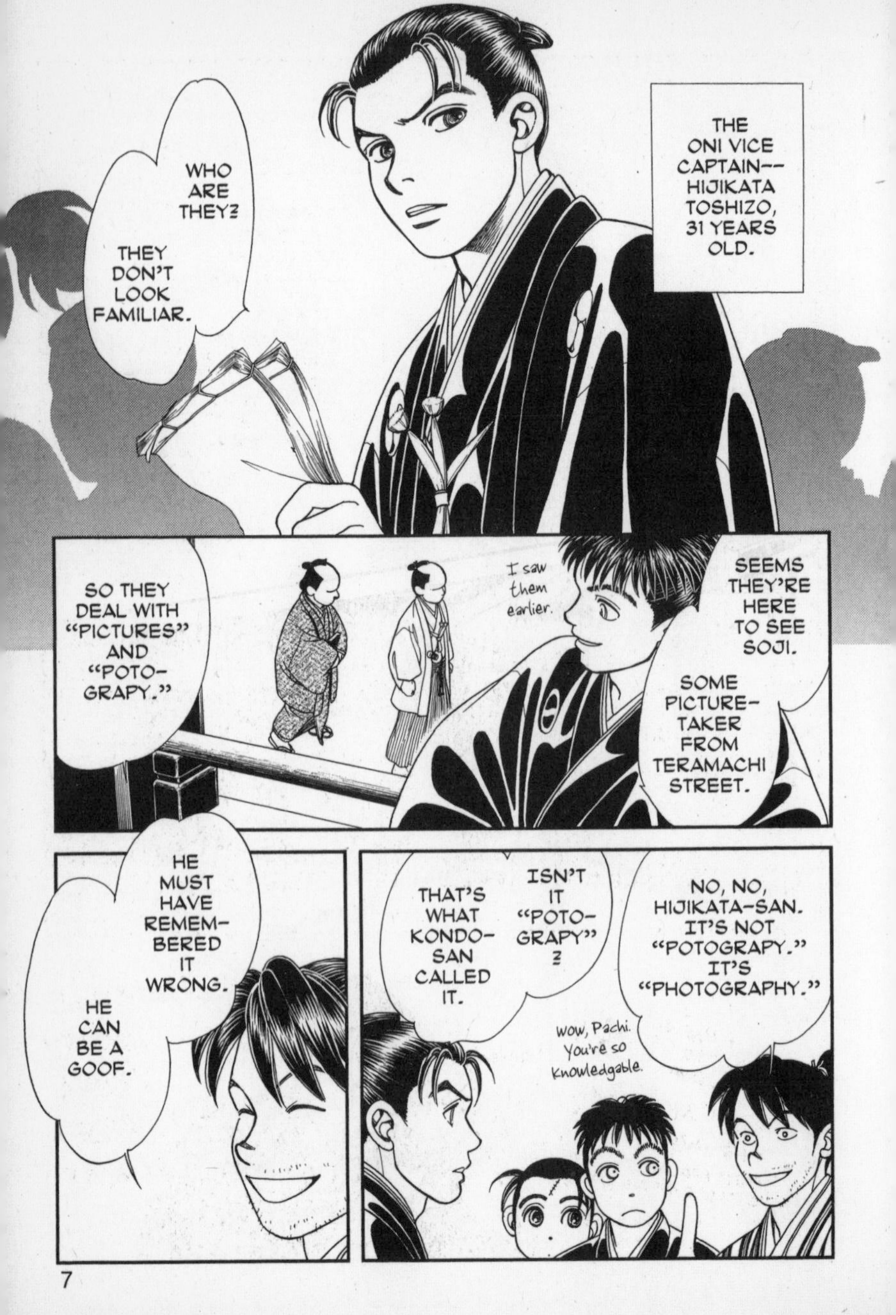
THE ONI VICE CAPTAIN--HIJIKATA TOSHIZO, 31 YEARS OLD.
WHO ARE THEY?
THEY DON'T LOOK FAMILIAR.
SEEMS THEY'RE HERE TO SEE SOJI.
SOME PICTURE-TAKER FROM TERAMACHI STREET.
I saw them earlier.
SO THEY DEAL WITH "PICTURES" AND "POTOGRAPY."
NO, NO, HIJIKATA-SAN. IT'S NOT "POTOGRAPY." IT'S "PHOTOGRAPHY."
Wow, Pachi. You're so knowledgable.
ISN'T IT "POTOGRAPY"?
THAT'S WHAT KONDO-SAN CALLED IT.
HE MUST HAVE REMEMBERED IT WRONG.
HE CAN BE A GOOF.

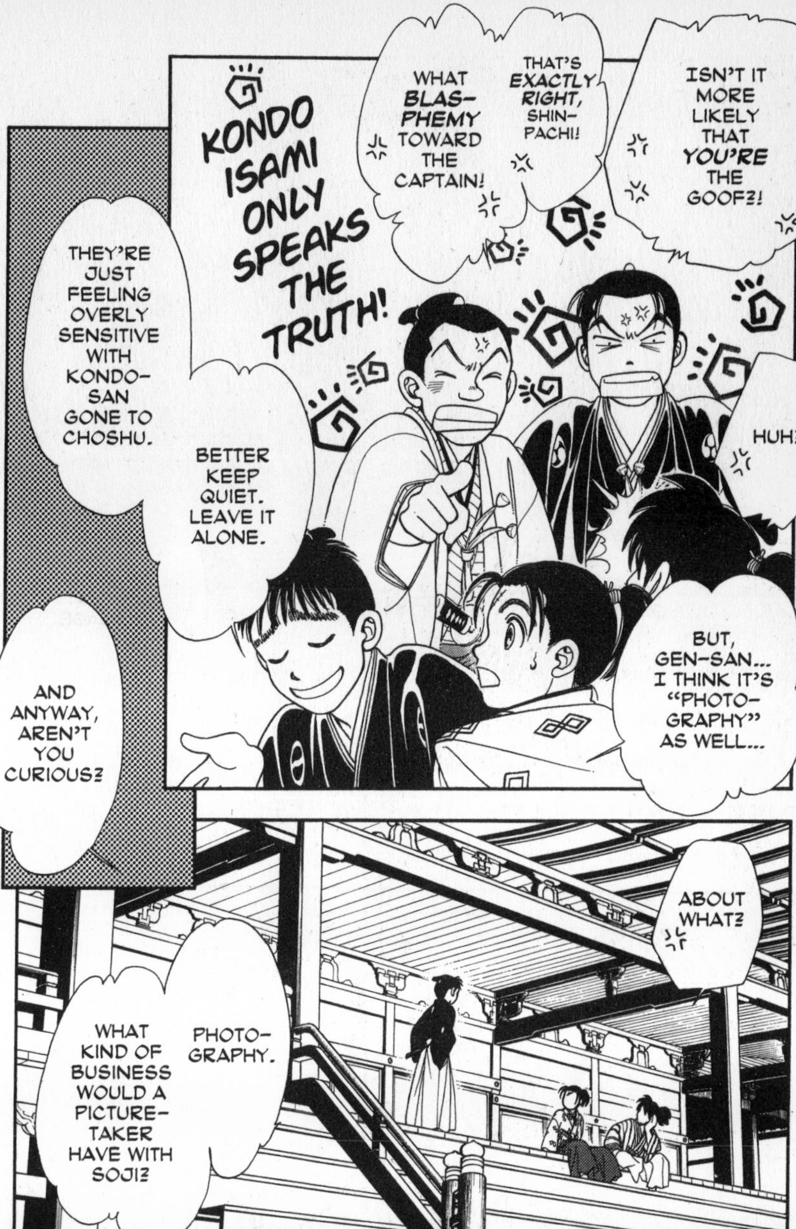
KONDO ISAMI ONLY SPEAKS THE TRUTH!
WHAT BLASPHEMY TOWARD THE CAPTAIN!
THAT'S EXACTLY RIGHT, SHINPACHI!
ISN'T IT MORE LIKELY THAT YOU'RE THE GOOF?!
HUH?!
BETTER KEEP QUIET. LEAVE IT ALONE.
THEY'RE JUST FEELING OVERLY SENSITIVE WITH KONDO-SAN GONE TO CHOSHU.
BUT, GEN-SAN... I THINK IT'S "PHOTOGRAPHY" AS WELL...
AND ANYWAY, AREN'T YOU CURIOUS?
ABOUT WHAT?
PHOTOGRAPHY.
WHAT KIND OF BUSINESS WOULD A PICTURE-TAKER HAVE WITH SOJI?

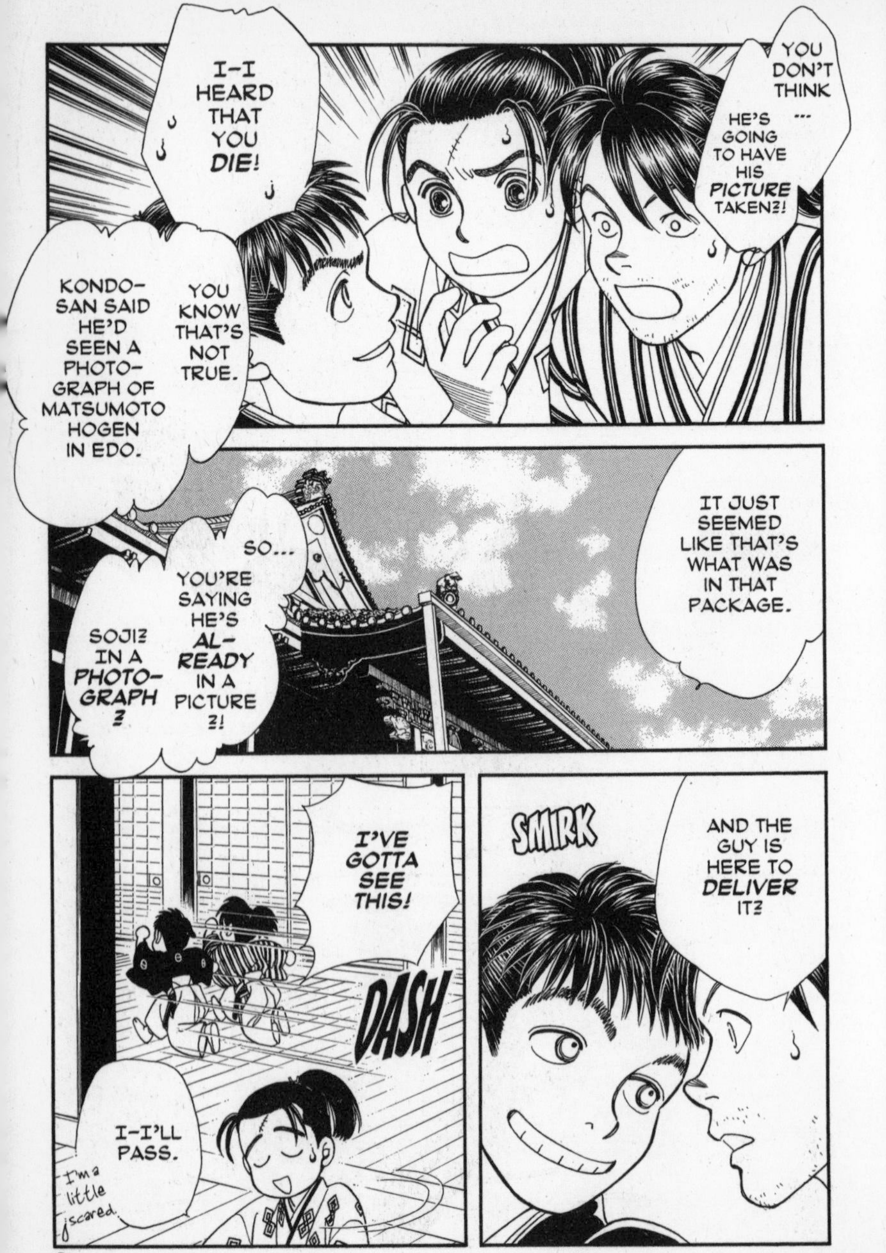
YOU DON'T THINK ... HE'S GOING TO HAVE HIS PICTURE TAKEN?!
I-I HEARD THAT YOU DIE!
YOU KNOW THAT'S NOT TRUE.
KONDO-SAN SAID HE'D SEEN A PHOTOGRAPH OF MATSUMOTO HOGEN IN EDO.
IT JUST SEEMED LIKE THAT'S WHAT WAS IN THAT PACKAGE.
SO... YOU'RE SAYING HE'S ALREADY IN A PICTURE?!
SOJI? IN A PHOTOGRAPH?
SMIRK
AND THE GUY IS HERE TO DELIVER IT?
I'VE GOTTA SEE THIS!
DASH
I-I'LL PASS.
I'm a little scared.

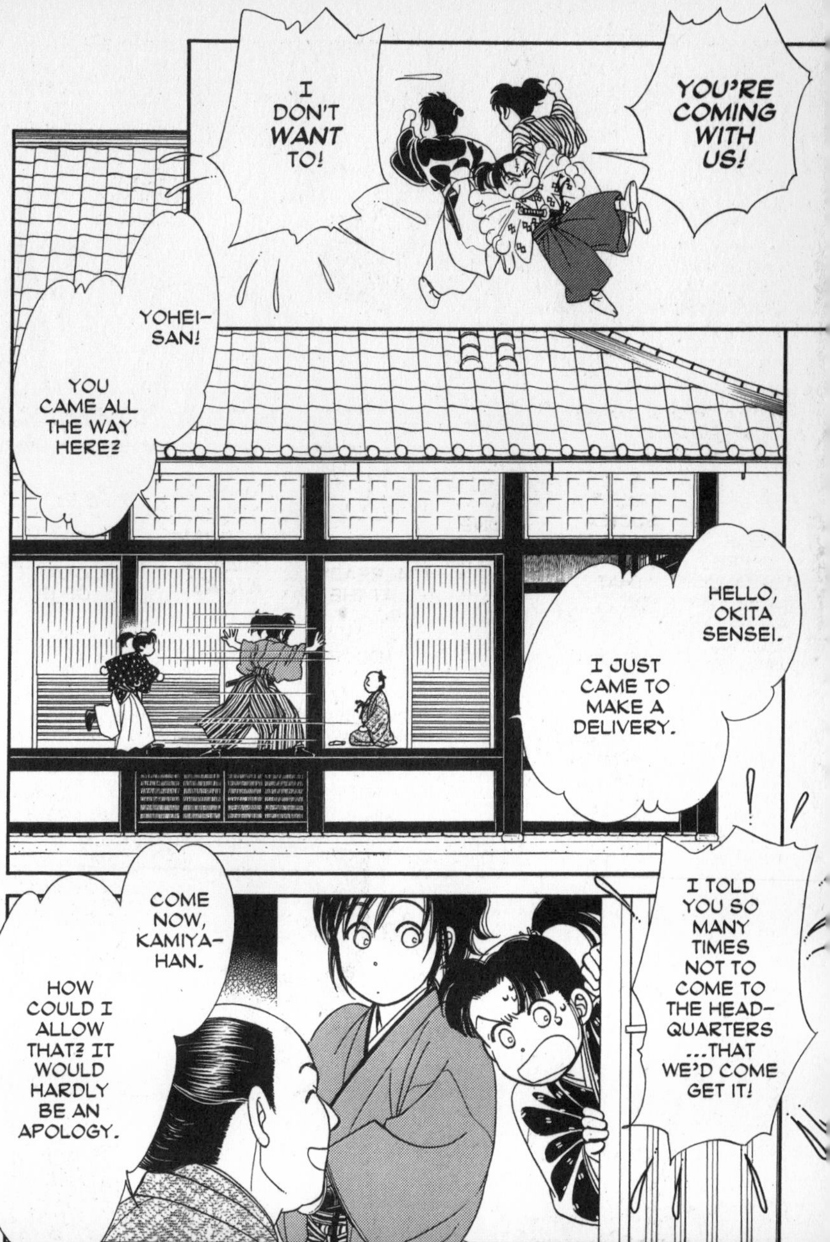
YOU'RE COMING WITH US!
I DON'T WANT TO!
YOHEI-SAN! YOU CAME ALL THE WAY HERE?
HELLO, OKITA SENSEI. I JUST CAME TO MAKE A DELIVERY.
I TOLD YOU SO MANY TIMES NOT TO COME TO THE HEAD-QUARTERS ...THAT WE'D COME GET IT!
COME NOW, KAMIYA-HAN.
HOW COULD I ALLOW THAT? IT WOULD HARDLY BE AN APOLOGY.

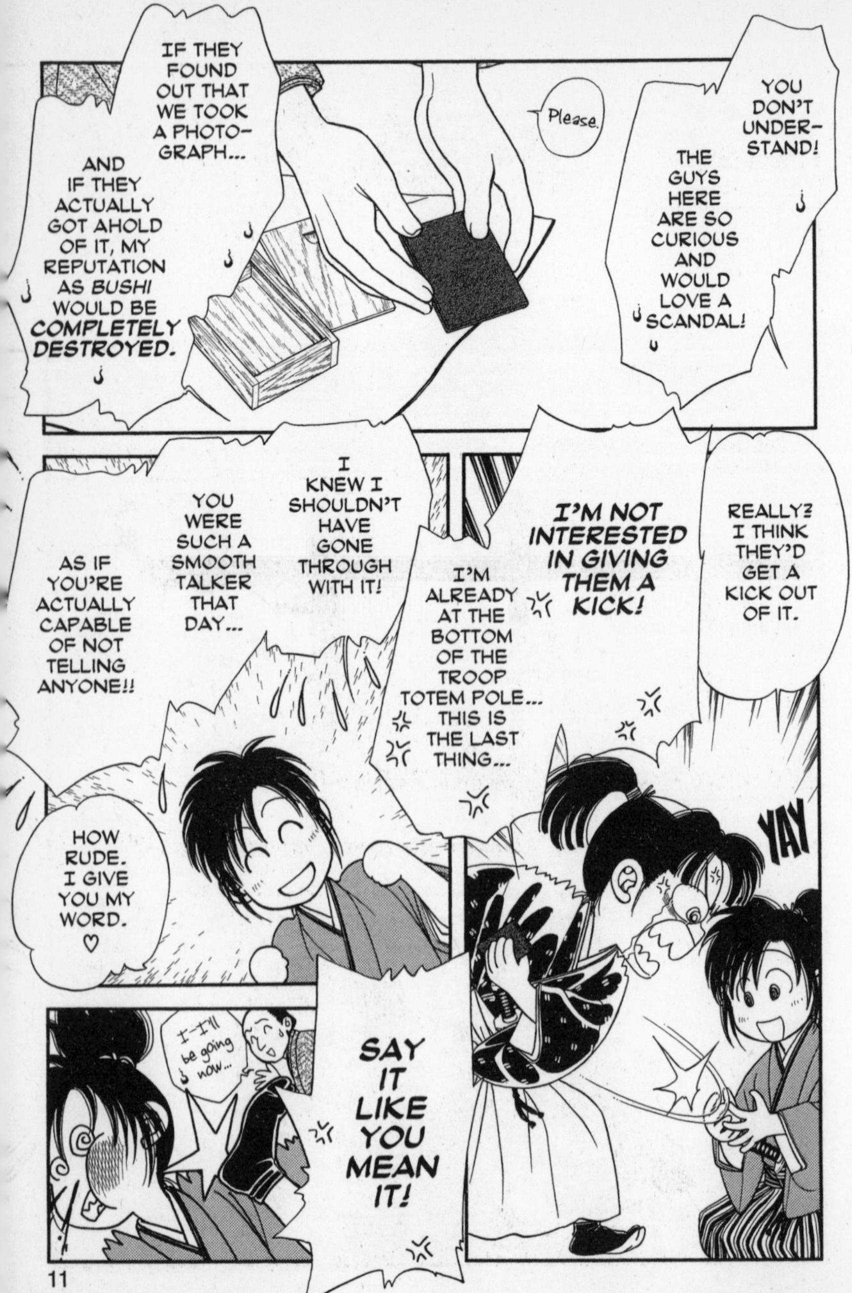
YOU DON'T UNDERSTAND!
THE GUYS HERE ARE SO CURIOUS AND WOULD LOVE A SCANDAL!
Please.
IF THEY FOUND OUT THAT WE TOOK A PHOTOGRAPH...
AND IF THEY ACTUALLY GOT AHOLD OF IT, MY REPUTATION AS *BUSHI* WOULD BE **COMPLETELY DESTROYED.**
REALLY? I THINK THEY'D GET A KICK OUT OF IT.
I'M NOT INTERESTED IN GIVING THEM A KICK!
I'M ALREADY AT THE BOTTOM OF THE TROOP TOTEM POLE... THIS IS THE LAST THING...
YAY
I KNEW I SHOULDN'T HAVE GONE THROUGH WITH IT!
YOU WERE SUCH A SMOOTH TALKER THAT DAY...
AS IF YOU'RE ACTUALLY CAPABLE OF NOT TELLING ANYONE!!
HOW RUDE. I GIVE YOU MY WORD. ♡
SAY IT LIKE YOU MEAN IT!
I-I'll be going now...

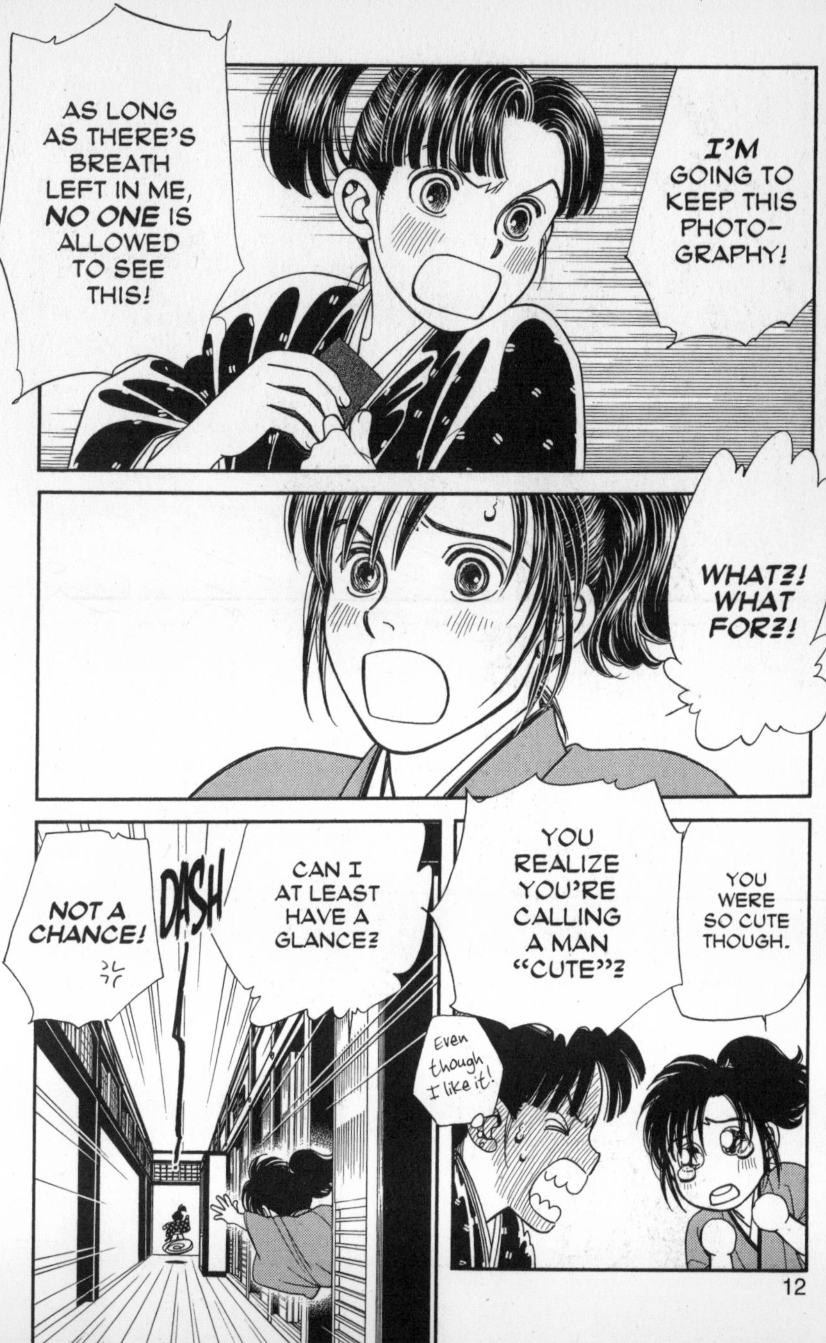
I'M GOING TO KEEP THIS PHOTOGRAPHY!
AS LONG AS THERE'S BREATH LEFT IN ME, NO ONE IS ALLOWED TO SEE THIS!
WHAT?! WHAT FOR?!
YOU WERE SO CUTE THOUGH.
YOU REALIZE YOU'RE CALLING A MAN "CUTE"?
Even though I like it!
CAN I AT LEAST HAVE A GLANCE?
DASH
NOT A CHANCE!

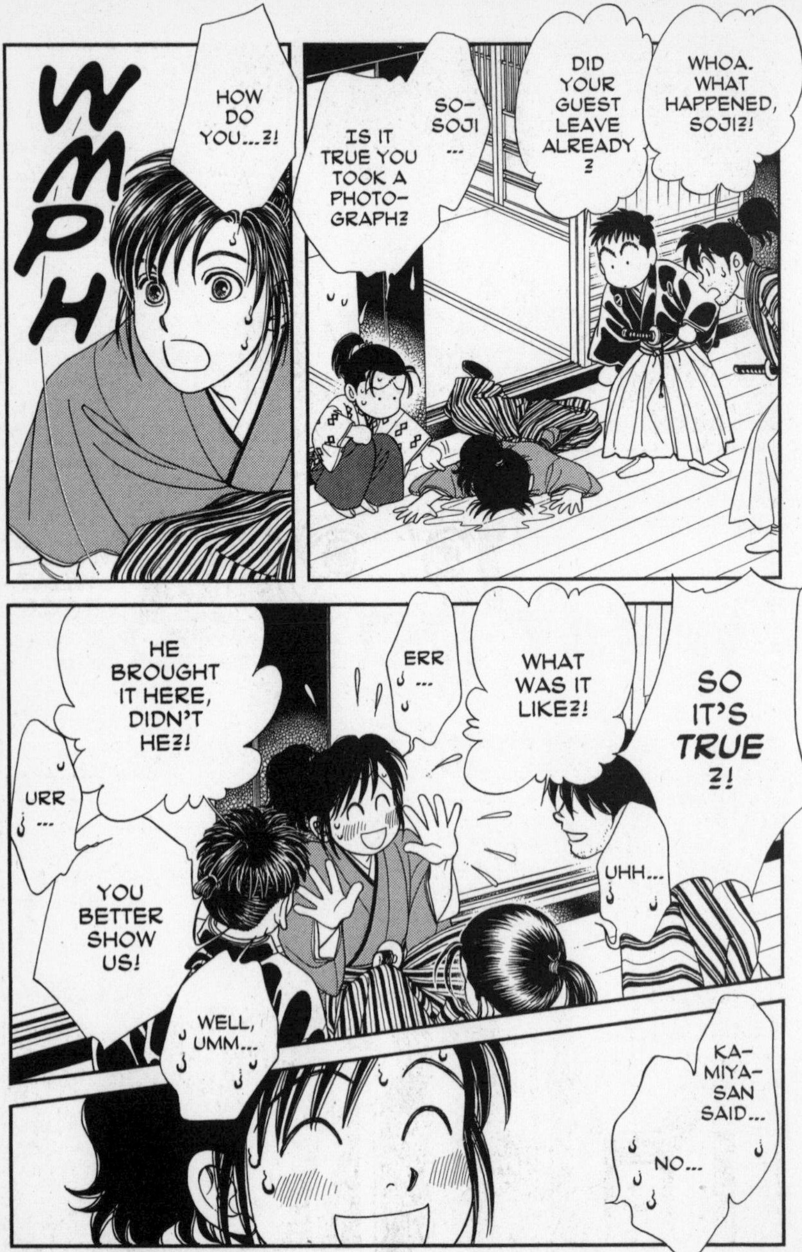
WHOA. WHAT HAPPENED, SOJI?!
DID YOUR GUEST LEAVE ALREADY?
SO-SOJI...
IS IT TRUE YOU TOOK A PHOTOGRAPH?
HOW DO YOU...?!
WMPH
SO IT'S TRUE?!
WHAT WAS IT LIKE?!
ERR...
HE BROUGHT IT HERE, DIDN'T HE?!
URR...
UHH...
YOU BETTER SHOW US!
WELL, UMM...
KA-MIYA-SAN SAID...
NO...

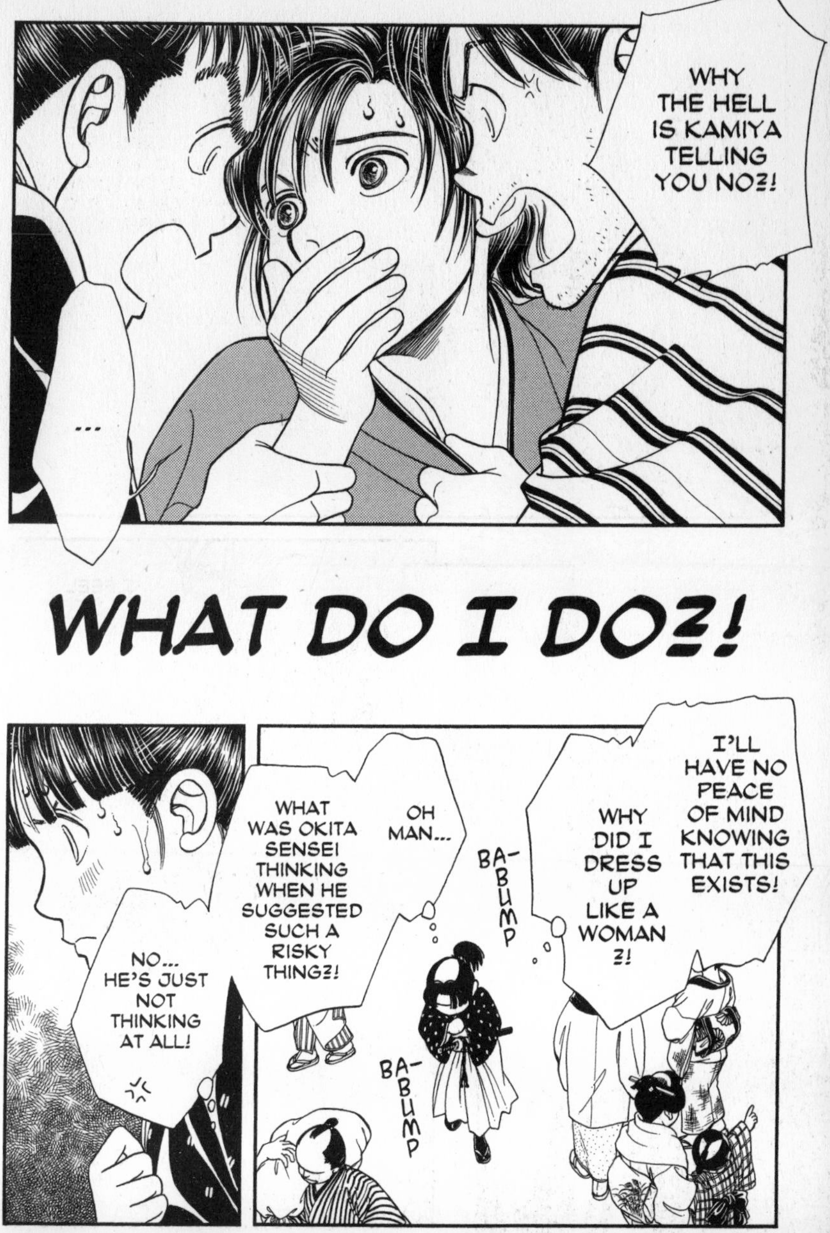
WHY THE HELL IS KAMIYA TELLING YOU NO?!
...
WHAT DO I DO?!
I'LL HAVE NO PEACE OF MIND KNOWING THAT THIS EXISTS!
WHY DID I DRESS UP LIKE A WOMAN?!
BA-BUMP
OH MAN...
WHAT WAS OKITA SENSEI THINKING WHEN HE SUGGESTED SUCH A RISKY THING?!
BA-BUMP
NO... HE'S JUST NOT THINKING AT ALL!

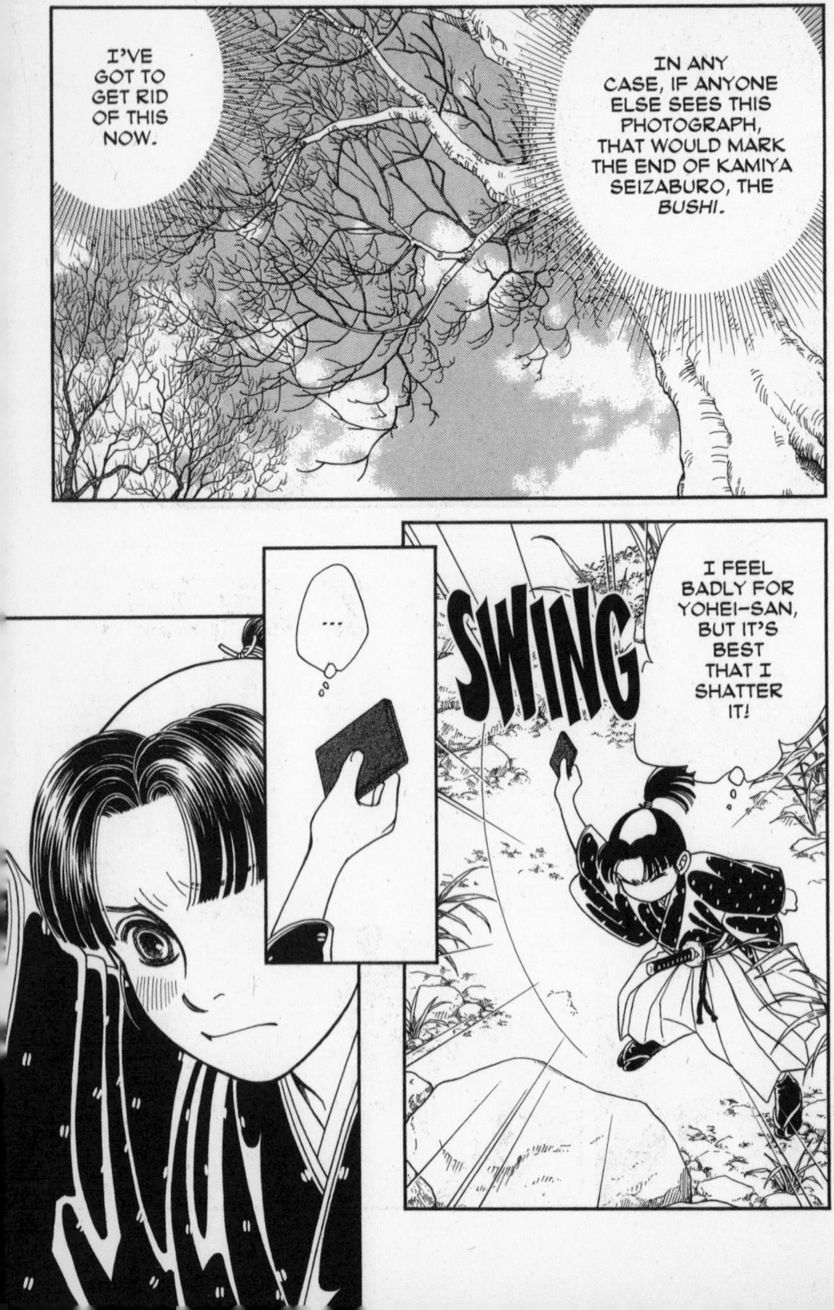
IN ANY CASE, IF ANYONE ELSE SEES THIS PHOTOGRAPH, THAT WOULD MARK THE END OF KAMIYA SEIZABURO, THE *BUSHI*.
I'VE GOT TO GET RID OF THIS NOW.
I FEEL BADLY FOR YOHEI-SAN, BUT IT'S BEST THAT I SHATTER IT!
SWING
...

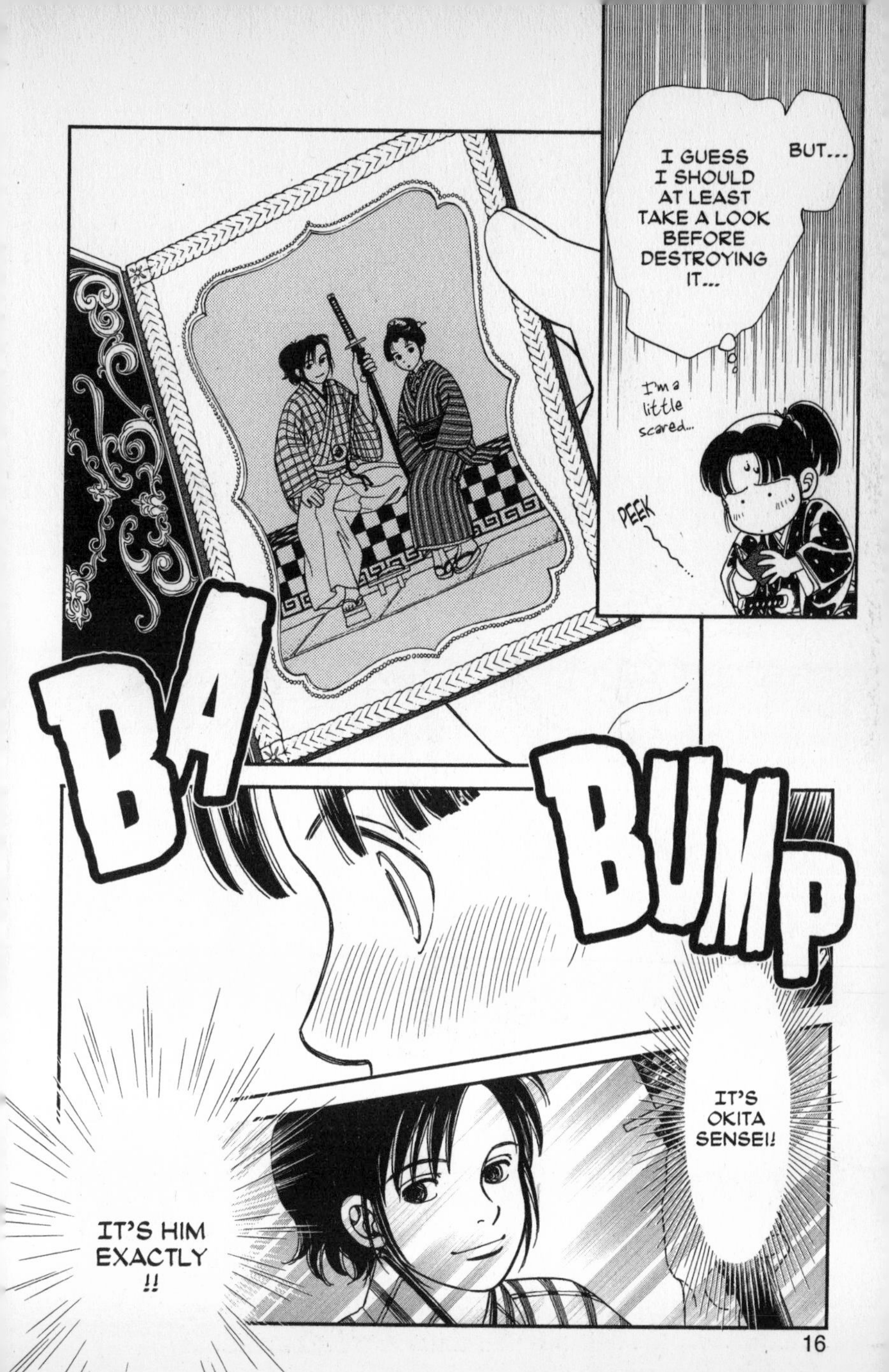
I GUESS I SHOULD AT LEAST TAKE A LOOK BEFORE DESTROYING IT...
BUT...
I'm a little scared...
PEEK
BA
BUMP
IT'S OKITA SENSEI!
IT'S HIM EXACTLY !!

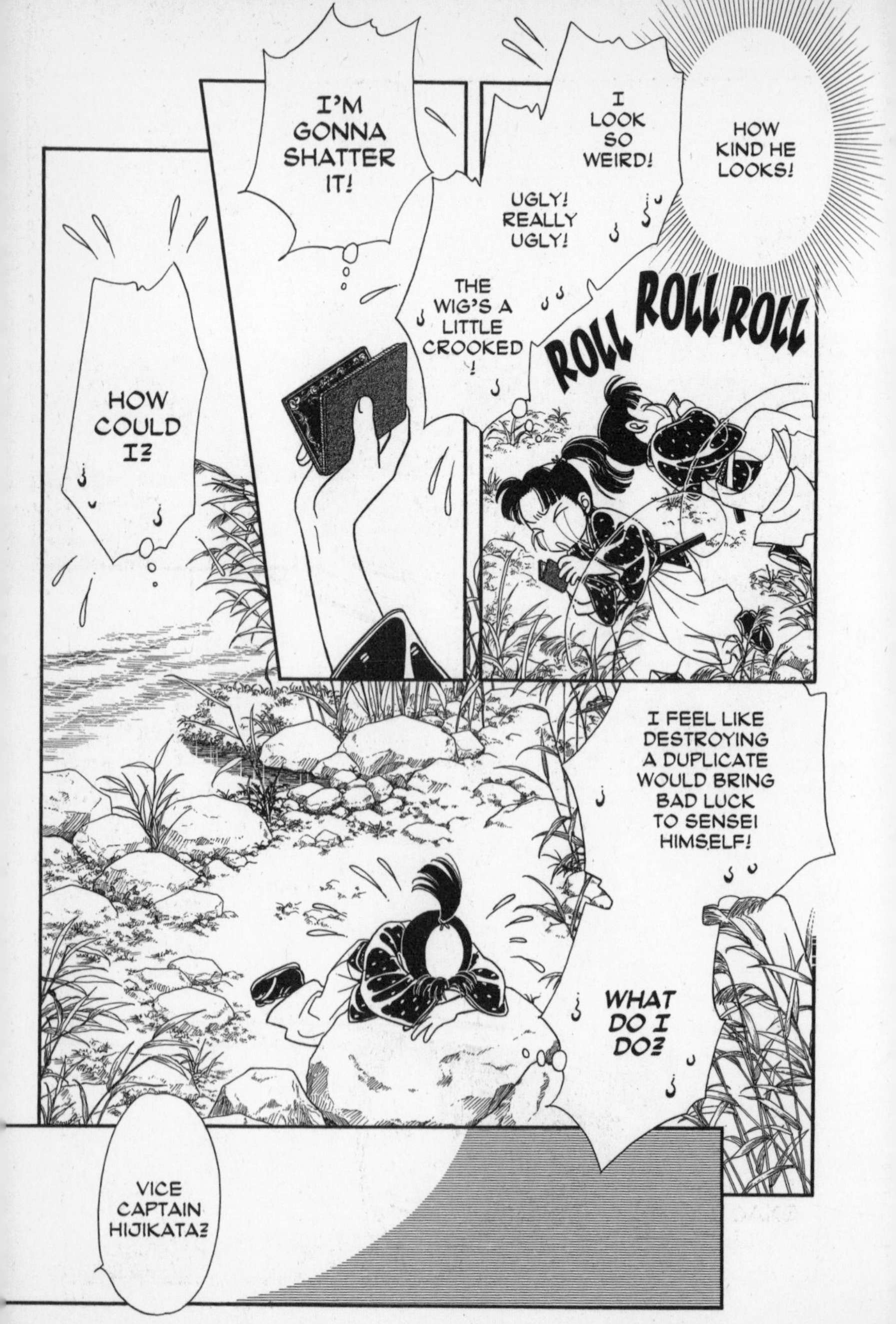
HOW KIND HE LOOKS!
I LOOK SO WEIRD!
UGLY! REALLY UGLY!
ROLL ROLL ROLL
THE WIG'S A LITTLE CROOKED!
I'M GONNA SHATTER IT!
HOW COULD I?
I FEEL LIKE DESTROYING A DUPLICATE WOULD BRING BAD LUCK TO SENSEI HIMSELF!
WHAT DO I DO?
VICE CAPTAIN HIJIKATA?

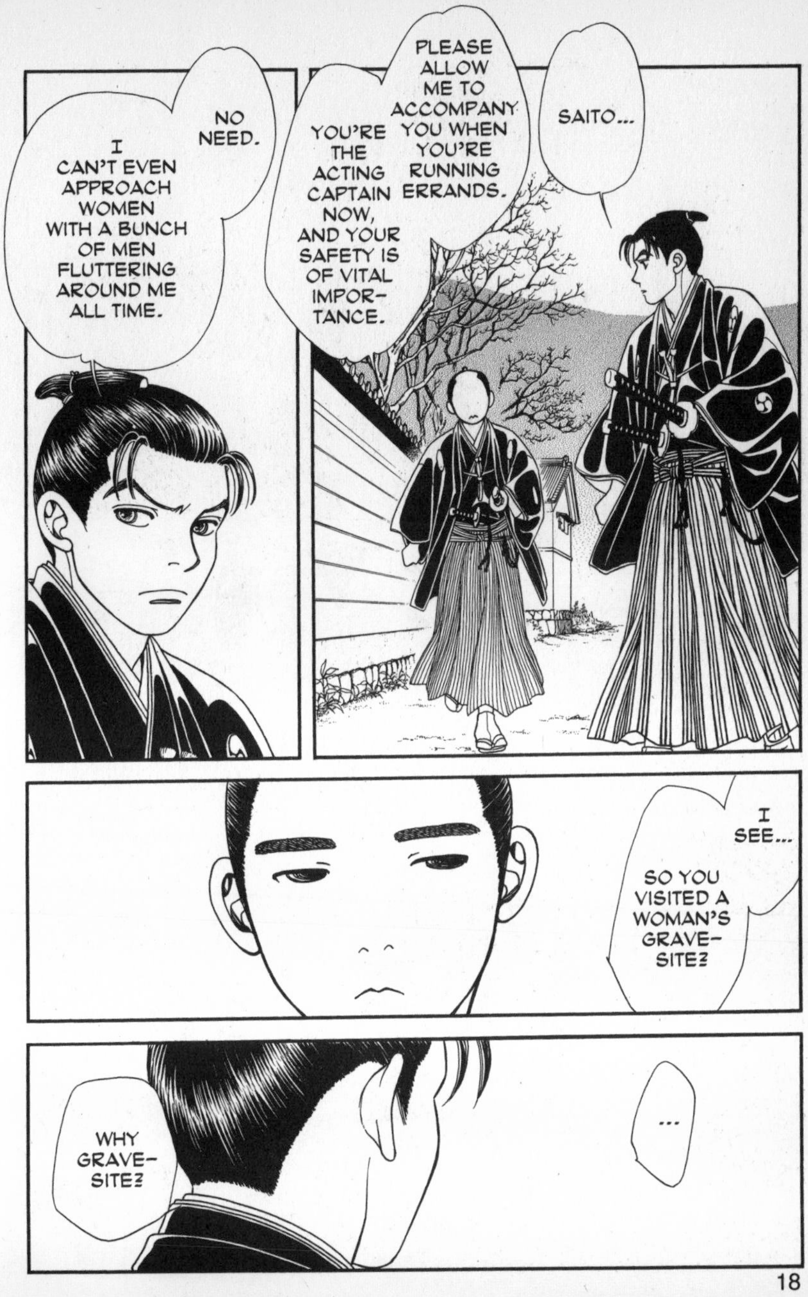
SAITO...
PLEASE ALLOW ME TO ACCOMPANY YOU WHEN YOU'RE RUNNING ERRANDS.
YOU'RE THE ACTING CAPTAIN NOW, AND YOUR SAFETY IS OF VITAL IMPOR-TANCE.
NO NEED.
I CAN'T EVEN APPROACH WOMEN WITH A BUNCH OF MEN FLUTTERING AROUND ME ALL TIME.
I SEE...
SO YOU VISITED A WOMAN'S GRAVE-SITE?
...
WHY GRAVE-SITE?

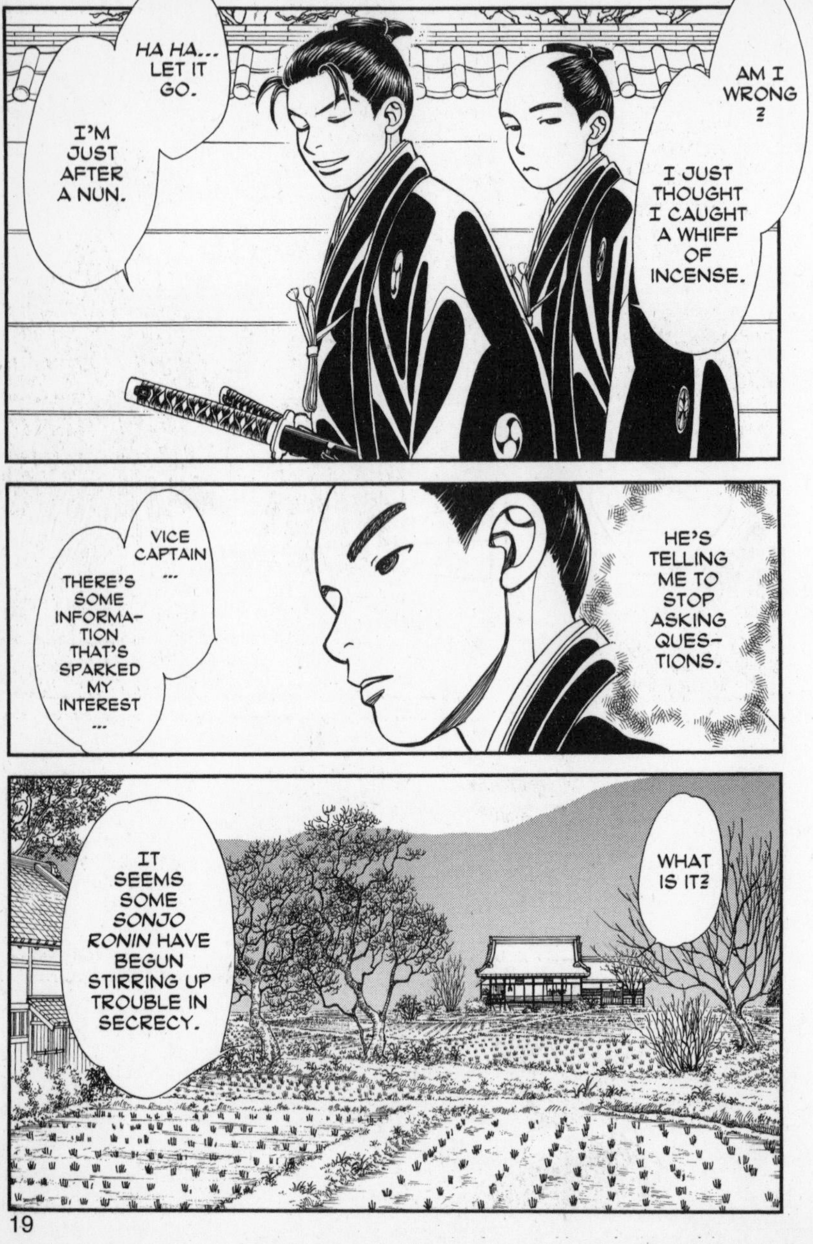
AM I WRONG?
I JUST THOUGHT I CAUGHT A WHIFF OF INCENSE.
HA HA... LET IT GO.
I'M JUST AFTER A NUN.
HE'S TELLING ME TO STOP ASKING QUES-TIONS.
VICE CAPTAIN...
THERE'S SOME INFORMA-TION THAT'S SPARKED MY INTEREST...
WHAT IS IT?
IT SEEMS SOME SONJO RONIN HAVE BEGUN STIRRING UP TROUBLE IN SECRECY.

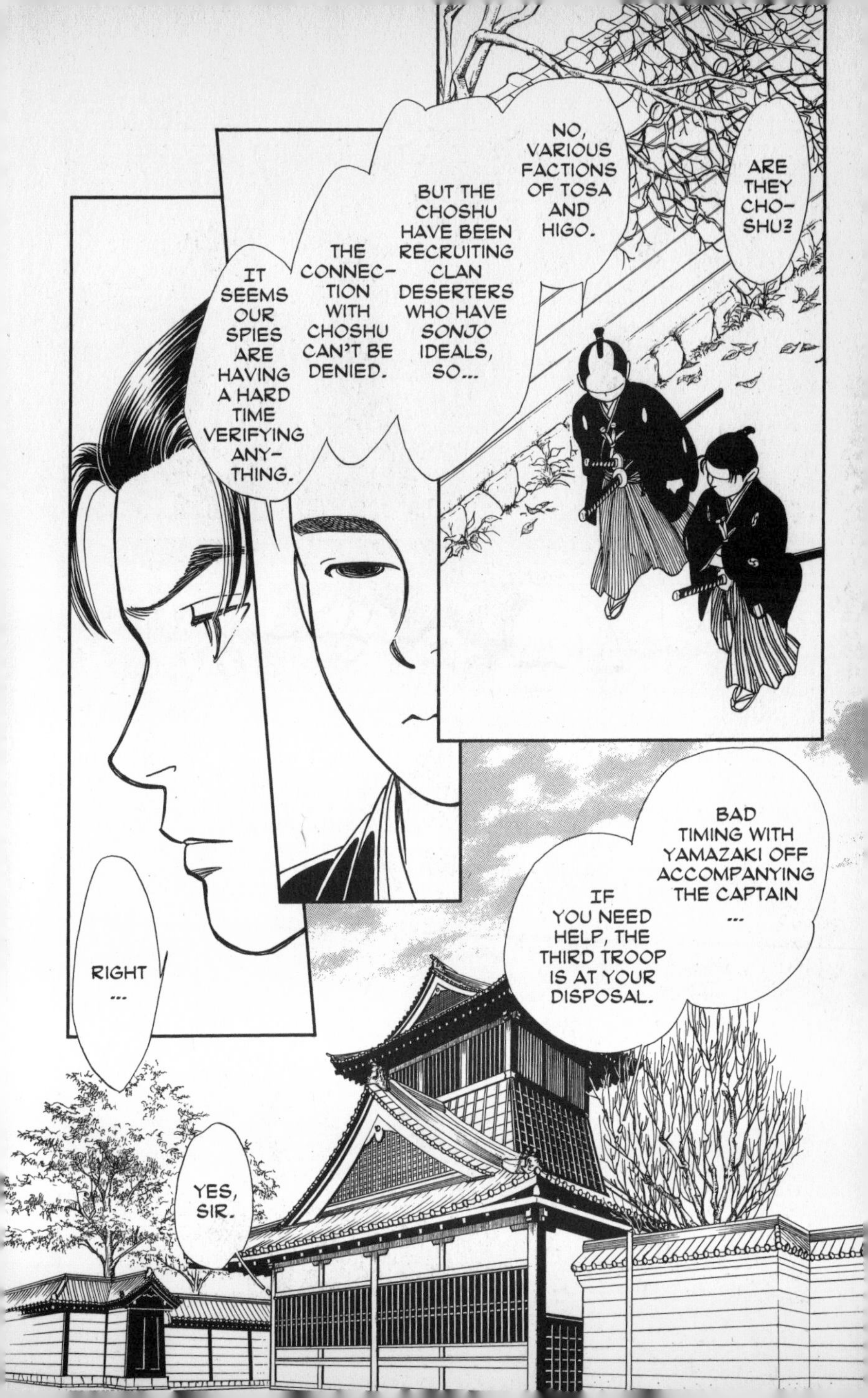
ARE THEY CHO-SHU?
NO, VARIOUS FACTIONS OF TOSA AND HIGO.
BUT THE CHOSHU HAVE BEEN RECRUITING CLAN DESERTERS WHO HAVE *SONJO* IDEALS, SO...
THE CONNECTION WITH CHOSHU CAN'T BE DENIED.
IT SEEMS OUR SPIES ARE HAVING A HARD TIME VERIFYING ANYTHING.
BAD TIMING WITH YAMAZAKI OFF ACCOMPANYING THE CAPTAIN...
IF YOU NEED HELP, THE THIRD TROOP IS AT YOUR DISPOSAL.
RIGHT...
YES, SIR.

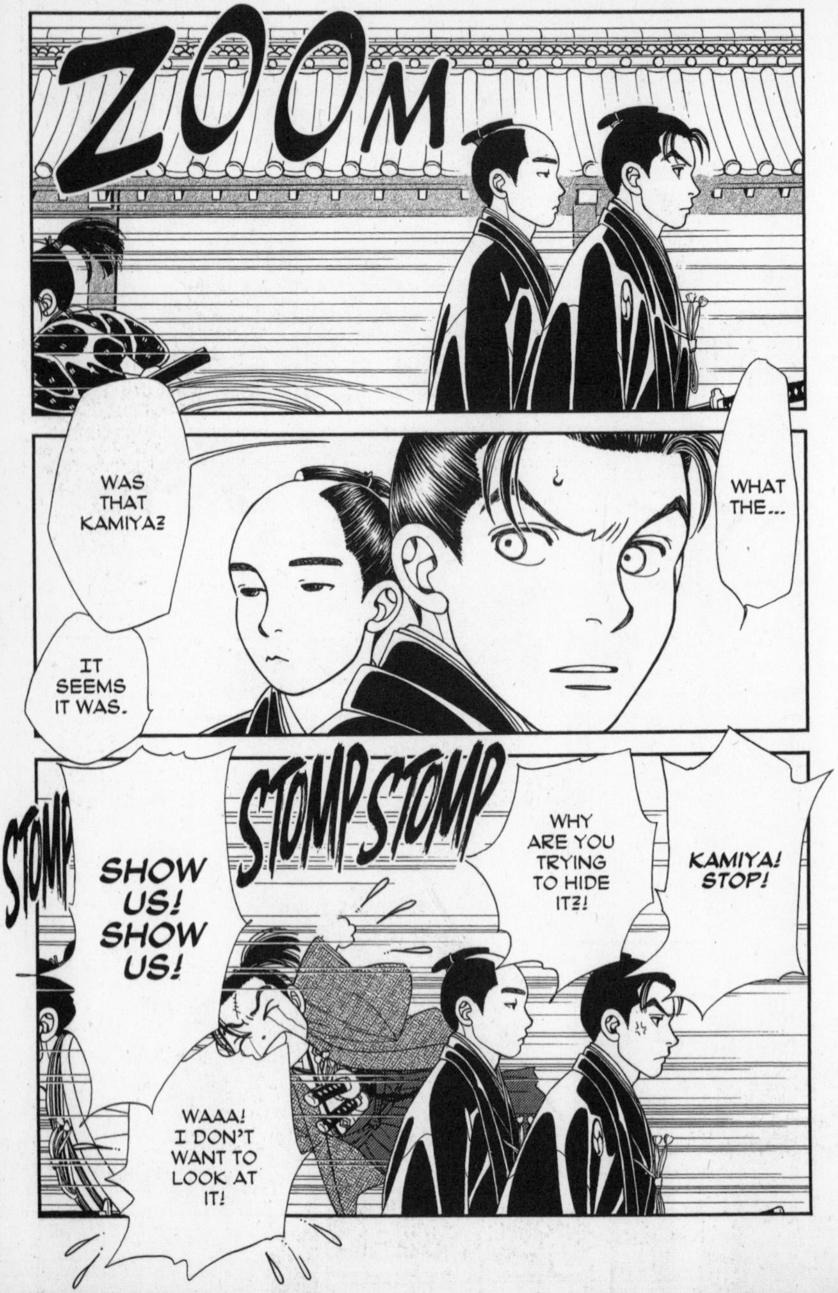
ZOOM
WHAT THE...
WAS THAT KAMIYA?
IT SEEMS IT WAS.
KAMIYA! STOP!
WHY ARE YOU TRYING TO HIDE IT?!
STOMP STOMP
SHOW US! SHOW US!
STOMP
WAAA! I DON'T WANT TO LOOK AT IT!

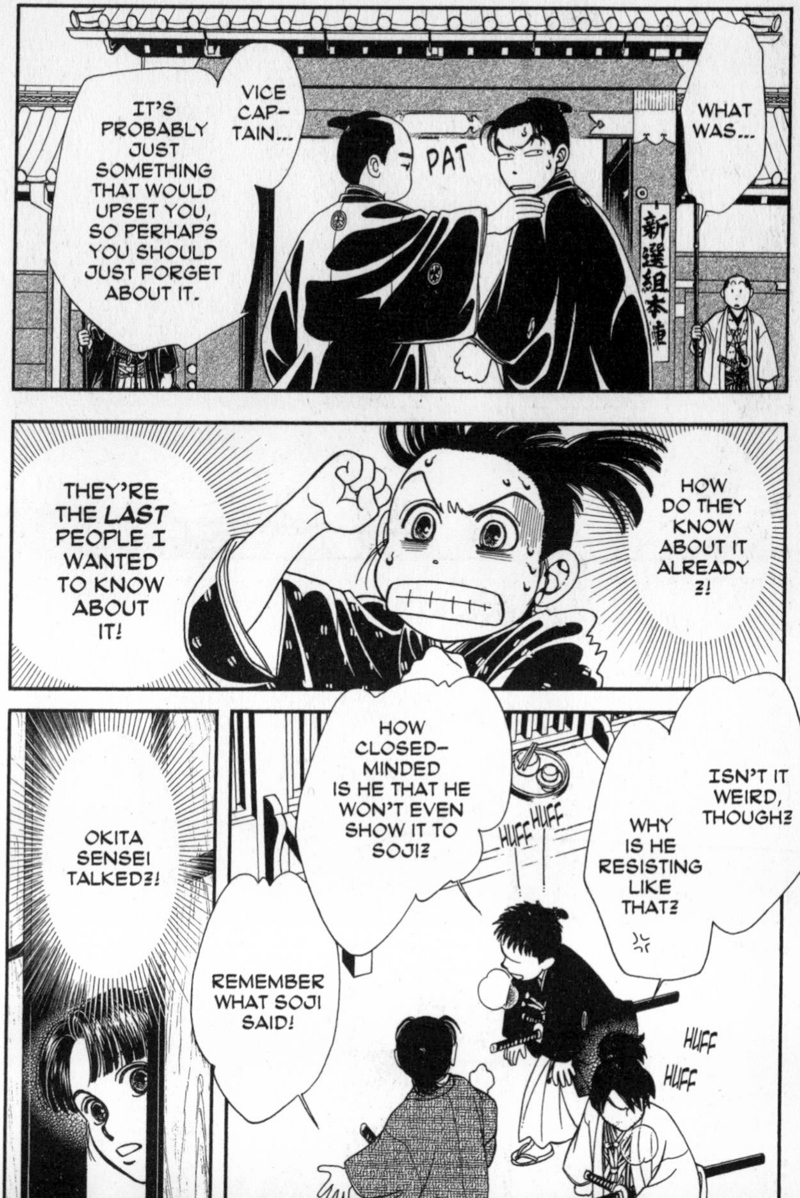
WHAT WAS...
PAT
VICE CAPTAIN...
IT'S PROBABLY JUST SOMETHING THAT WOULD UPSET YOU, SO PERHAPS YOU SHOULD JUST FORGET ABOUT IT.
新選組本陣
HOW DO THEY KNOW ABOUT IT ALREADY?!
THEY'RE THE *LAST* PEOPLE I WANTED TO KNOW ABOUT IT!
ISN'T IT WEIRD, THOUGH?
WHY IS HE RESISTING LIKE THAT?
HOW CLOSED-MINDED IS HE THAT HE WON'T EVEN SHOW IT TO SOJI?
HUFF HUFF
REMEMBER WHAT SOJI SAID!
HUFF
HUFF
OKITA SENSEI TALKED?!

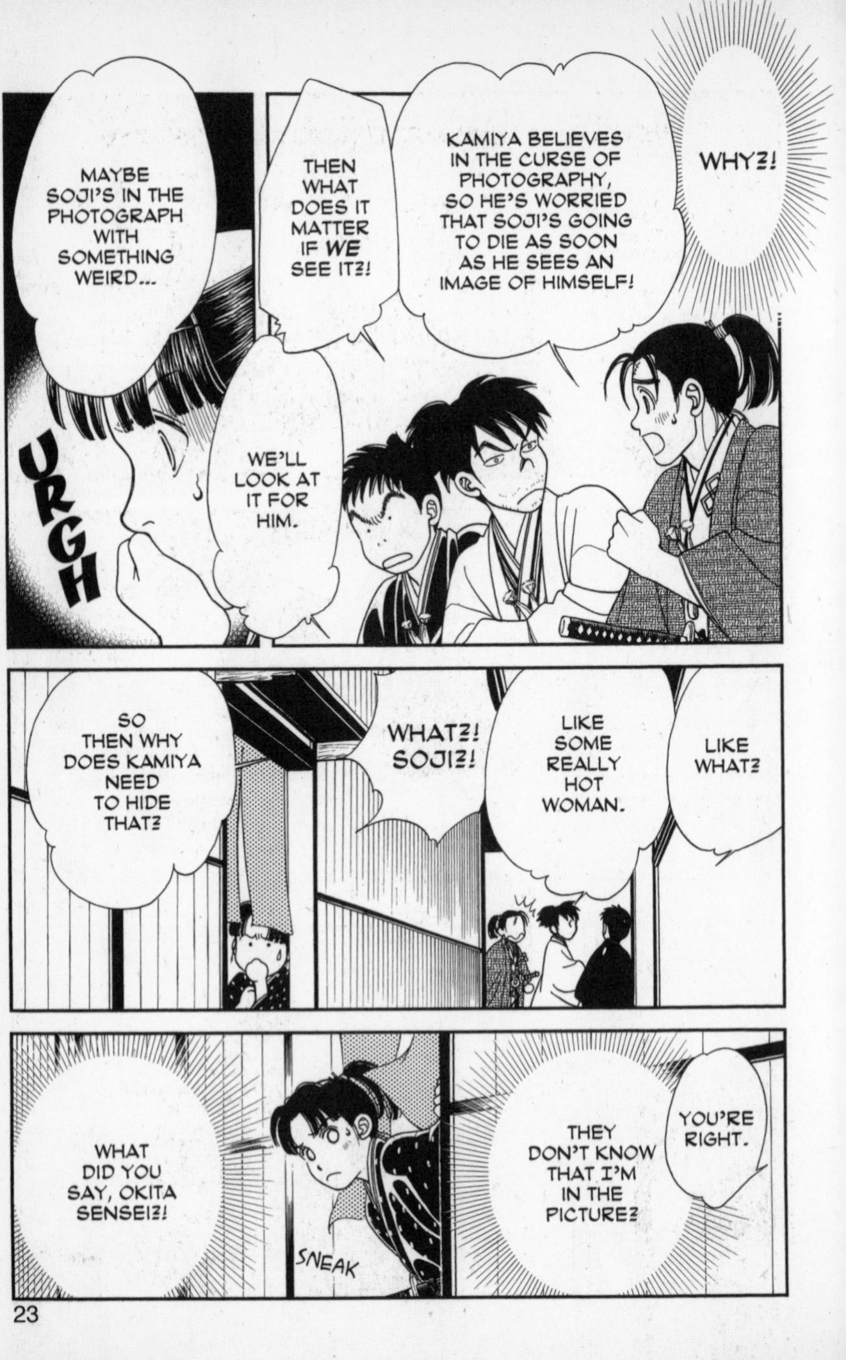
WHY?!
KAMIYA BELIEVES IN THE CURSE OF PHOTOGRAPHY, SO HE'S WORRIED THAT SOJI'S GOING TO DIE AS SOON AS HE SEES AN IMAGE OF HIMSELF!
THEN WHAT DOES IT MATTER IF *WE* SEE IT?!
WE'LL LOOK AT IT FOR HIM.
MAYBE SOJI'S IN THE PHOTOGRAPH WITH SOMETHING WEIRD...
URGH
LIKE WHAT?
LIKE SOME REALLY HOT WOMAN.
WHAT?! SOJI?!
SO THEN WHY DOES KAMIYA NEED TO HIDE THAT?
YOU'RE RIGHT.
THEY DON'T KNOW THAT I'M IN THE PICTURE?
SNEAK
WHAT DID YOU SAY, OKITA SENSEI?!

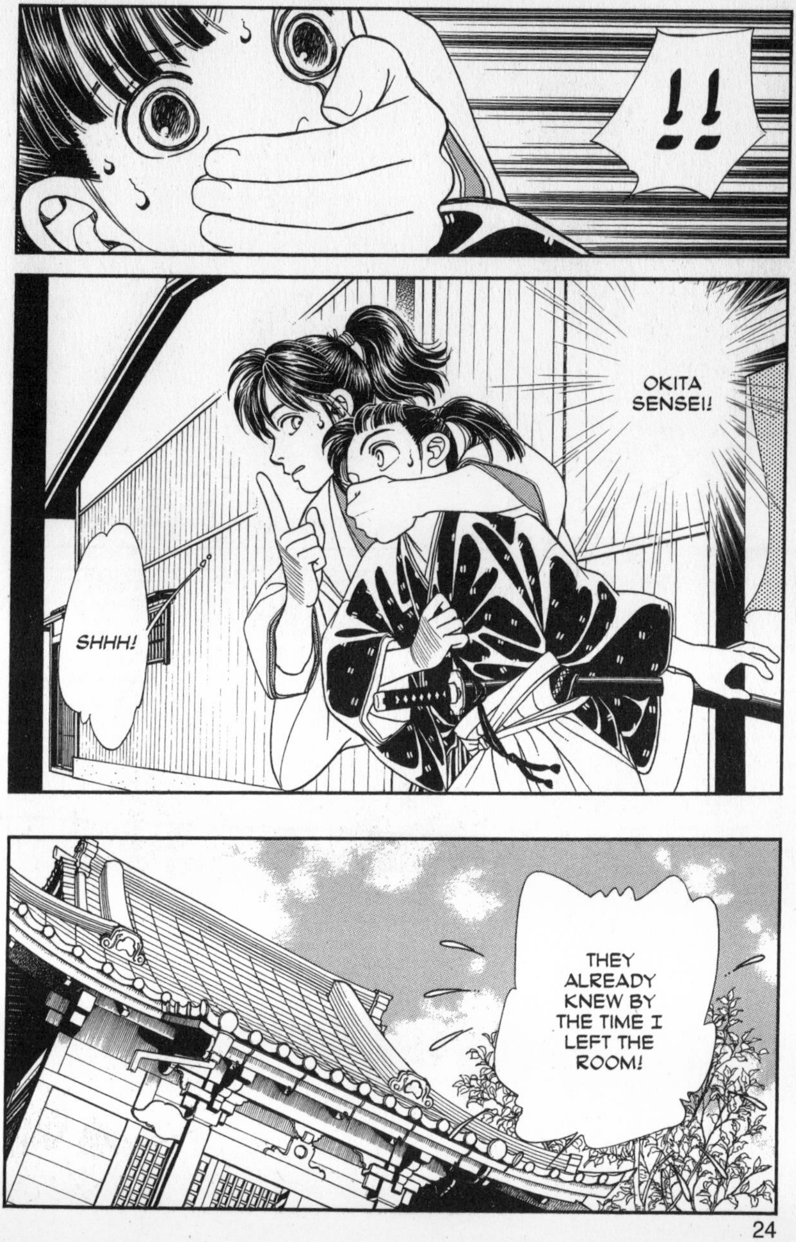
!!
OKITA SENSEI!
SHHH!
THEY ALREADY KNEW BY THE TIME I LEFT THE ROOM!

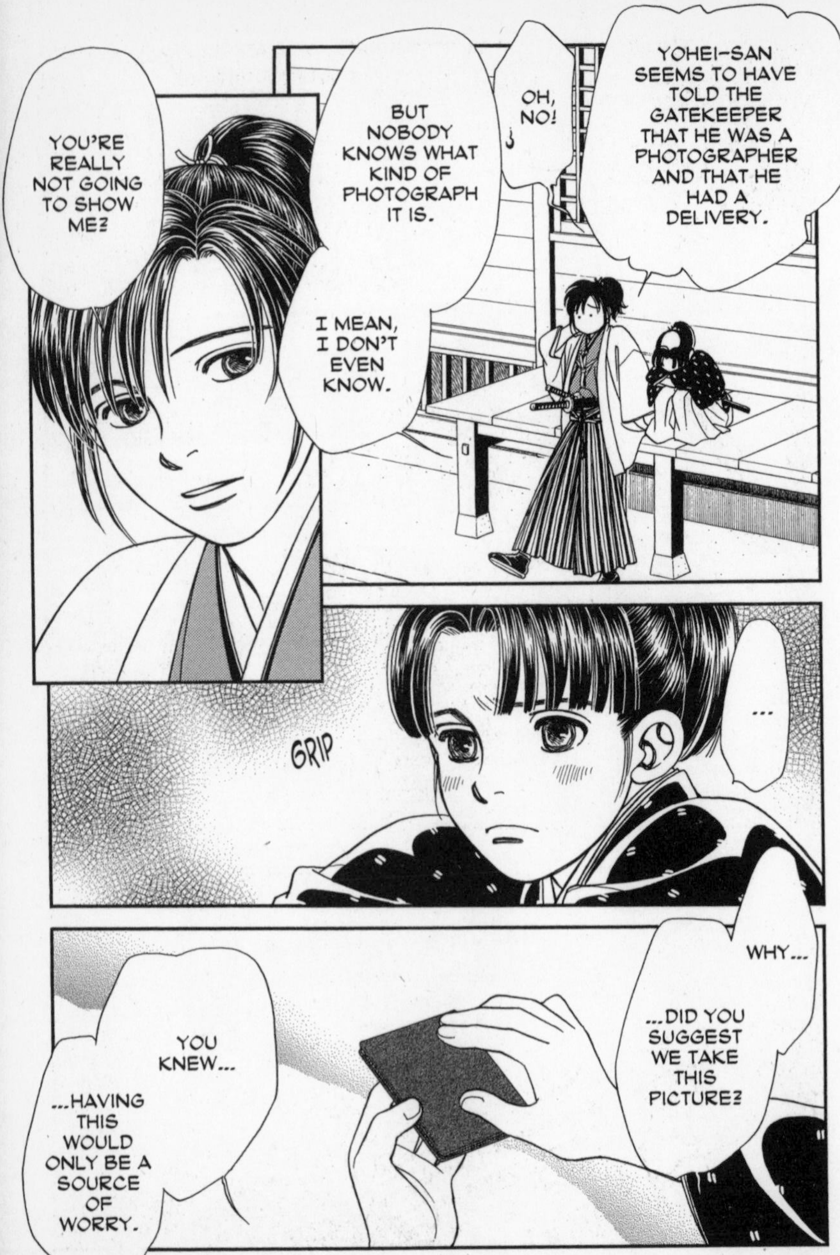
YOHEI-SAN SEEMS TO HAVE TOLD THE GATEKEEPER THAT HE WAS A PHOTOGRAPHER AND THAT HE HAD A DELIVERY.
OH, NO!
BUT NOBODY KNOWS WHAT KIND OF PHOTOGRAPH IT IS.
I MEAN, I DON'T EVEN KNOW.
YOU'RE REALLY NOT GOING TO SHOW ME?
...
GRIP
WHY...
...DID YOU SUGGEST WE TAKE THIS PICTURE?
YOU KNEW...
...HAVING THIS WOULD ONLY BE A SOURCE OF WORRY.

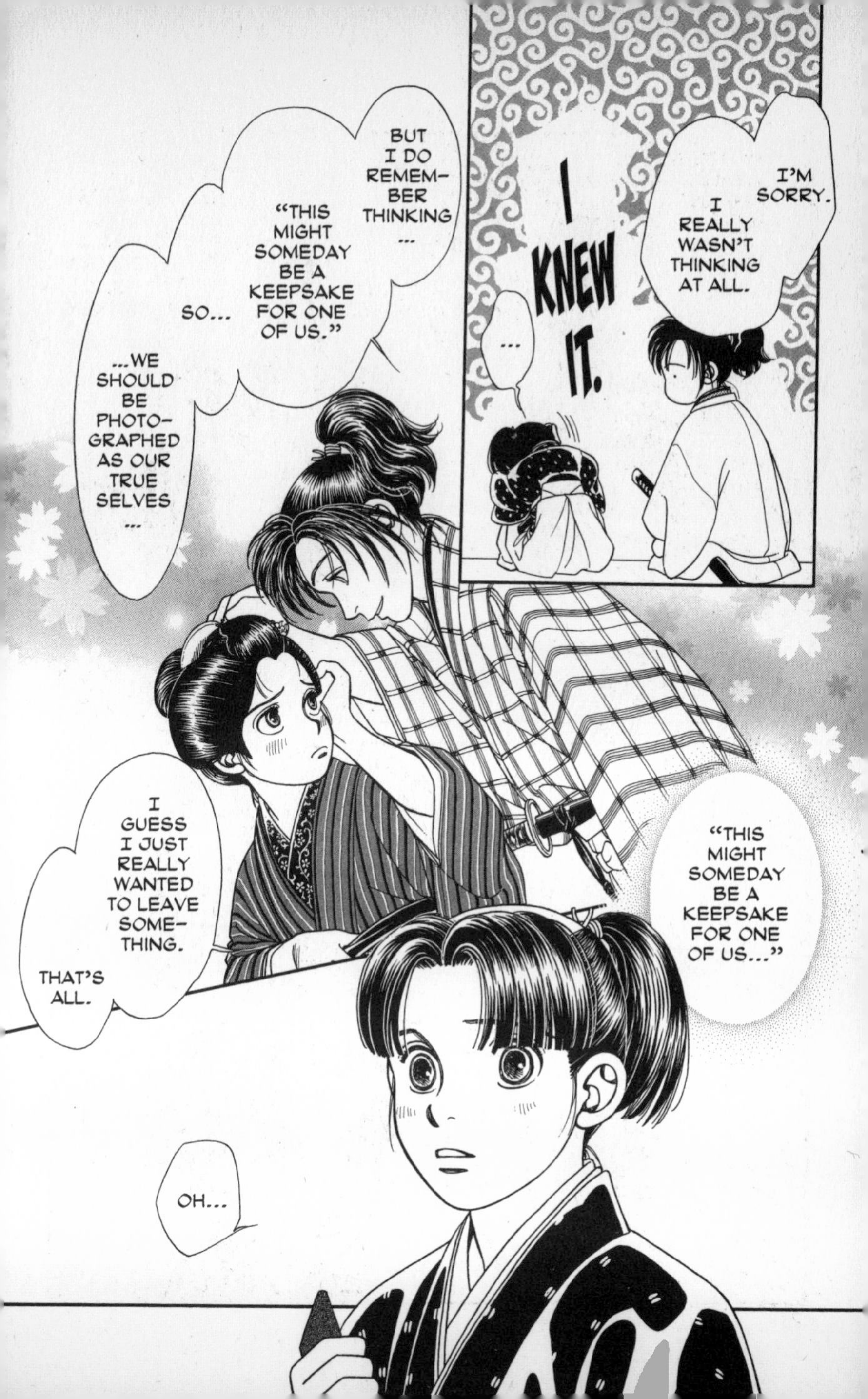
I'M SORRY. I REALLY WASN'T THINKING AT ALL.
I KNEW IT.
...
BUT I DO REMEMBER THINKING...
"THIS MIGHT SOMEDAY BE A KEEPSAKE FOR ONE OF US."
SO...
...WE SHOULD BE PHOTOGRAPHED AS OUR TRUE SELVES...
I GUESS I JUST REALLY WANTED TO LEAVE SOMETHING.
THAT'S ALL.
"THIS MIGHT SOMEDAY BE A KEEPSAKE FOR ONE OF US..."
OH...

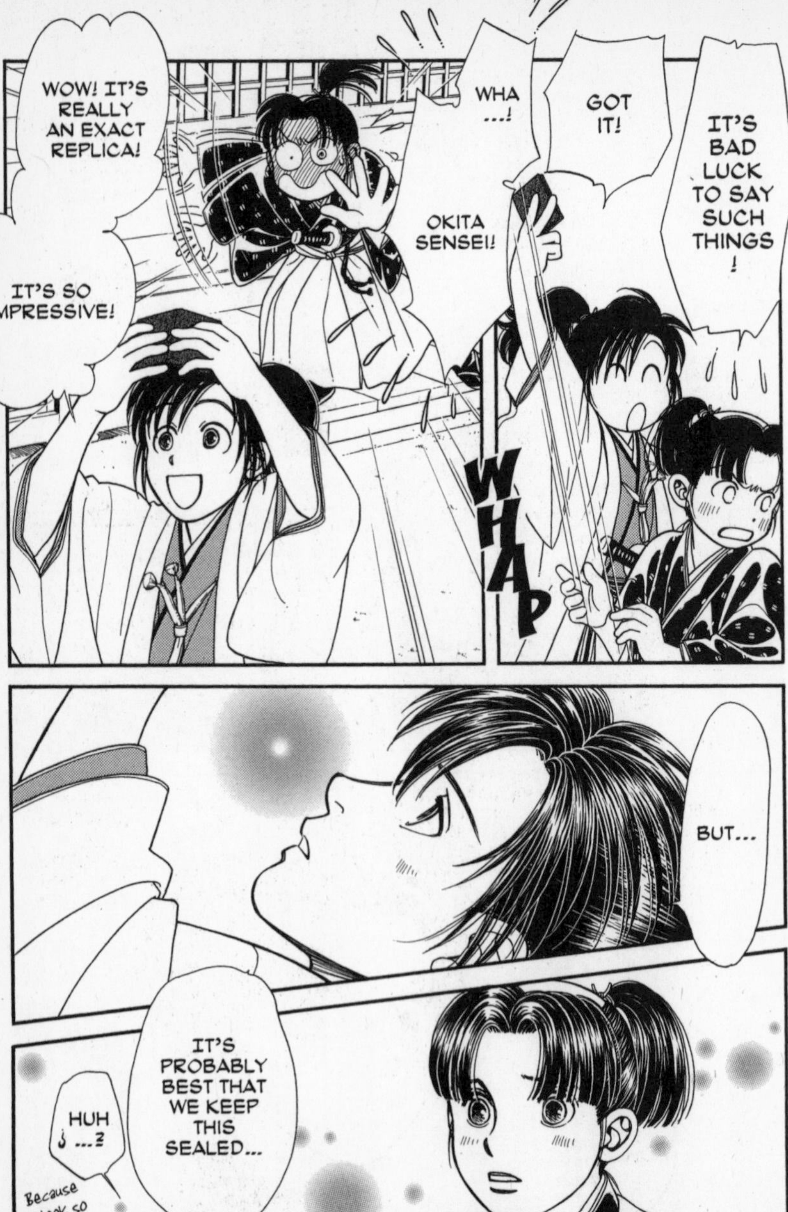
IT'S BAD LUCK TO SAY SUCH THINGS!
GOT IT!
WHA...!
OKITA SENSEI!
WHAP
WOW! IT'S REALLY AN EXACT REPLICA!
IT'S SO IMPRESSIVE!
BUT...
IT'S PROBABLY BEST THAT WE KEEP THIS SEALED...
HUH ¿...?
Because I look so terrible?!

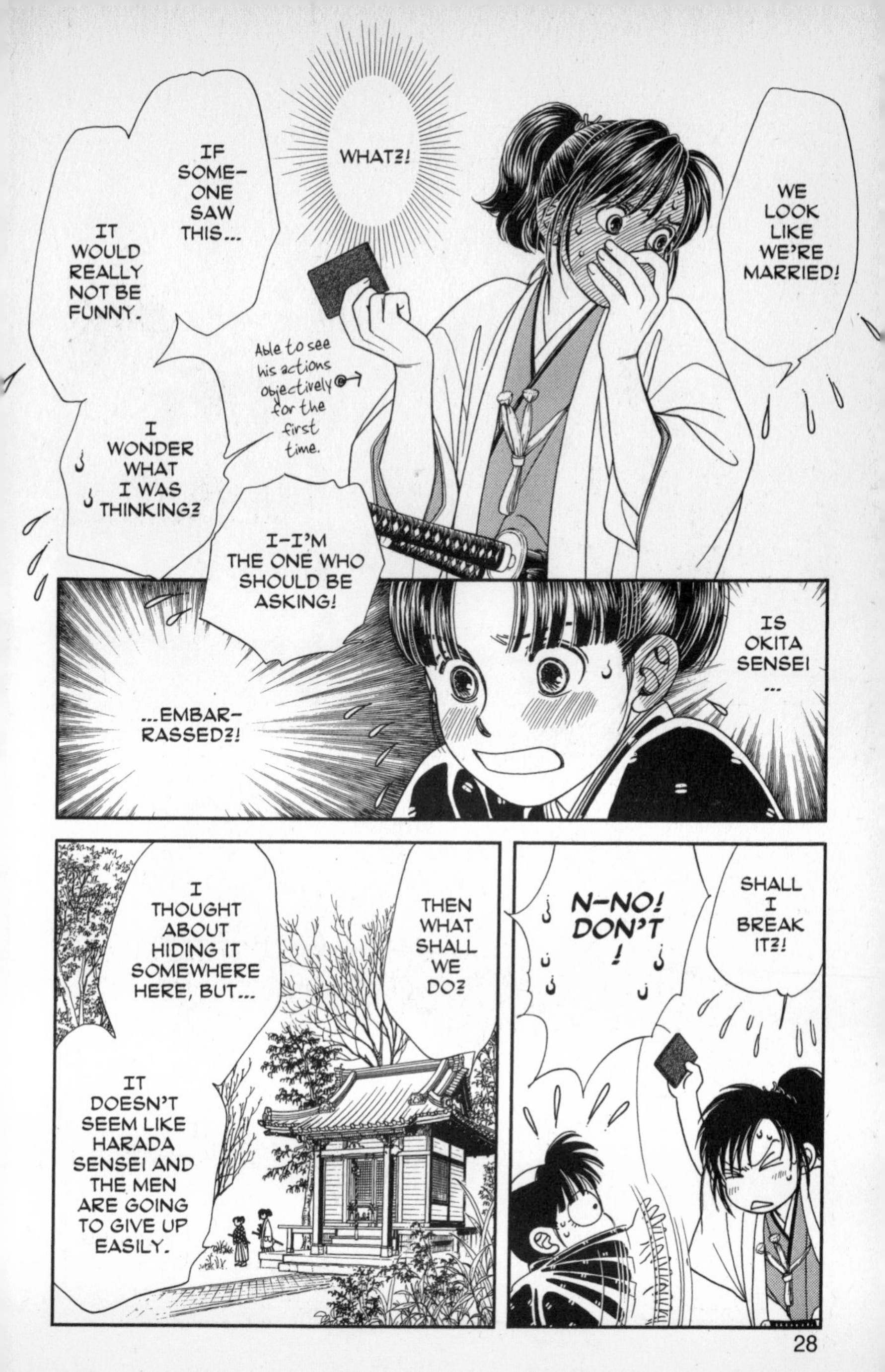
WE LOOK LIKE WE'RE MARRIED!
WHAT?!
IF SOME-ONE SAW THIS...
IT WOULD REALLY NOT BE FUNNY.
Able to see his actions objectively for the first time.
I WONDER WHAT I WAS THINKING?
I-I'M THE ONE WHO SHOULD BE ASKING!
IS OKITA SENSEI ...
...EMBAR-RASSED?!
SHALL I BREAK IT?!
N-NO! DON'T!
THEN WHAT SHALL WE DO?
I THOUGHT ABOUT HIDING IT SOMEWHERE HERE, BUT...
IT DOESN'T SEEM LIKE HARADA SENSEI AND THE MEN ARE GOING TO GIVE UP EASILY.

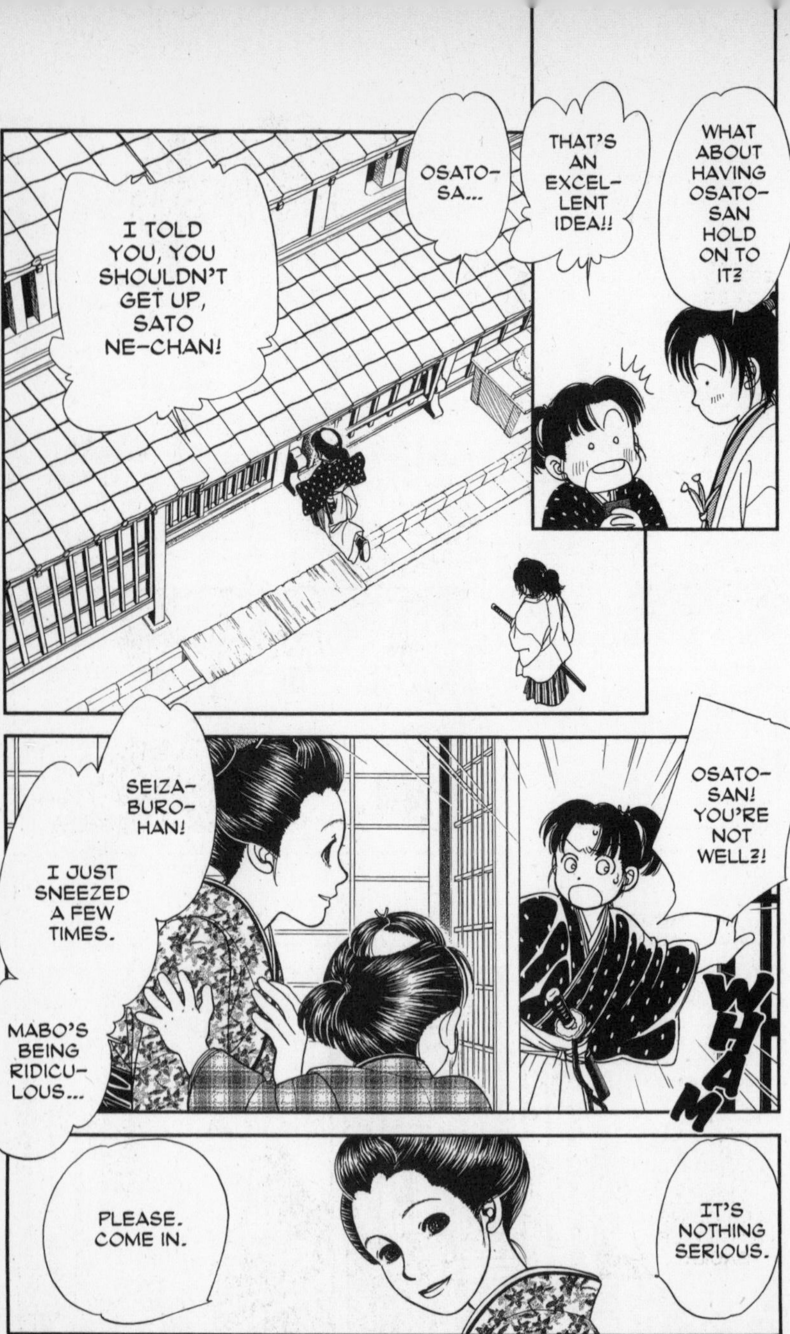
WHAT ABOUT HAVING OSATO-SAN HOLD ON TO IT?
THAT'S AN EXCEL-LENT IDEA!!
OSATO-SA...
I TOLD YOU, YOU SHOULDN'T GET UP, SATO NE-CHAN!
OSATO-SAN! YOU'RE NOT WELL?!
WHAM
SEIZA-BURO-HAN!
I JUST SNEEZED A FEW TIMES.
MABO'S BEING RIDICU-LOUS...
IT'S NOTHING SERIOUS.
PLEASE. COME IN.

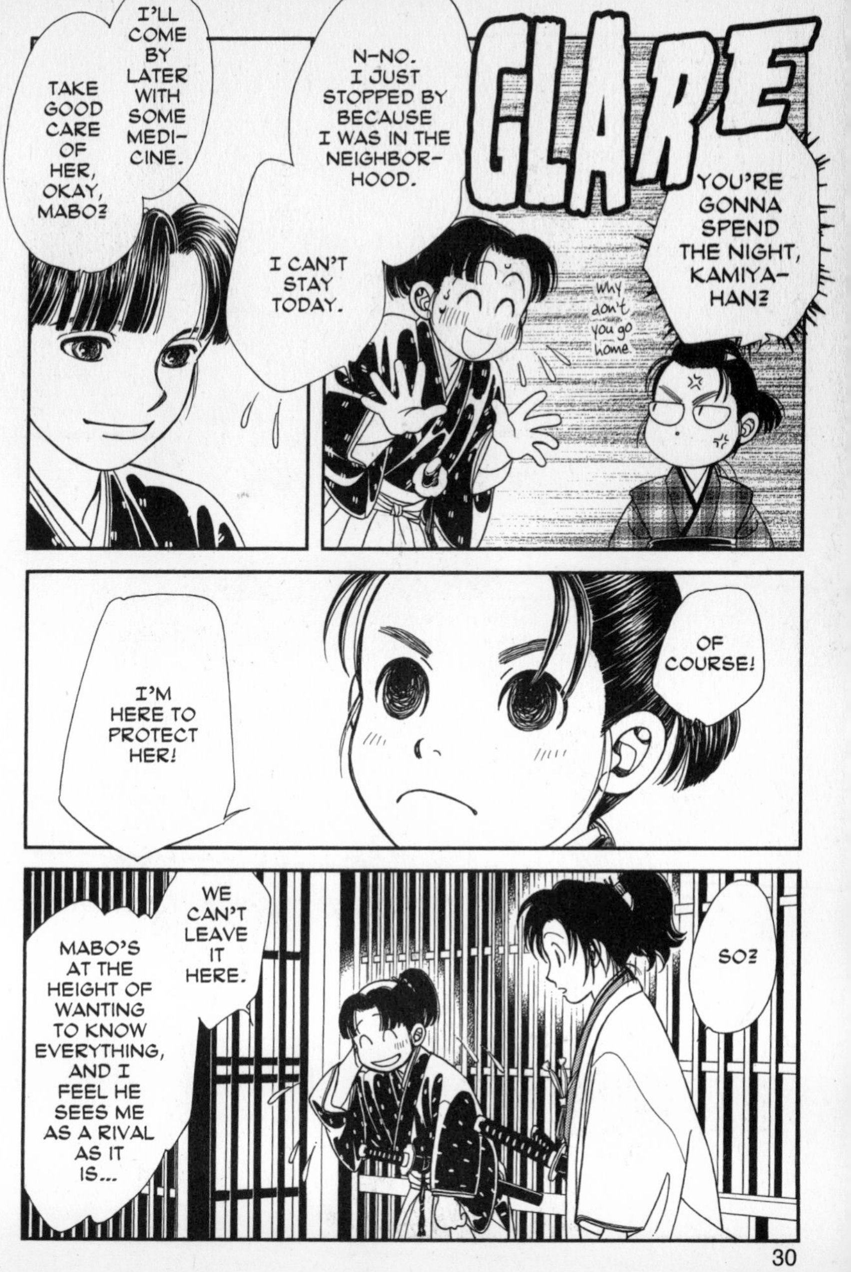
GLARE
YOU'RE GONNA SPEND THE NIGHT, KAMIYA-HAN?
Why don't you go home
N-NO. I JUST STOPPED BY BECAUSE I WAS IN THE NEIGHBOR-HOOD.
I CAN'T STAY TODAY.
I'LL COME BY LATER WITH SOME MEDI-CINE.
TAKE GOOD CARE OF HER, OKAY, MABO?
OF COURSE!
I'M HERE TO PROTECT HER!
SO?
WE CAN'T LEAVE IT HERE.
MABO'S AT THE HEIGHT OF WANTING TO KNOW EVERYTHING, AND I FEEL HE SEES ME AS A RIVAL AS IT IS...

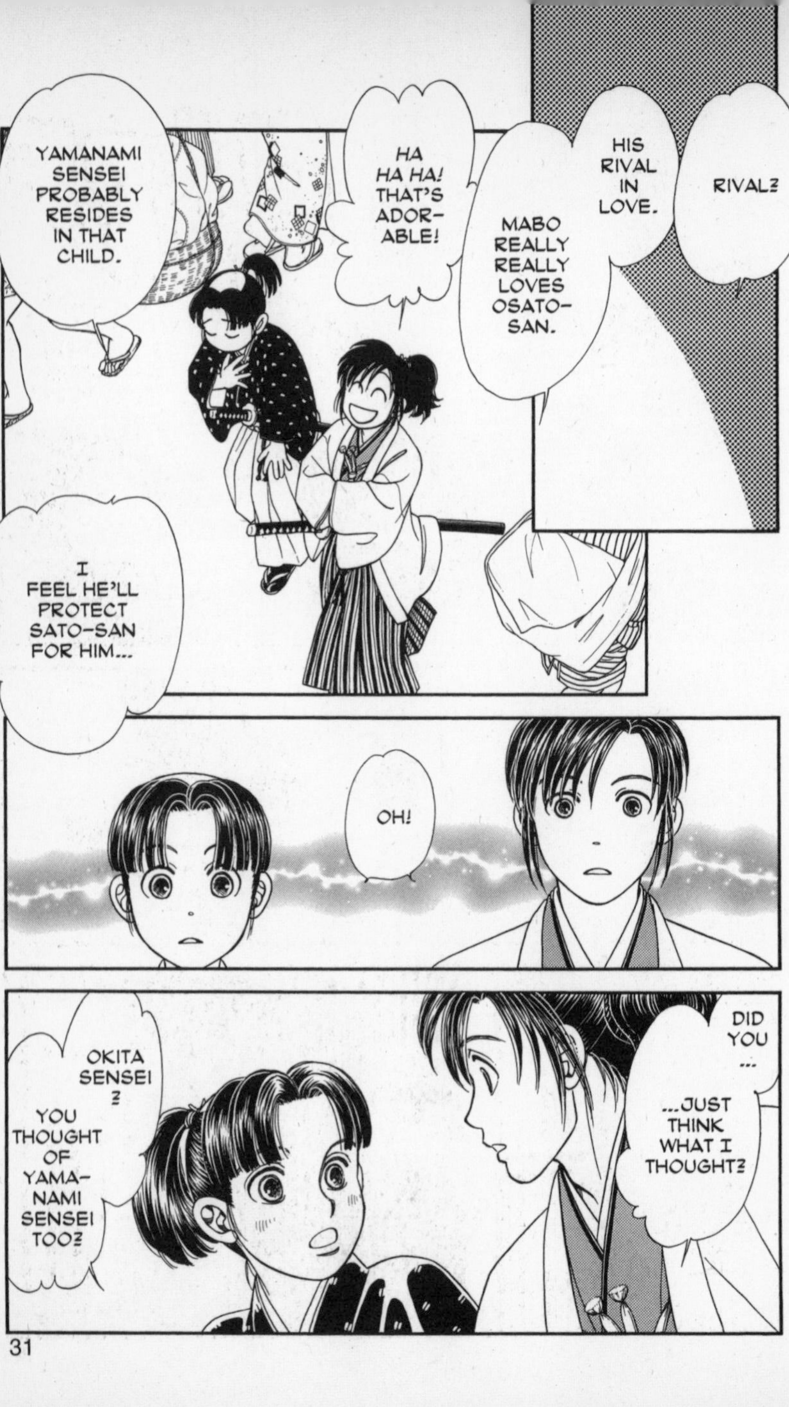
RIVAL?
HIS RIVAL IN LOVE.
MABO REALLY REALLY LOVES OSATO-SAN.
HA HA HA! THAT'S ADORABLE!
YAMANAMI SENSEI PROBABLY RESIDES IN THAT CHILD.
I FEEL HE'LL PROTECT SATO-SAN FOR HIM...
OH!
DID YOU ...
...JUST THINK WHAT I THOUGHT?
OKITA SENSEI?
YOU THOUGHT OF YAMANAMI SENSEI TOO?

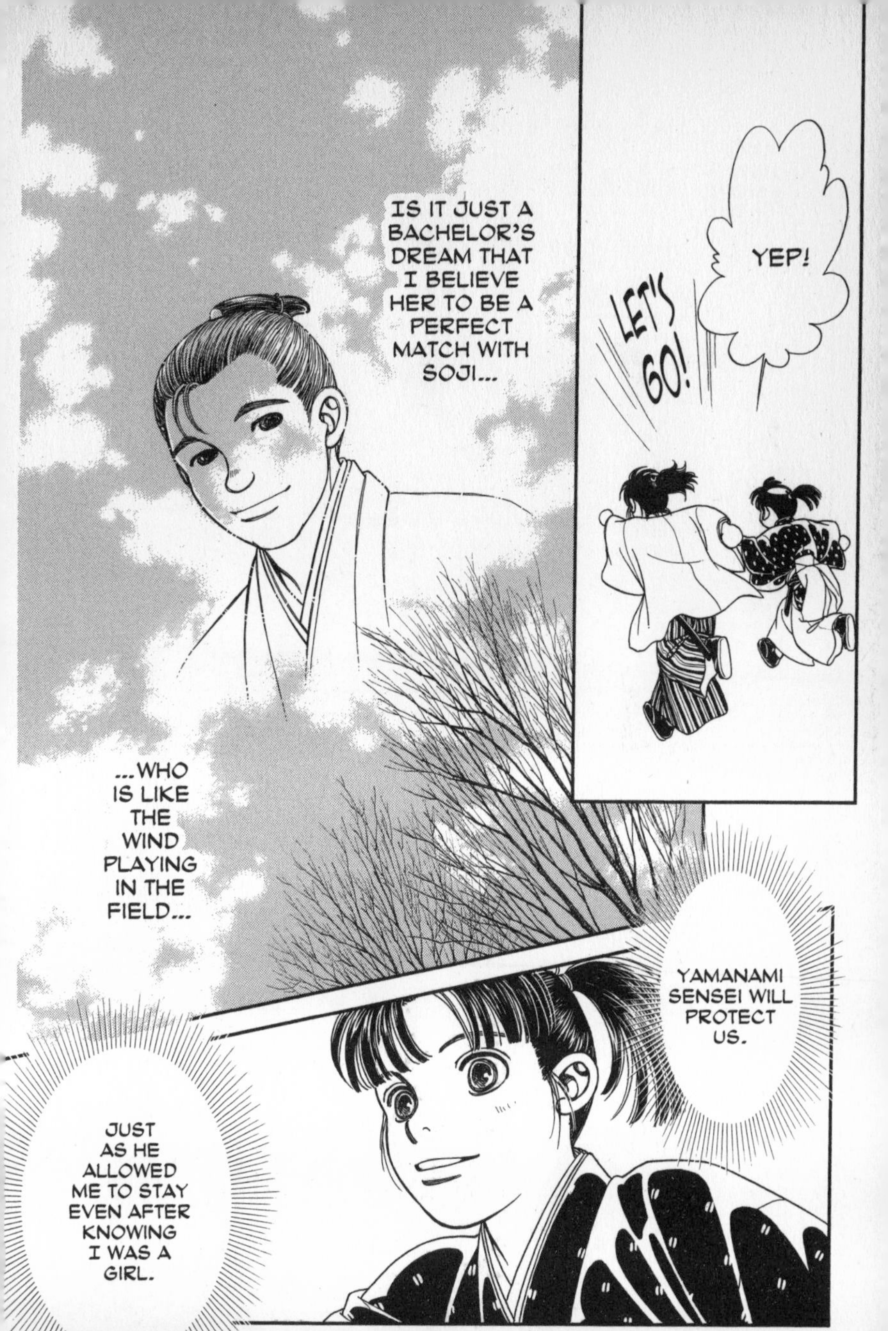
YEP!
LET'S GO!
IS IT JUST A BACHELOR'S DREAM THAT I BELIEVE HER TO BE A PERFECT MATCH WITH SOJI...
...WHO IS LIKE THE WIND PLAYING IN THE FIELD...
YAMANAMI SENSEI WILL PROTECT US.
JUST AS HE ALLOWED ME TO STAY EVEN AFTER KNOWING I WAS A GIRL.

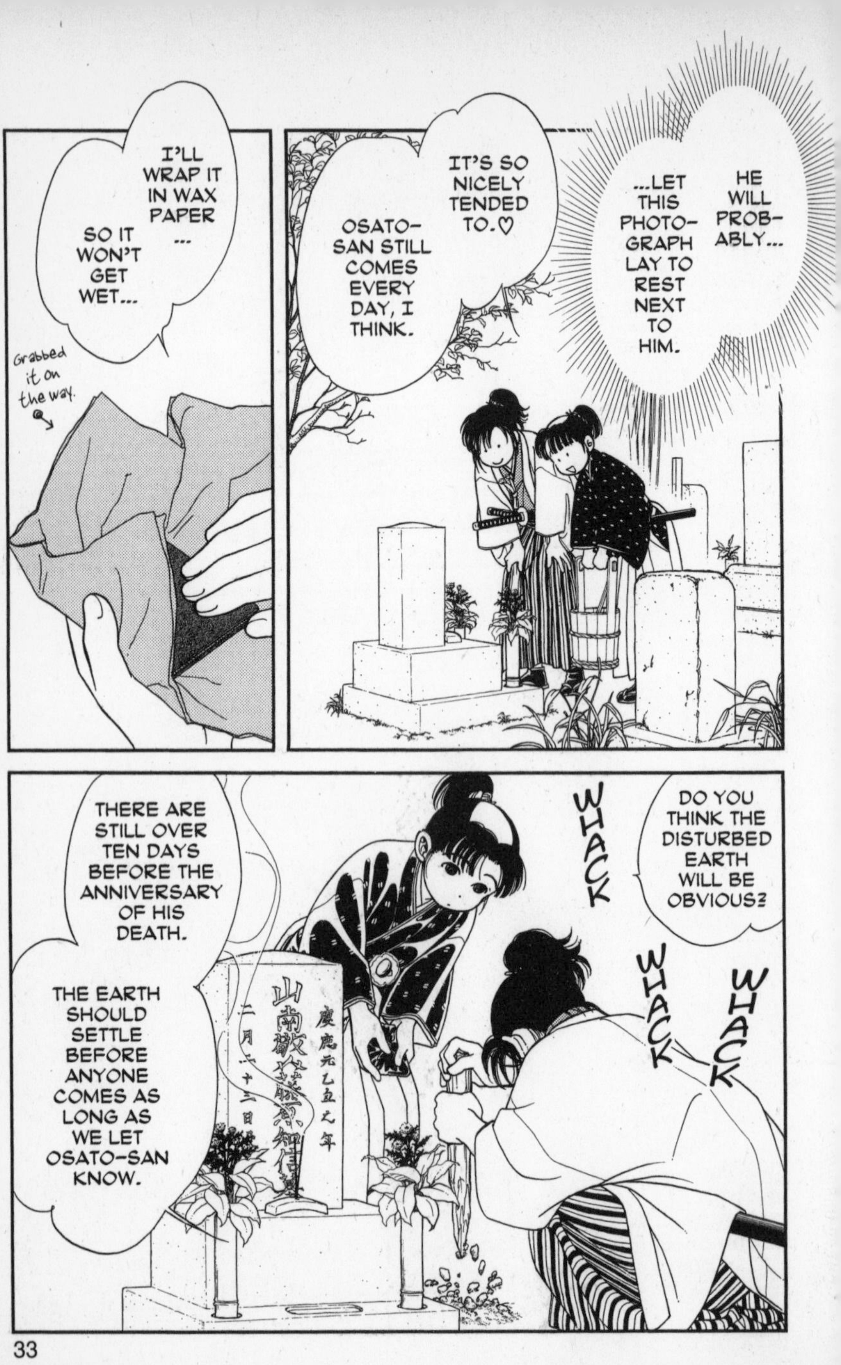
HE WILL PROBABLY...
...LET THIS PHOTOGRAPH LAY TO REST NEXT TO HIM.
IT'S SO NICELY TENDED TO.♡
OSATO-SAN STILL COMES EVERY DAY, I THINK.
I'LL WRAP IT IN WAX PAPER ...
SO IT WON'T GET WET...
Grabbed it on the way.
DO YOU THINK THE DISTURBED EARTH WILL BE OBVIOUS?
WHACK
WHACK
WHACK
THERE ARE STILL OVER TEN DAYS BEFORE THE ANNIVERSARY OF HIS DEATH.
THE EARTH SHOULD SETTLE BEFORE ANYONE COMES AS LONG AS WE LET OSATO-SAN KNOW.

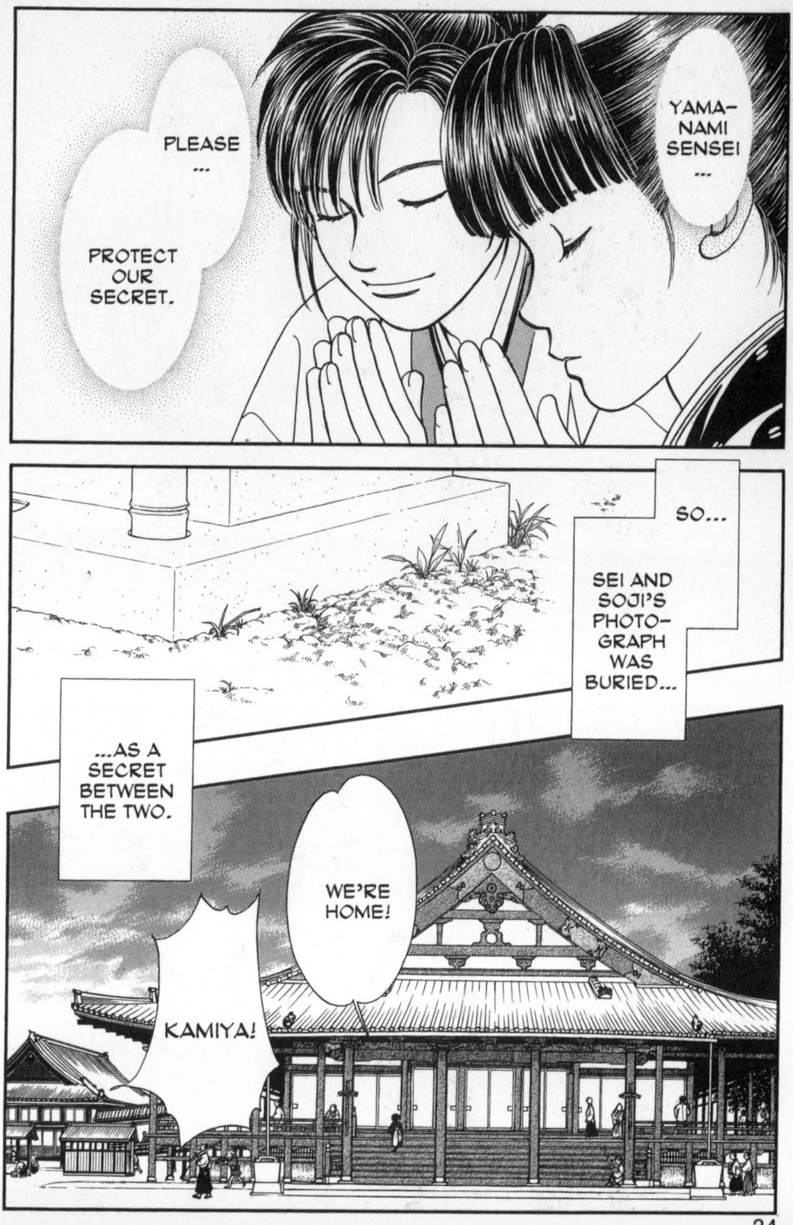
YAMA-NAMI SENSEI ...
PLEASE ...
PROTECT OUR SECRET.
SO...
SEI AND SOJI'S PHOTO-GRAPH WAS BURIED...
...AS A SECRET BETWEEN THE TWO.
WE'RE HOME!
KAMIYA!

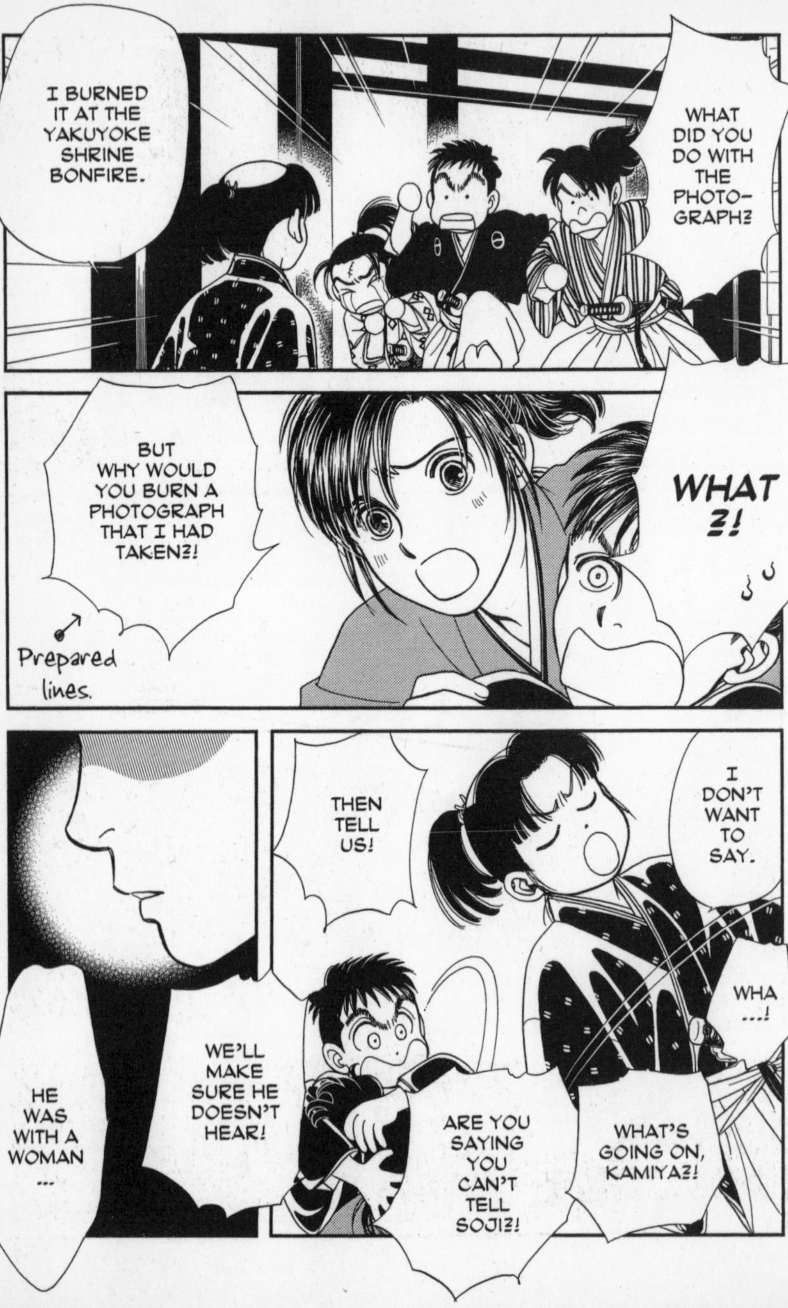
WHAT DID YOU DO WITH THE PHOTOGRAPH?
I BURNED IT AT THE YAKUYOKE SHRINE BONFIRE.
WHAT?!
BUT WHY WOULD YOU BURN A PHOTOGRAPH THAT I HAD TAKEN?!
Prepared lines.
I DON'T WANT TO SAY.
THEN TELL US!
WHA...!
WHAT'S GOING ON, KAMIYA?!
ARE YOU SAYING YOU CAN'T TELL SOJI?!
WE'LL MAKE SURE HE DOESN'T HEAR!
HE WAS WITH A WOMAN...

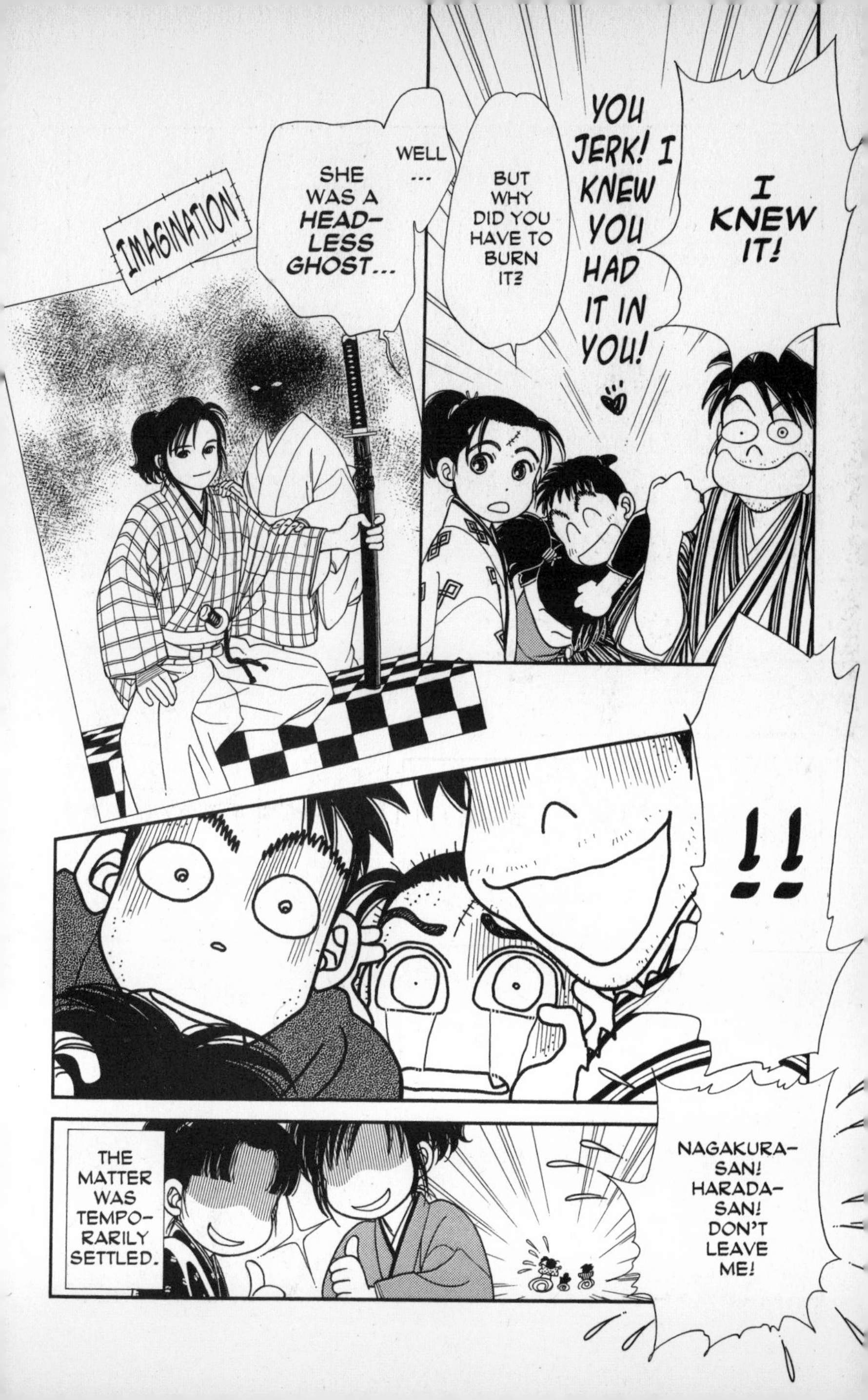
I KNEW IT!
YOU JERK! I KNEW YOU HAD IT IN YOU!
BUT WHY DID YOU HAVE TO BURN IT?
WELL ...
SHE WAS A HEADLESS GHOST...
IMAGINATION
!!
NAGAKURA-SAN! HARADA-SAN! DON'T LEAVE ME!
THE MATTER WAS TEMPORARILY SETTLED.

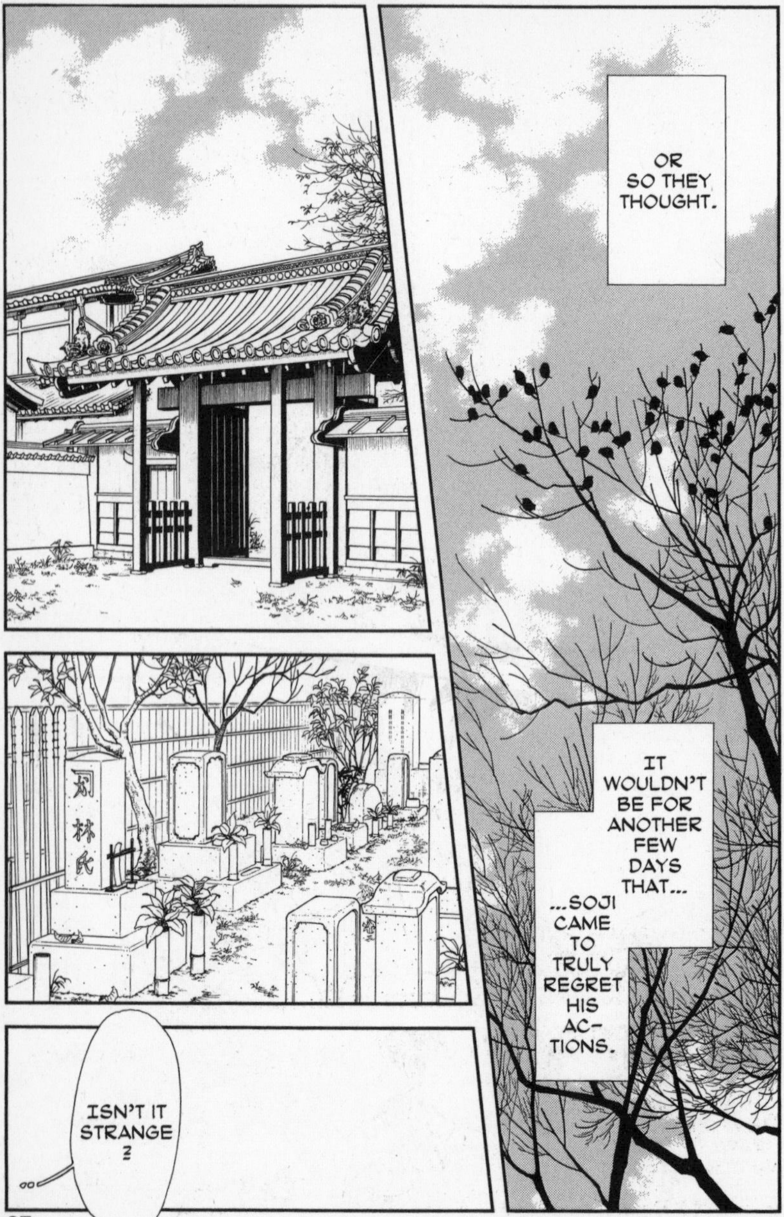
OR SO THEY THOUGHT.
IT WOULDN'T BE FOR ANOTHER FEW DAYS THAT...
...SOJI CAME TO TRULY REGRET HIS AC-TIONS.
ISN'T IT STRANGE?

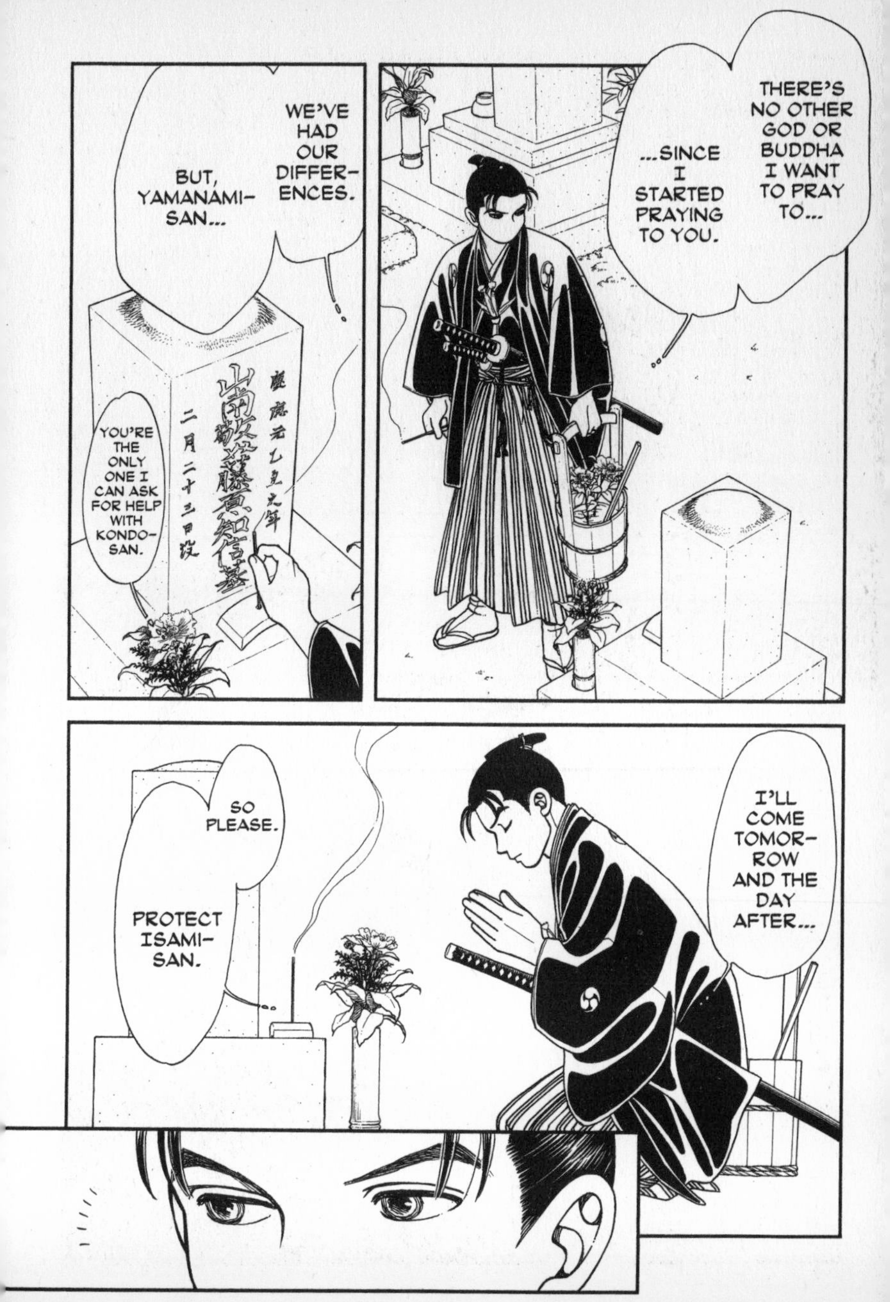
THERE'S NO OTHER GOD OR BUDDHA I WANT TO PRAY TO...
...SINCE I STARTED PRAYING TO YOU.
WE'VE HAD OUR DIFFER-ENCES.
BUT, YAMANAMI-SAN...
慶應元乙丑之年
山南敬助藤原知信墓
二月二十三日没
YOU'RE THE ONLY ONE I CAN ASK FOR HELP WITH KONDO-SAN.
I'LL COME TOMOR-ROW AND THE DAY AFTER...
SO PLEASE.
PROTECT ISAMI-SAN.

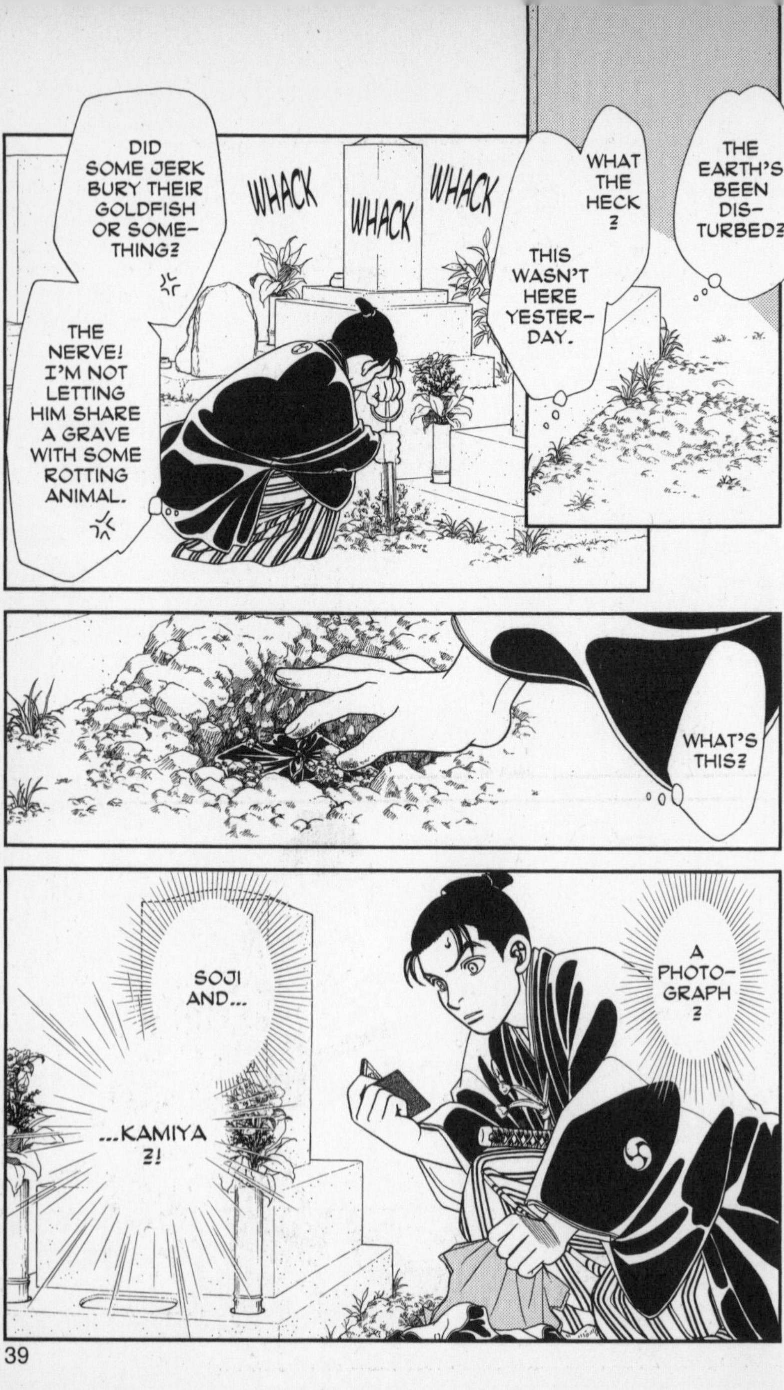
THE EARTH'S BEEN DIS-TURBED?
WHAT THE HECK?
THIS WASN'T HERE YESTER-DAY.
WHACK
WHACK
WHACK
DID SOME JERK BURY THEIR GOLDFISH OR SOME-THING?
THE NERVE! I'M NOT LETTING HIM SHARE A GRAVE WITH SOME ROTTING ANIMAL.
WHAT'S THIS?
A PHOTO-GRAPH?
SOJI AND...
...KAMIYA?!

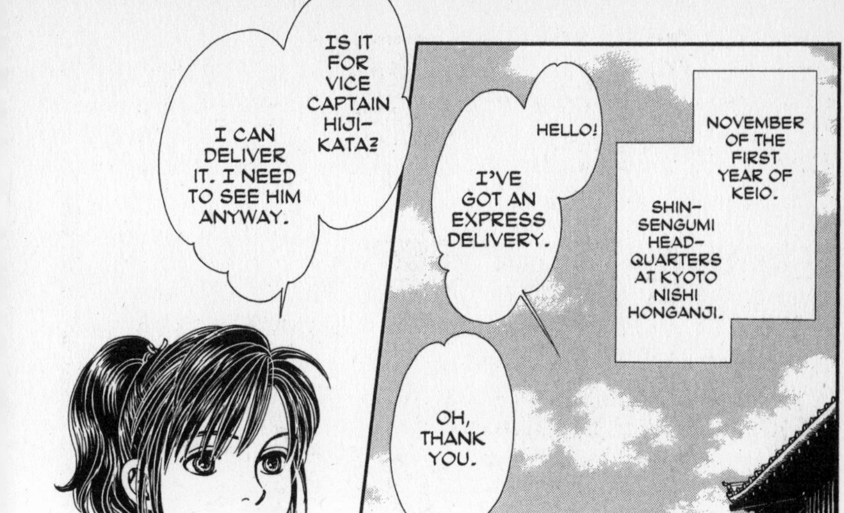
NOVEMBER OF THE FIRST YEAR OF KEIO.
SHIN-SENGUMI HEAD-QUARTERS AT KYOTO NISHI HONGANJI.
HELLO!
I'VE GOT AN EXPRESS DELIVERY.
OH, THANK YOU.
IS IT FOR VICE CAPTAIN HIJI-KATA?
I CAN DELIVER IT. I NEED TO SEE HIM ANYWAY.

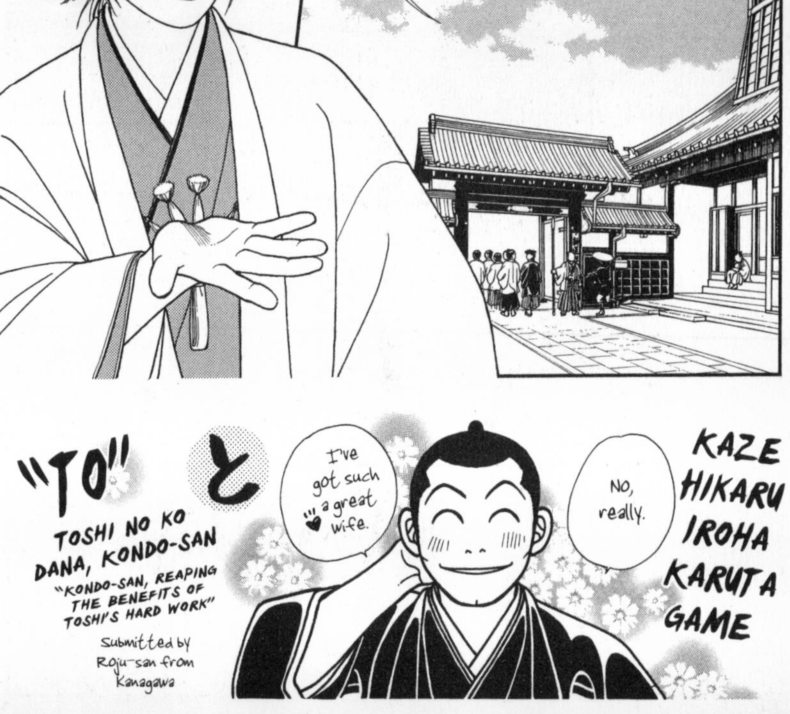
KAZE HIKARU IROHA KARUTA GAME
No, really.
I've got such a great wife.
"TO" と
TOSHI NO KO DANA, KONDO-SAN
"KONDO-SAN, REAPING THE BENEFITS OF TOSHI'S HARD WORK"
Submitted by Roju-san from Kanagawa

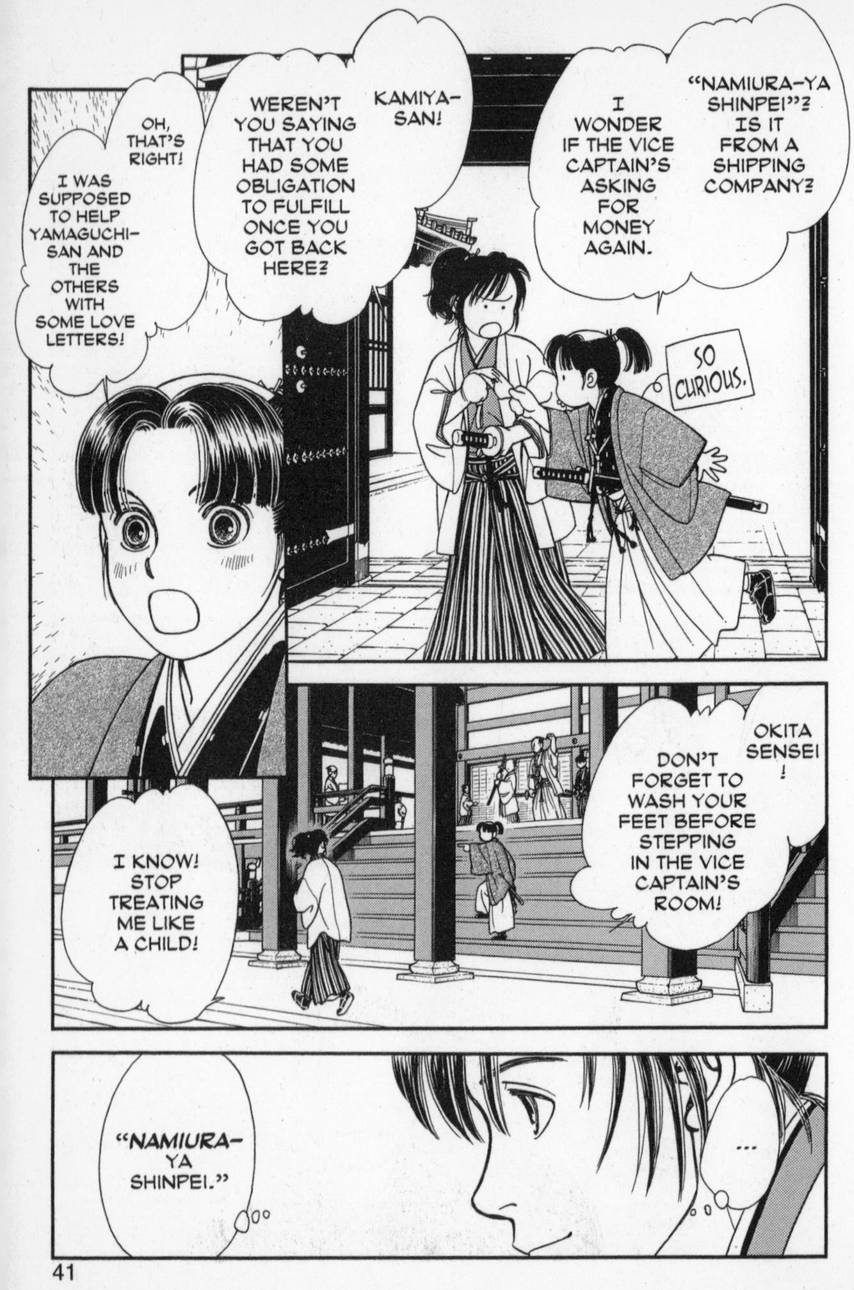
"NAMIURA-YA SHINPEI"? IS IT FROM A SHIPPING COMPANY?
I WONDER IF THE VICE CAPTAIN'S ASKING FOR MONEY AGAIN.
SO CURIOUS.
KAMIYA-SAN!
WEREN'T YOU SAYING THAT YOU HAD SOME OBLIGATION TO FULFILL ONCE YOU GOT BACK HERE?
OH, THAT'S RIGHT!
I WAS SUPPOSED TO HELP YAMAGUCHI-SAN AND THE OTHERS WITH SOME LOVE LETTERS!
OKITA SENSEI!
DON'T FORGET TO WASH YOUR FEET BEFORE STEPPING IN THE VICE CAPTAIN'S ROOM!
I KNOW! STOP TREATING ME LIKE A CHILD!
...
"NAMIURA-YA SHINPEI."

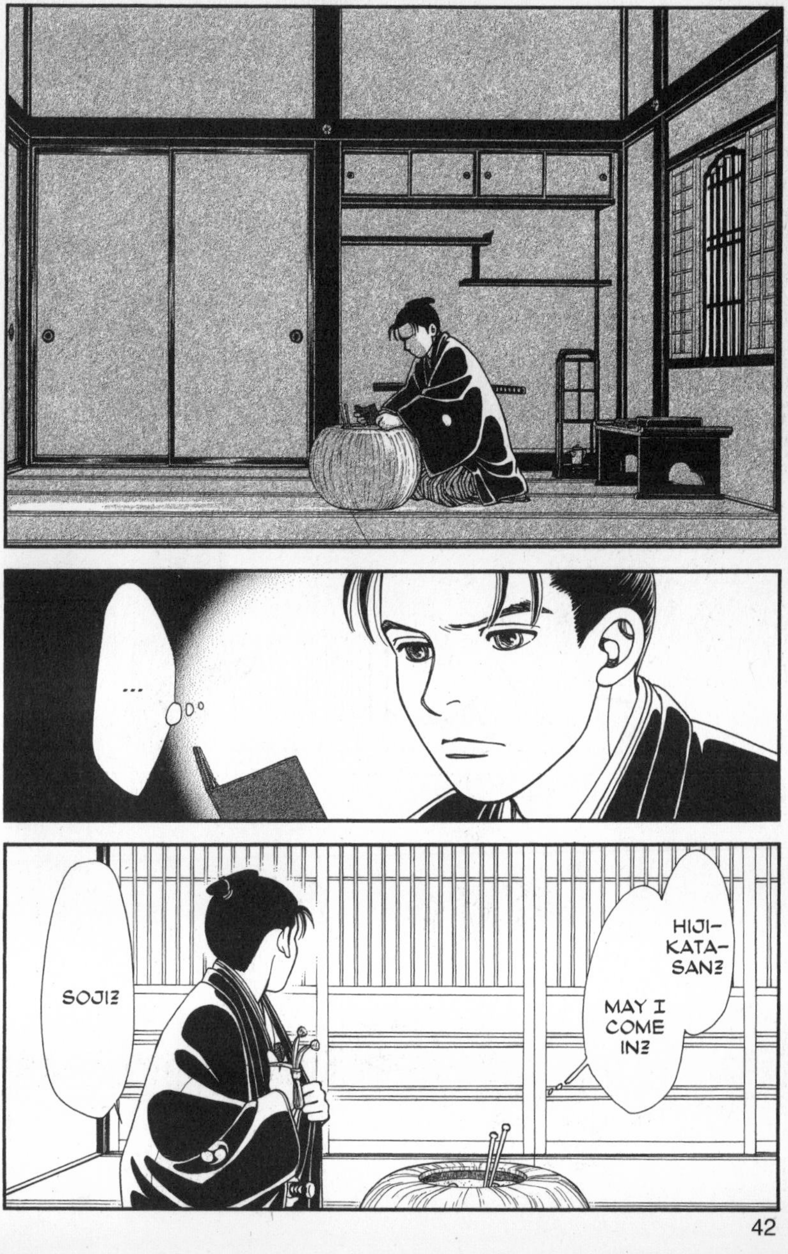
...
HIJI-KATA-SAN?
MAY I COME IN?
SOJI?

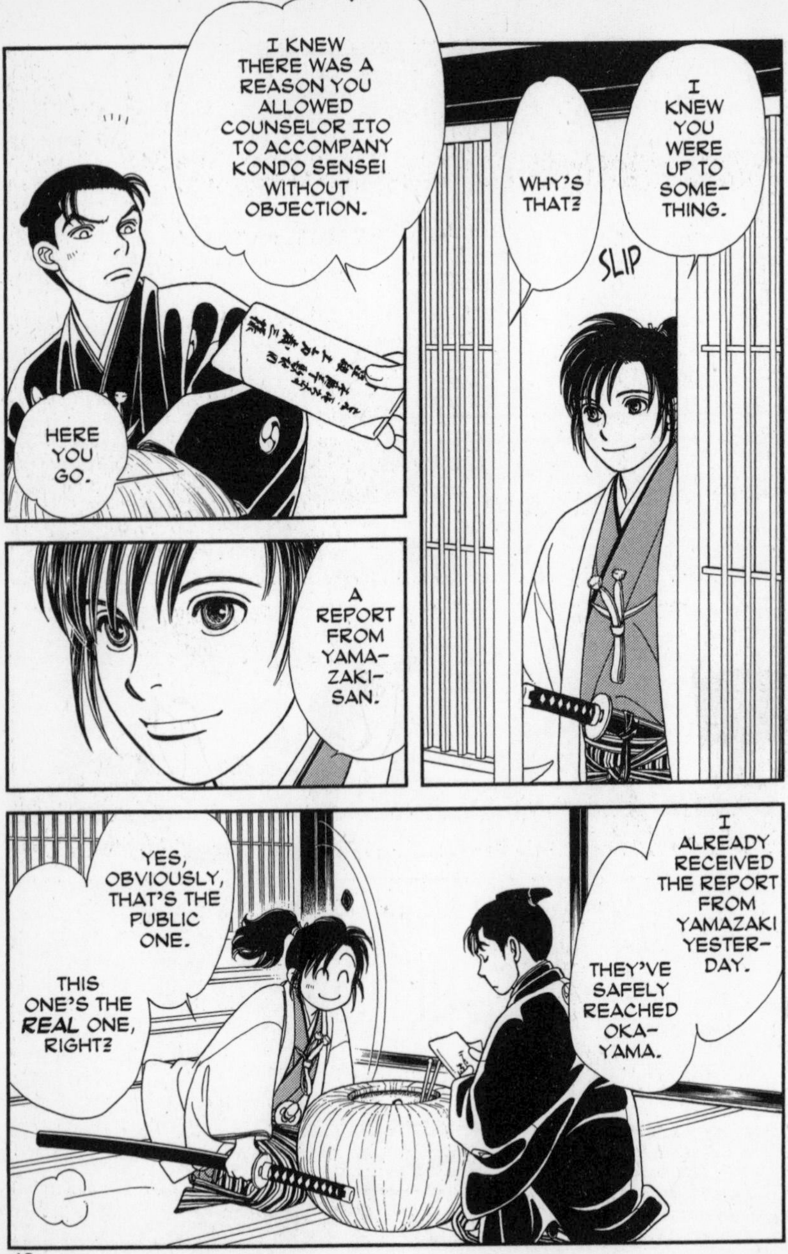
I KNEW YOU WERE UP TO SOME-THING.
WHY'S THAT?
SLIP
I KNEW THERE WAS A REASON YOU ALLOWED COUNSELOR ITO TO ACCOMPANY KONDO SENSEI WITHOUT OBJECTION.
HERE YOU GO.
A REPORT FROM YAMA-ZAKI-SAN.
I ALREADY RECEIVED THE REPORT FROM YAMAZAKI YESTER-DAY.
THEY'VE SAFELY REACHED OKA-YAMA.
YES, OBVIOUSLY, THAT'S THE PUBLIC ONE.
THIS ONE'S THE *REAL* ONE, RIGHT?

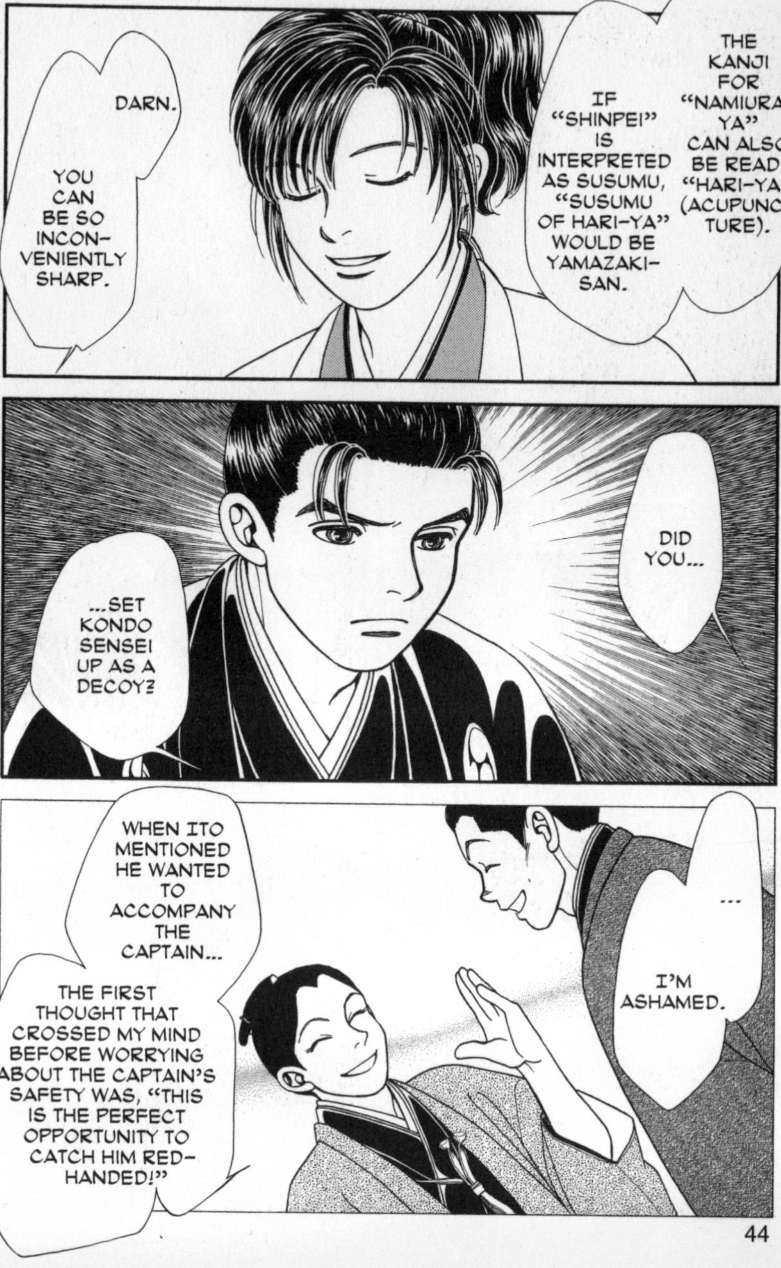
THE KANJI FOR "NAMIURA-YA" CAN ALSO BE READ, "HARI-YA" (ACUPUNCTURE).
IF "SHINPEI" IS INTERPRETED AS SUSUMU, "SUSUMU OF HARI-YA" WOULD BE YAMAZAKI-SAN.
DARN.
YOU CAN BE SO INCONVENIENTLY SHARP.
DID YOU...
...SET KONDO SENSEI UP AS A DECOY?
...
I'M ASHAMED.
WHEN ITO MENTIONED HE WANTED TO ACCOMPANY THE CAPTAIN...
THE FIRST THOUGHT THAT CROSSED MY MIND BEFORE WORRYING ABOUT THE CAPTAIN'S SAFETY WAS, "THIS IS THE PERFECT OPPORTUNITY TO CATCH HIM RED-HANDED!"

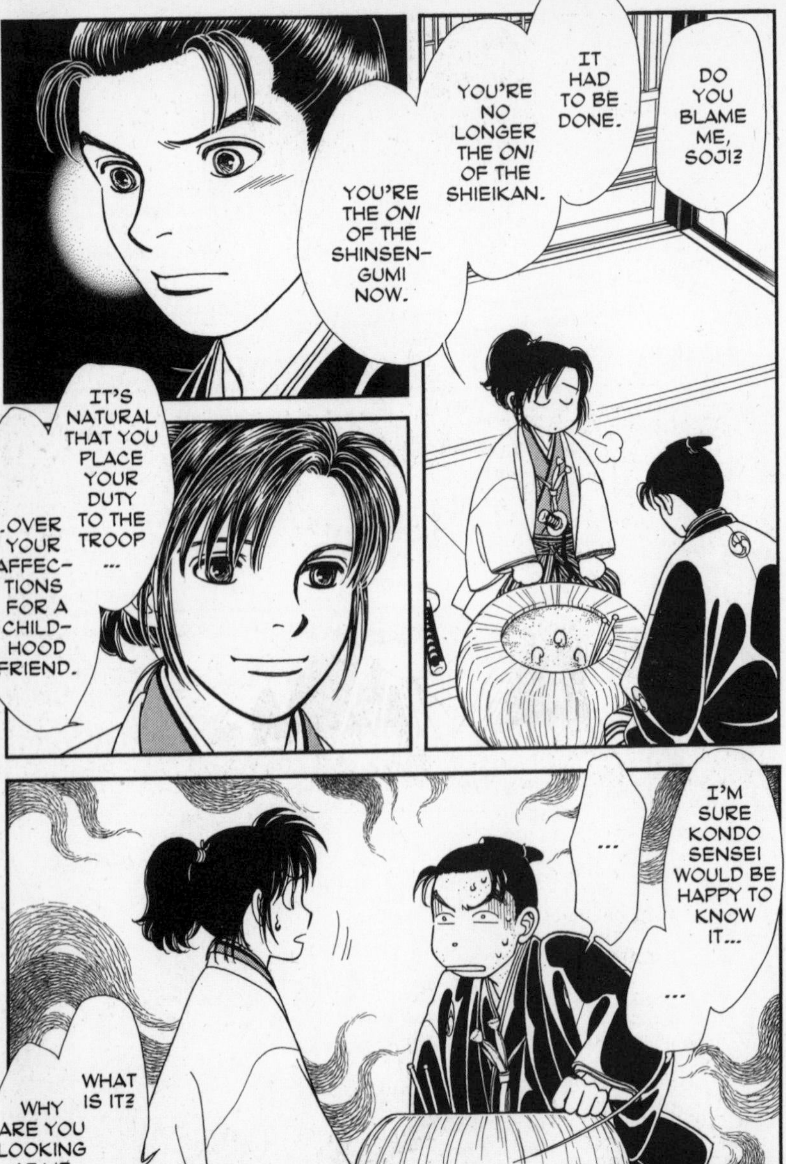
DO YOU BLAME ME, SOJI?
IT HAD TO BE DONE.
YOU'RE NO LONGER THE *ONI* OF THE SHIEIKAN.
YOU'RE THE *ONI* OF THE SHINSEN-GUMI NOW.
IT'S NATURAL THAT YOU PLACE YOUR DUTY TO THE TROOP ...
...OVER YOUR AFFECTIONS FOR A CHILDHOOD FRIEND.
I'M SURE KONDO SENSEI WOULD BE HAPPY TO KNOW IT...
...
...
WHAT IS IT?
WHY ARE YOU LOOKING AT ME LIKE THAT?

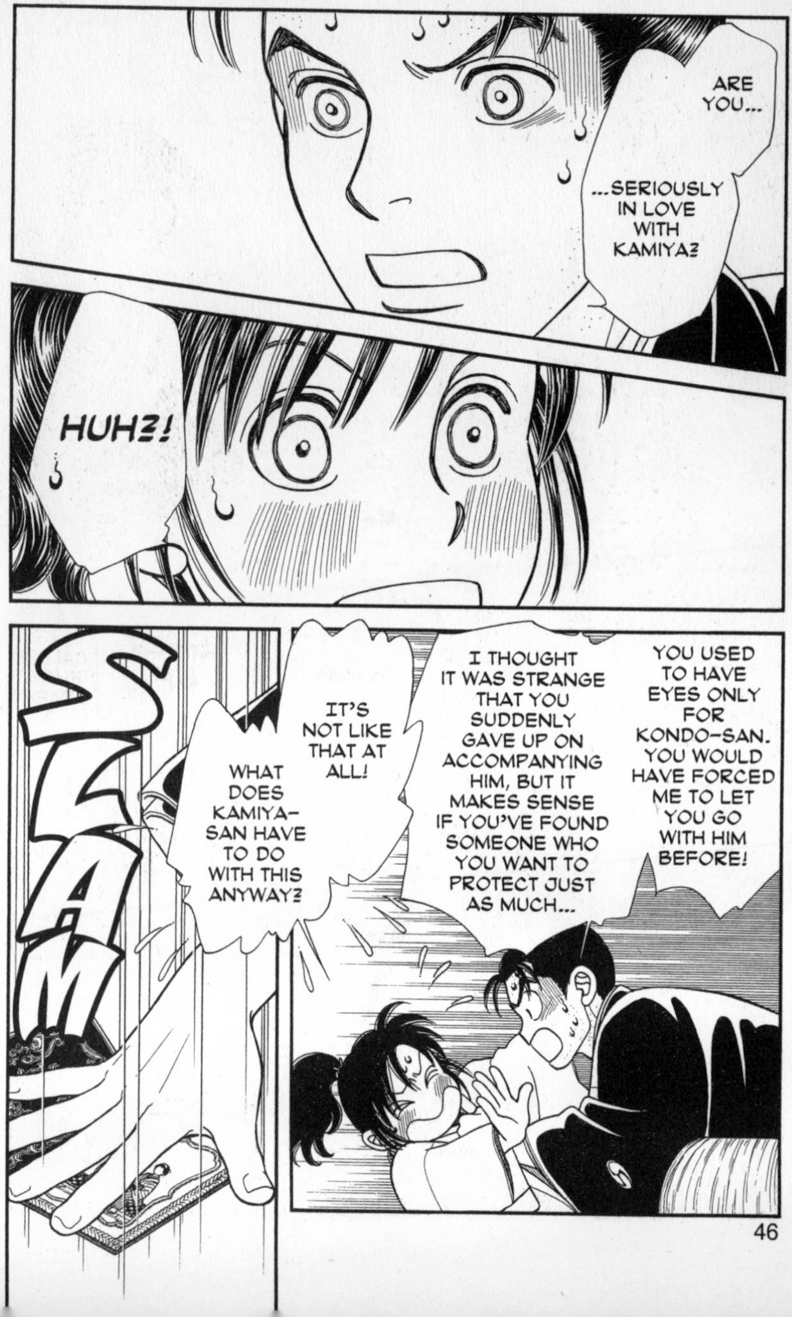
ARE YOU...
...SERIOUSLY IN LOVE WITH KAMIYA?
HUH?!
YOU USED TO HAVE EYES ONLY FOR KONDO-SAN. YOU WOULD HAVE FORCED ME TO LET YOU GO WITH HIM BEFORE!
I THOUGHT IT WAS STRANGE THAT YOU SUDDENLY GAVE UP ON ACCOMPANYING HIM, BUT IT MAKES SENSE IF YOU'VE FOUND SOMEONE WHO YOU WANT TO PROTECT JUST AS MUCH...
IT'S NOT LIKE THAT AT ALL!
WHAT DOES KAMIYA-SAN HAVE TO DO WITH THIS ANYWAY?
SLAM

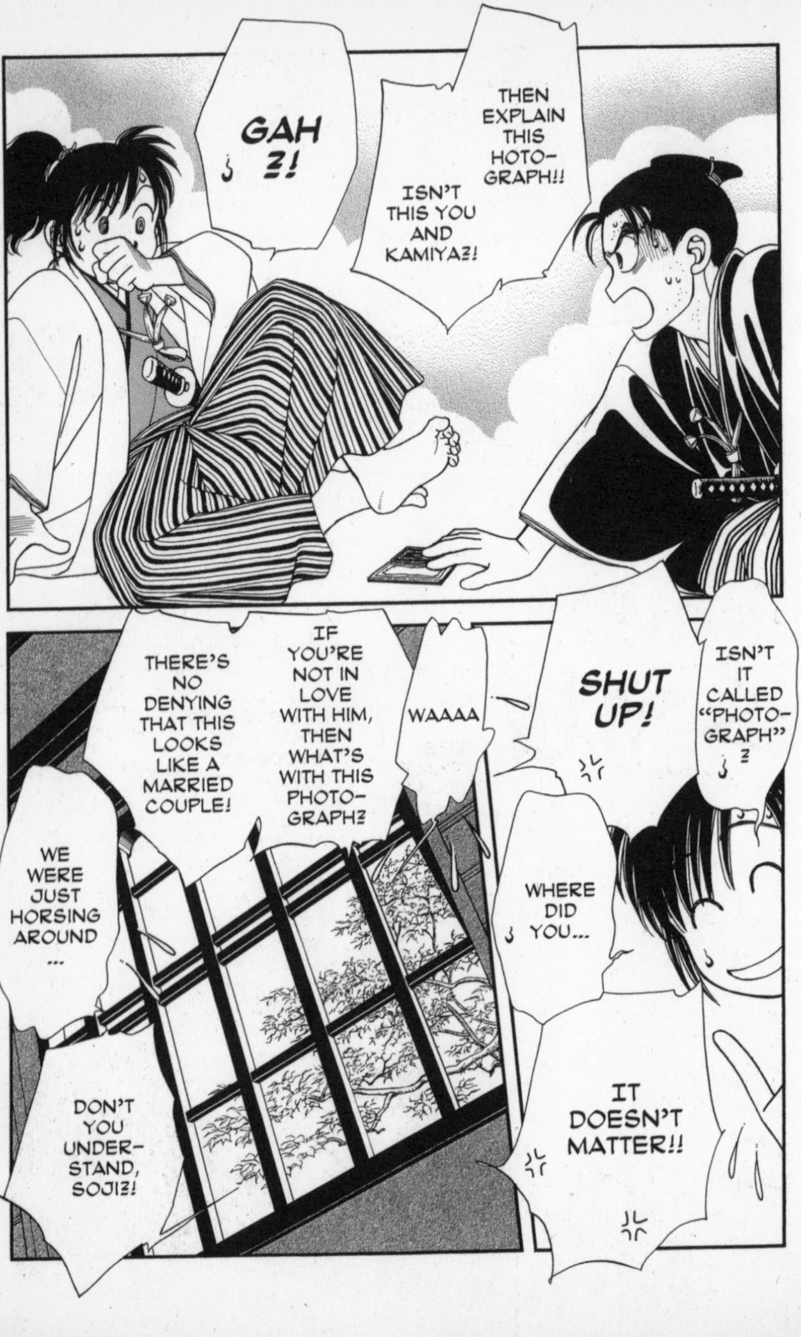
THEN EXPLAIN THIS HOTOGRAPH!! ISN'T THIS YOU AND KAMIYA?!
GAH?!
ISN'T IT CALLED "PHOTOGRAPH"?
SHUT UP!
WAAAA
IF YOU'RE NOT IN LOVE WITH HIM, THEN WHAT'S WITH THIS PHOTOGRAPH?
THERE'S NO DENYING THAT THIS LOOKS LIKE A MARRIED COUPLE!
WHERE DID YOU...
WE WERE JUST HORSING AROUND...
IT DOESN'T MATTER!!
DON'T YOU UNDERSTAND, SOJI?!

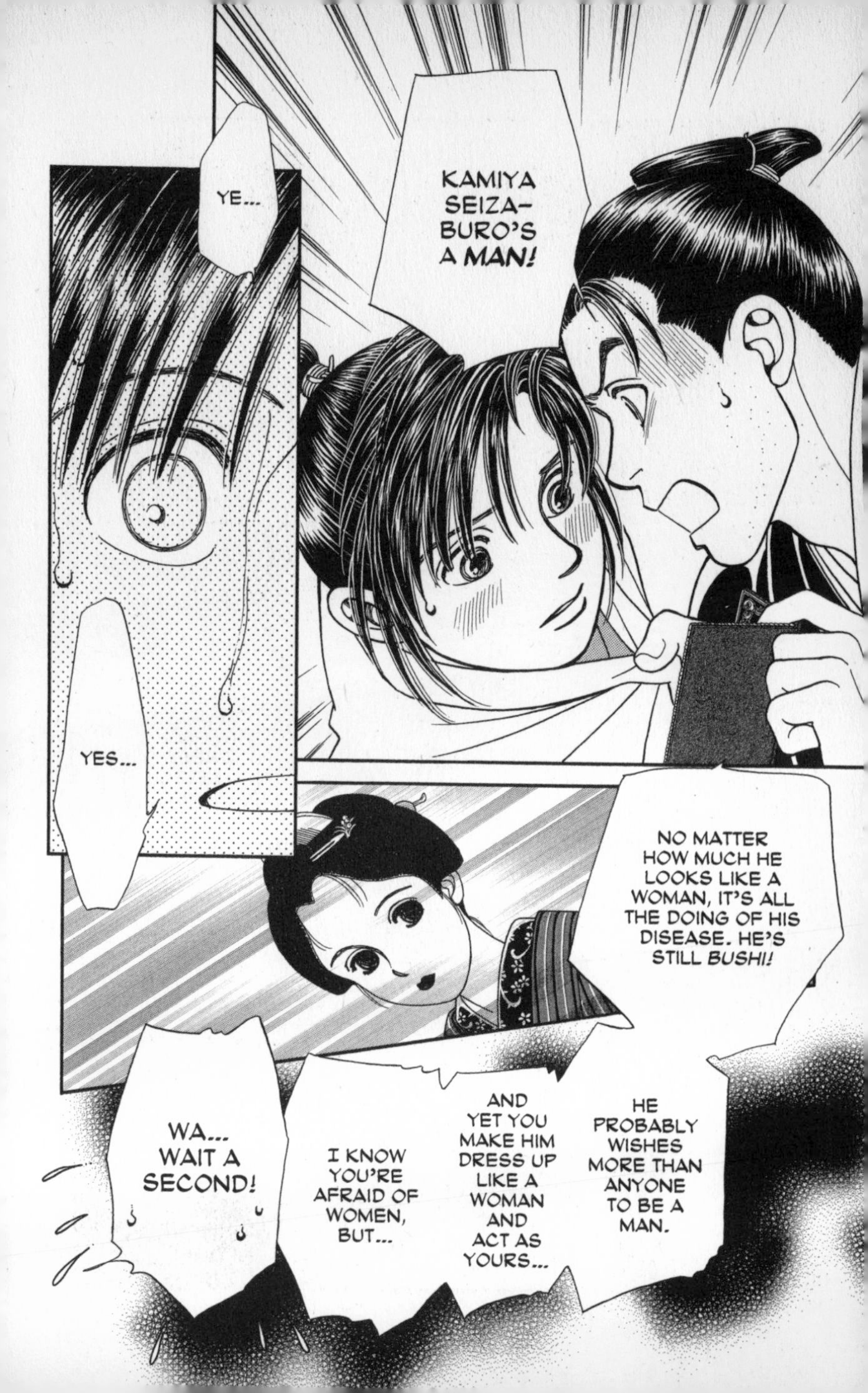
KAMIYA SEIZABURO'S A *MAN!*
YE...
YES...
NO MATTER HOW MUCH HE LOOKS LIKE A WOMAN, IT'S ALL THE DOING OF HIS DISEASE. HE'S STILL *BUSHI!*
HE PROBABLY WISHES MORE THAN ANYONE TO BE A MAN.
AND YET YOU MAKE HIM DRESS UP LIKE A WOMAN AND ACT AS YOURS...
I KNOW YOU'RE AFRAID OF WOMEN, BUT...
WA... WAIT A SECOND!

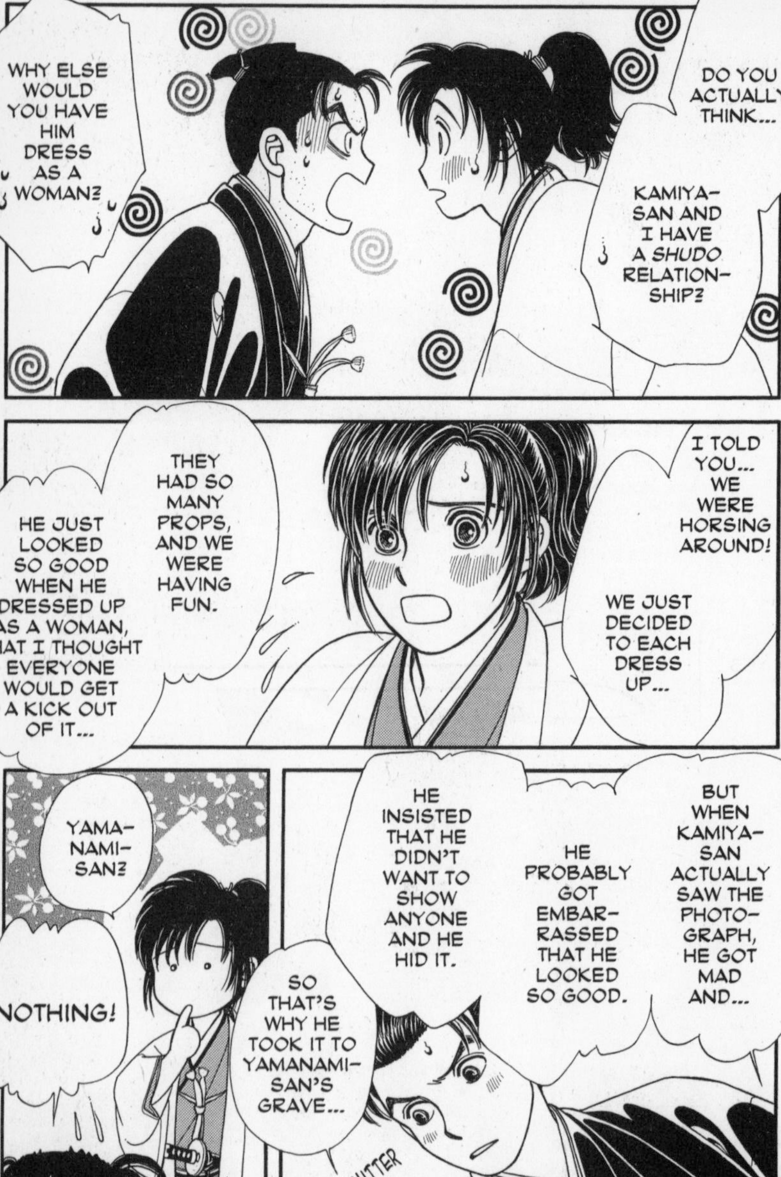
DO YOU ACTUALLY THINK...
KAMIYA-SAN AND I HAVE A *SHUDO* RELATIONSHIP?
WHY ELSE WOULD YOU HAVE HIM DRESS AS A WOMAN?
I TOLD YOU... WE WERE HORSING AROUND!
WE JUST DECIDED TO EACH DRESS UP...
THEY HAD SO MANY PROPS, AND WE WERE HAVING FUN.
HE JUST LOOKED SO GOOD WHEN HE DRESSED UP AS A WOMAN, THAT I THOUGHT EVERYONE WOULD GET A KICK OUT OF IT...
BUT WHEN KAMIYA-SAN ACTUALLY SAW THE PHOTOGRAPH, HE GOT MAD AND...
HE PROBABLY GOT EMBARRASSED THAT HE LOOKED SO GOOD.
HE INSISTED THAT HE DIDN'T WANT TO SHOW ANYONE AND HE HID IT.
SO THAT'S WHY HE TOOK IT TO YAMANAMI-SAN'S GRAVE...
MUTTER
YAMANAMI-SAN?
NOTHING!

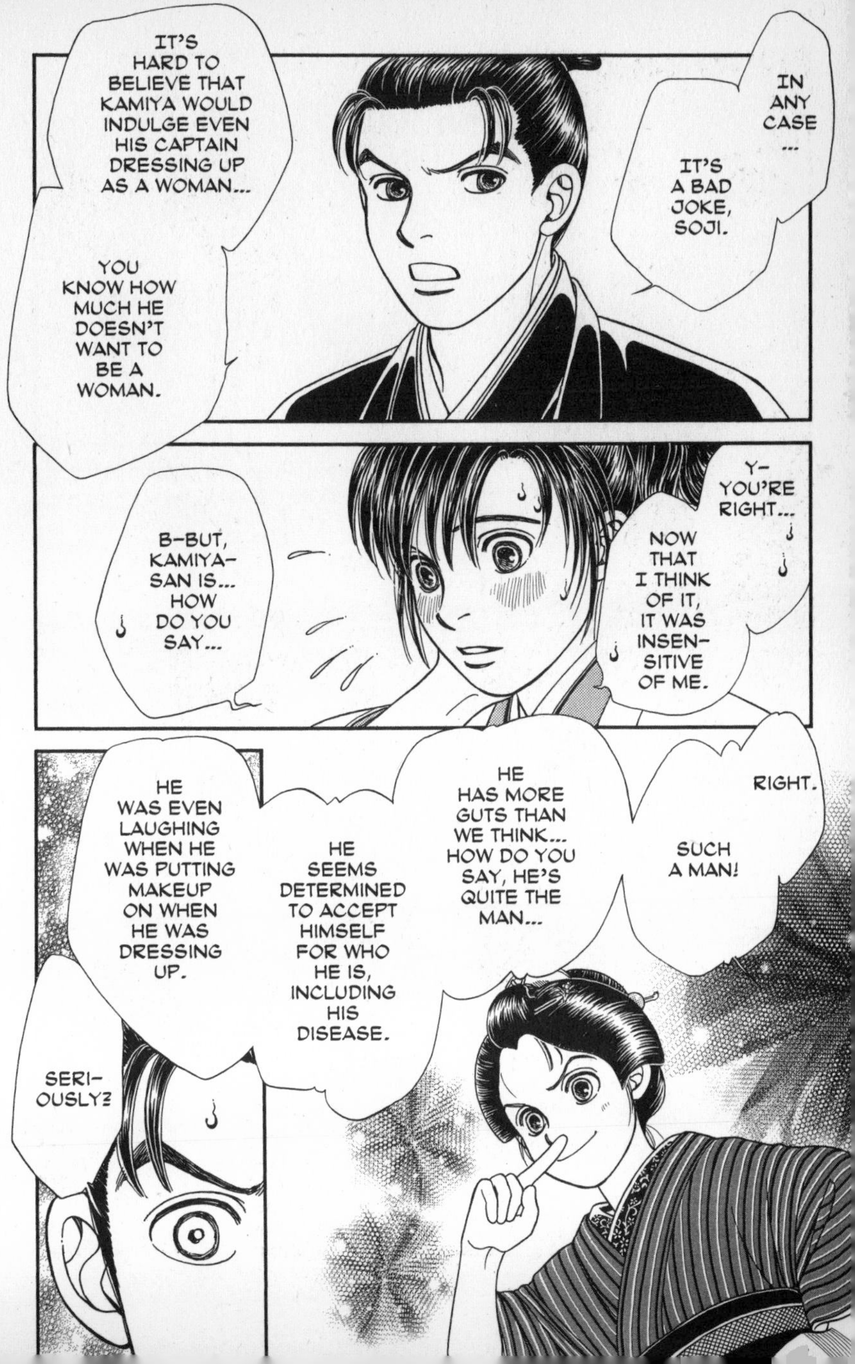
IN ANY CASE...
IT'S A BAD JOKE, SOJI.
IT'S HARD TO BELIEVE THAT KAMIYA WOULD INDULGE EVEN HIS CAPTAIN DRESSING UP AS A WOMAN...
YOU KNOW HOW MUCH HE DOESN'T WANT TO BE A WOMAN.
Y-YOU'RE RIGHT...
NOW THAT I THINK OF IT, IT WAS INSEN-SITIVE OF ME.
B-BUT, KAMIYA-SAN IS... HOW DO YOU SAY...
RIGHT.
SUCH A MAN!
HE HAS MORE GUTS THAN WE THINK... HOW DO YOU SAY, HE'S QUITE THE MAN...
HE SEEMS DETERMINED TO ACCEPT HIMSELF FOR WHO HE IS, INCLUDING HIS DISEASE.
HE WAS EVEN LAUGHING WHEN HE WAS PUTTING MAKEUP ON WHEN HE WAS DRESSING UP.
SERI-OUSLY?

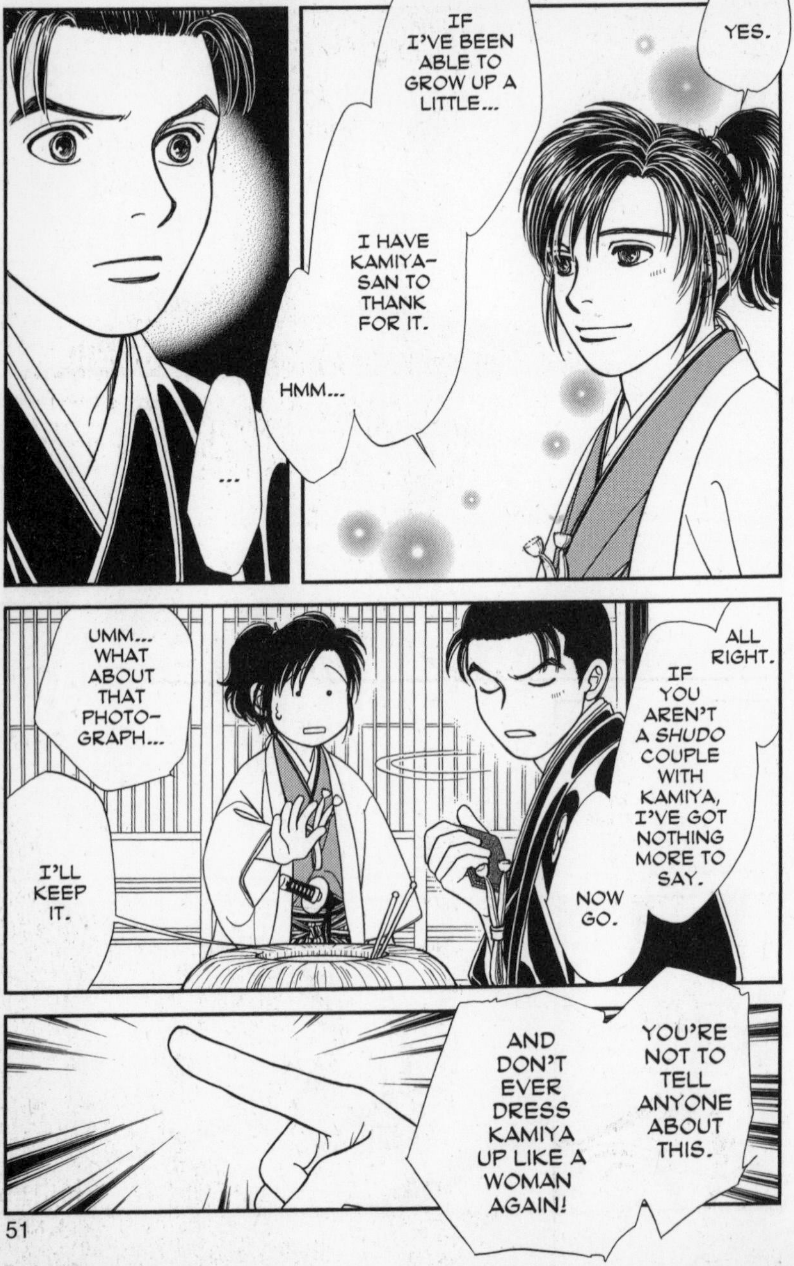
YES.
IF I'VE BEEN ABLE TO GROW UP A LITTLE...
I HAVE KAMIYA-SAN TO THANK FOR IT.
HMM...
...
ALL RIGHT.
IF YOU AREN'T A *SHUDO* COUPLE WITH KAMIYA, I'VE GOT NOTHING MORE TO SAY.
NOW GO.
UMM... WHAT ABOUT THAT PHOTOGRAPH...
I'LL KEEP IT.
YOU'RE NOT TO TELL ANYONE ABOUT THIS.
AND DON'T EVER DRESS KAMIYA UP LIKE A WOMAN AGAIN!

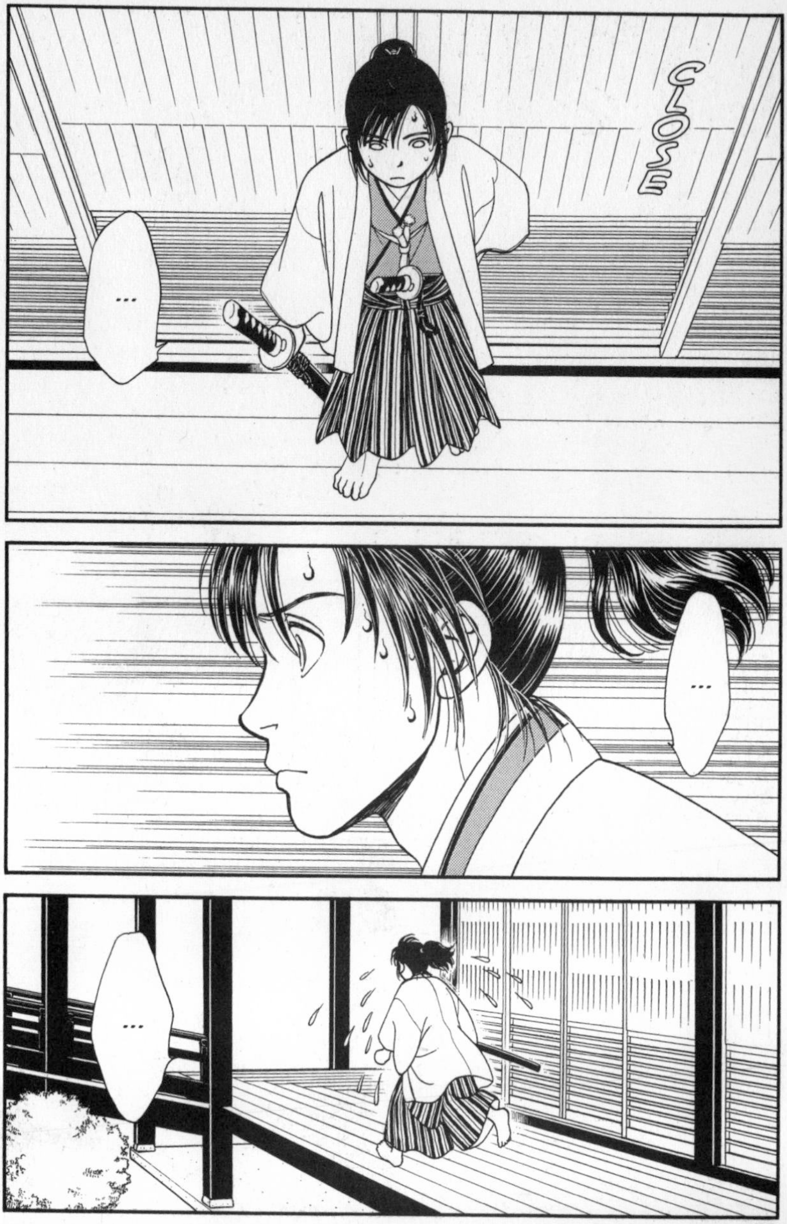
CLOSE
...
...
...

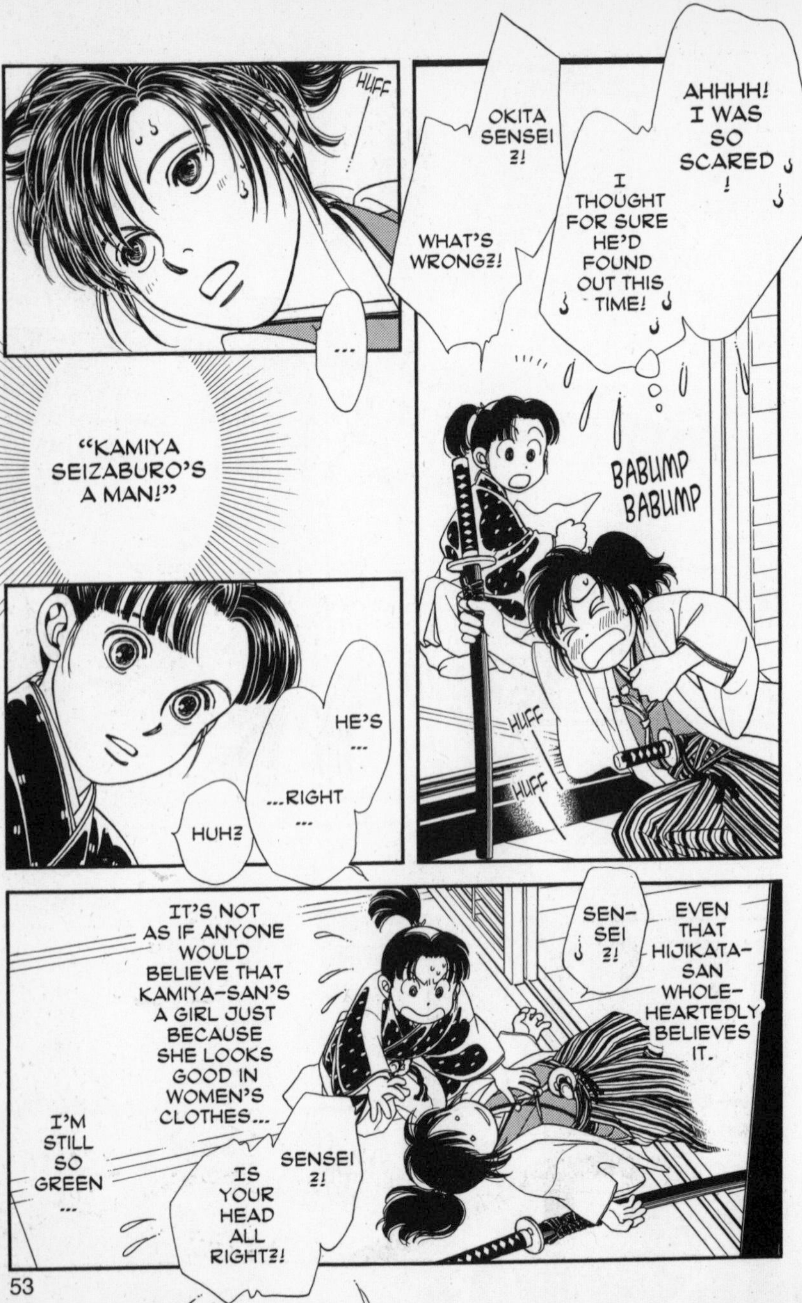
AHHHH! I WAS SO SCARED!
I THOUGHT FOR SURE HE'D FOUND OUT THIS TIME!
OKITA SENSEI?!
WHAT'S WRONG?!
BABUMP BABUMP
HUFF
HUFF
HUFF
...
"KAMIYA SEIZABURO'S A MAN!"
HE'S...
...RIGHT...
HUH?
EVEN THAT HIJIKATA-SAN WHOLE-HEARTEDLY BELIEVES IT.
SEN-SEI?!
IT'S NOT AS IF ANYONE WOULD BELIEVE THAT KAMIYA-SAN'S A GIRL JUST BECAUSE SHE LOOKS GOOD IN WOMEN'S CLOTHES...
SENSEI?!
IS YOUR HEAD ALL RIGHT?!
I'M STILL SO GREEN...

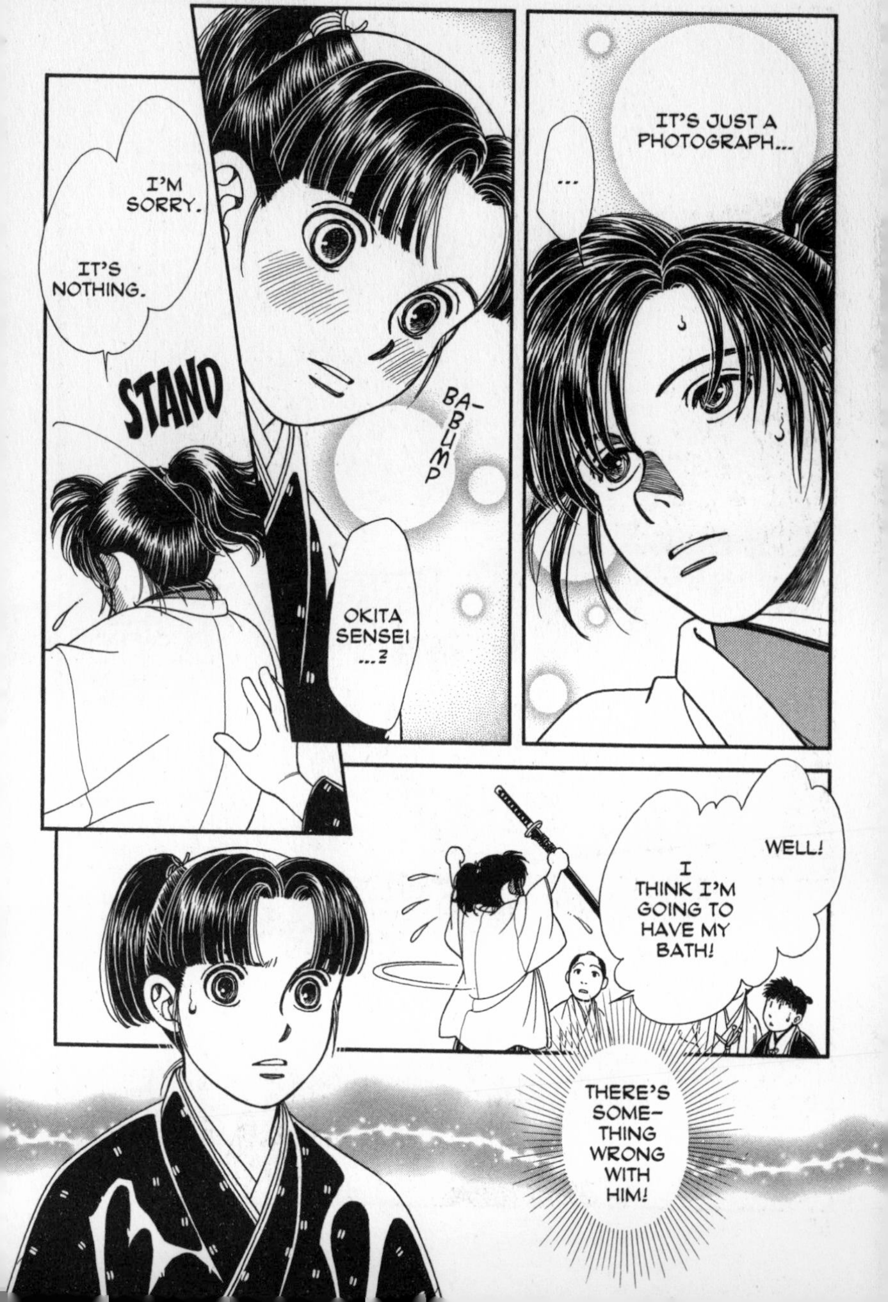
IT'S JUST A PHOTOGRAPH...
...
BA-BUMP
OKITA SENSEI ...?
I'M SORRY.
IT'S NOTHING.
STAND
WELL!
I THINK I'M GOING TO HAVE MY BATH!
THERE'S SOME-THING WRONG WITH HIM!

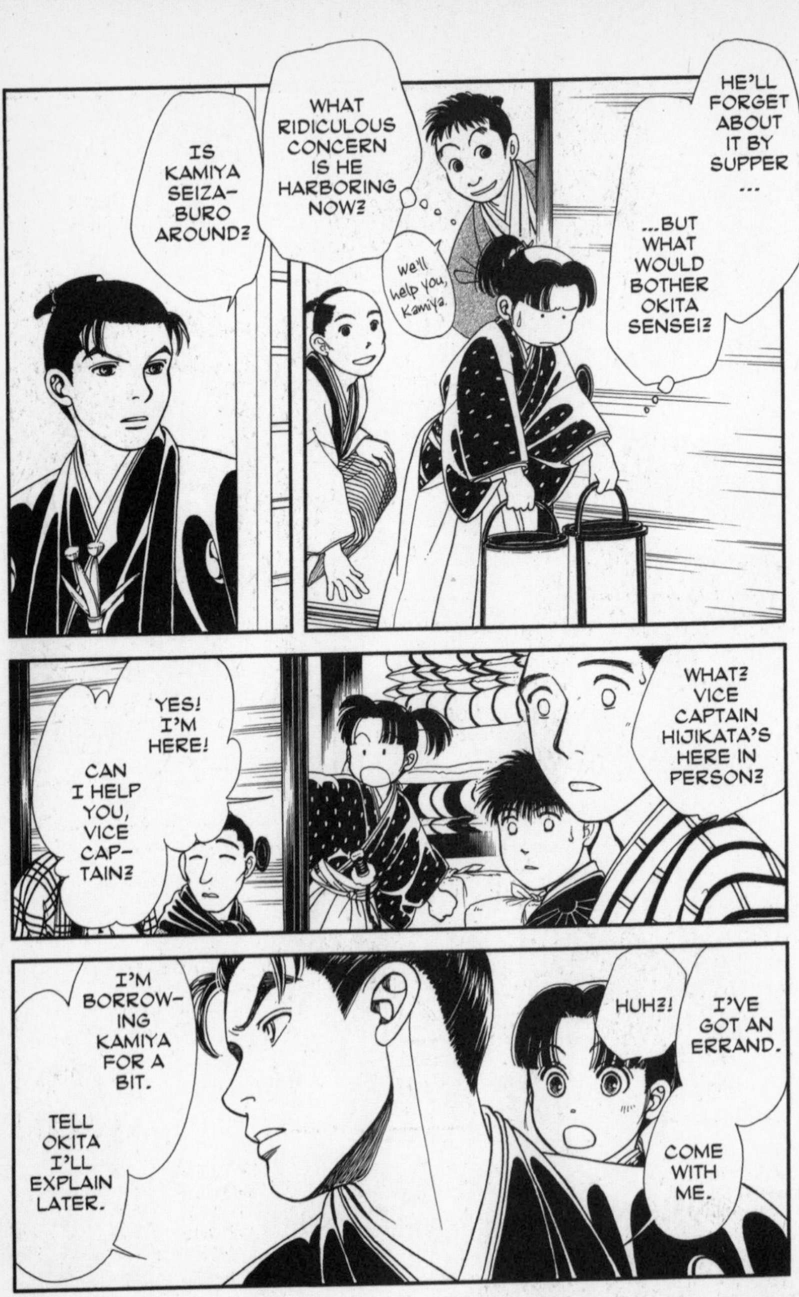
HE'LL FORGET ABOUT IT BY SUPPER ...
...BUT WHAT WOULD BOTHER OKITA SENSEI?
WHAT RIDICULOUS CONCERN IS HE HARBORING NOW?
We'll help you, Kamiya.
IS KAMIYA SEIZA-BURO AROUND?
WHAT? VICE CAPTAIN HIJIKATA'S HERE IN PERSON?
YES! I'M HERE!
CAN I HELP YOU, VICE CAP-TAIN?
I'VE GOT AN ERRAND.
HUH?!
COME WITH ME.
I'M BORROW-ING KAMIYA FOR A BIT.
TELL OKITA I'LL EXPLAIN LATER.

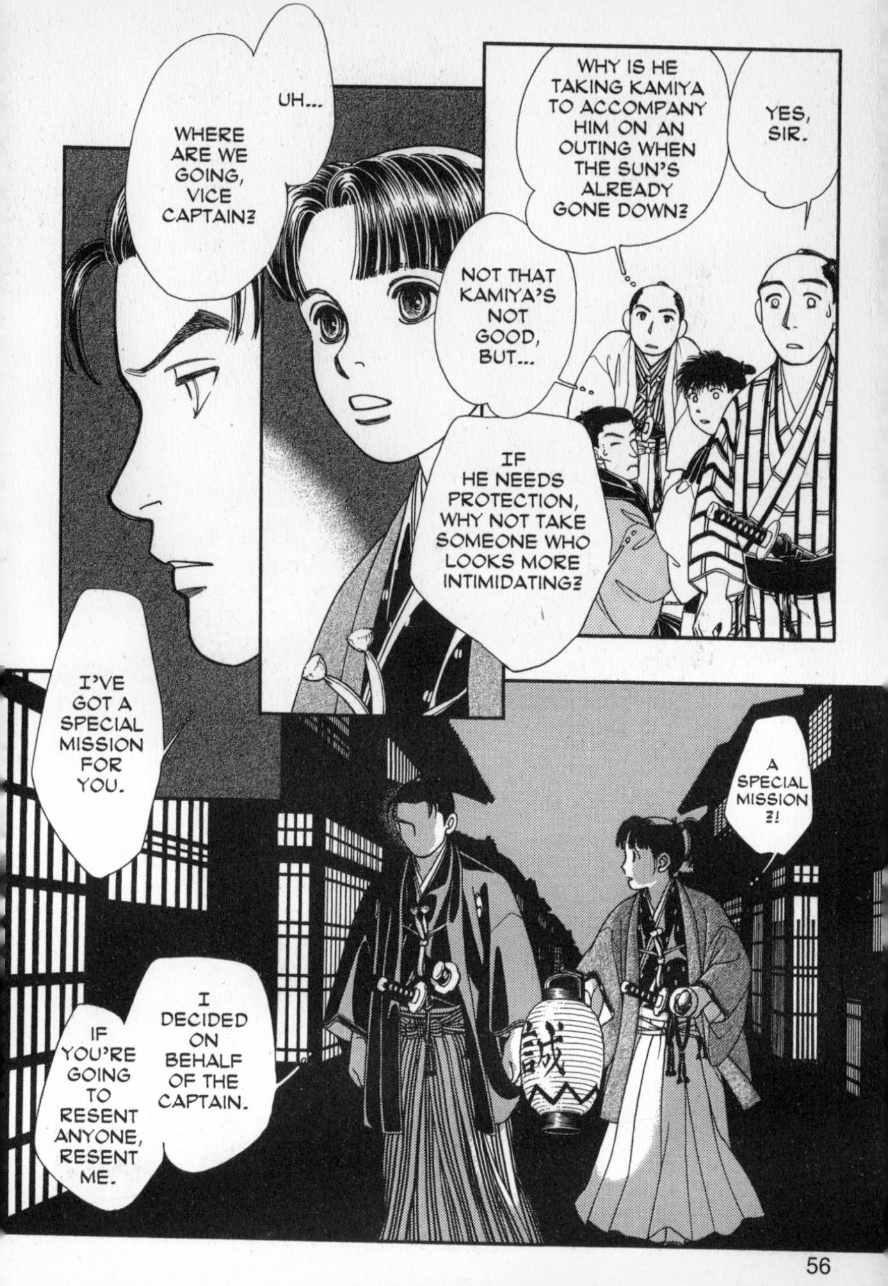
YES, SIR.
WHY IS HE TAKING KAMIYA TO ACCOMPANY HIM ON AN OUTING WHEN THE SUN'S ALREADY GONE DOWN?
NOT THAT KAMIYA'S NOT GOOD, BUT...
IF HE NEEDS PROTECTION, WHY NOT TAKE SOMEONE WHO LOOKS MORE INTIMIDATING?
UH...
WHERE ARE WE GOING, VICE CAPTAIN?
I'VE GOT A SPECIAL MISSION FOR YOU.
A SPECIAL MISSION?!
I DECIDED ON BEHALF OF THE CAPTAIN.
IF YOU'RE GOING TO RESENT ANYONE, RESENT ME.

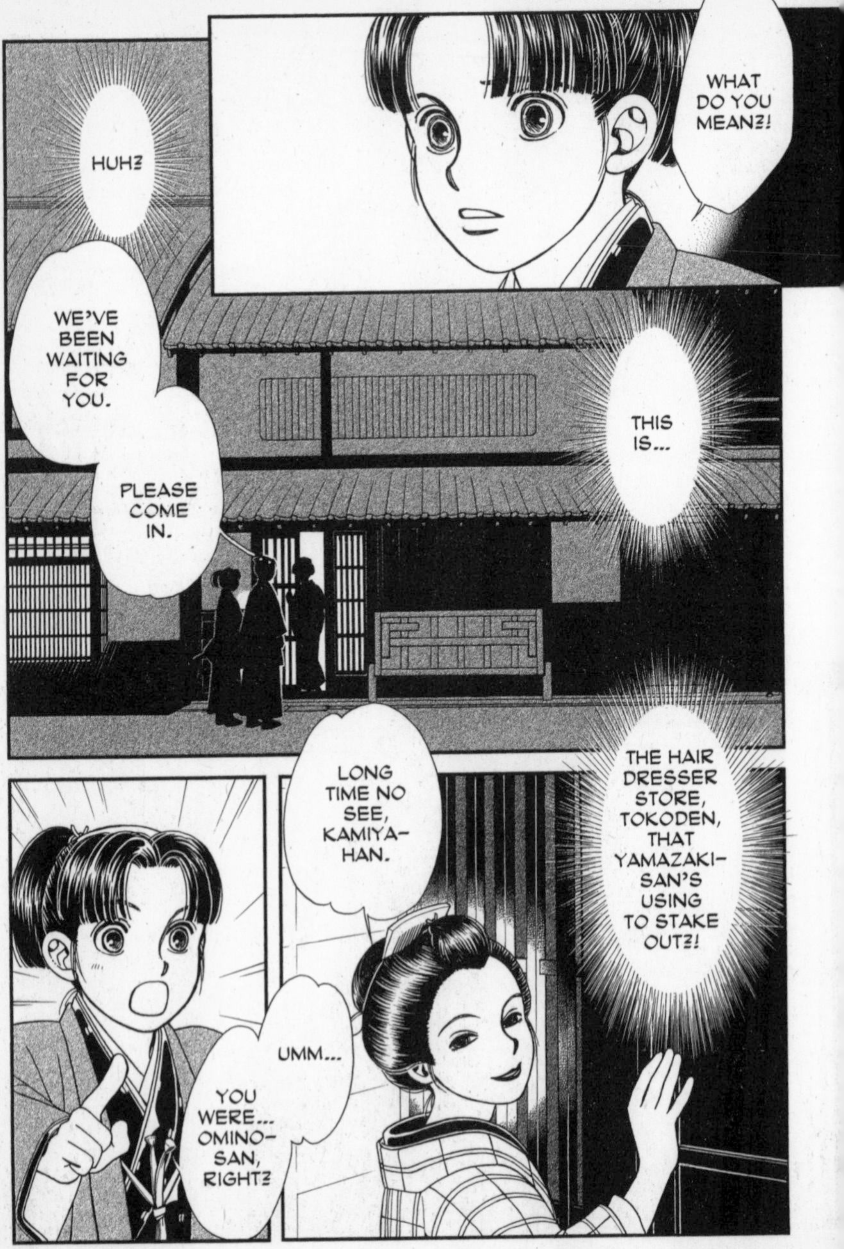
WHAT DO YOU MEAN?!
HUH?
WE'VE BEEN WAITING FOR YOU.
PLEASE COME IN.
THIS IS...
THE HAIR DRESSER STORE, TOKODEN, THAT YAMAZAKI-SAN'S USING TO STAKE OUT?!
LONG TIME NO SEE, KAMIYA-HAN.
UMM...
YOU WERE... OMINO-SAN, RIGHT?

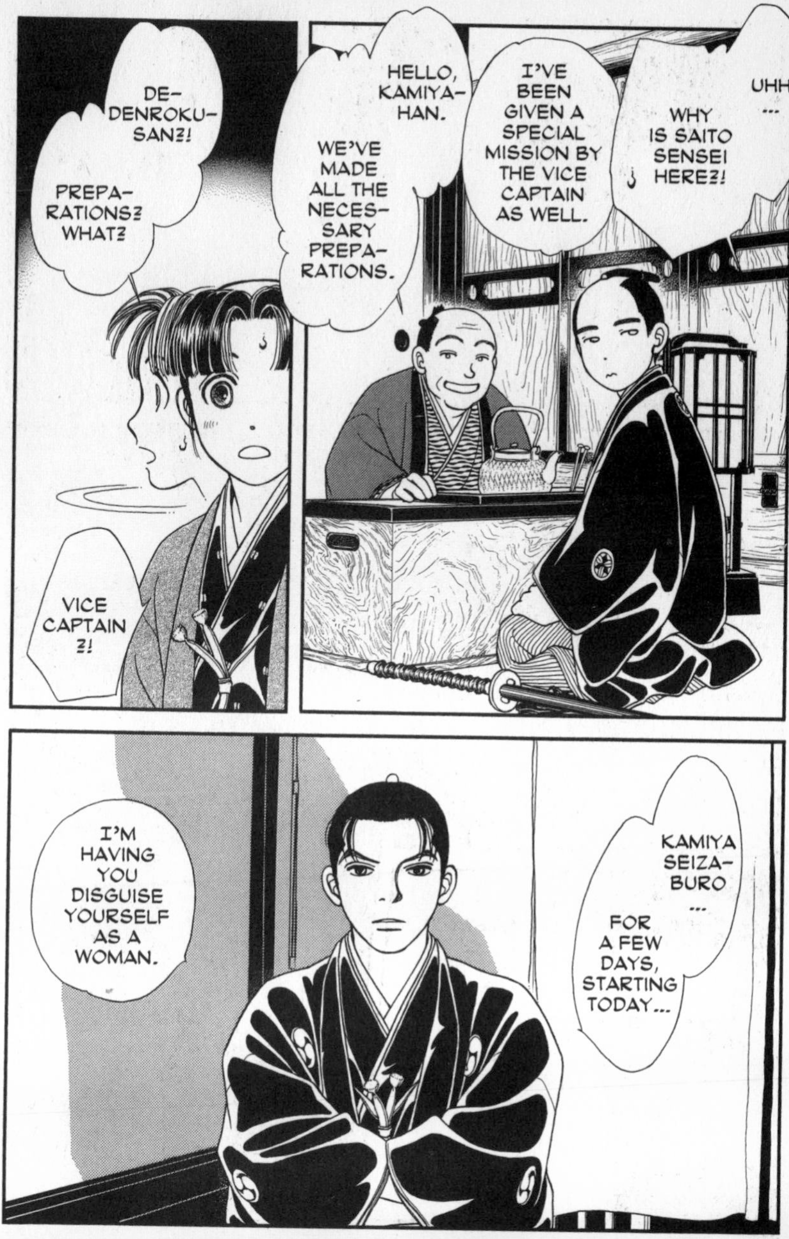

UHH ...
WHY IS SAITO SENSEI HERE?!
I'VE BEEN GIVEN A SPECIAL MISSION BY THE VICE CAPTAIN AS WELL.
HELLO, KAMIYA-HAN.
WE'VE MADE ALL THE NECES-SARY PREPA-RATIONS.
DE-DENROKU-SAN?!
PREPA-RATIONS? WHAT?
VICE CAPTAIN ?!
KAMIYA SEIZA-BURO ...
FOR A FEW DAYS, STARTING TODAY...
I'M HAVING YOU DISGUISE YOURSELF AS A WOMAN.

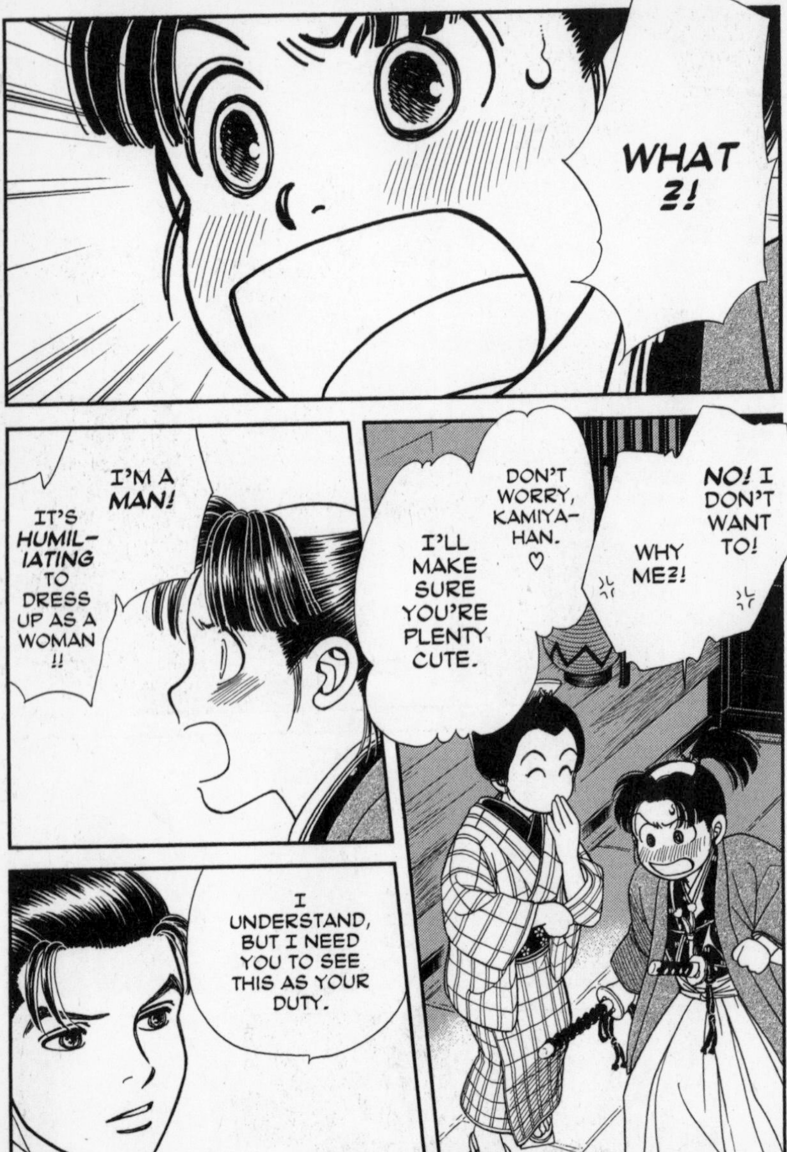
WHAT?!
NO! I DON'T WANT TO!
WHY ME?!
DON'T WORRY, KAMIYA-HAN. ♡
I'LL MAKE SURE YOU'RE PLENTY CUTE.
I'M A MAN!
IT'S HUMILIATING TO DRESS UP AS A WOMAN!!
I UNDERSTAND, BUT I NEED YOU TO SEE THIS AS YOUR DUTY.

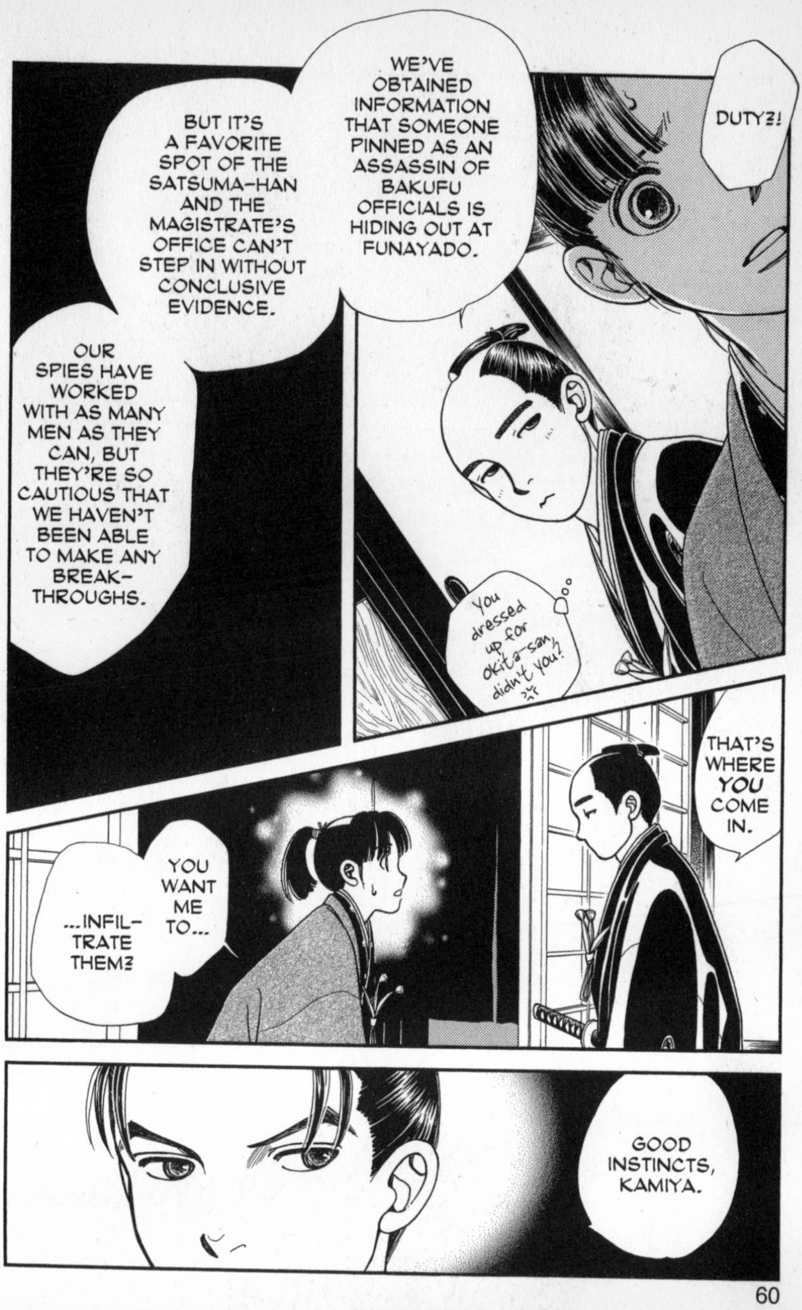
DUTY?!
WE'VE OBTAINED INFORMATION THAT SOMEONE PINNED AS AN ASSASSIN OF BAKUFU OFFICIALS IS HIDING OUT AT FUNAYADO.
You dressed up for Okita-san, didn't you?
BUT IT'S A FAVORITE SPOT OF THE SATSUMA-HAN AND THE MAGISTRATE'S OFFICE CAN'T STEP IN WITHOUT CONCLUSIVE EVIDENCE.
OUR SPIES HAVE WORKED WITH AS MANY MEN AS THEY CAN, BUT THEY'RE SO CAUTIOUS THAT WE HAVEN'T BEEN ABLE TO MAKE ANY BREAK-THROUGHS.
THAT'S WHERE *YOU* COME IN.
YOU WANT ME TO...
...INFIL-TRATE THEM?
GOOD INSTINCTS, KAMIYA.

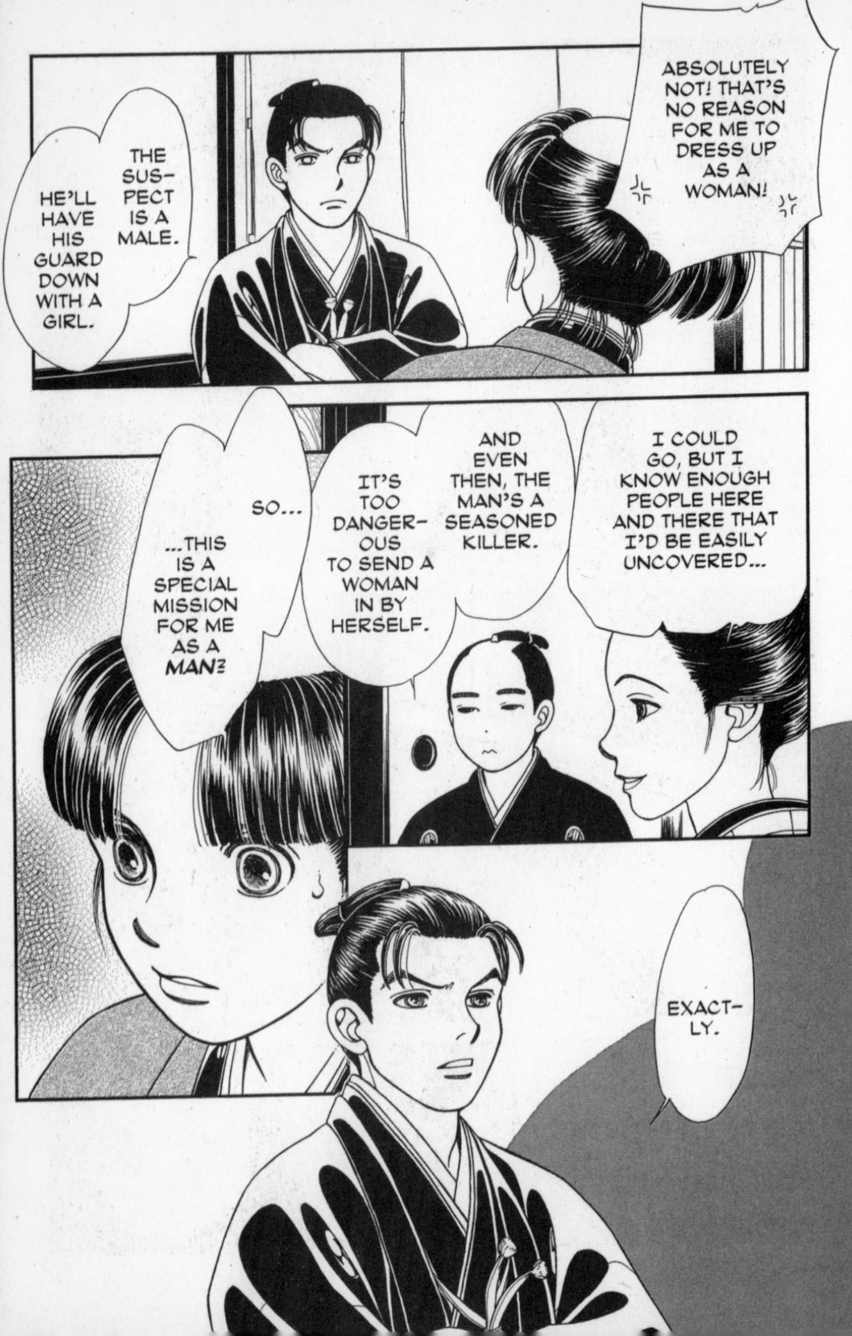
ABSOLUTELY NOT! THAT'S NO REASON FOR ME TO DRESS UP AS A WOMAN!
THE SUSPECT IS A MALE.
HE'LL HAVE HIS GUARD DOWN WITH A GIRL.
I COULD GO, BUT I KNOW ENOUGH PEOPLE HERE AND THERE THAT I'D BE EASILY UNCOVERED...
AND EVEN THEN, THE MAN'S A SEASONED KILLER.
IT'S TOO DANGEROUS TO SEND A WOMAN IN BY HERSELF.
SO...
...THIS IS A SPECIAL MISSION FOR ME AS A MAN?
EXACTLY.

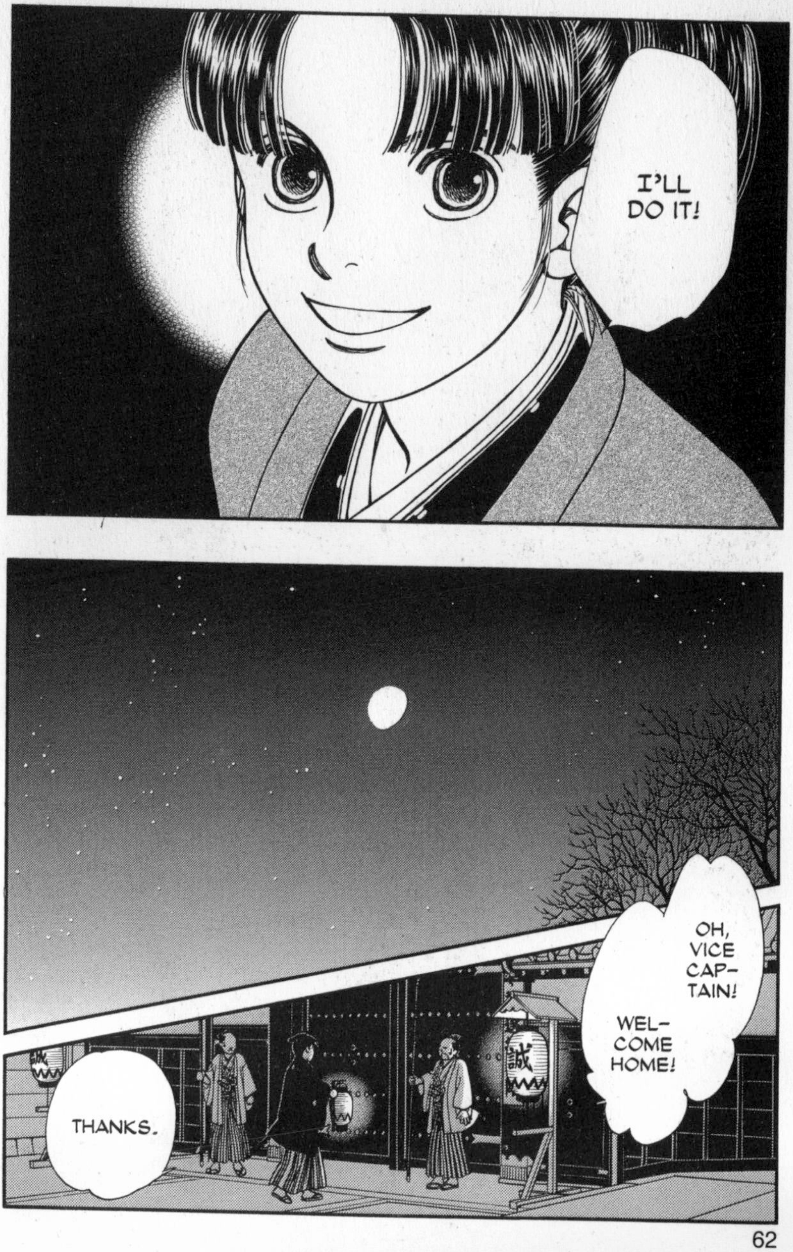
I'LL DO IT!
OH, VICE CAP-TAIN!
WEL-COME HOME!
THANKS.

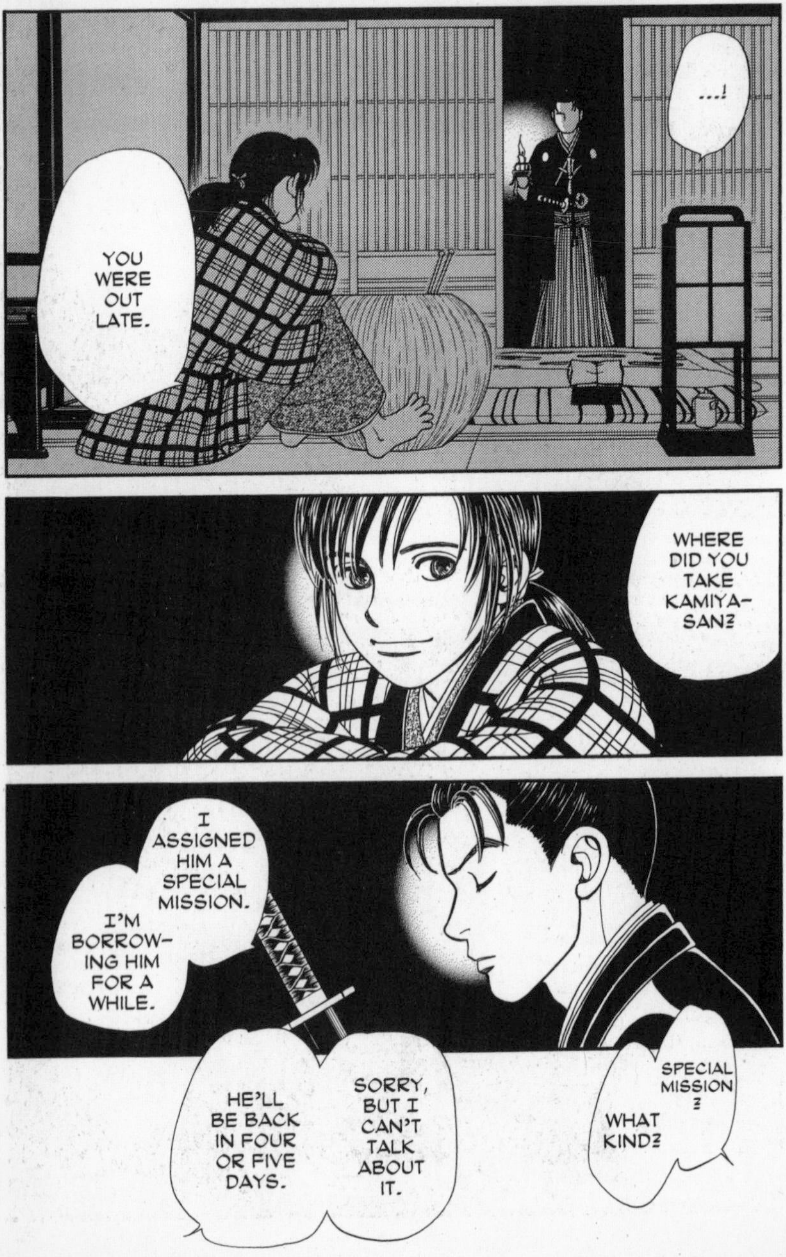
...!
YOU WERE OUT LATE.
WHERE DID YOU TAKE KAMIYA-SAN?
I ASSIGNED HIM A SPECIAL MISSION.
I'M BORROWING HIM FOR A WHILE.
SPECIAL MISSION?
WHAT KIND?
SORRY, BUT I CAN'T TALK ABOUT IT.
HE'LL BE BACK IN FOUR OR FIVE DAYS.

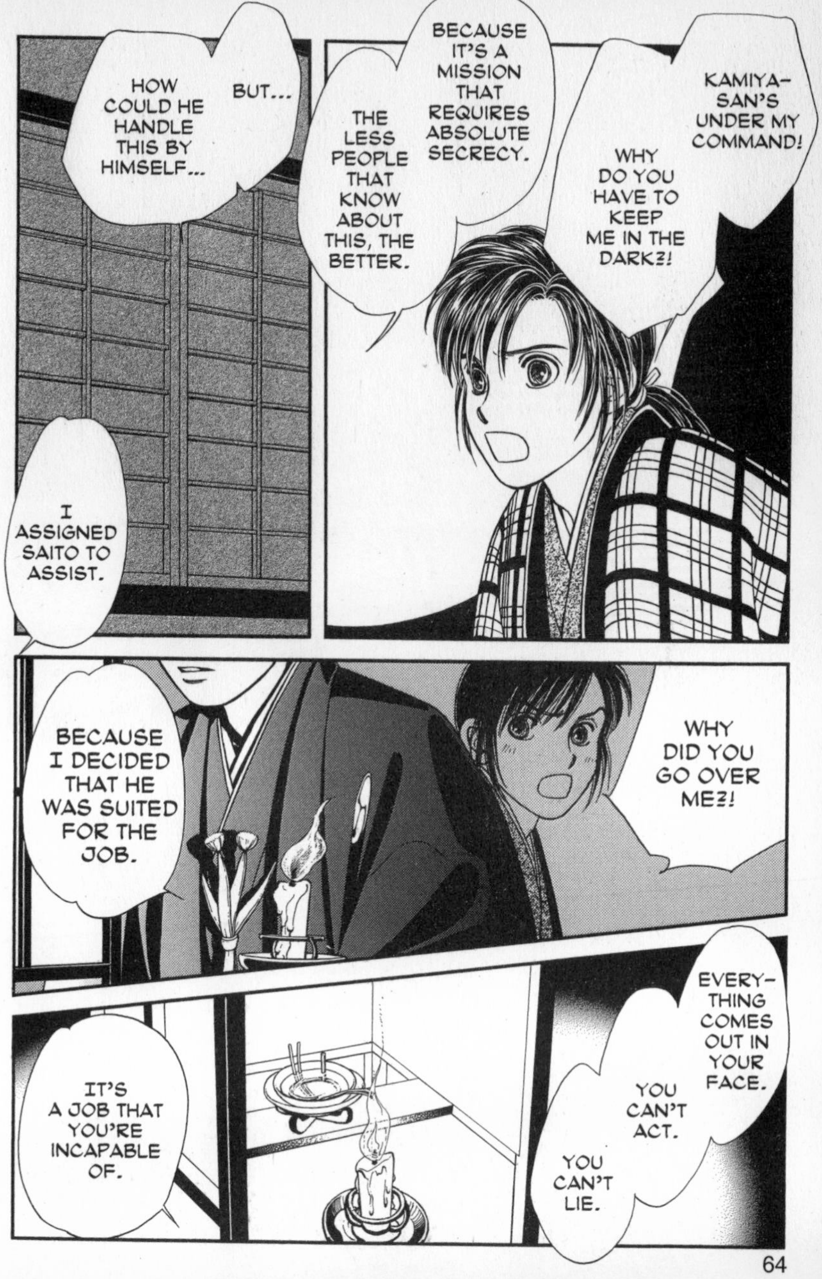
KAMIYA-SAN'S UNDER MY COMMAND!
WHY DO YOU HAVE TO KEEP ME IN THE DARK?!
BECAUSE IT'S A MISSION THAT REQUIRES ABSOLUTE SECRECY.
THE LESS PEOPLE THAT KNOW ABOUT THIS, THE BETTER.
BUT...
HOW COULD HE HANDLE THIS BY HIMSELF...
I ASSIGNED SAITO TO ASSIST.
WHY DID YOU GO OVER ME?!
BECAUSE I DECIDED THAT HE WAS SUITED FOR THE JOB.
EVERY-THING COMES OUT IN YOUR FACE.
YOU CAN'T ACT.
YOU CAN'T LIE.
IT'S A JOB THAT YOU'RE INCAPABLE OF.

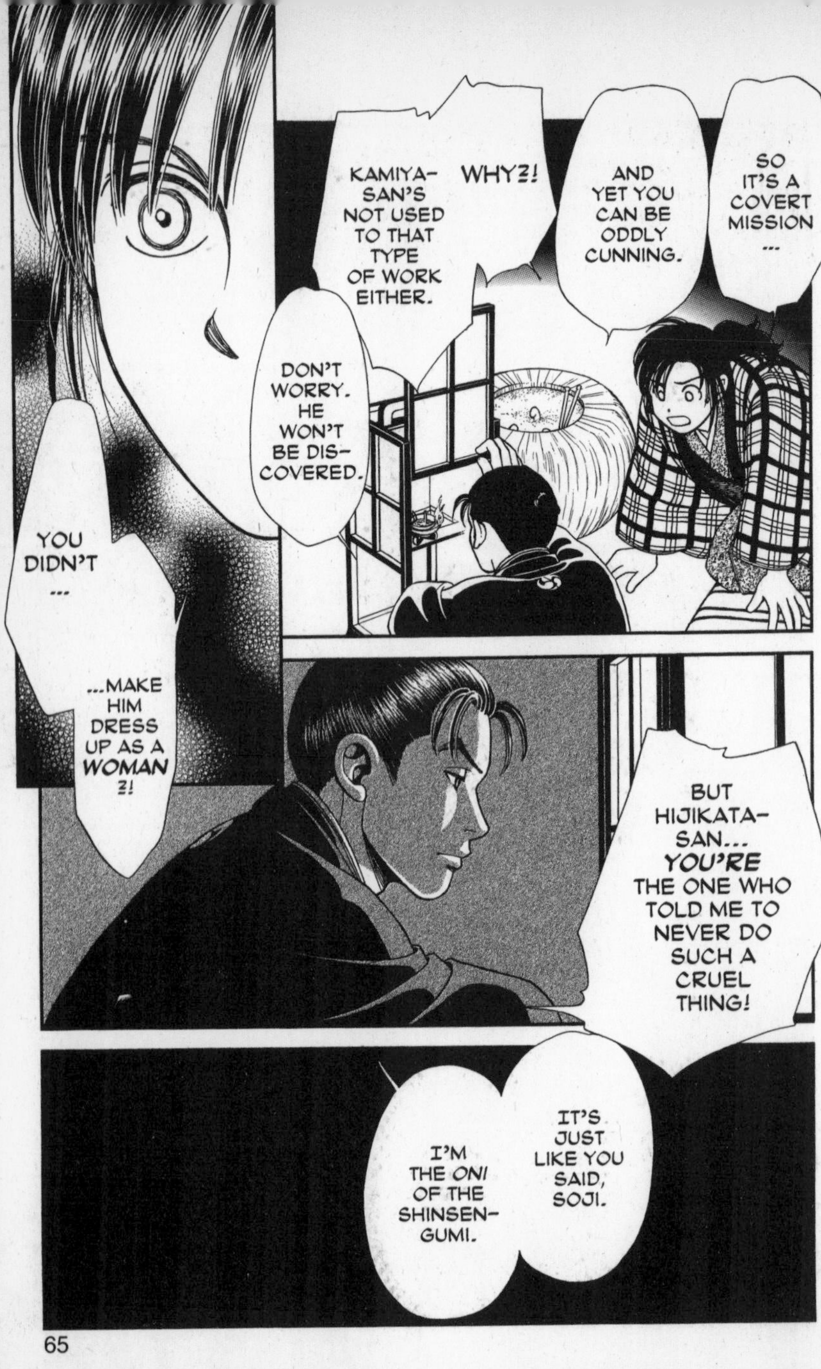
SO IT'S A COVERT MISSION ...
AND YET YOU CAN BE ODDLY CUNNING.
WHY?!
KAMIYA-SAN'S NOT USED TO THAT TYPE OF WORK EITHER.
DON'T WORRY. HE WON'T BE DIS-COVERED.
YOU DIDN'T ...
...MAKE HIM DRESS UP AS A *WOMAN* ?!
BUT HIJIKATA-SAN... *YOU'RE* THE ONE WHO TOLD ME TO NEVER DO SUCH A CRUEL THING!
IT'S JUST LIKE YOU SAID, SOJI.
I'M THE *ONI* OF THE SHINSEN-GUMI.

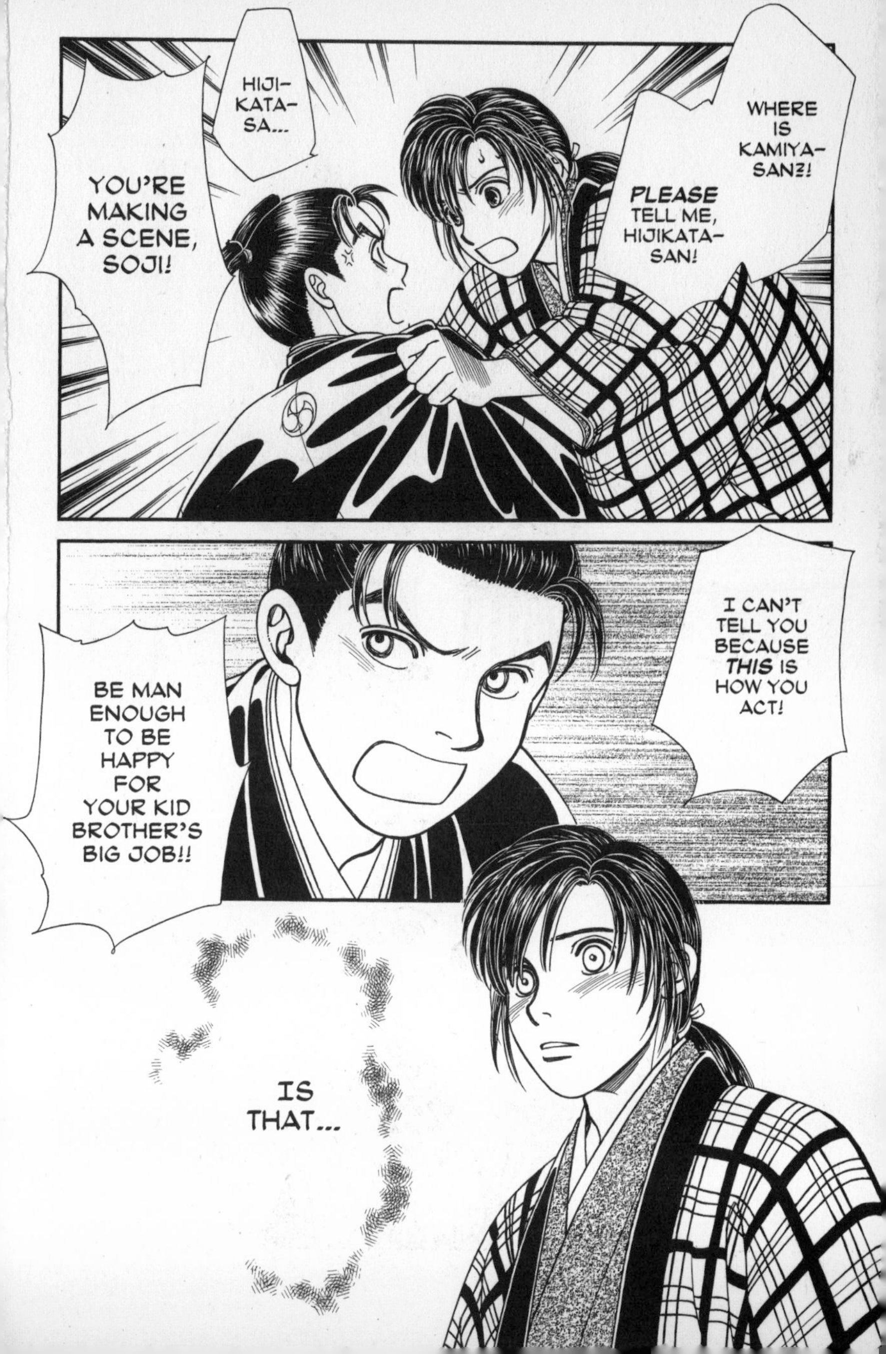
WHERE IS KAMIYA-SAN?!
PLEASE TELL ME, HIJIKATA-SAN!
HIJI-KATA-SA...
YOU'RE MAKING A SCENE, SOJI!
I CAN'T TELL YOU BECAUSE THIS IS HOW YOU ACT!
BE MAN ENOUGH TO BE HAPPY FOR YOUR KID BROTHER'S BIG JOB!!
IS THAT...

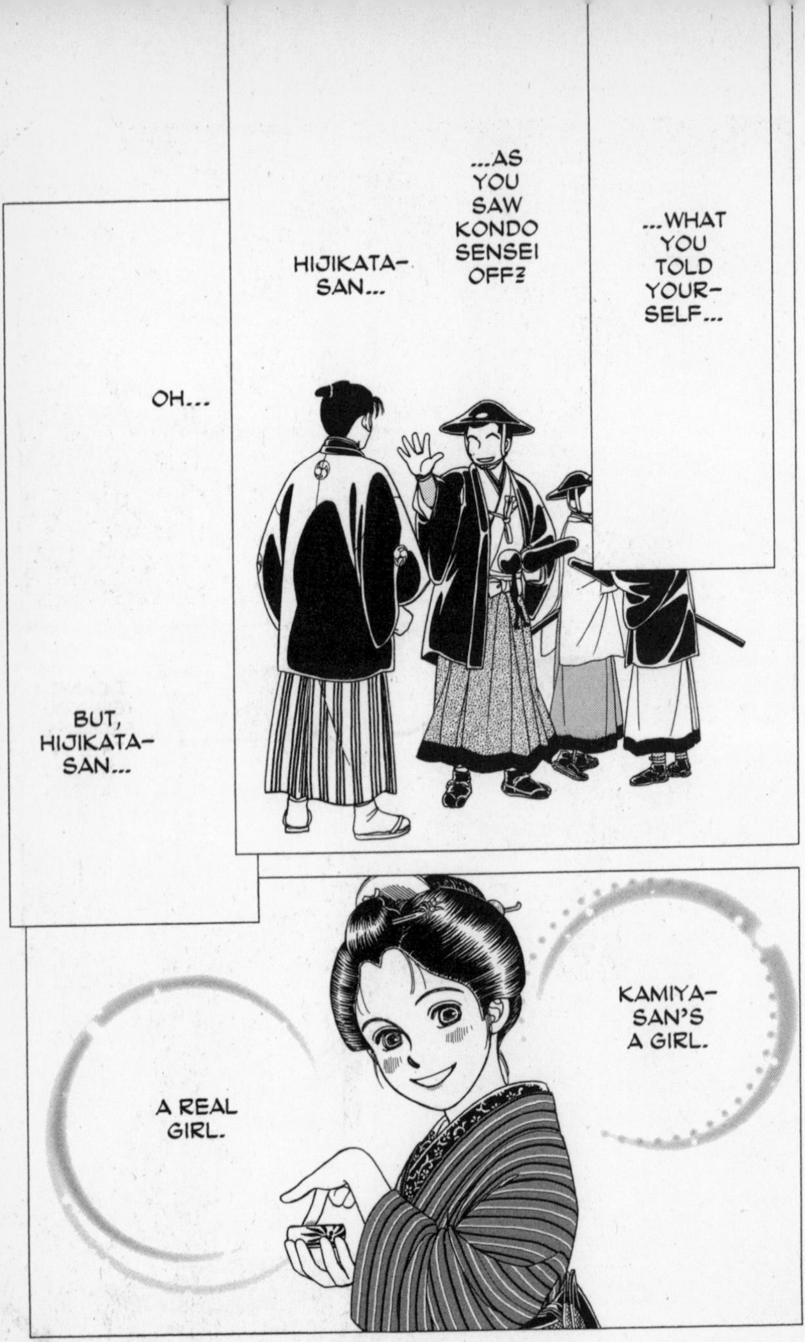
...WHAT YOU TOLD YOURSELF...
...AS YOU SAW KONDO SENSEI OFF?
HIJIKATA-SAN...
OH...
BUT, HIJIKATA-SAN...
KAMIYA-SAN'S A GIRL.
A REAL GIRL.

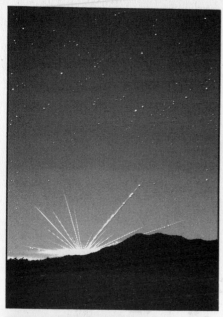

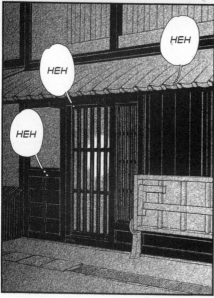

HEH

HEH

HEH

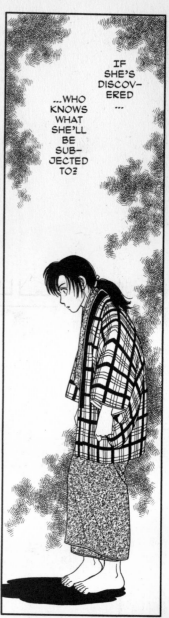

IF SHE'S DISCOVERED...

...WHO KNOWS WHAT SHE'LL BE SUBJECTED TO?

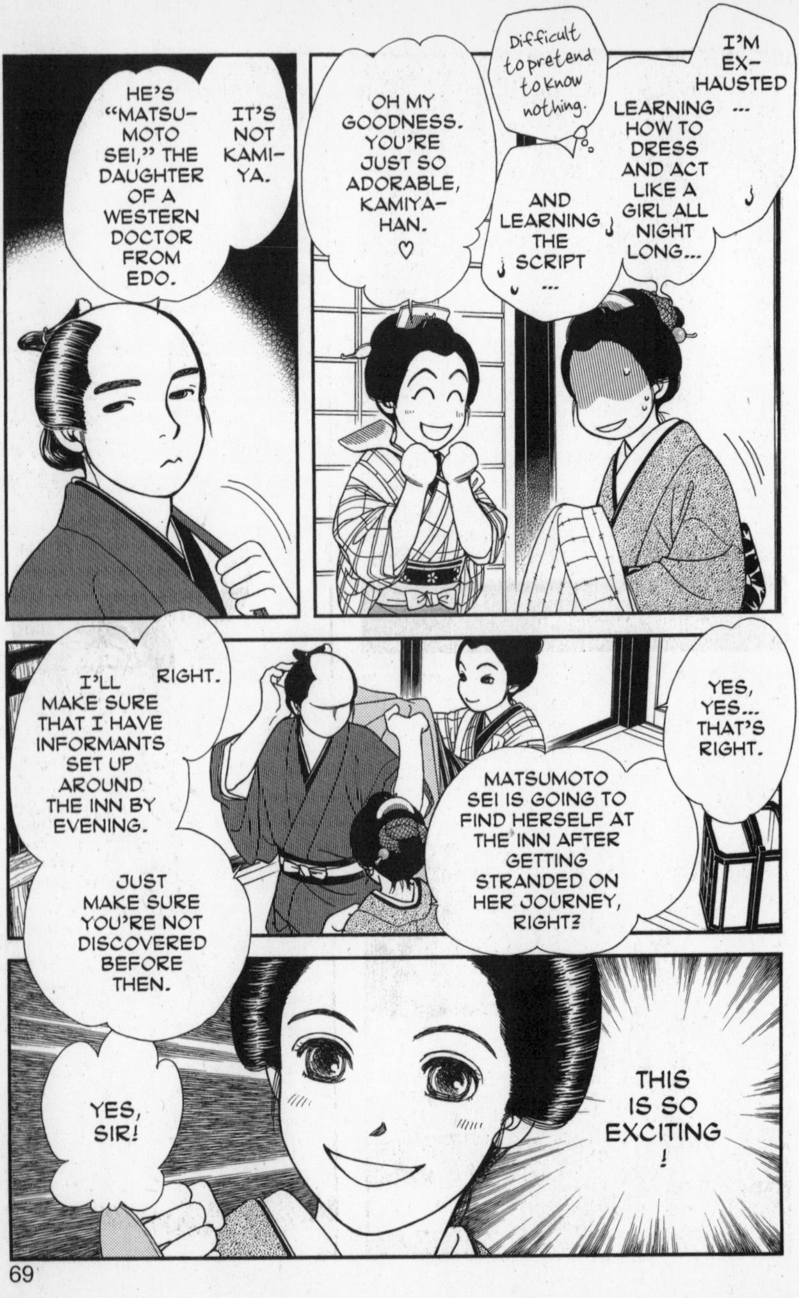
I'M EX-HAUSTED ... LEARNING HOW TO DRESS AND ACT LIKE A GIRL ALL NIGHT LONG...
Difficult to pretend to know nothing.
AND LEARNING THE SCRIPT ...
OH MY GOODNESS. YOU'RE JUST SO ADORABLE, KAMIYA-HAN. ♡
IT'S NOT KAMIYA.
HE'S "MATSUMOTO SEI," THE DAUGHTER OF A WESTERN DOCTOR FROM EDO.
YES, YES... THAT'S RIGHT.
MATSUMOTO SEI IS GOING TO FIND HERSELF AT THE INN AFTER GETTING STRANDED ON HER JOURNEY, RIGHT?
RIGHT. I'LL MAKE SURE THAT I HAVE INFORMANTS SET UP AROUND THE INN BY EVENING.
JUST MAKE SURE YOU'RE NOT DISCOVERED BEFORE THEN.
THIS IS SO EXCITING!
YES, SIR!

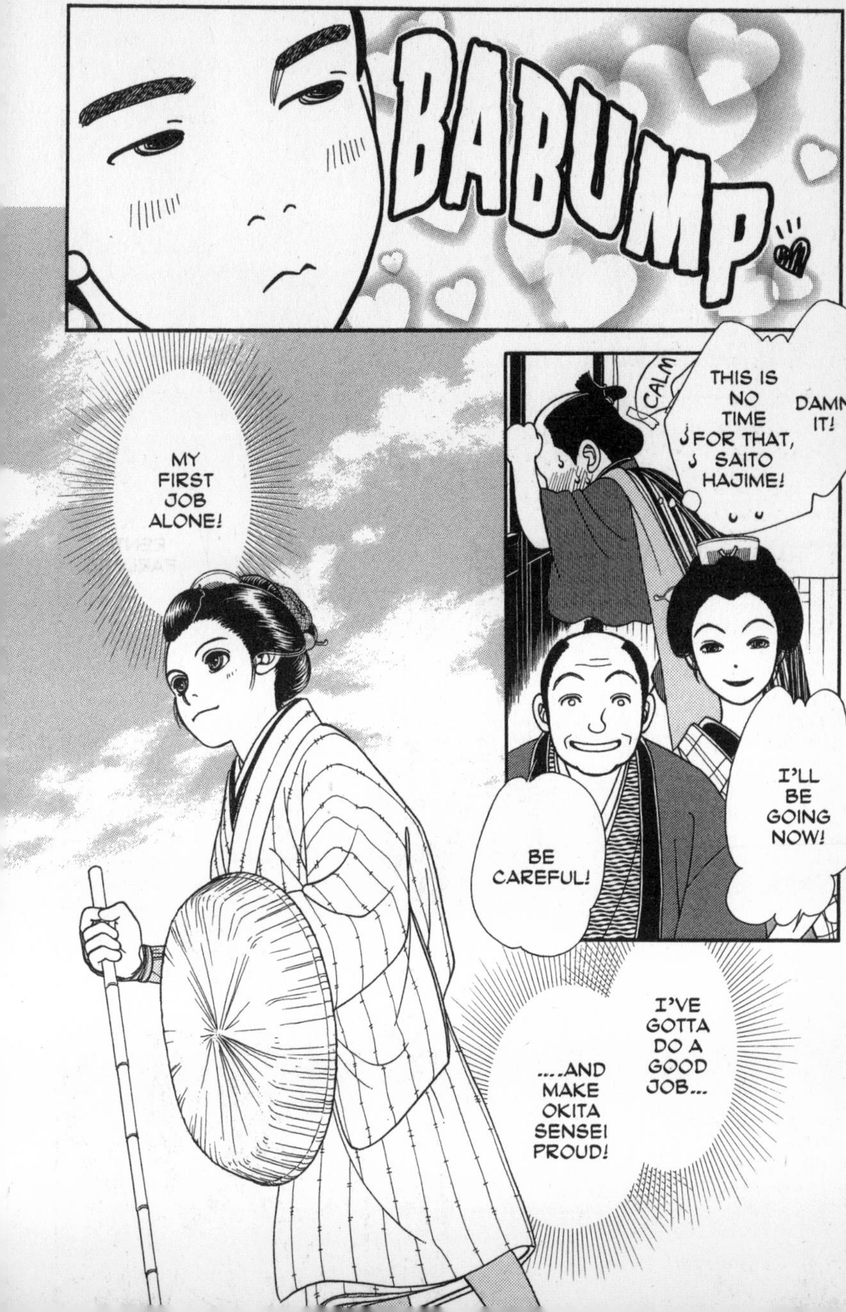
BABUMP
DAMN IT!
THIS IS NO TIME FOR THAT, SAITO HAJIME!
CALM
I'LL BE GOING NOW!
BE CAREFUL!
MY FIRST JOB ALONE!
I'VE GOTTA DO A GOOD JOB...
....AND MAKE OKITA SENSEI PROUD!

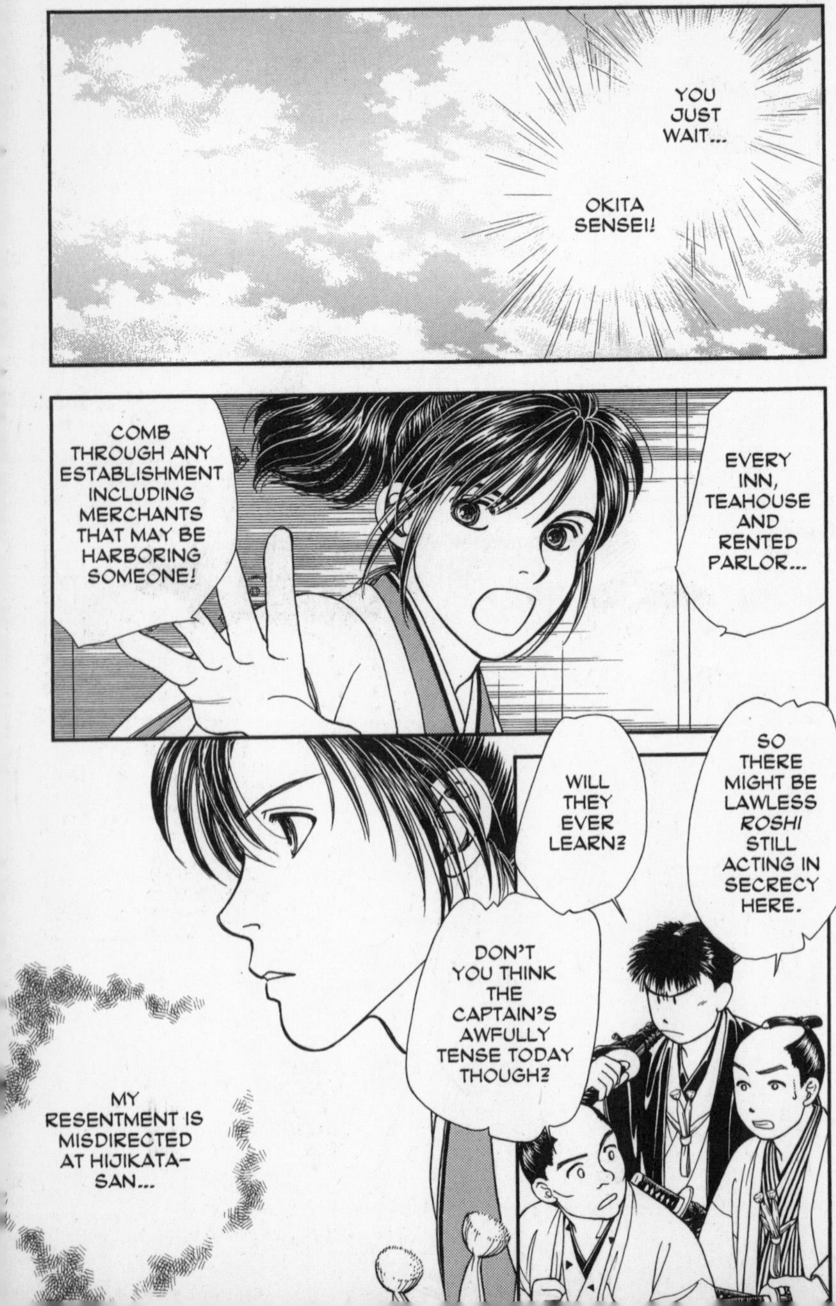
YOU JUST WAIT...
OKITA SENSEI!
EVERY INN, TEAHOUSE AND RENTED PARLOR...
COMB THROUGH ANY ESTABLISHMENT INCLUDING MERCHANTS THAT MAY BE HARBORING SOMEONE!
SO THERE MIGHT BE LAWLESS *ROSHI* STILL ACTING IN SECRECY HERE.
WILL THEY EVER LEARN?
DON'T YOU THINK THE CAPTAIN'S AWFULLY TENSE TODAY THOUGH?
MY RESENTMENT IS MISDIRECTED AT HIJIKATA-SAN...

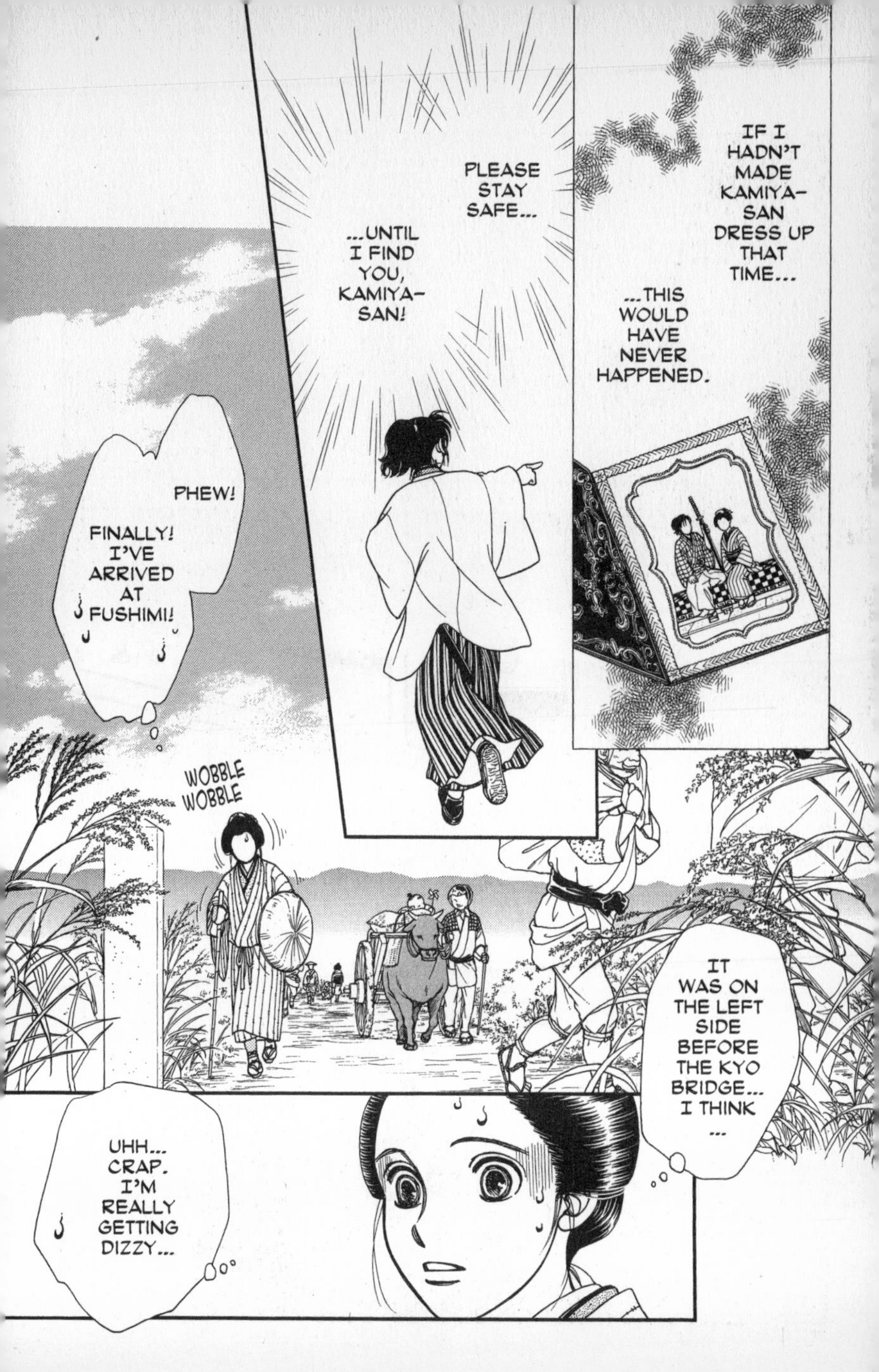
IF I HADN'T MADE KAMIYA-SAN DRESS UP THAT TIME...
...THIS WOULD HAVE NEVER HAPPENED.
PLEASE STAY SAFE...
...UNTIL I FIND YOU, KAMIYA-SAN!
PHEW! FINALLY! I'VE ARRIVED AT FUSHIMI!
WOBBLE WOBBLE
IT WAS ON THE LEFT SIDE BEFORE THE KYO BRIDGE... I THINK ...
UHH... CRAP. I'M REALLY GETTING DIZZY...

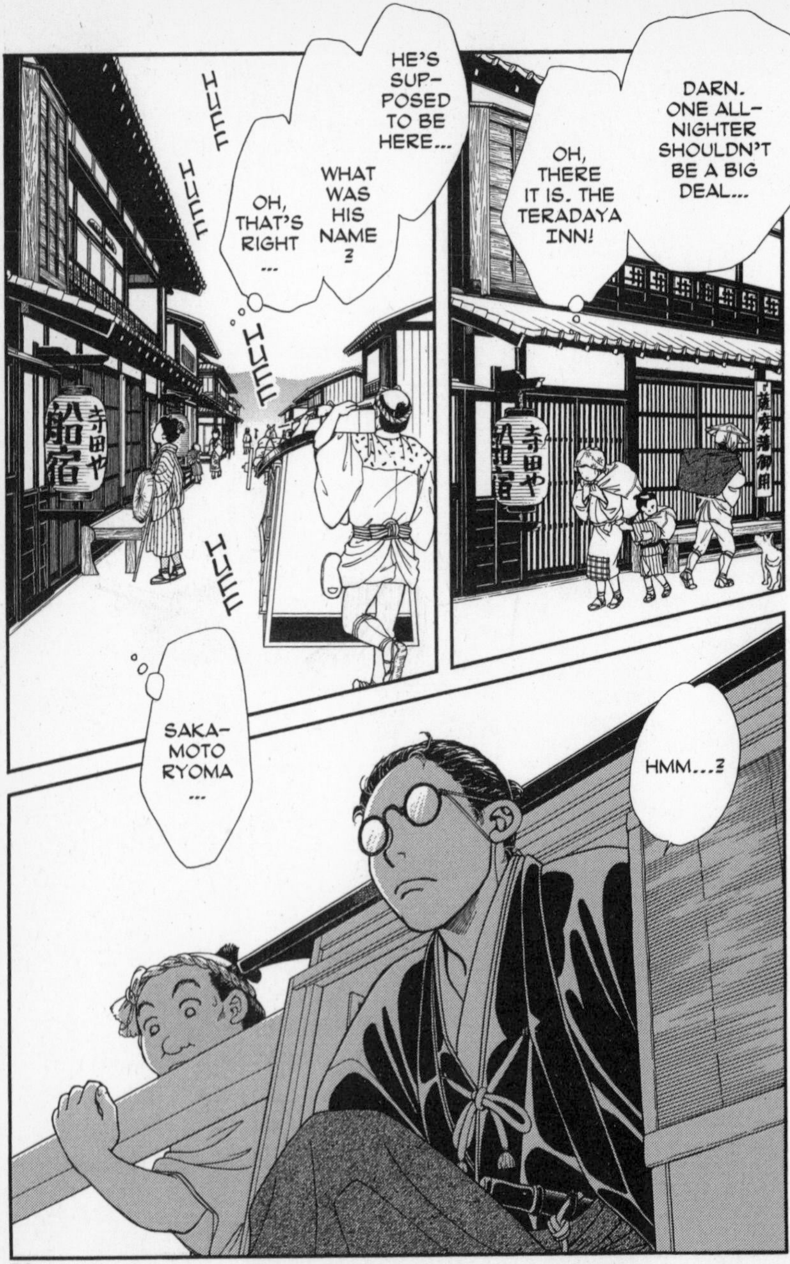
DARN. ONE ALL-NIGHTER SHOULDN'T BE A BIG DEAL...
OH, THERE IT IS. THE TERADAYA INN!
寺田や 船宿
薩摩藩御用
HE'S SUP-POSED TO BE HERE...
WHAT WAS HIS NAME?
OH, THAT'S RIGHT...
HUFF HUFF HUFF HUFF
寺田や 船宿
HMM...?
SAKA-MOTO RYOMA...

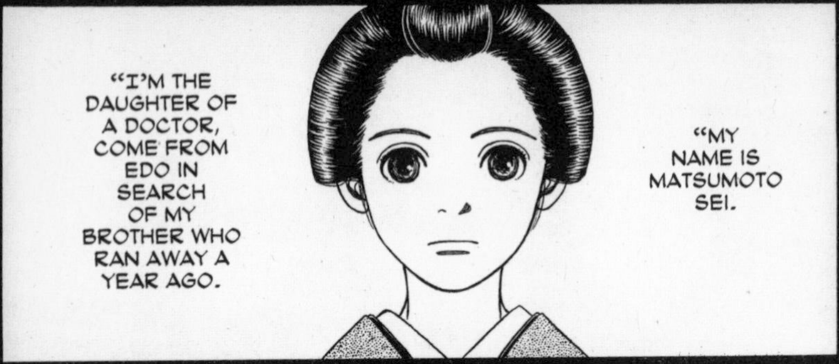
"MY NAME IS MATSUMOTO SEI.
"I'M THE DAUGHTER OF A DOCTOR, COME FROM EDO IN SEARCH OF MY BROTHER WHO RAN AWAY A YEAR AGO.

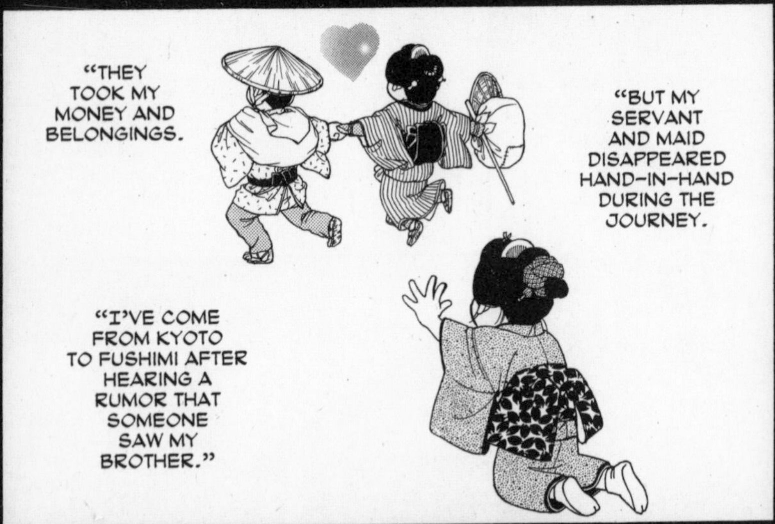
"BUT MY SERVANT AND MAID DISAPPEARED HAND-IN-HAND DURING THE JOURNEY.
"THEY TOOK MY MONEY AND BELONGINGS.
"I'VE COME FROM KYOTO TO FUSHIMI AFTER HEARING A RUMOR THAT SOMEONE SAW MY BROTHER."

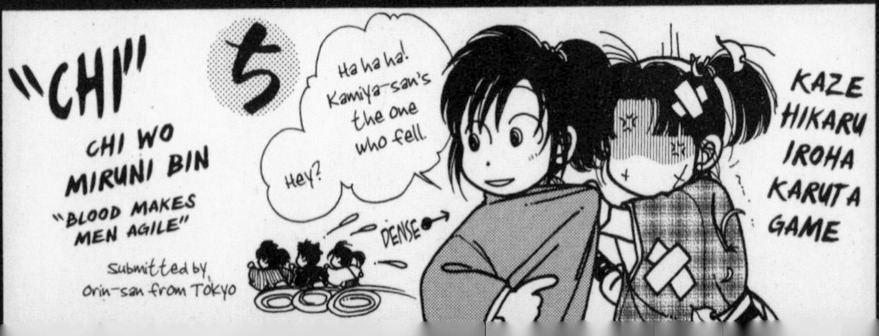
KAZE HIKARU IROHA KARUTA GAME
Ha ha ha! Kamiya-san's the one who fell.
Hey?
DENSE
ち
"CHI"
CHI WO MIRUNI BIN
"BLOOD MAKES MEN AGILE"
Submitted by Orin-san from Tokyo

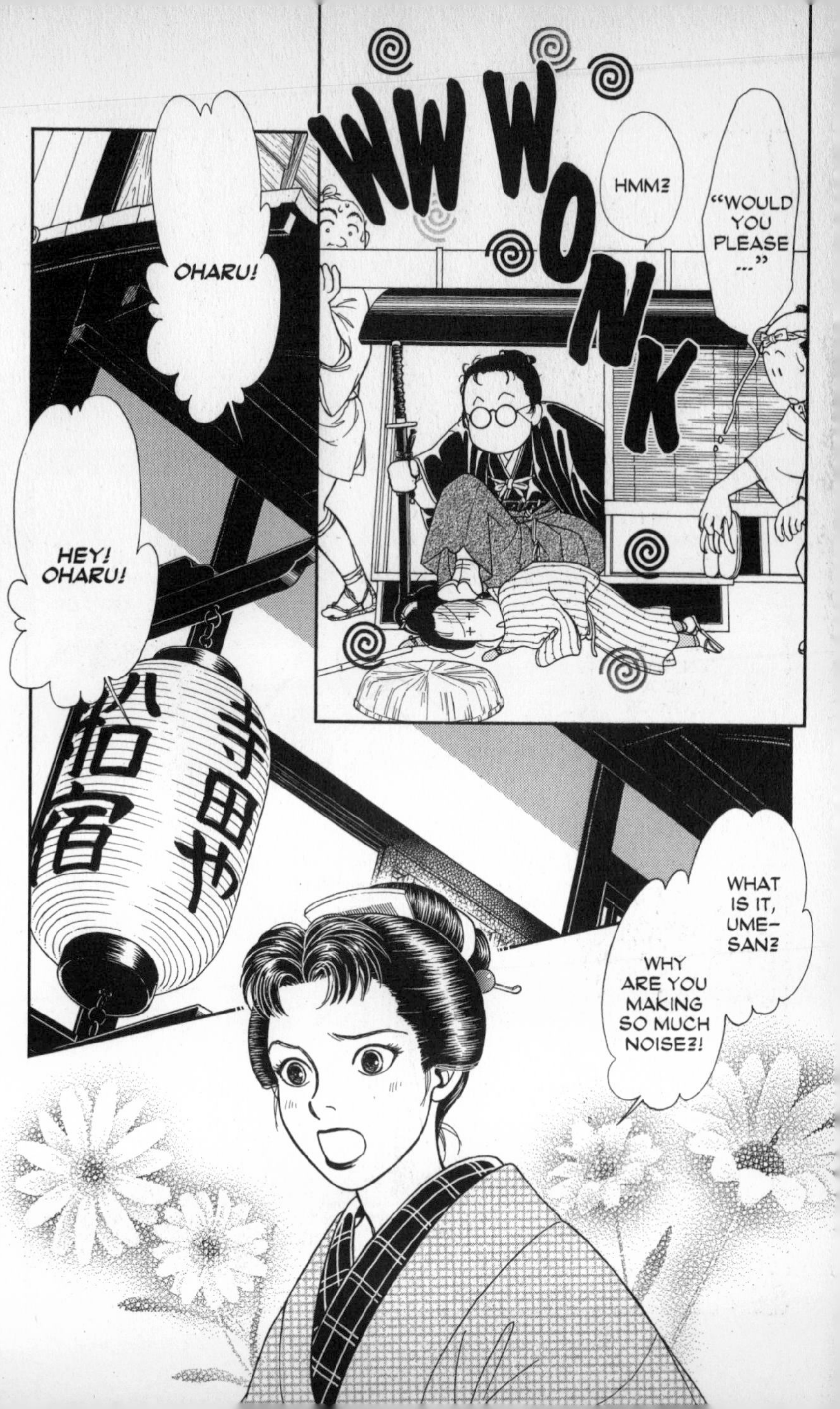
"WOULD YOU PLEASE ..."
HMM?
WWWONK
OHARU!
HEY! OHARU!
寺田や
船宿
WHAT IS IT, UME-SAN?
WHY ARE YOU MAKING SO MUCH NOISE?!

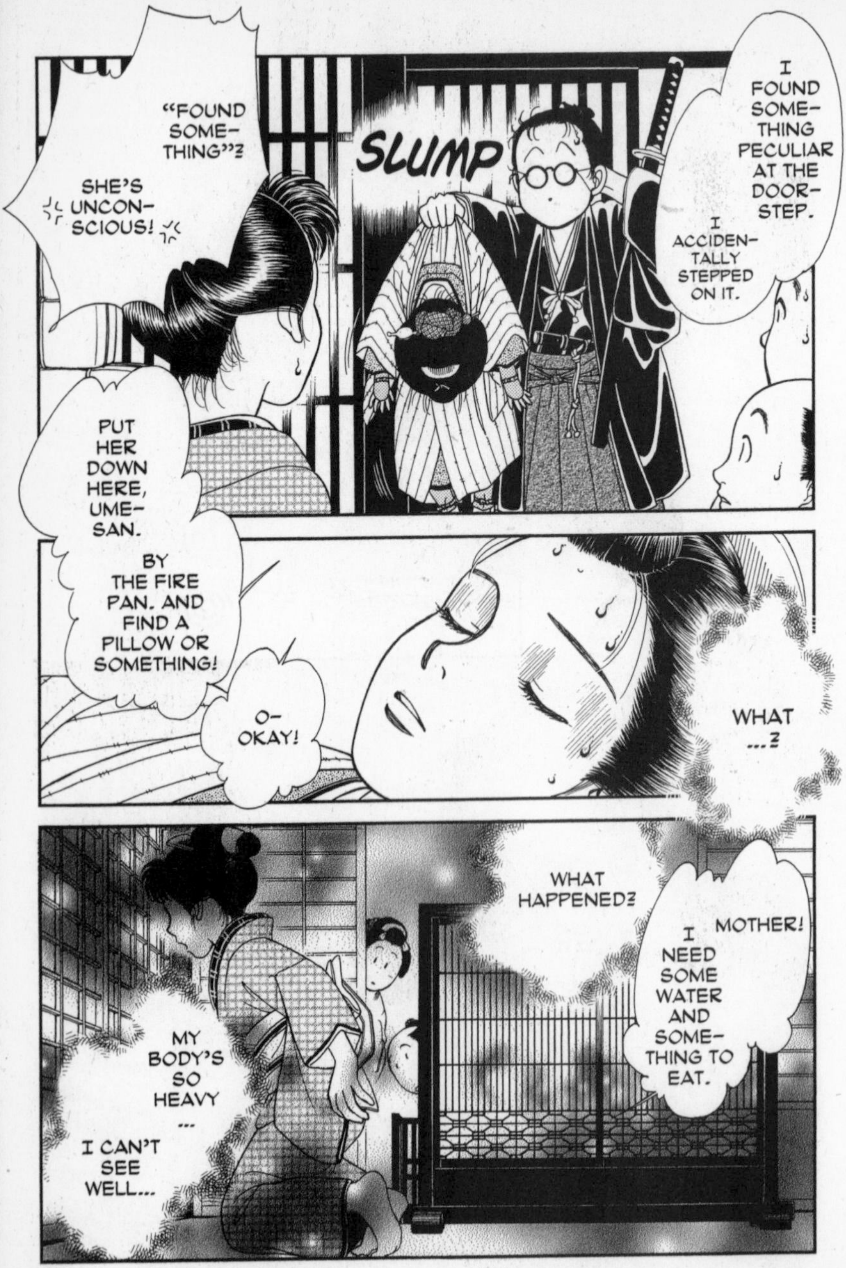
I FOUND SOMETHING PECULIAR AT THE DOORSTEP.
I ACCIDENTALLY STEPPED ON IT.
SLUMP
"FOUND SOMETHING"?
SHE'S UNCONSCIOUS!
PUT HER DOWN HERE, UME-SAN.
BY THE FIRE PAN. AND FIND A PILLOW OR SOMETHING!
WHAT ...?
O-OKAY!
WHAT HAPPENED?
MOTHER!
I NEED SOME WATER AND SOMETHING TO EAT.
MY BODY'S SO HEAVY ...
I CAN'T SEE WELL...

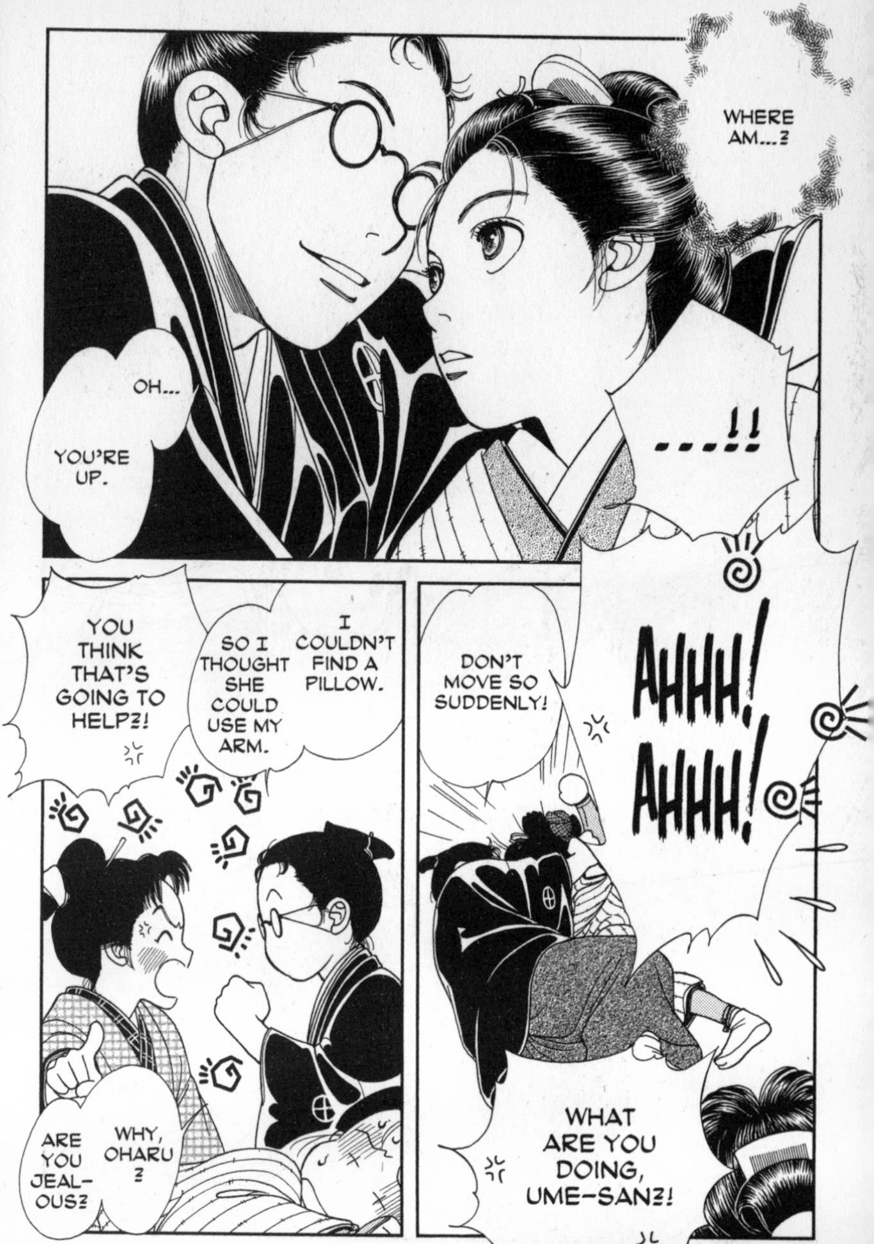
WHERE AM...?
...!!
OH...
YOU'RE UP.
AHHH! AHHH!
DON'T MOVE SO SUDDENLY!
WHAT ARE YOU DOING, UME-SAN?!
I COULDN'T FIND A PILLOW.
SO I THOUGHT SHE COULD USE MY ARM.
YOU THINK THAT'S GOING TO HELP?!
WHY, OHARU?
ARE YOU JEAL-OUS?

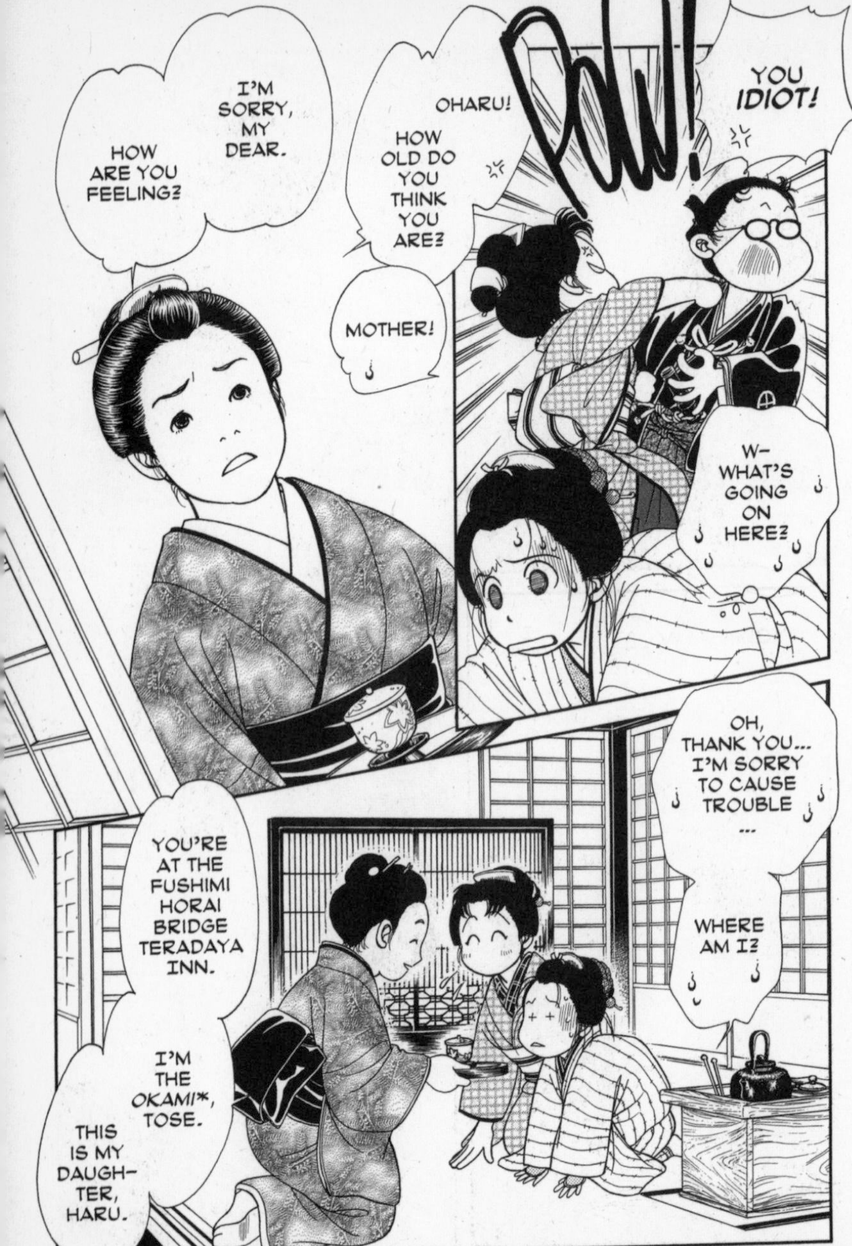
YOU IDIOT!
POW!
OHARU!
HOW OLD DO YOU THINK YOU ARE?
MOTHER!
W-WHAT'S GOING ON HERE?
I'M SORRY, MY DEAR.
HOW ARE YOU FEELING?
OH, THANK YOU... I'M SORRY TO CAUSE TROUBLE...
WHERE AM I?
YOU'RE AT THE FUSHIMI HORAI BRIDGE TERADAYA INN.
I'M THE OKAMI*, TOSE.
THIS IS MY DAUGHTER, HARU.

*The head lady of the establishment.

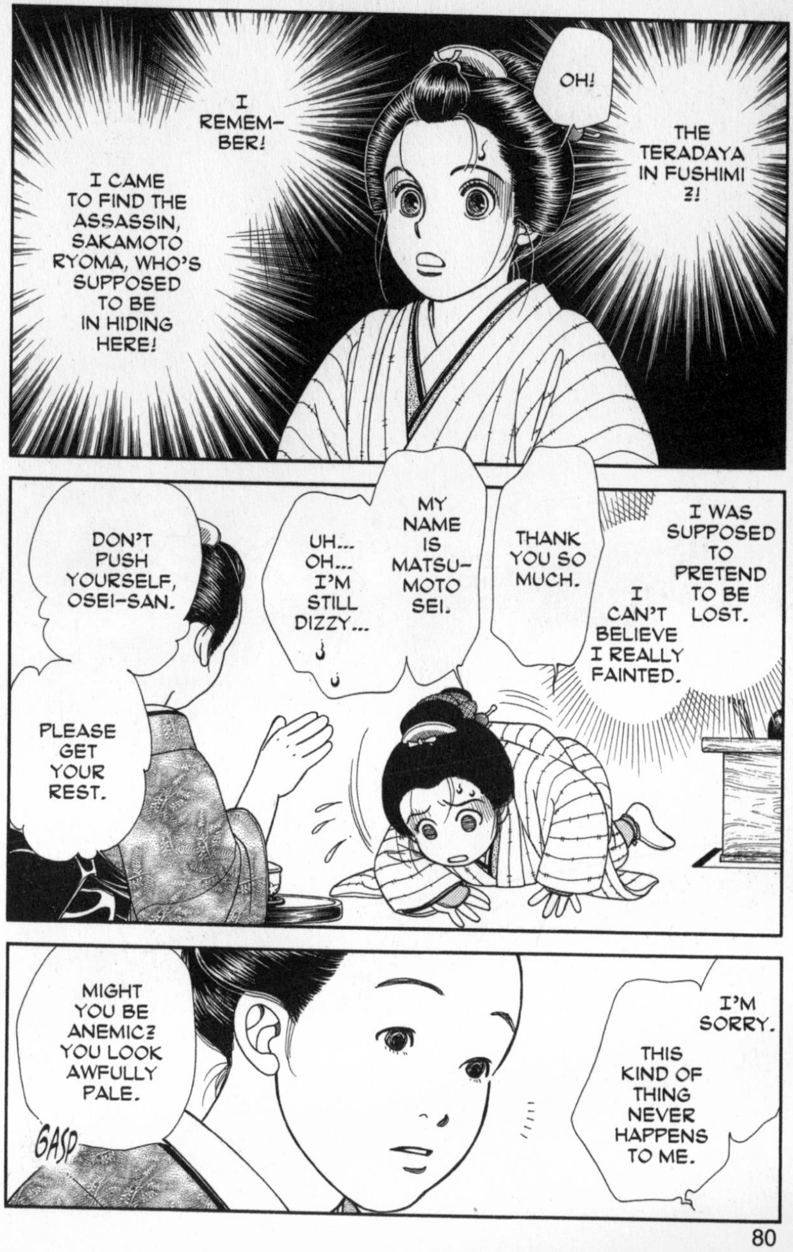
OH!
THE TERADAYA IN FUSHIMI?!
I REMEMBER!
I CAME TO FIND THE ASSASSIN, SAKAMOTO RYOMA, WHO'S SUPPOSED TO BE IN HIDING HERE!
I WAS SUPPOSED TO PRETEND TO BE LOST.
I CAN'T BELIEVE I REALLY FAINTED.
THANK YOU SO MUCH.
MY NAME IS MATSUMOTO SEI.
UH... OH... I'M STILL DIZZY...
DON'T PUSH YOURSELF, OSEI-SAN.
PLEASE GET YOUR REST.
I'M SORRY.
THIS KIND OF THING NEVER HAPPENS TO ME.
MIGHT YOU BE ANEMIC? YOU LOOK AWFULLY PALE.
GASP

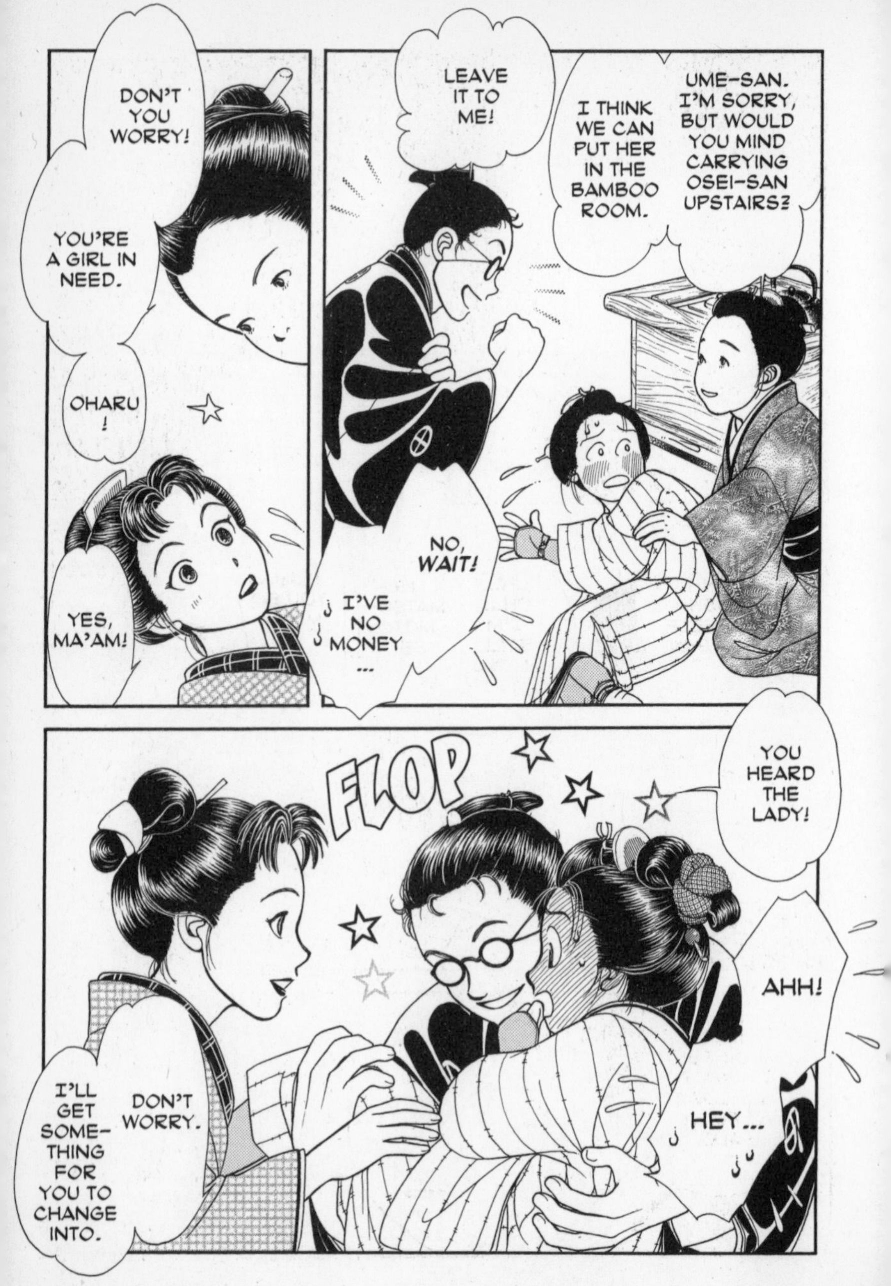
UME-SAN. I'M SORRY, BUT WOULD YOU MIND CARRYING OSEI-SAN UPSTAIRS?
I THINK WE CAN PUT HER IN THE BAMBOO ROOM.
LEAVE IT TO ME!
NO, *WAIT!*
I'VE NO MONEY ...
DON'T YOU WORRY!
YOU'RE A GIRL IN NEED.
OHARU!
YES, MA'AM!
YOU HEARD THE LADY!
FLOP
AHH!
HEY...
DON'T WORRY.
I'LL GET SOME-THING FOR YOU TO CHANGE INTO.

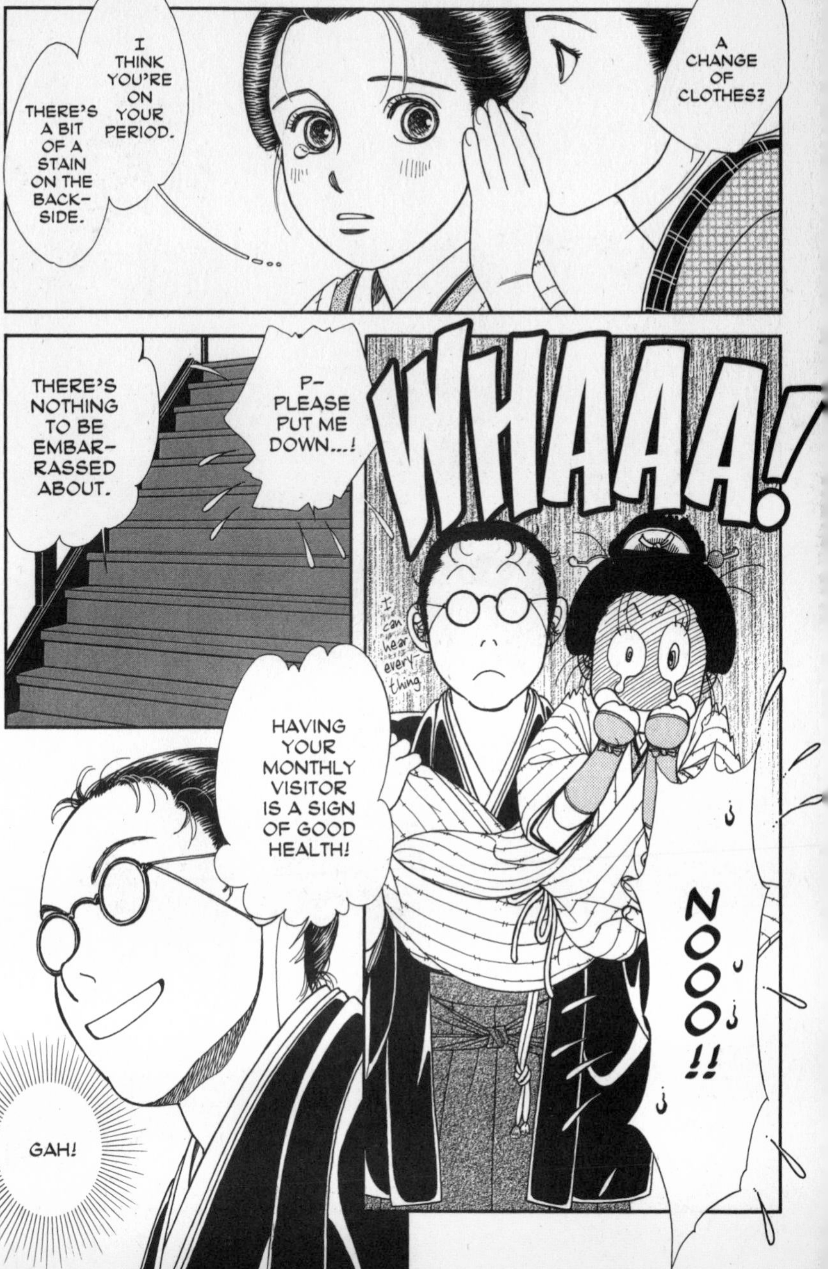
A CHANGE OF CLOTHES?
I THINK YOU'RE ON YOUR PERIOD.
THERE'S A BIT OF A STAIN ON THE BACKSIDE.
WHAAAA!
I can hear every-thing
NOOOO!!
P-PLEASE PUT ME DOWN...!
THERE'S NOTHING TO BE EMBARRASSED ABOUT.
HAVING YOUR MONTHLY VISITOR IS A SIGN OF GOOD HEALTH!
GAH!

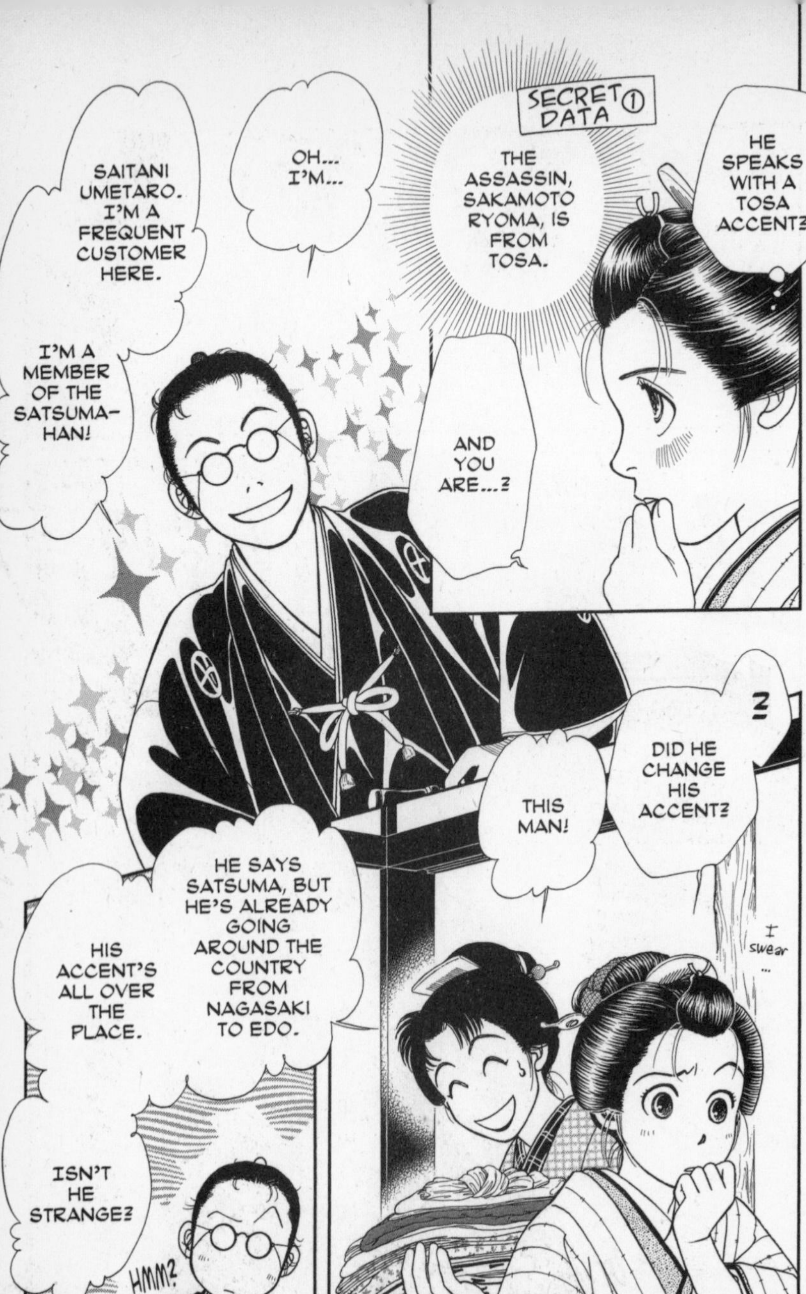
HE SPEAKS WITH A TOSA ACCENT?
SECRET DATA ①
THE ASSASSIN, SAKAMOTO RYOMA, IS FROM TOSA.
AND YOU ARE...?
OH... I'M...
SAITANI UMETARO. I'M A FREQUENT CUSTOMER HERE.
I'M A MEMBER OF THE SATSUMA-HAN!
?
DID HE CHANGE HIS ACCENT?
THIS MAN!
I swear...
HE SAYS SATSUMA, BUT HE'S ALREADY GOING AROUND THE COUNTRY FROM NAGASAKI TO EDO.
HIS ACCENT'S ALL OVER THE PLACE.
ISN'T HE STRANGE?
HMM?

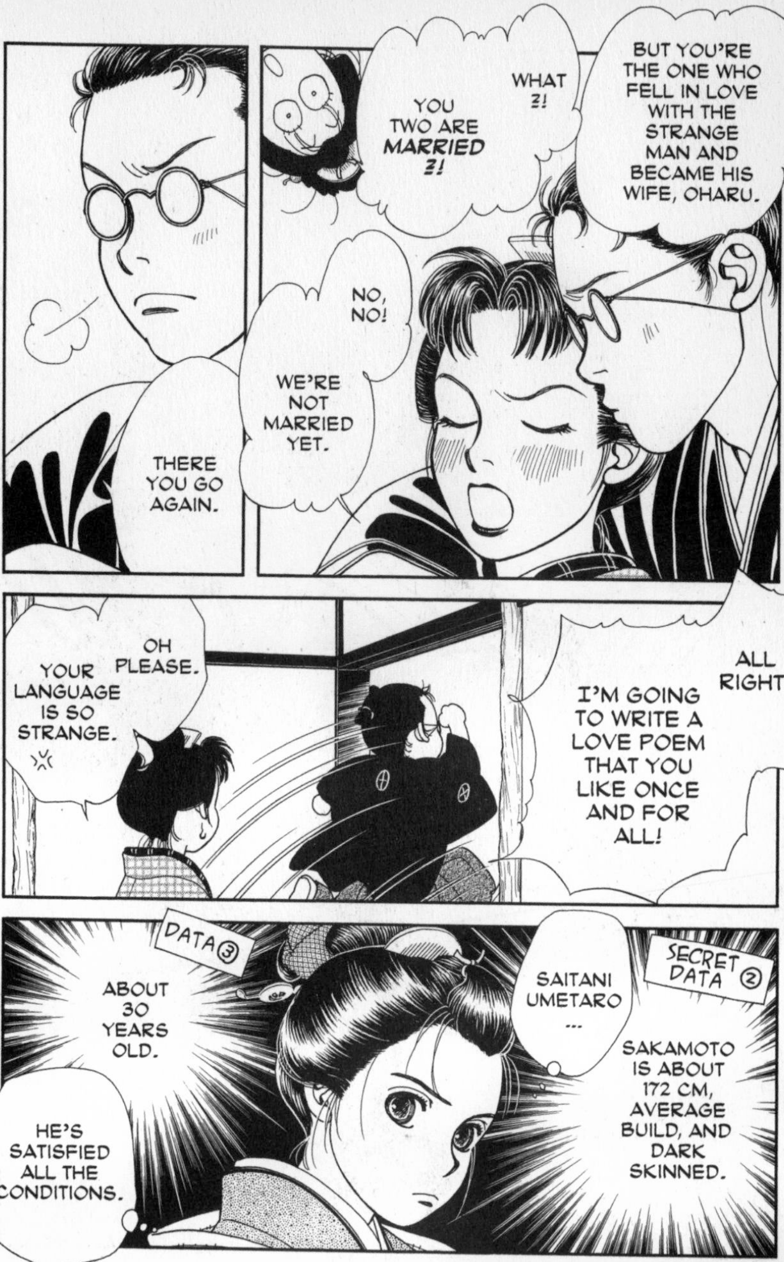
BUT YOU'RE THE ONE WHO FELL IN LOVE WITH THE STRANGE MAN AND BECAME HIS WIFE, OHARU.
WHAT ?!
YOU TWO ARE MARRIED ?!
NO, NO!
WE'RE NOT MARRIED YET.
THERE YOU GO AGAIN.
ALL RIGHT!
I'M GOING TO WRITE A LOVE POEM THAT YOU LIKE ONCE AND FOR ALL!
OH PLEASE.
YOUR LANGUAGE IS SO STRANGE.
SECRET DATA ②
SAKAMOTO IS ABOUT 172 CM, AVERAGE BUILD, AND DARK SKINNED.
SAITANI UMETARO ...
DATA ③
ABOUT 30 YEARS OLD.
HE'S SATISFIED ALL THE CONDITIONS.

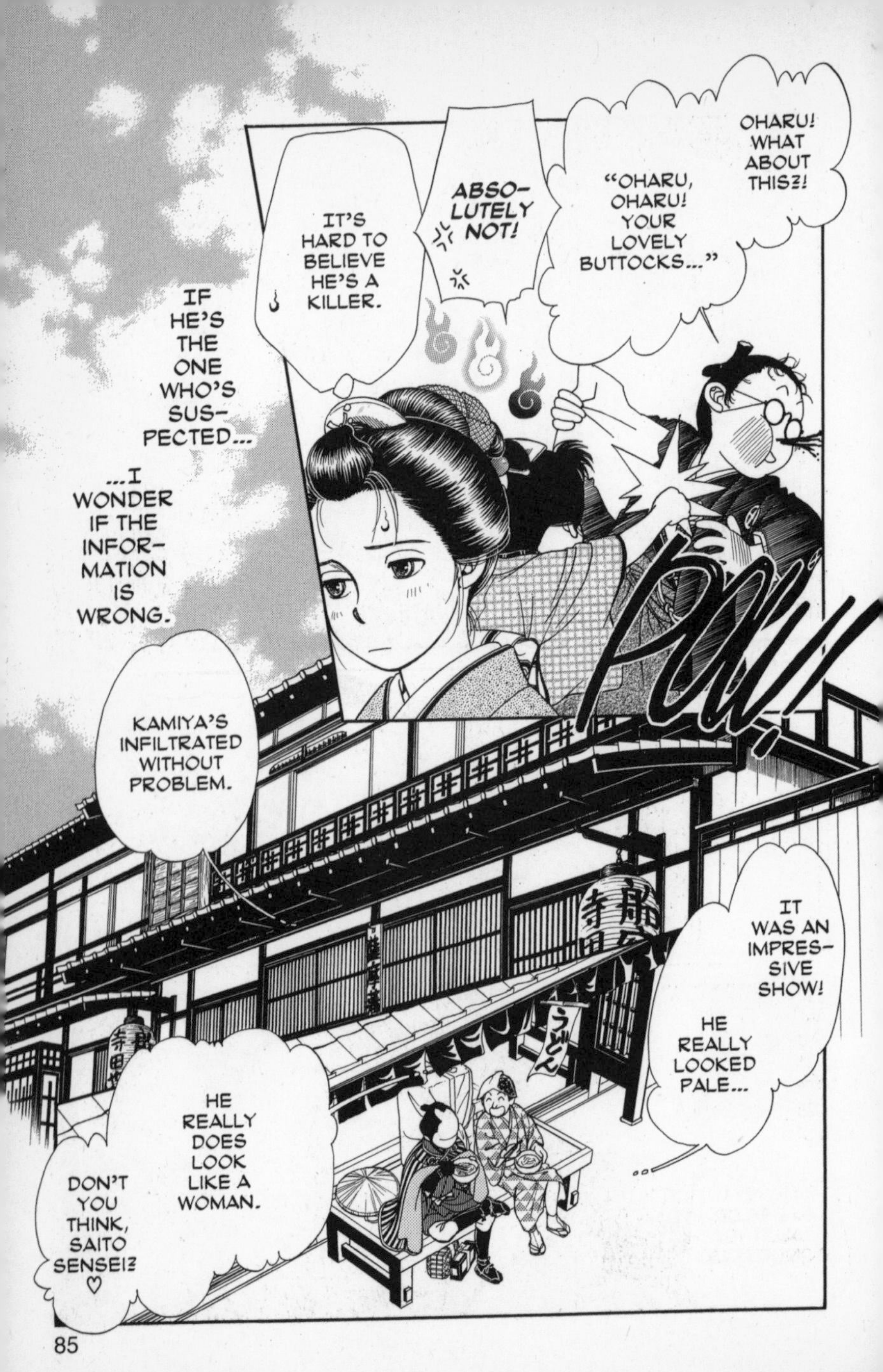
OHARU! WHAT ABOUT THIS?!
"OHARU, OHARU! YOUR LOVELY BUTTOCKS..."
ABSO-LUTELY NOT!
IT'S HARD TO BELIEVE HE'S A KILLER.
POW!
IF HE'S THE ONE WHO'S SUS-PECTED...
...I WONDER IF THE INFOR-MATION IS WRONG.
IT WAS AN IMPRES-SIVE SHOW!
HE REALLY LOOKED PALE...
KAMIYA'S INFILTRATED WITHOUT PROBLEM.
HE REALLY DOES LOOK LIKE A WOMAN.
DON'T YOU THINK, SAITO SENSEI?! ♡

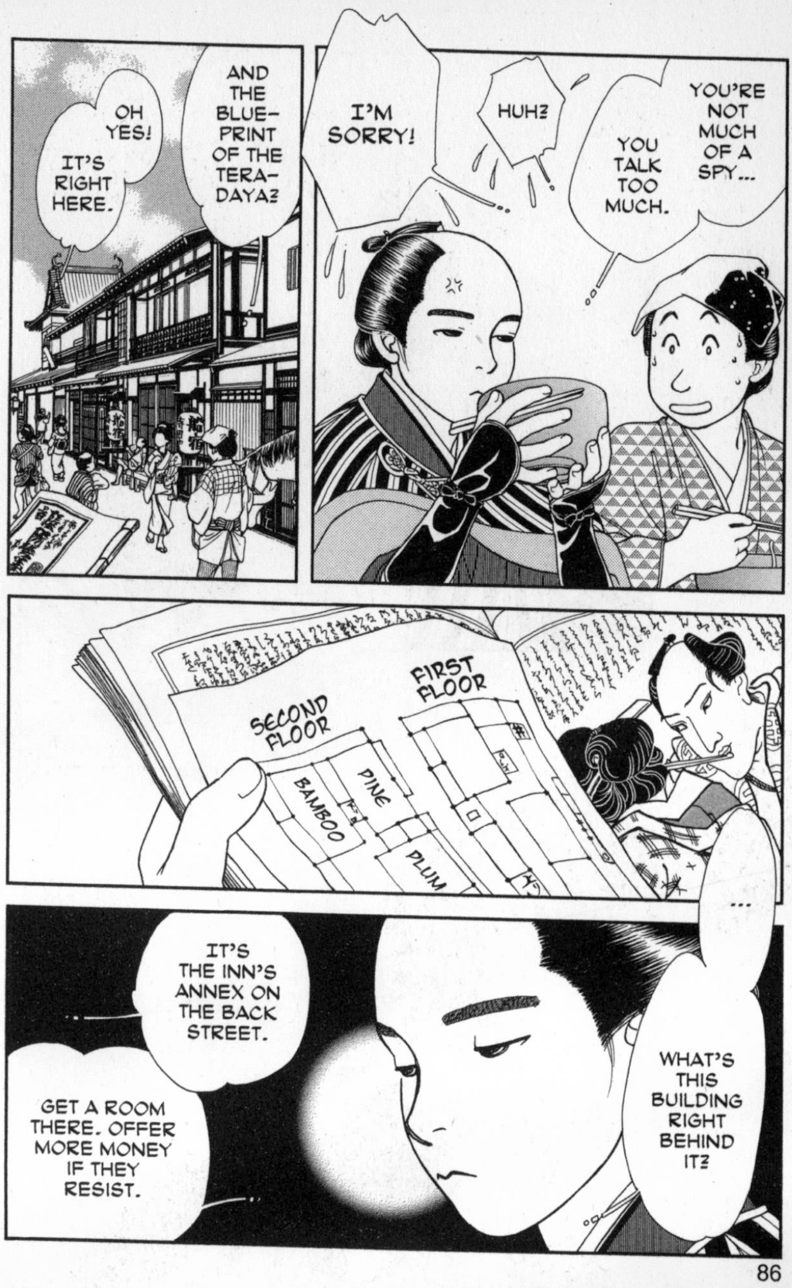
YOU'RE NOT MUCH OF A SPY...
YOU TALK TOO MUCH.
HUH?
I'M SORRY!
AND THE BLUE-PRINT OF THE TERA-DAYA?
OH YES! IT'S RIGHT HERE.
FIRST FLOOR
SECOND FLOOR
PINE
BAMBOO
PLUM
...
WHAT'S THIS BUILDING RIGHT BEHIND IT?
IT'S THE INN'S ANNEX ON THE BACK STREET.
GET A ROOM THERE. OFFER MORE MONEY IF THEY RESIST.

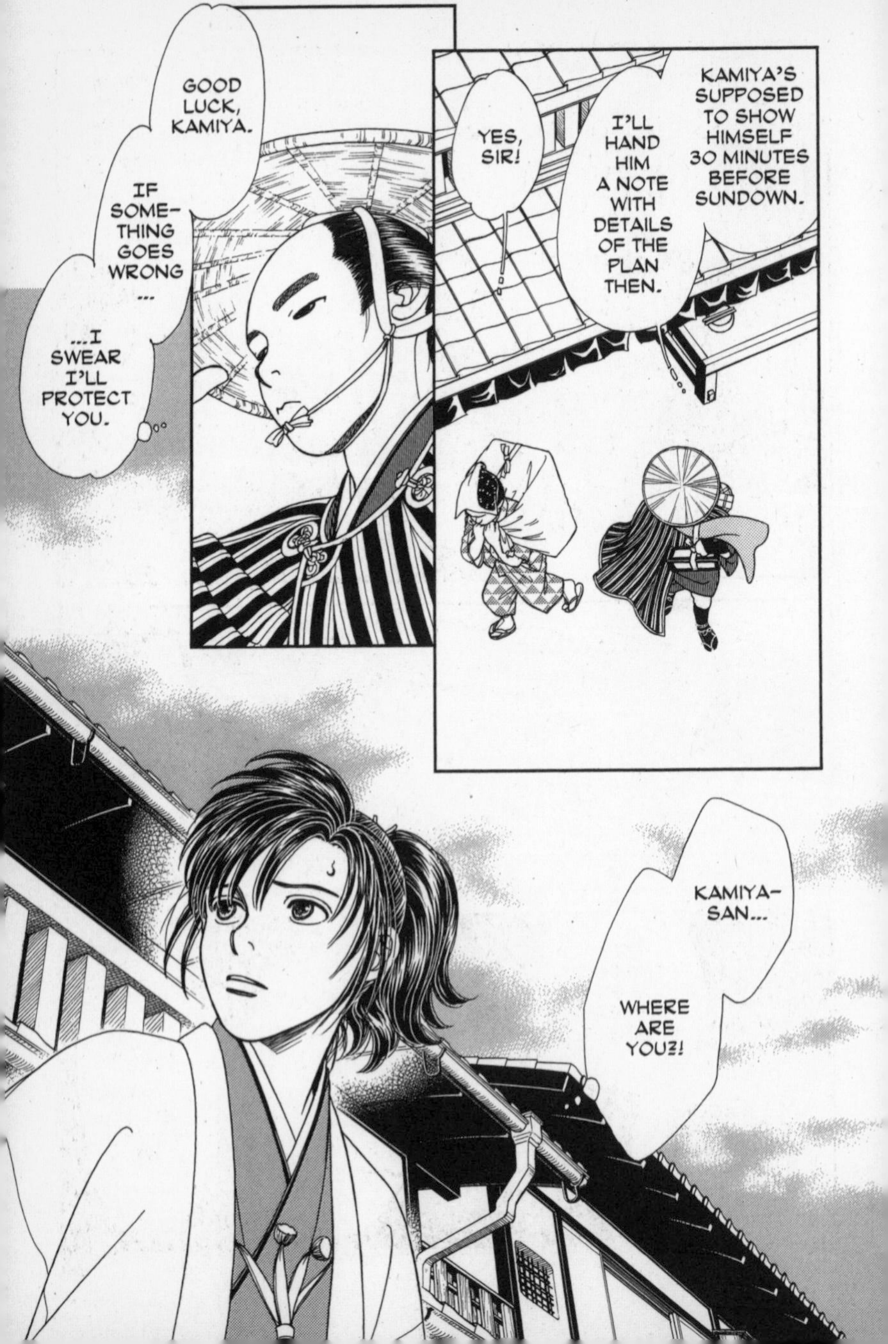
KAMIYA'S SUPPOSED TO SHOW HIMSELF 30 MINUTES BEFORE SUNDOWN.
I'LL HAND HIM A NOTE WITH DETAILS OF THE PLAN THEN.
YES, SIR!
GOOD LUCK, KAMIYA.
IF SOME-THING GOES WRONG...
...I SWEAR I'LL PROTECT YOU.
KAMIYA-SAN...
WHERE ARE YOU?!

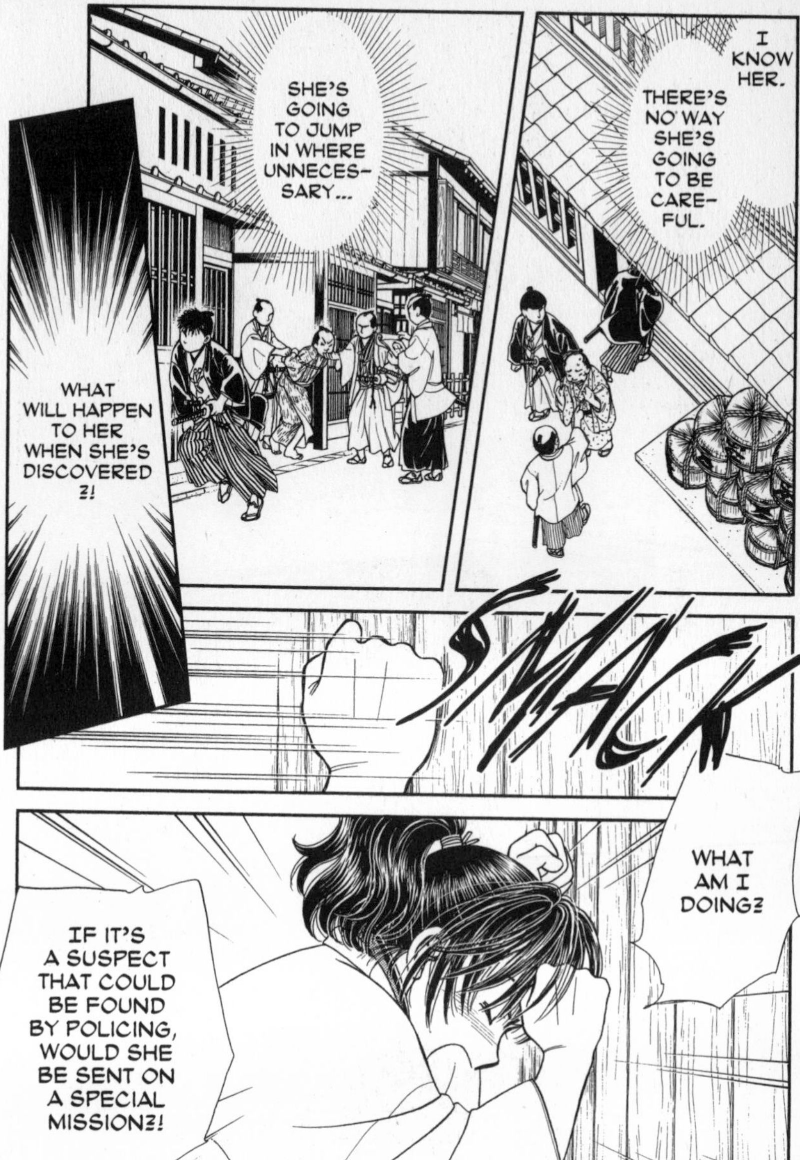

I KNOW HER.
THERE'S NO WAY SHE'S GOING TO BE CARE-FUL.
SHE'S GOING TO JUMP IN WHERE UNNECES-SARY...
WHAT WILL HAPPEN TO HER WHEN SHE'S DISCOVERED?!
SMACK
WHAT AM I DOING?
IF IT'S A SUSPECT THAT COULD BE FOUND BY POLICING, WOULD SHE BE SENT ON A SPECIAL MISSION?!

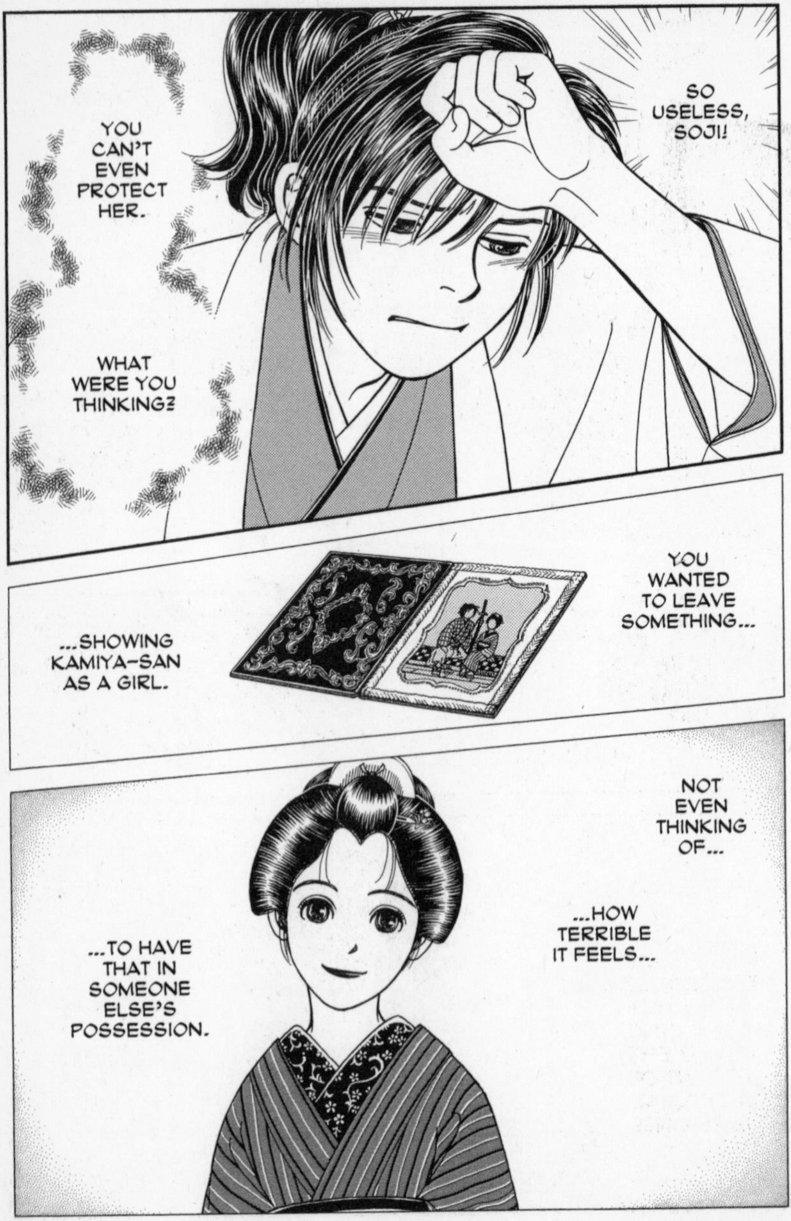
SO USELESS, SOJI!
YOU CAN'T EVEN PROTECT HER.
WHAT WERE YOU THINKING?
YOU WANTED TO LEAVE SOMETHING...
...SHOWING KAMIYA-SAN AS A GIRL.
NOT EVEN THINKING OF...
...HOW TERRIBLE IT FEELS...
...TO HAVE THAT IN SOMEONE ELSE'S POSSESSION.

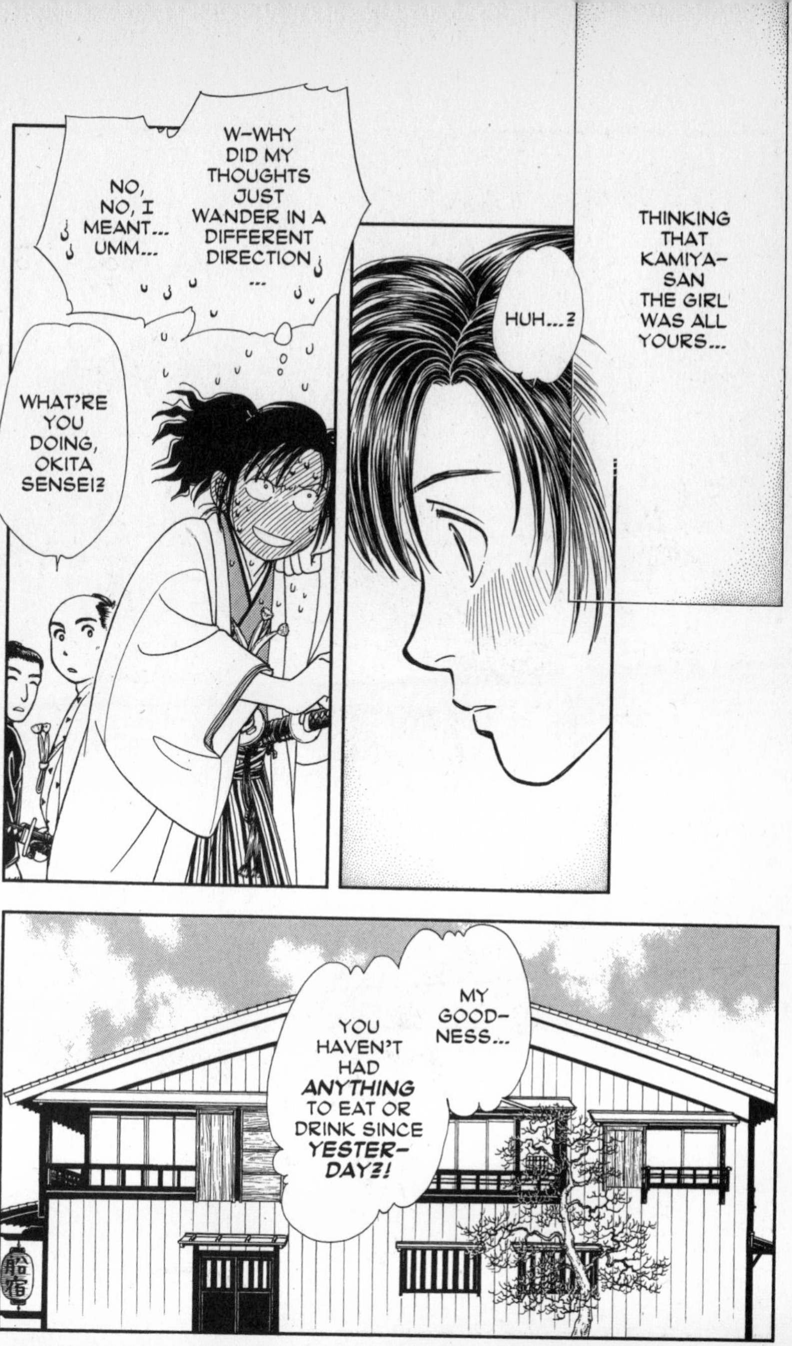
THINKING THAT KAMIYA-SAN THE GIRL WAS ALL YOURS...
HUH...?
W-WHY DID MY THOUGHTS JUST WANDER IN A DIFFERENT DIRECTION...
NO, NO, I MEANT... UMM...
WHAT'RE YOU DOING, OKITA SENSEI!?
MY GOODNESS...
YOU HAVEN'T HAD ANYTHING TO EAT OR DRINK SINCE YESTERDAY?!
船宿

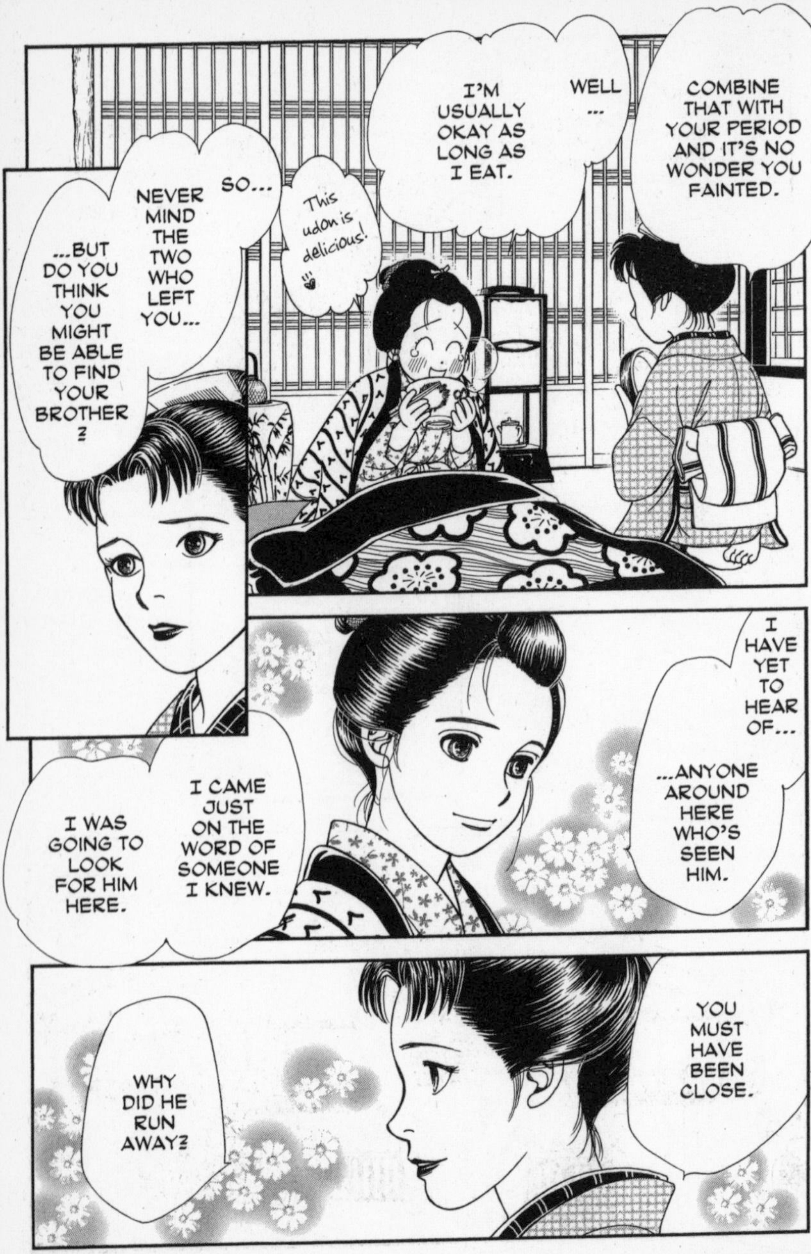
COMBINE THAT WITH YOUR PERIOD AND IT'S NO WONDER YOU FAINTED.
WELL...
I'M USUALLY OKAY AS LONG AS I EAT.
This udon is delicious!
SO...
NEVER MIND THE TWO WHO LEFT YOU...
...BUT DO YOU THINK YOU MIGHT BE ABLE TO FIND YOUR BROTHER?
I HAVE YET TO HEAR OF...
...ANYONE AROUND HERE WHO'S SEEN HIM.
I CAME JUST ON THE WORD OF SOMEONE I KNEW.
I WAS GOING TO LOOK FOR HIM HERE.
YOU MUST HAVE BEEN CLOSE.
WHY DID HE RUN AWAY?

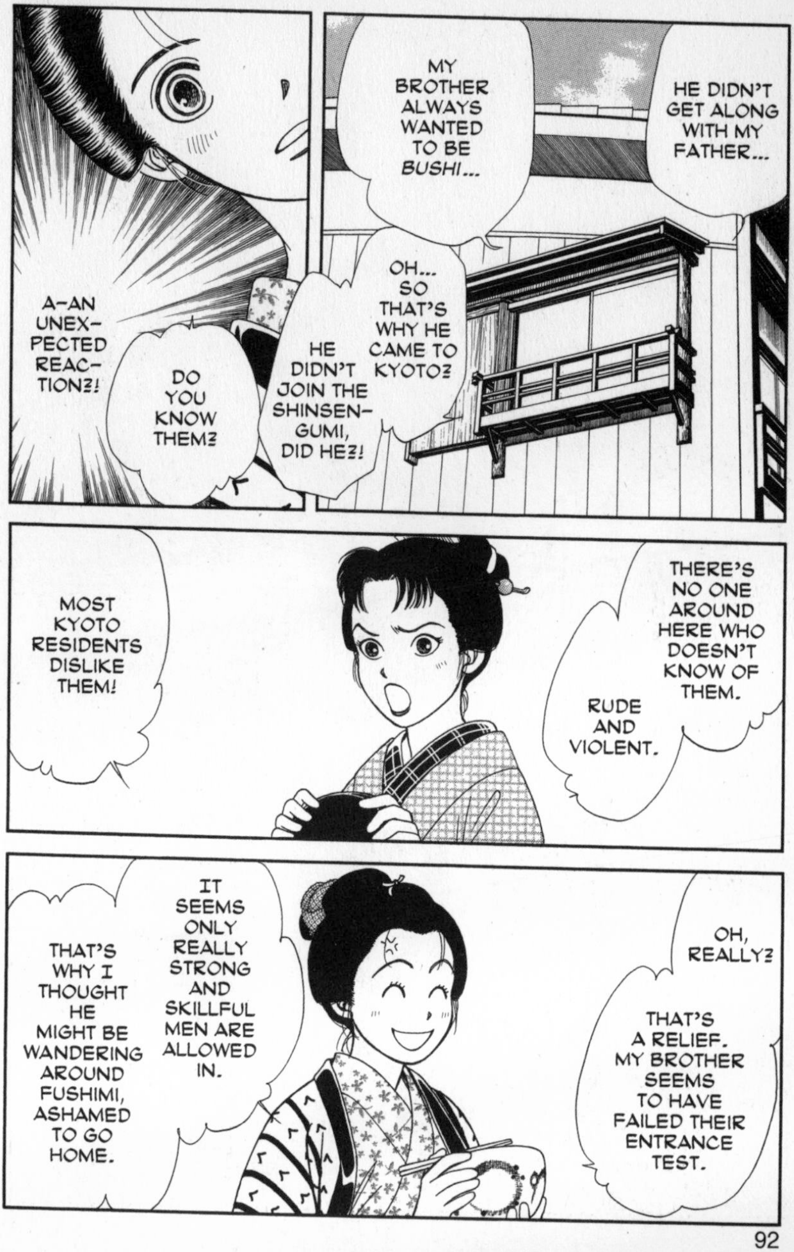
HE DIDN'T GET ALONG WITH MY FATHER...
MY BROTHER ALWAYS WANTED TO BE *BUSHI*...
OH... SO THAT'S WHY HE CAME TO KYOTO?
HE DIDN'T JOIN THE SHINSEN-GUMI, DID HE?!
DO YOU KNOW THEM?
A-AN UNEXPECTED REACTION?!
THERE'S NO ONE AROUND HERE WHO DOESN'T KNOW OF THEM.
RUDE AND VIOLENT.
MOST KYOTO RESIDENTS DISLIKE THEM!
OH, REALLY?
THAT'S A RELIEF. MY BROTHER SEEMS TO HAVE FAILED THEIR ENTRANCE TEST.
IT SEEMS ONLY REALLY STRONG AND SKILLFUL MEN ARE ALLOWED IN.
THAT'S WHY I THOUGHT HE MIGHT BE WANDERING AROUND FUSHIMI, ASHAMED TO GO HOME.

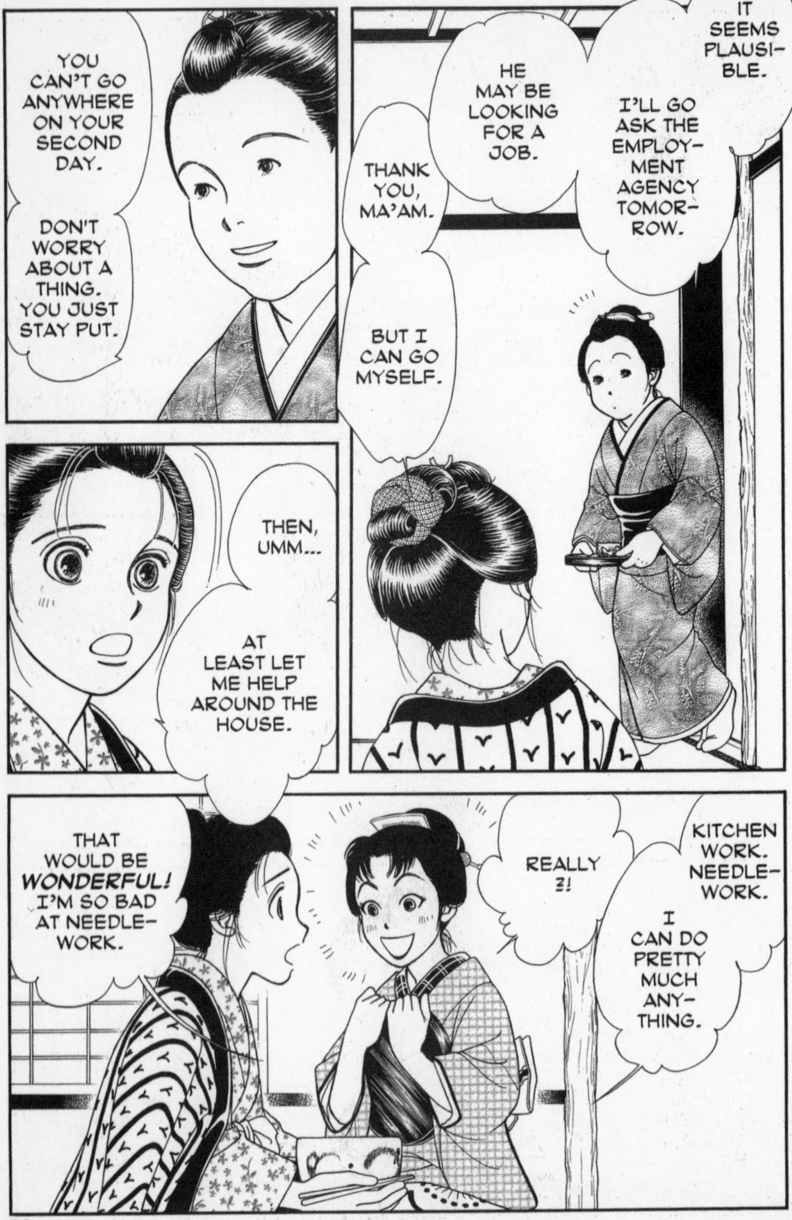
IT SEEMS PLAUSIBLE.
I'LL GO ASK THE EMPLOYMENT AGENCY TOMORROW.
HE MAY BE LOOKING FOR A JOB.
THANK YOU, MA'AM.
BUT I CAN GO MYSELF.
YOU CAN'T GO ANYWHERE ON YOUR SECOND DAY.
DON'T WORRY ABOUT A THING. YOU JUST STAY PUT.
THEN, UMM...
AT LEAST LET ME HELP AROUND THE HOUSE.
KITCHEN WORK. NEEDLEWORK.
I CAN DO PRETTY MUCH ANYTHING.
REALLY?!
THAT WOULD BE WONDERFUL! I'M SO BAD AT NEEDLEWORK.

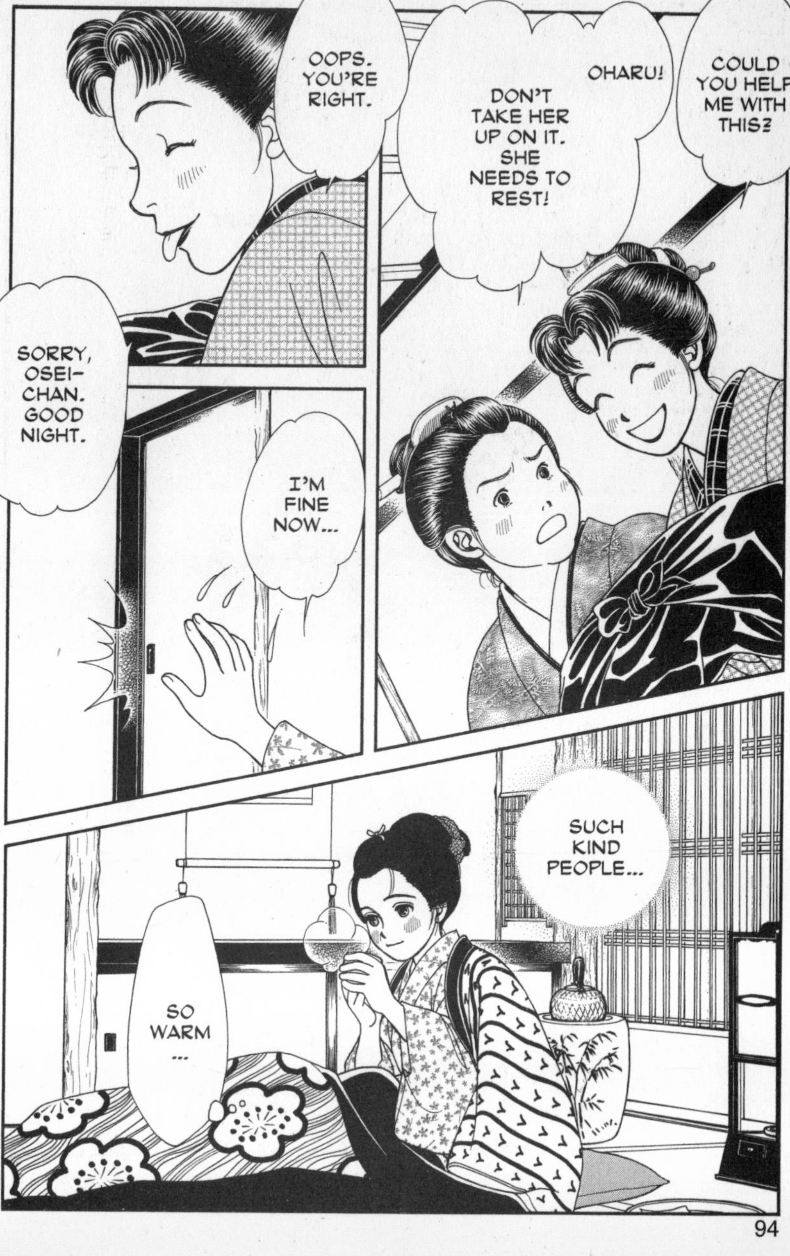
COULD YOU HELP ME WITH THIS?
OHARU!
DON'T TAKE HER UP ON IT. SHE NEEDS TO REST!
OOPS. YOU'RE RIGHT.
I'M FINE NOW...
SORRY, OSEI-CHAN. GOOD NIGHT.
SUCH KIND PEOPLE...
SO WARM ...

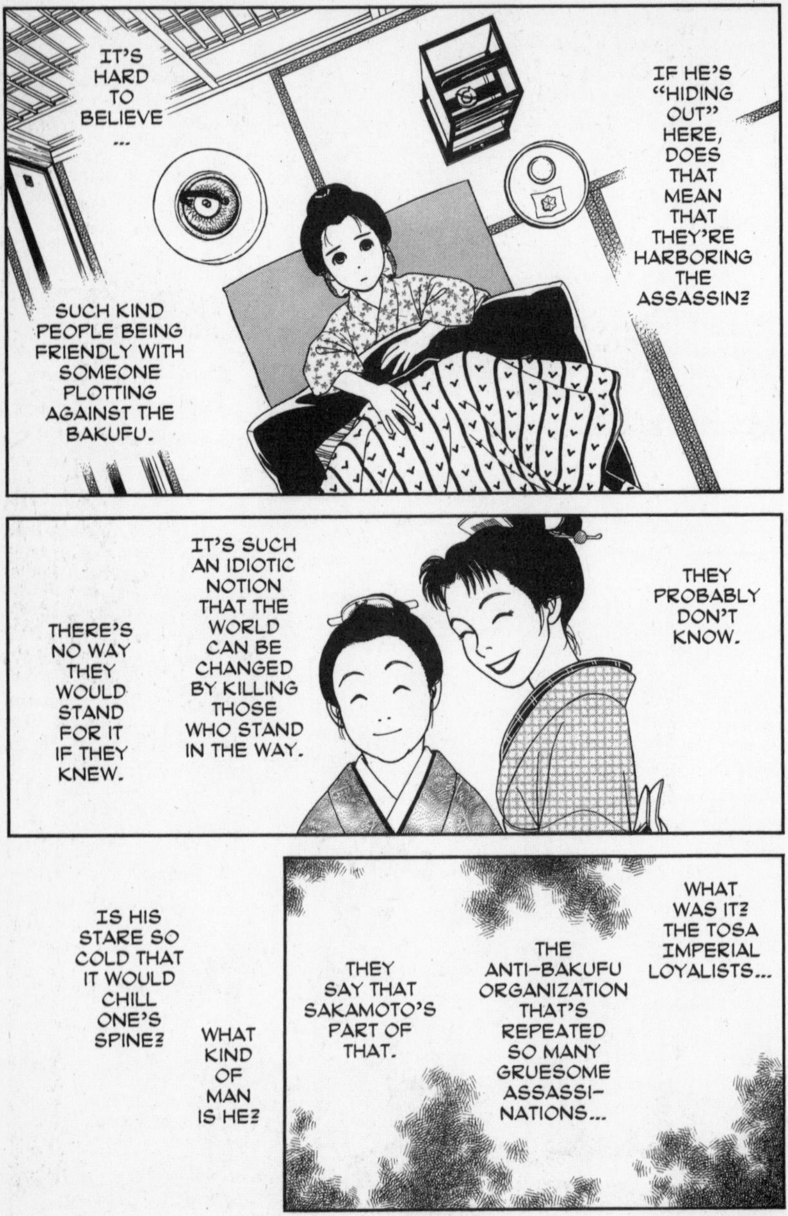
IF HE'S "HIDING OUT" HERE, DOES THAT MEAN THAT THEY'RE HARBORING THE ASSASSIN?
IT'S HARD TO BELIEVE...
SUCH KIND PEOPLE BEING FRIENDLY WITH SOMEONE PLOTTING AGAINST THE BAKUFU.
THEY PROBABLY DON'T KNOW.
IT'S SUCH AN IDIOTIC NOTION THAT THE WORLD CAN BE CHANGED BY KILLING THOSE WHO STAND IN THE WAY.
THERE'S NO WAY THEY WOULD STAND FOR IT IF THEY KNEW.
WHAT WAS IT? THE TOSA IMPERIAL LOYALISTS...
THE ANTI-BAKUFU ORGANIZATION THAT'S REPEATED SO MANY GRUESOME ASSASSI-NATIONS...
THEY SAY THAT SAKAMOTO'S PART OF THAT.
WHAT KIND OF MAN IS HE?
IS HIS STARE SO COLD THAT IT WOULD CHILL ONE'S SPINE?

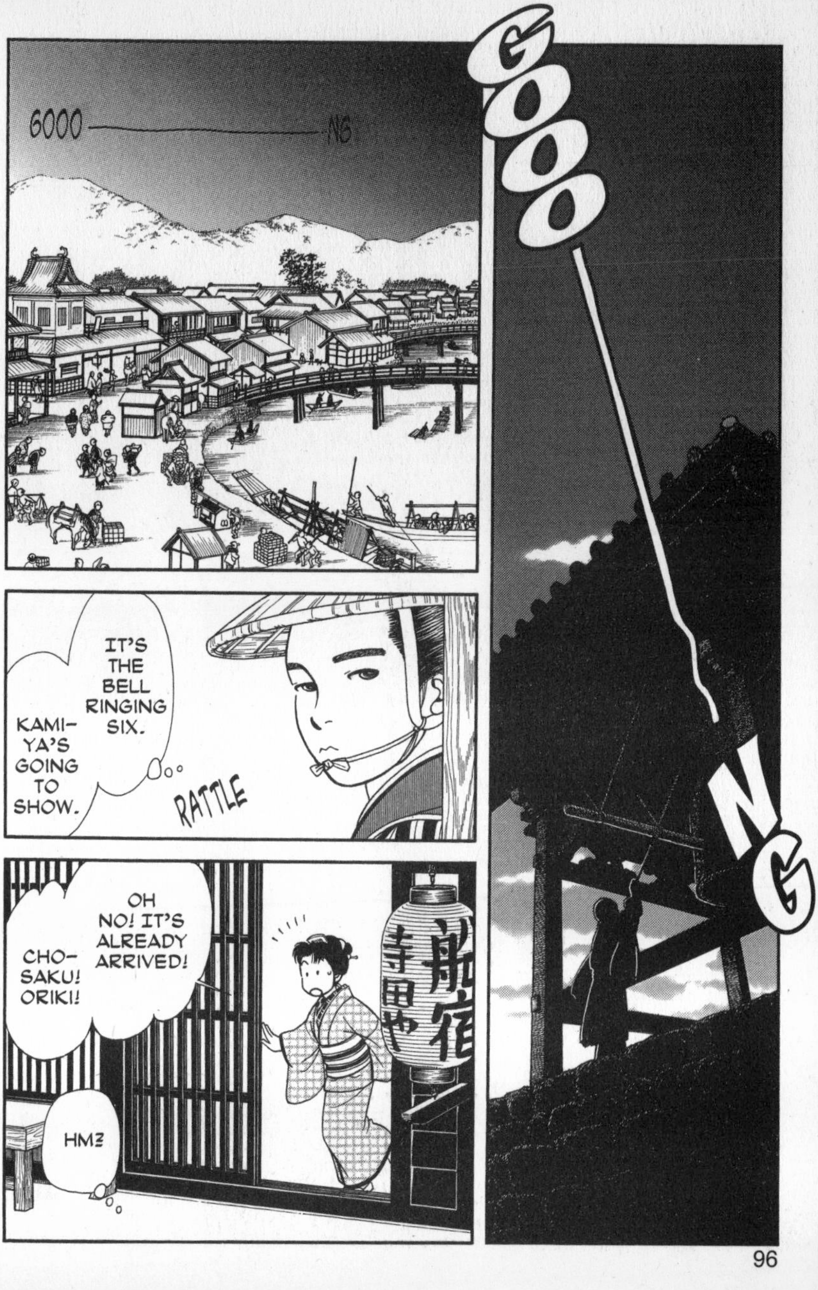
GOOOO
NG
GOOO——NG
IT'S THE BELL RINGING SIX.
KAMI-YA'S GOING TO SHOW.
RATTLE
OH NO! IT'S ALREADY ARRIVED!
CHO-SAKU! ORIKI!
旅宿
寺田や
HM?

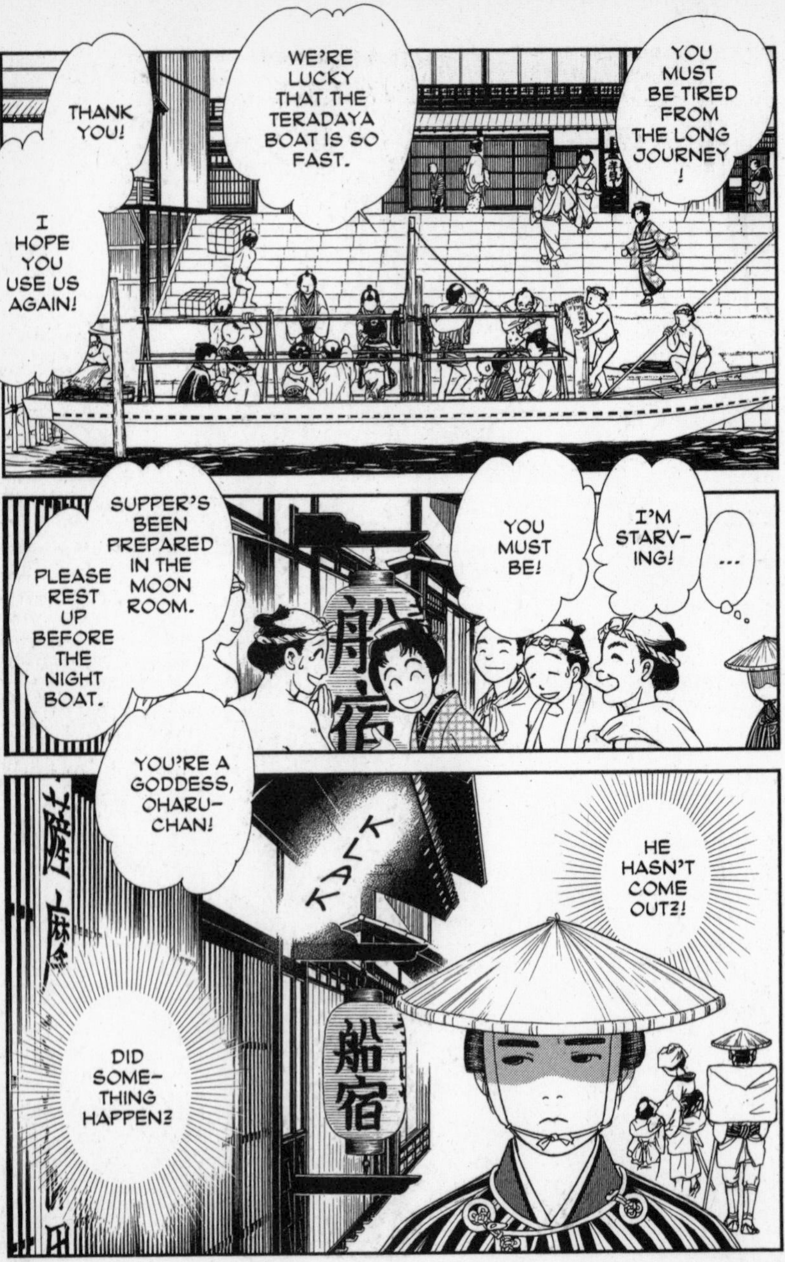
YOU MUST BE TIRED FROM THE LONG JOURNEY!
WE'RE LUCKY THAT THE TERADAYA BOAT IS SO FAST.
THANK YOU!
I HOPE YOU USE US AGAIN!
...
I'M STARV-ING!
YOU MUST BE!
SUPPER'S BEEN PREPARED IN THE MOON ROOM.
PLEASE REST UP BEFORE THE NIGHT BOAT.
YOU'RE A GODDESS, OHARU-CHAN!
HE HASN'T COME OUT?!
KLAK
船宿
DID SOME-THING HAPPEN?

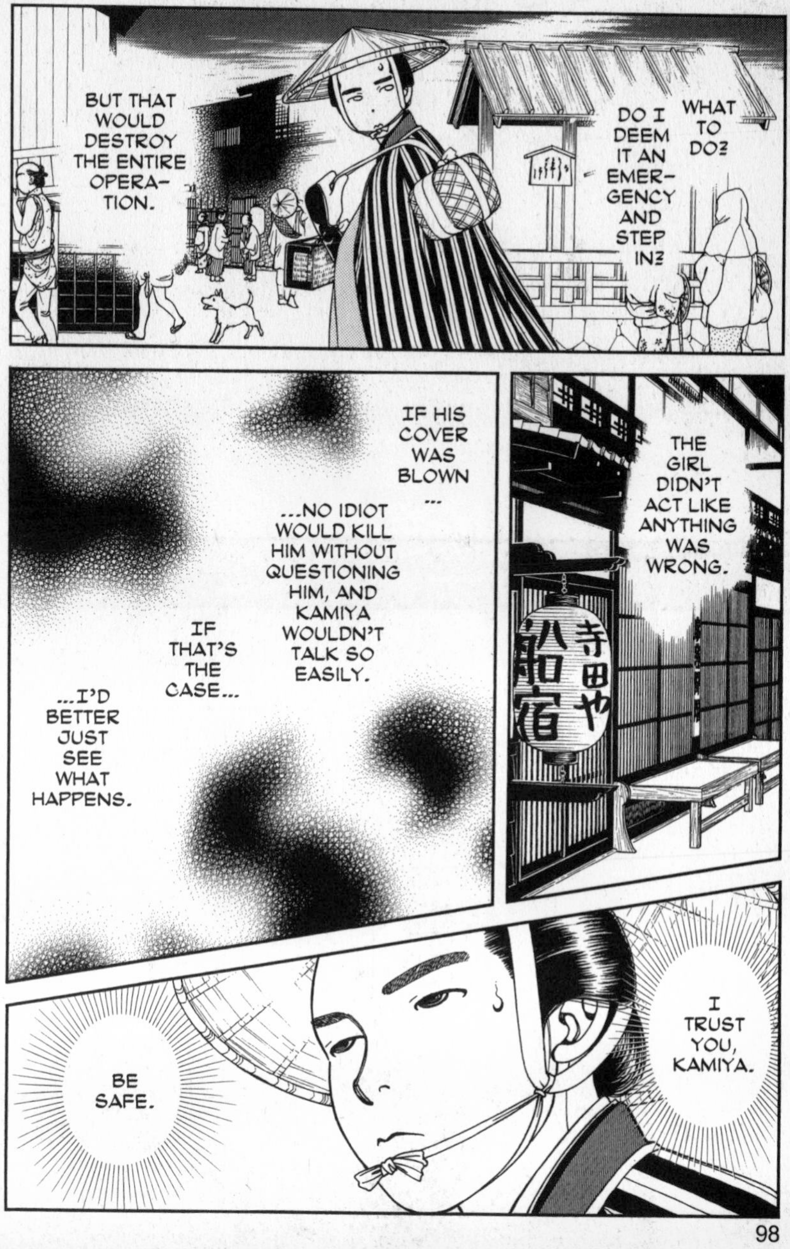
WHAT TO DO?
DO I DEEM IT AN EMERGENCY AND STEP IN?
BUT THAT WOULD DESTROY THE ENTIRE OPERATION.
THE GIRL DIDN'T ACT LIKE ANYTHING WAS WRONG.
寺田や
船宿
IF HIS COVER WAS BLOWN...
...NO IDIOT WOULD KILL HIM WITHOUT QUESTIONING HIM, AND KAMIYA WOULDN'T TALK SO EASILY.
IF THAT'S THE CASE...
...I'D BETTER JUST SEE WHAT HAPPENS.
I TRUST YOU, KAMIYA.
BE SAFE.

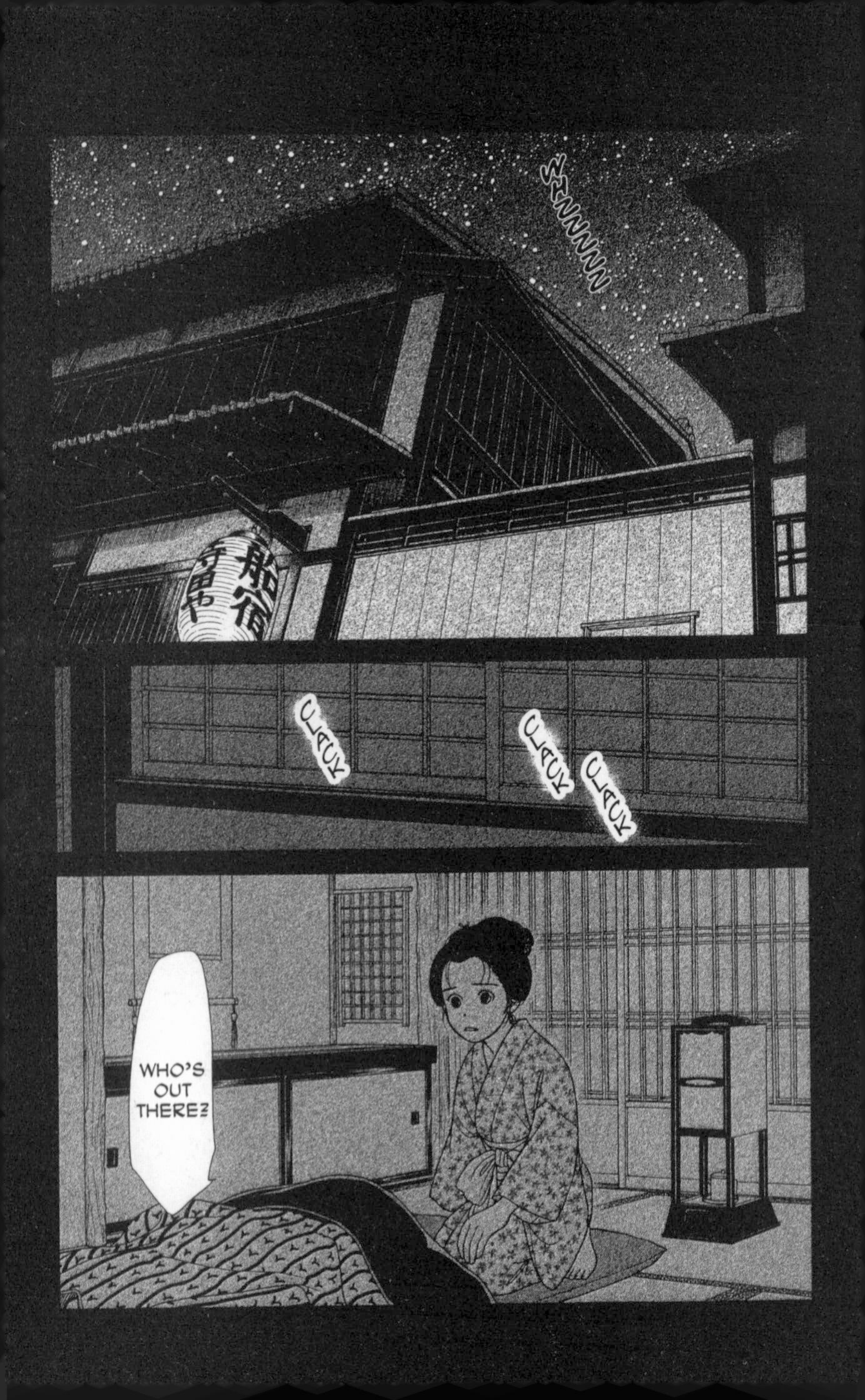
WHNNNNN
CLACK
CLACK
CLACK
WHO'S OUT THERE?

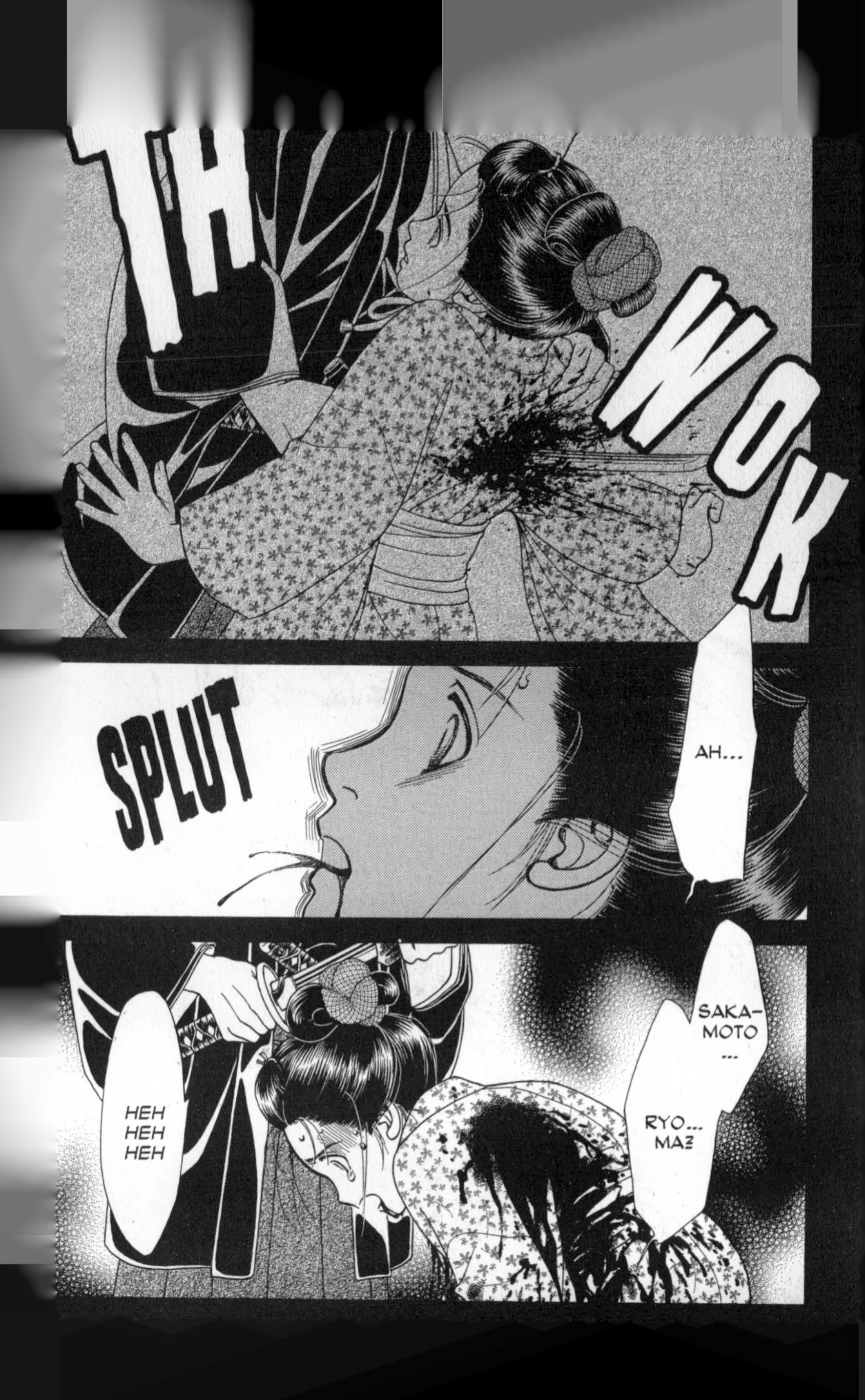
THWOK
AH...
SPLUT
SAKAMOTO...
RYO... MA?
HEH HEH HEH

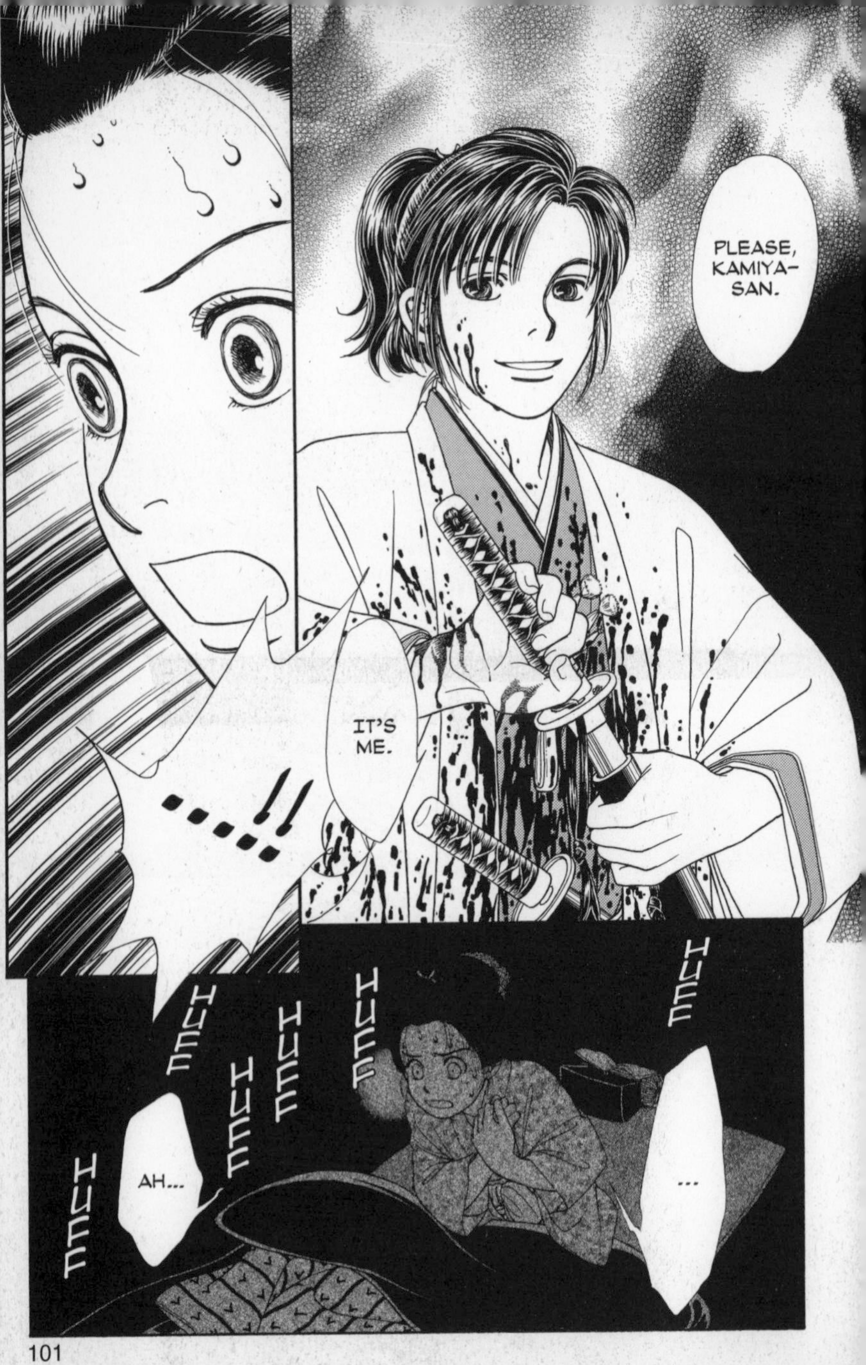
PLEASE, KAMIYA-SAN.
IT'S ME.
...!!
HUFF
...
HUFF
HUFF
HUFF
HUFF
AH...
HUFF

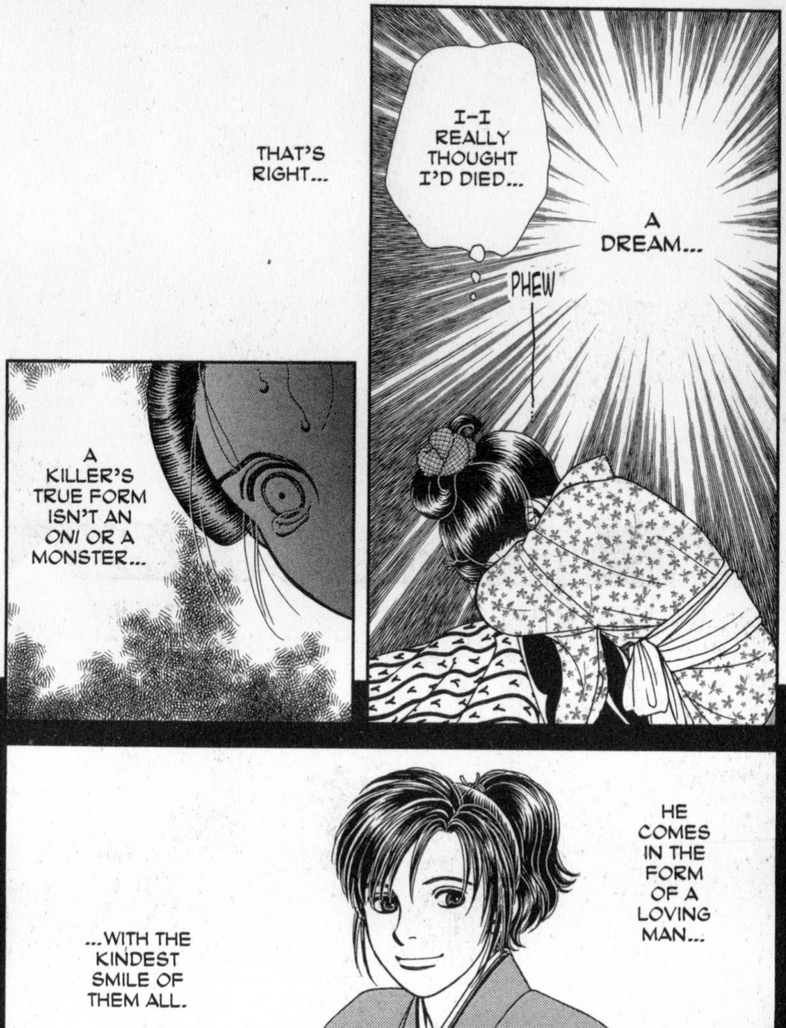
I-I REALLY THOUGHT I'D DIED...
A DREAM...
PHEW
THAT'S RIGHT...
A KILLER'S TRUE FORM ISN'T AN *ONI* OR A MONSTER...
HE COMES IN THE FORM OF A LOVING MAN...
...WITH THE KINDEST SMILE OF THEM ALL.

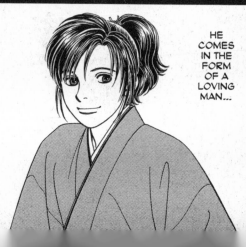

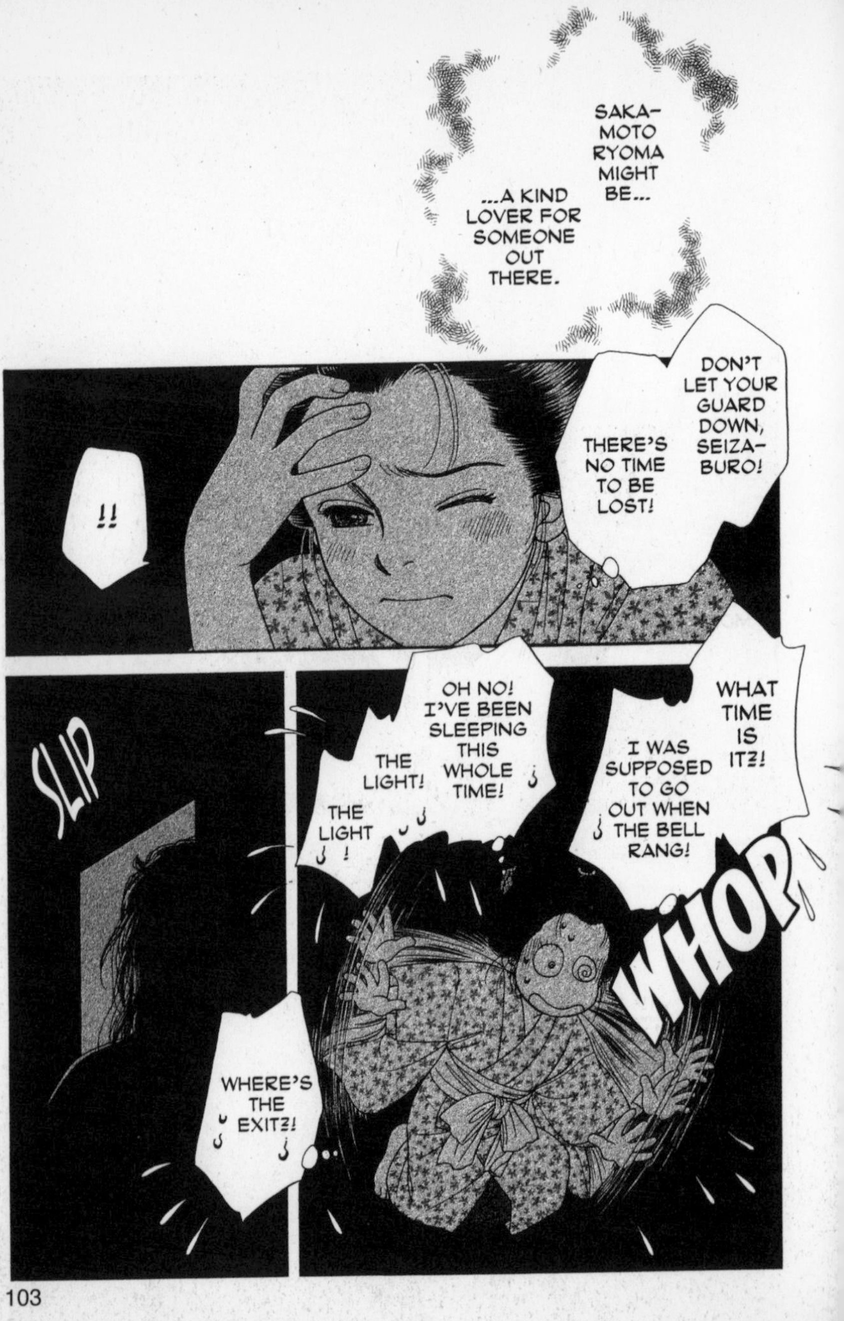
SAKAMOTO RYOMA MIGHT BE...
...A KIND LOVER FOR SOMEONE OUT THERE.
DON'T LET YOUR GUARD DOWN, SEIZABURO!
THERE'S NO TIME TO BE LOST!
!!
WHAT TIME IS IT?!
I WAS SUPPOSED TO GO OUT WHEN THE BELL RANG!
OH NO! I'VE BEEN SLEEPING THIS WHOLE TIME!
THE LIGHT!
THE LIGHT!
WHOP
WHERE'S THE EXIT?!
SLIP

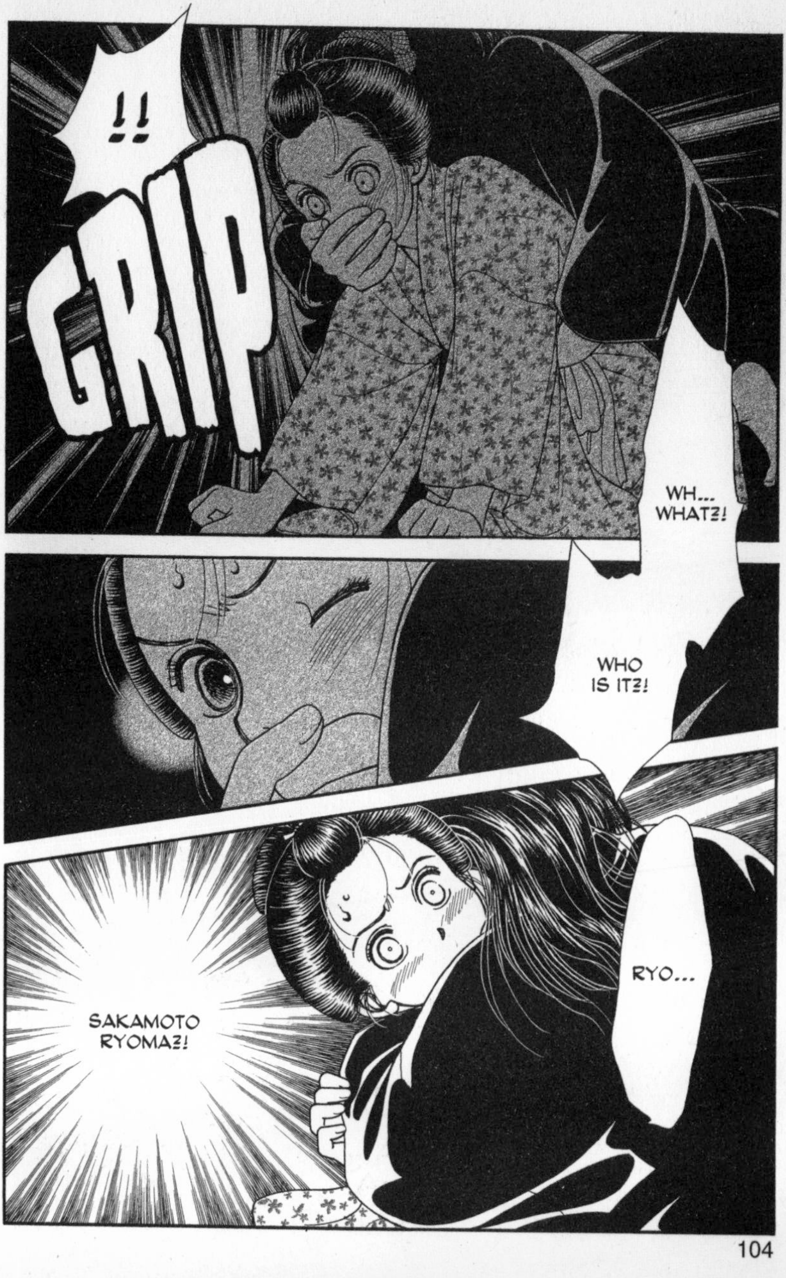
!!
GRIP
WH... WHAT?!
WHO IS IT?!
RYO...
SAKAMOTO RYOMA?!

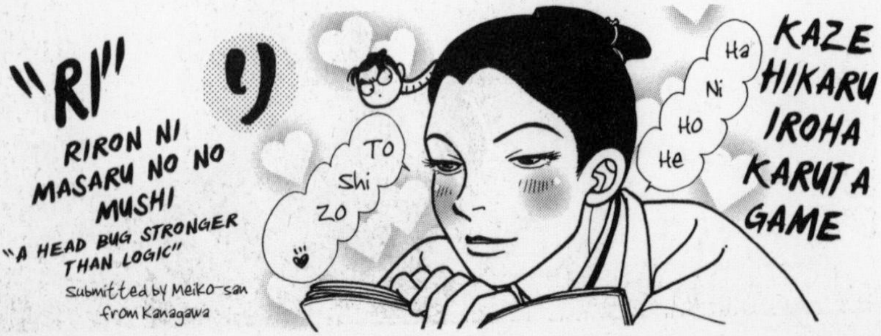
KAZE HIKARU IROHA KARUTA GAME
Ha
Ni
Ho
He
TO
Shi
ZO
"RI"
り
RIRON NI MASARU NO NO MUSHI
"A HEAD BUG STRONGER THAN LOGIC"
Submitted by Meiko-san from Kanagawa

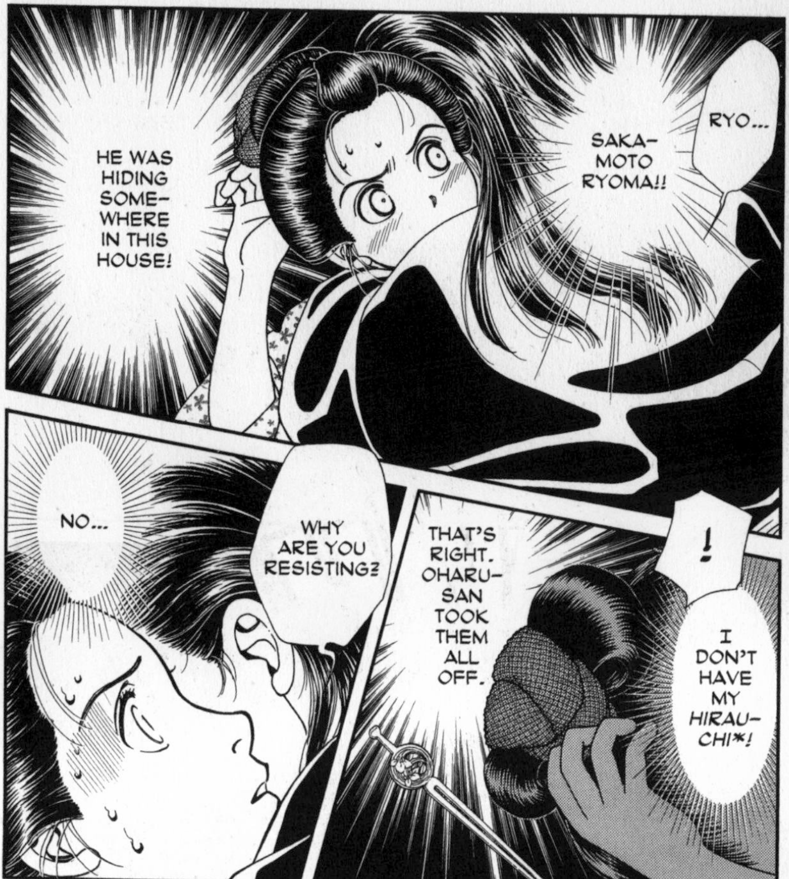
RYO...
SAKA-MOTO RYOMA!!
HE WAS HIDING SOME-WHERE IN THIS HOUSE!
!
I DON'T HAVE MY HIRAU-CHI*!
THAT'S RIGHT. OHARU-SAN TOOK THEM ALL OFF.
WHY ARE YOU RESISTING?
NO...

*A flat hammered metal hair pin that was used by some girls for protection.

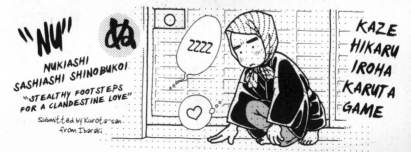

KAZE HIKARU IROHA KARUTA GAME

"NU" ぬ

NUKIASHI SASHIASHI SHINOBUKOI

"STEALTHY FOOTSTEPS FOR A CLANDESTINE LOVE"

Submitted by Kurota-san from Ibaraki

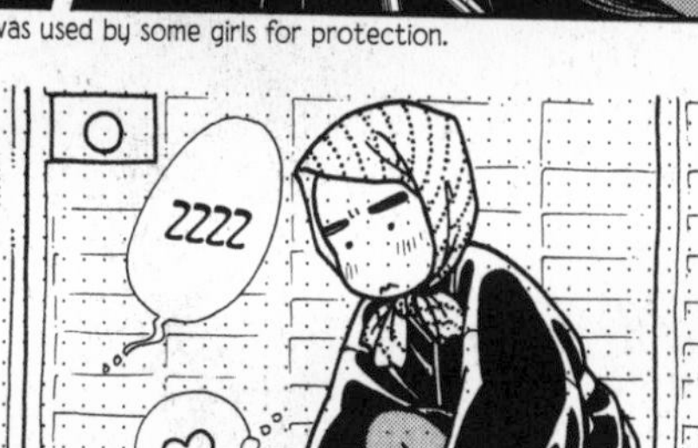
ZZZZ

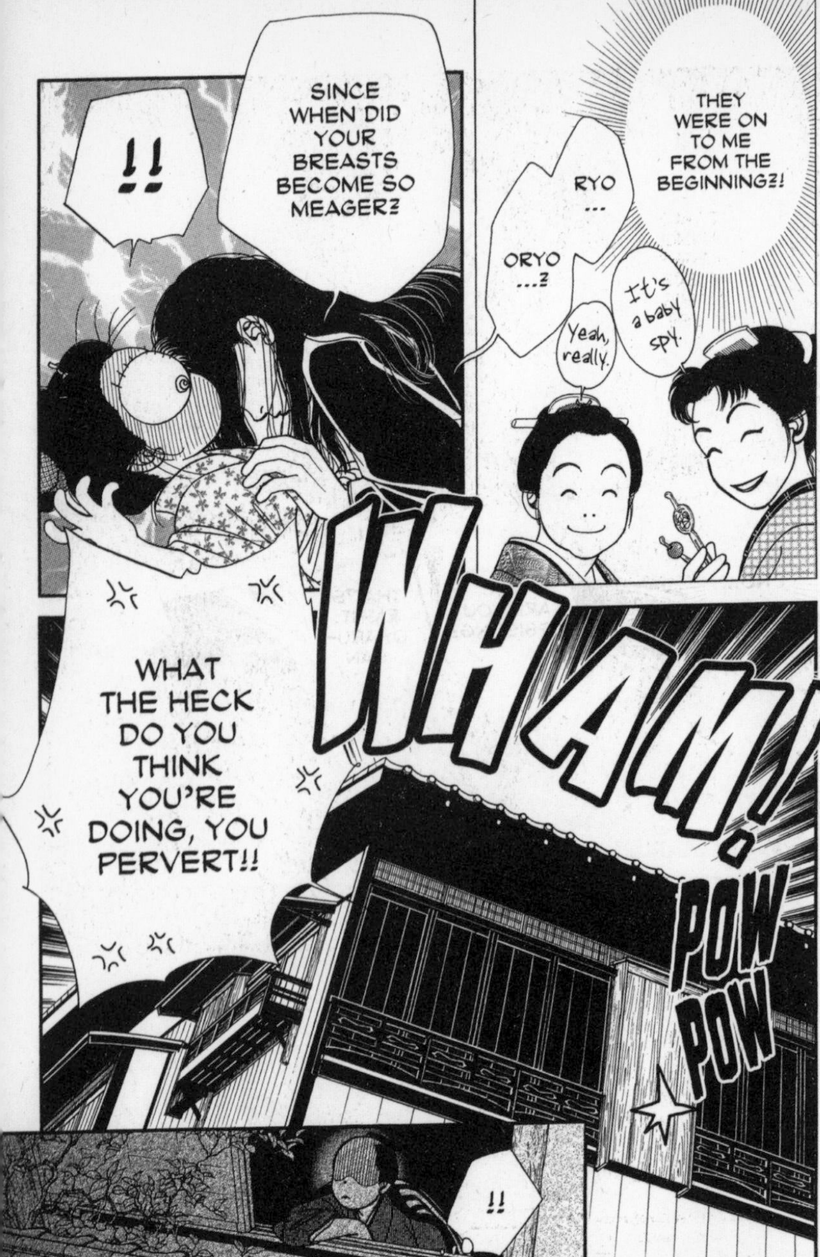
THEY WERE ON TO ME FROM THE BEGINNING?!
RYO... ORYO...?
It's a baby spy.
Yeah, really.
SINCE WHEN DID YOUR BREASTS BECOME SO MEAGER?
!!
WHAT THE HECK DO YOU THINK YOU'RE DOING, YOU PERVERT!!
WHAM!
POW POW
!!

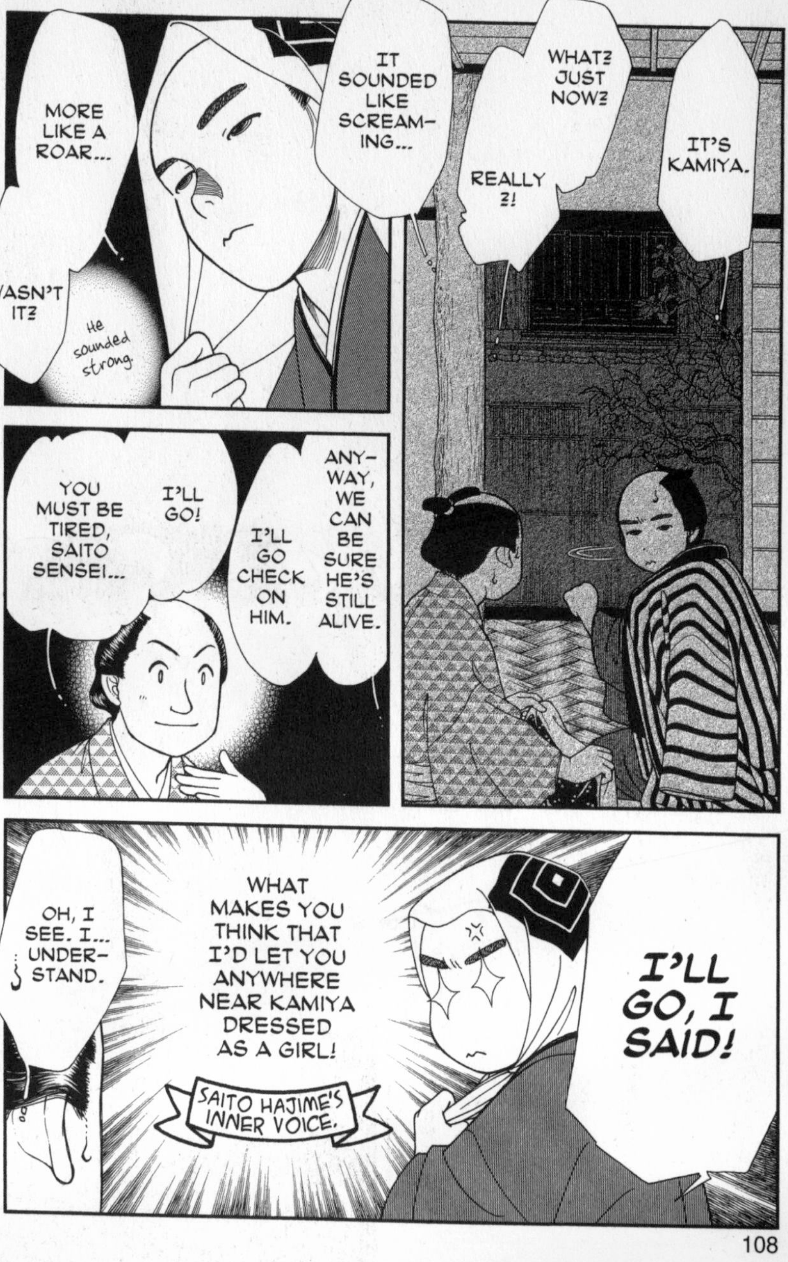
IT'S KAMIYA.
WHAT? JUST NOW?
REALLY?!
IT SOUNDED LIKE SCREAMING...
MORE LIKE A ROAR...
WASN'T IT?
He sounded strong.
ANYWAY, WE CAN BE SURE HE'S STILL ALIVE.
I'LL GO CHECK ON HIM.
I'LL GO!
YOU MUST BE TIRED, SAITO SENSEI...
I'LL GO, I SAID!
WHAT MAKES YOU THINK THAT I'D LET YOU ANYWHERE NEAR KAMIYA DRESSED AS A GIRL!
SAITO HAJIME'S INNER VOICE.
OH, I SEE. I... UNDERSTAND.

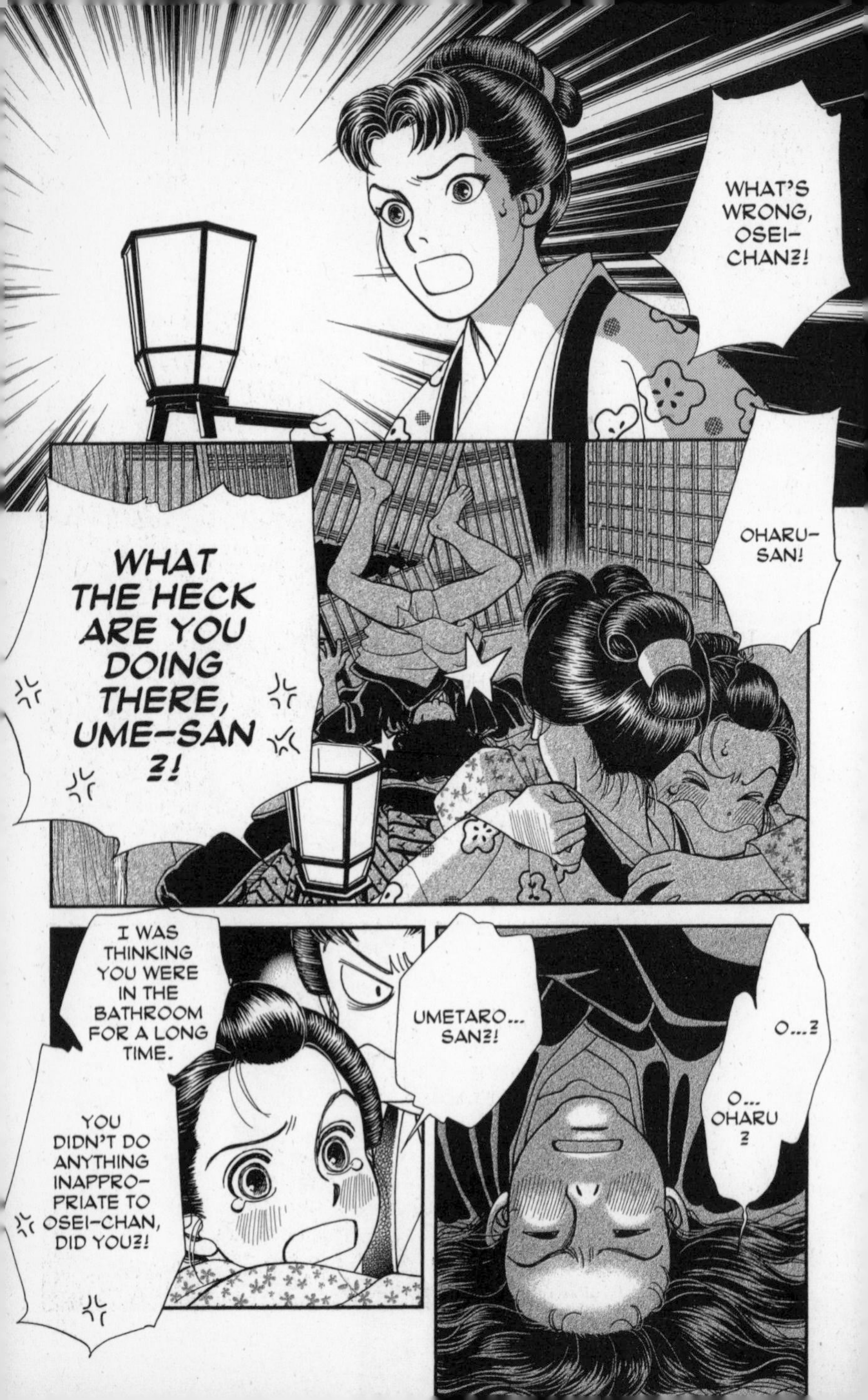
WHAT'S WRONG, OSEI-CHAN?!
OHARU-SAN!
WHAT THE HECK ARE YOU DOING THERE, UME-SAN?!
O...?
O... OHARU?
UMETARO... SAN?!
I WAS THINKING YOU WERE IN THE BATHROOM FOR A LONG TIME.
YOU DIDN'T DO ANYTHING INAPPROPRIATE TO OSEI-CHAN, DID YOU?!

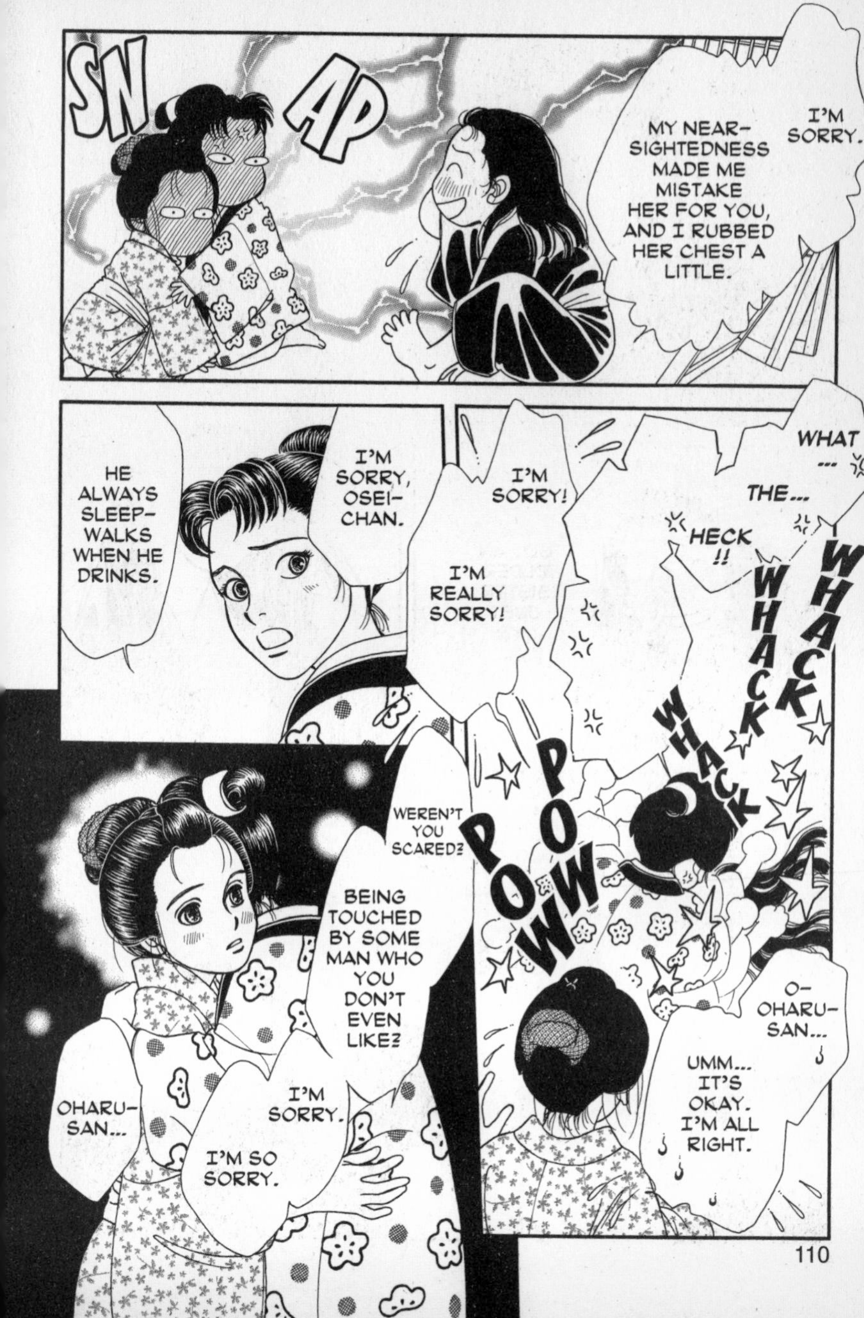
I'M SORRY.
MY NEAR-SIGHTEDNESS MADE ME MISTAKE HER FOR YOU, AND I RUBBED HER CHEST A LITTLE.
SNAP
WHAT ... THE... HECK!!
WHACK
WHACK
WHACK
I'M SORRY!
I'M REALLY SORRY!
POW
POW
O-OHARU-SAN...
UMM... IT'S OKAY. I'M ALL RIGHT.
I'M SORRY, OSEI-CHAN.
HE ALWAYS SLEEP-WALKS WHEN HE DRINKS.
WEREN'T YOU SCARED?
BEING TOUCHED BY SOME MAN WHO YOU DON'T EVEN LIKE?
I'M SORRY.
I'M SO SORRY.
OHARU-SAN...

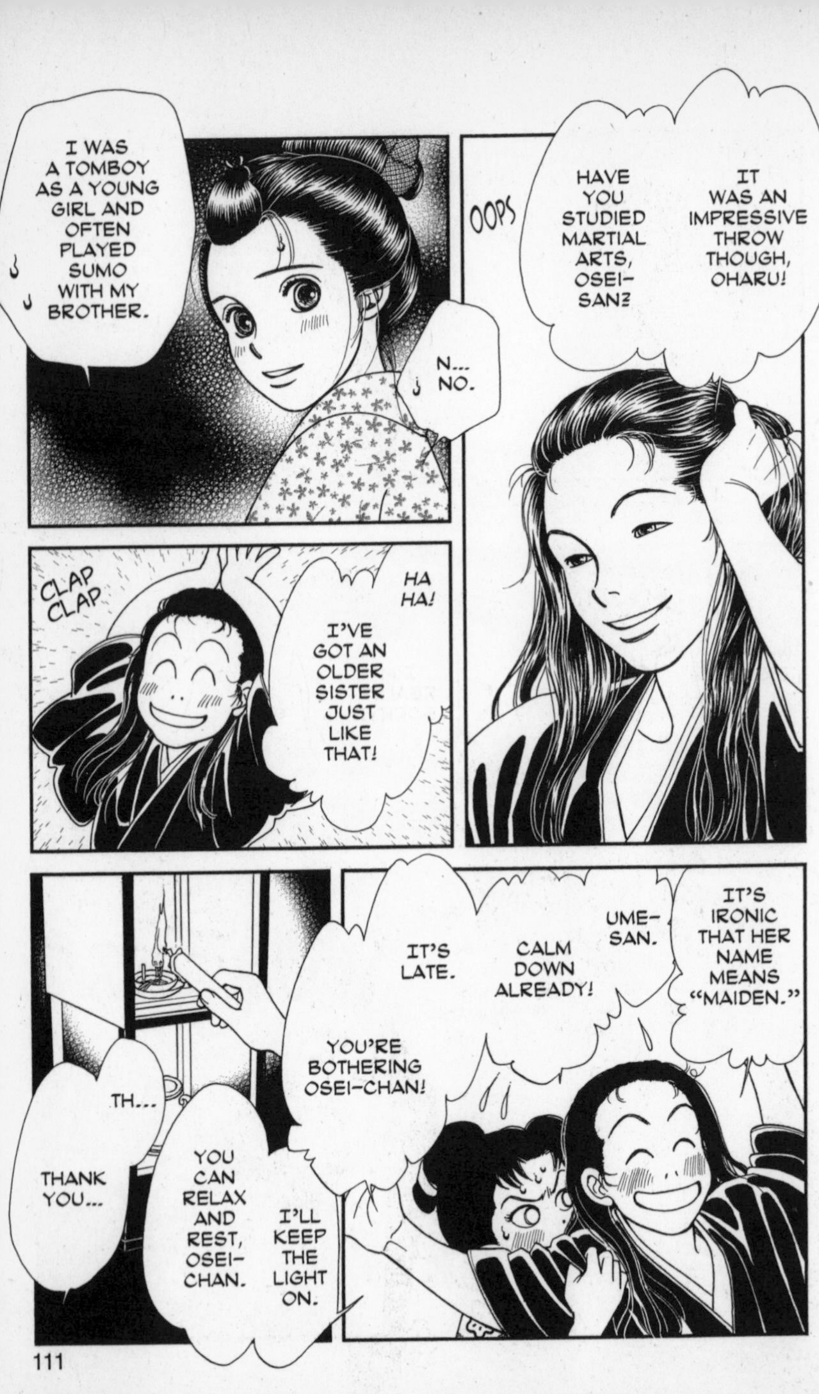
IT WAS AN IMPRESSIVE THROW THOUGH, OHARU!
HAVE YOU STUDIED MARTIAL ARTS, OSEI-SAN?
OOPS
N... NO.
I WAS A TOMBOY AS A YOUNG GIRL AND OFTEN PLAYED SUMO WITH MY BROTHER.
HA HA!
I'VE GOT AN OLDER SISTER JUST LIKE THAT!
CLAP CLAP
IT'S IRONIC THAT HER NAME MEANS "MAIDEN."
UME-SAN.
CALM DOWN ALREADY!
IT'S LATE.
YOU'RE BOTHERING OSEI-CHAN!
I'LL KEEP THE LIGHT ON.
YOU CAN RELAX AND REST, OSEI-CHAN.
TH...
THANK YOU...

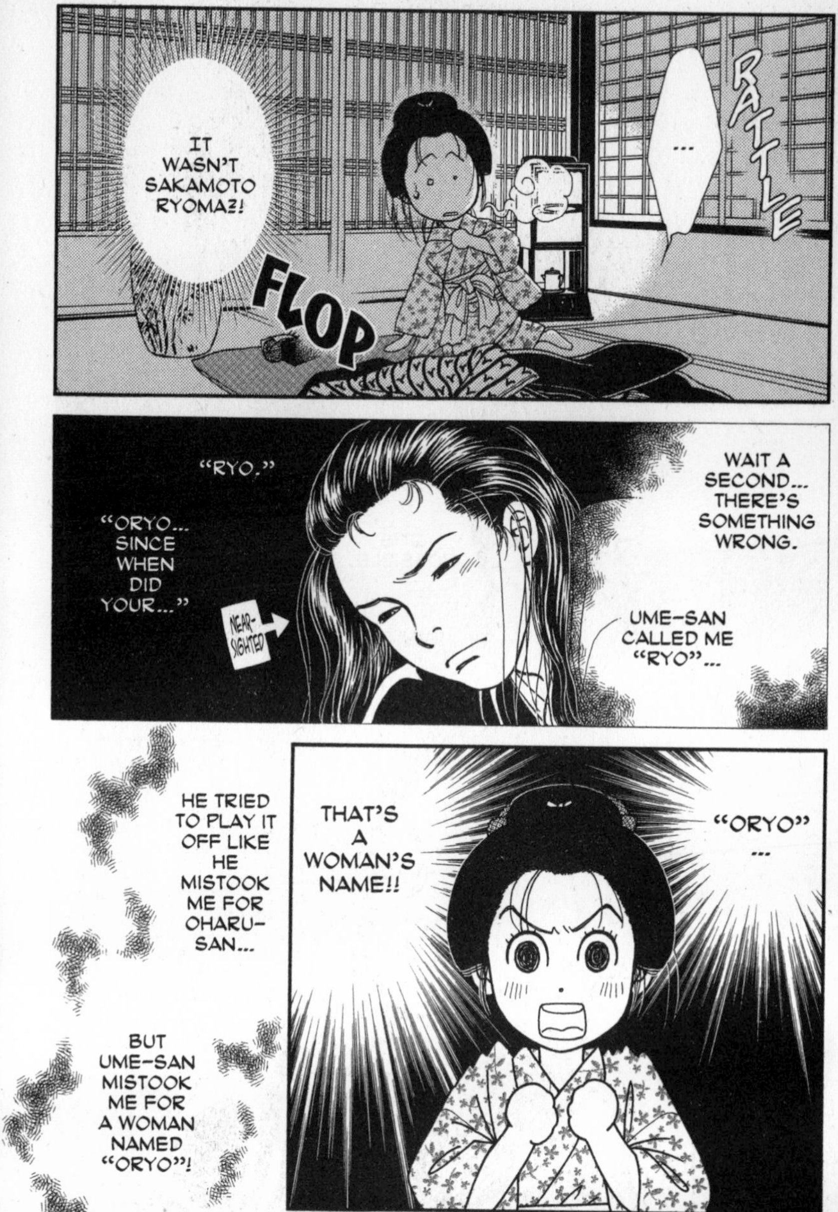
...
RATTLE
IT WASN'T SAKAMOTO RYOMA?!
FLOP
WAIT A SECOND... THERE'S SOMETHING WRONG.
UME-SAN CALLED ME "RYO"...
"RYO."
"ORYO... SINCE WHEN DID YOUR..."
NEAR-SIGHTED
"ORYO" ...
THAT'S A WOMAN'S NAME!!
HE TRIED TO PLAY IT OFF LIKE HE MISTOOK ME FOR OHARU-SAN...
BUT UME-SAN MISTOOK ME FOR A WOMAN NAMED "ORYO"!

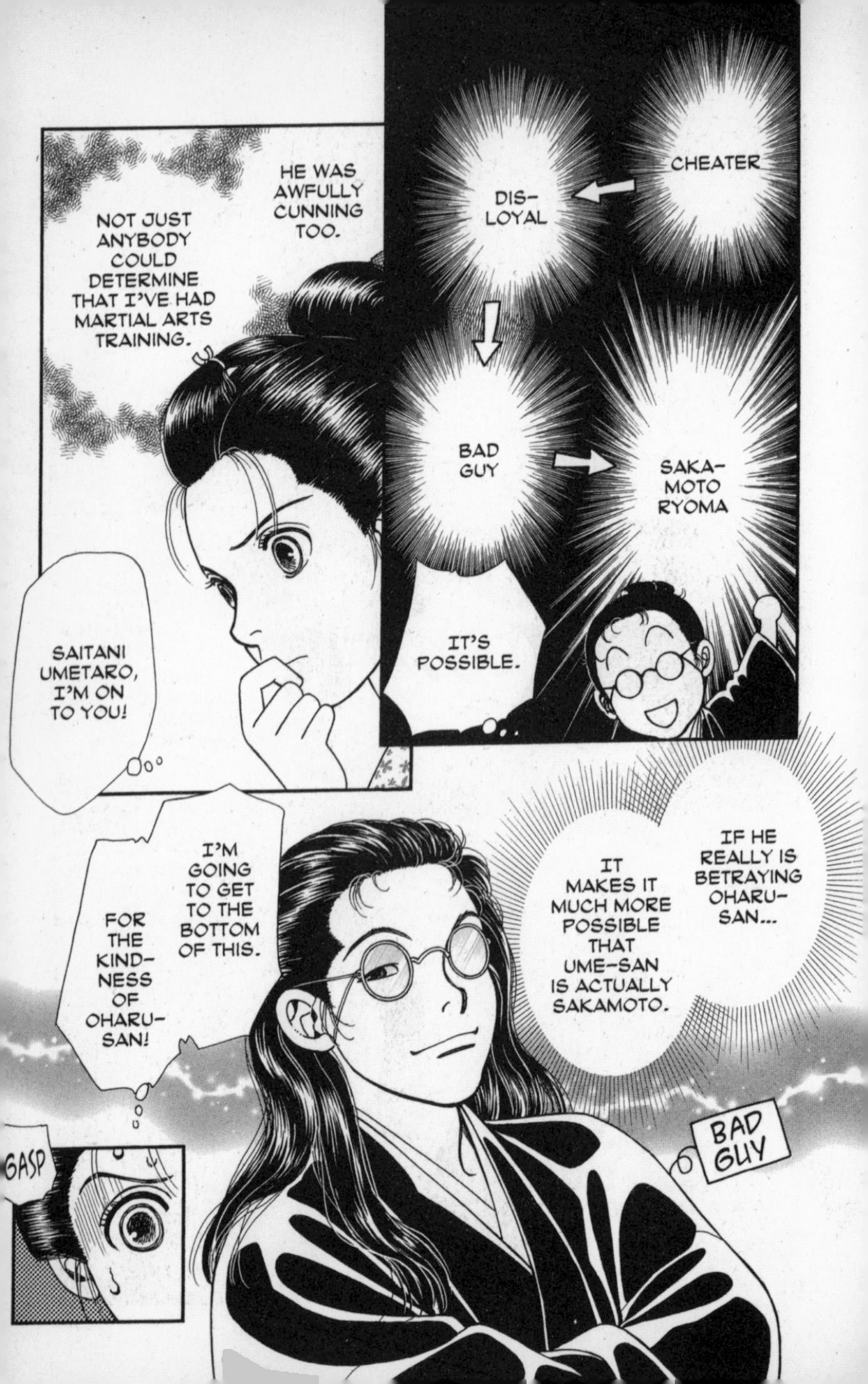
CHEATER
DIS-LOYAL
BAD GUY
SAKA-MOTO RYOMA
IT'S POSSIBLE.
HE WAS AWFULLY CUNNING TOO.
NOT JUST ANYBODY COULD DETERMINE THAT I'VE HAD MARTIAL ARTS TRAINING.
SAITANI UMETARO, I'M ON TO YOU!
IF HE REALLY IS BETRAYING OHARU-SAN...
IT MAKES IT MUCH MORE POSSIBLE THAT UME-SAN IS ACTUALLY SAKAMOTO.
BAD GUY
I'M GOING TO GET TO THE BOTTOM OF THIS.
FOR THE KINDNESS OF OHARU-SAN!
GASP

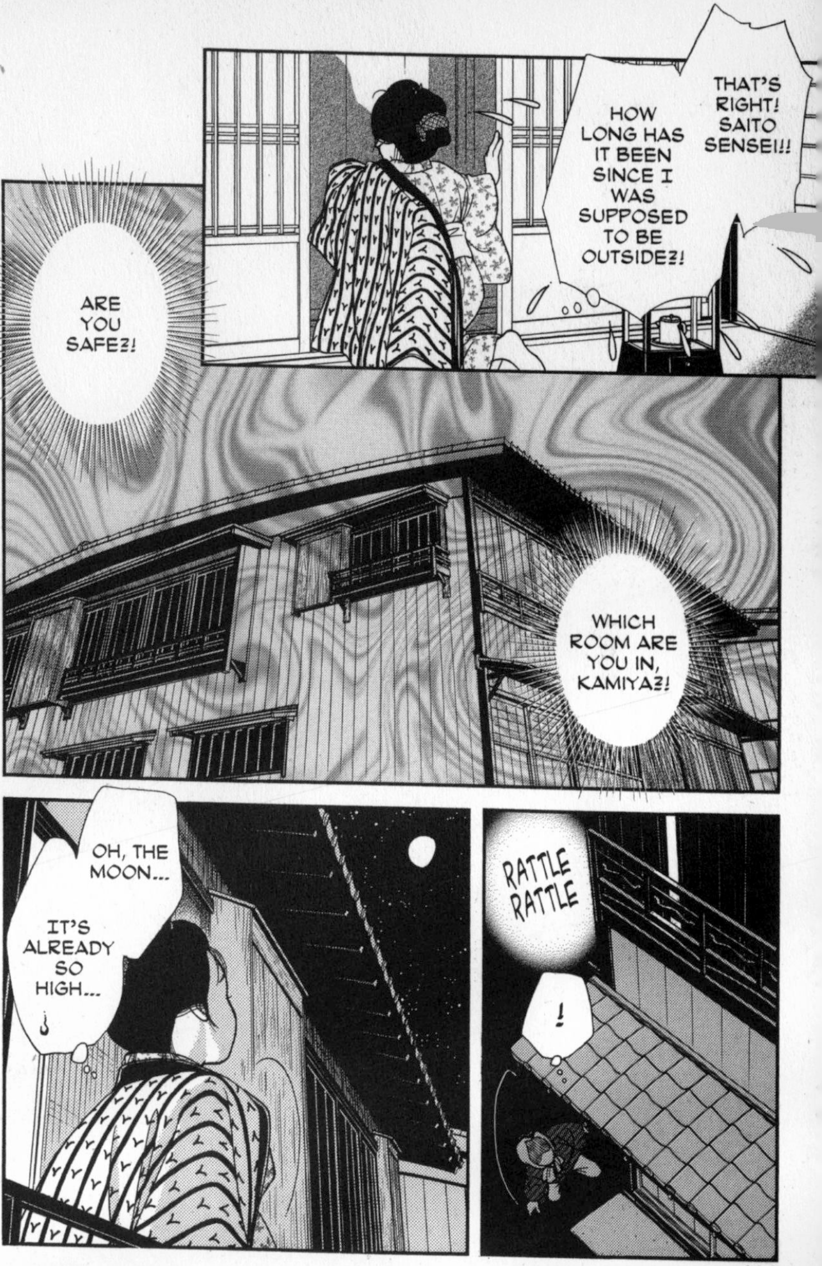
THAT'S RIGHT! SAITO SENSEI!!!
HOW LONG HAS IT BEEN SINCE I WAS SUPPOSED TO BE OUTSIDE?!
ARE YOU SAFE?!
WHICH ROOM ARE YOU IN, KAMIYA?!
RATTLE RATTLE
!
OH, THE MOON...
IT'S ALREADY SO HIGH...

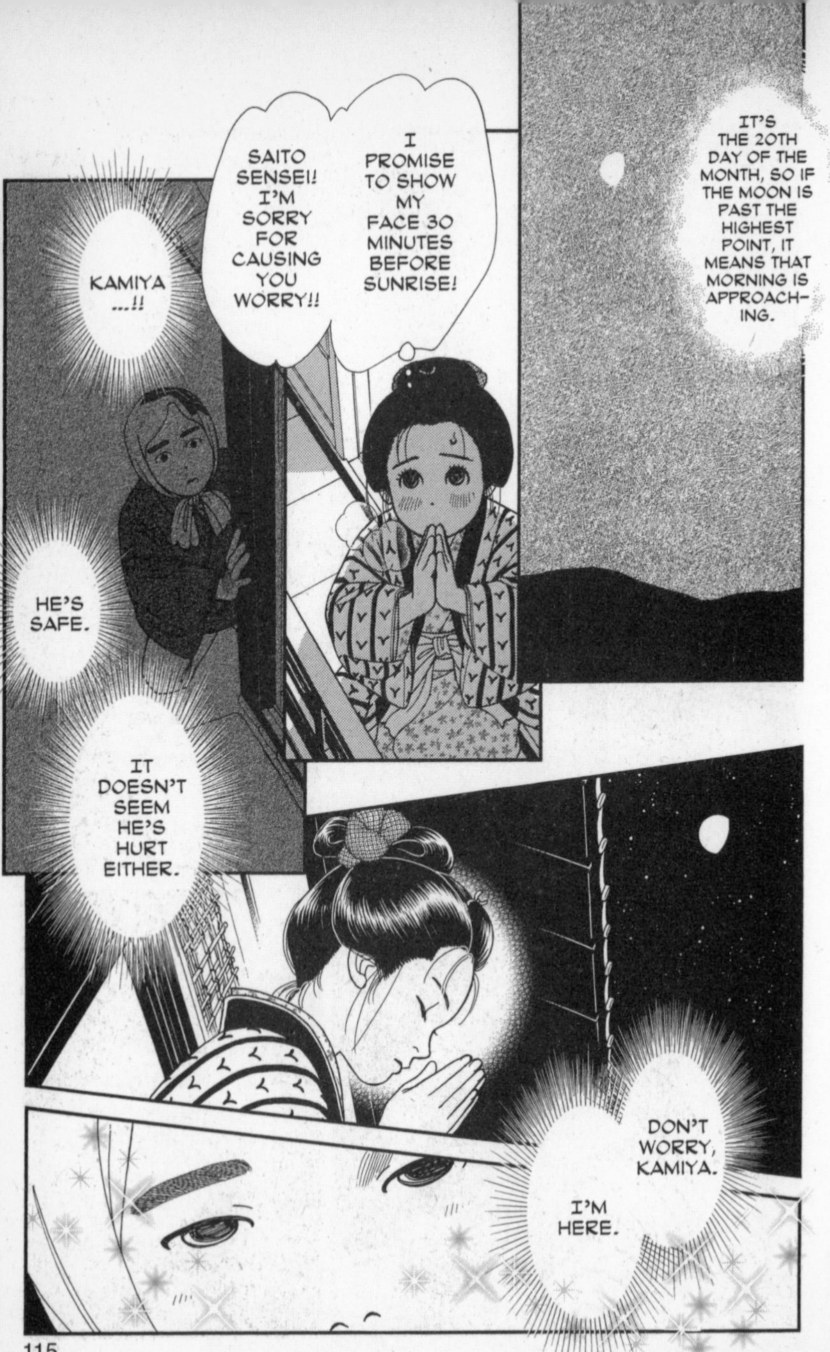
IT'S THE 20TH DAY OF THE MONTH, SO IF THE MOON IS PAST THE HIGHEST POINT, IT MEANS THAT MORNING IS APPROACH-ING.
I PROMISE TO SHOW MY FACE 30 MINUTES BEFORE SUNRISE!
SAITO SENSEI! I'M SORRY FOR CAUSING YOU WORRY!!
KAMIYA ...!!
HE'S SAFE.
IT DOESN'T SEEM HE'S HURT EITHER.
DON'T WORRY, KAMIYA.
I'M HERE.

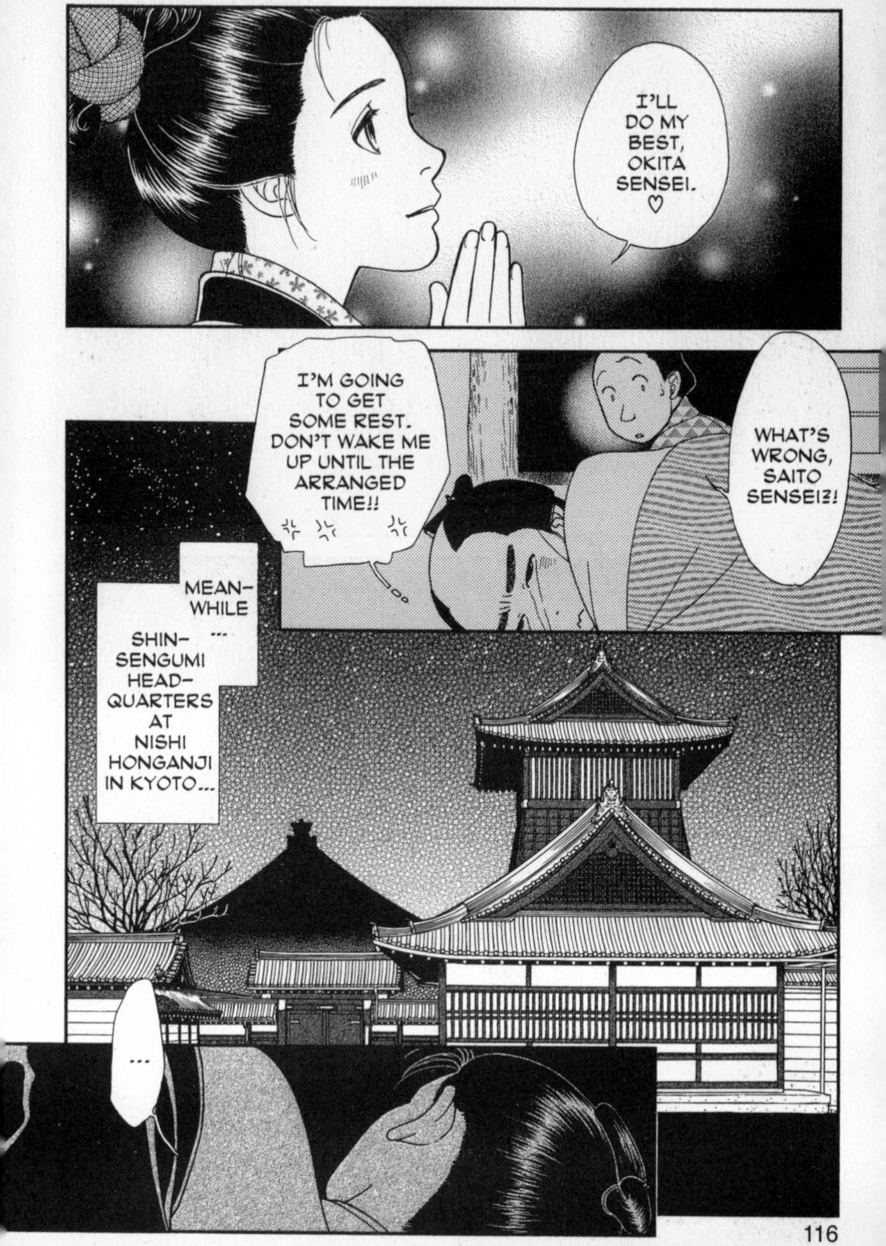
I'LL DO MY BEST, OKITA SENSEI. ♡
WHAT'S WRONG, SAITO SENSEI!?!
I'M GOING TO GET SOME REST. DON'T WAKE ME UP UNTIL THE ARRANGED TIME!!
MEAN-WHILE ...
SHIN-SENGUMI HEAD-QUARTERS AT NISHI HONGANJI IN KYOTO...
...

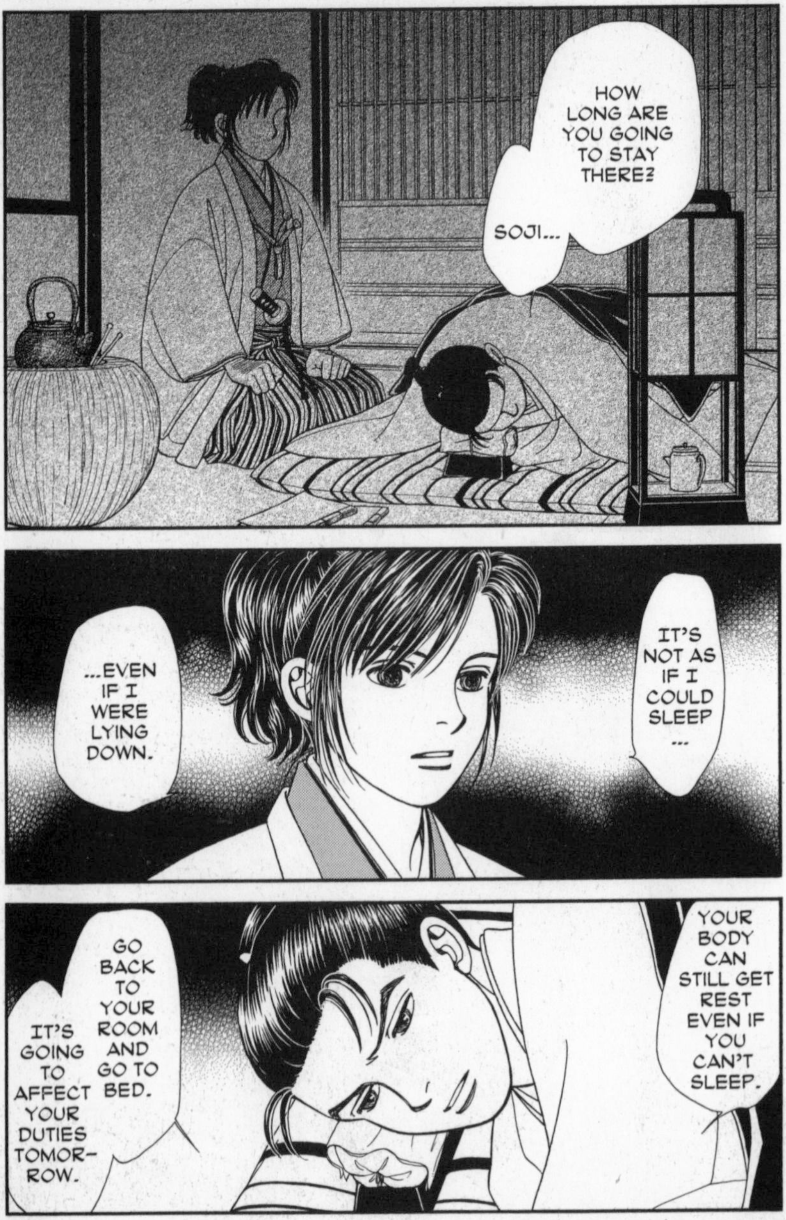
HOW LONG ARE YOU GOING TO STAY THERE?
SOJI...
IT'S NOT AS IF I COULD SLEEP...
...EVEN IF I WERE LYING DOWN.
YOUR BODY CAN STILL GET REST EVEN IF YOU CAN'T SLEEP.
GO BACK TO YOUR ROOM AND GO TO BED.
IT'S GOING TO AFFECT YOUR DUTIES TOMORROW.

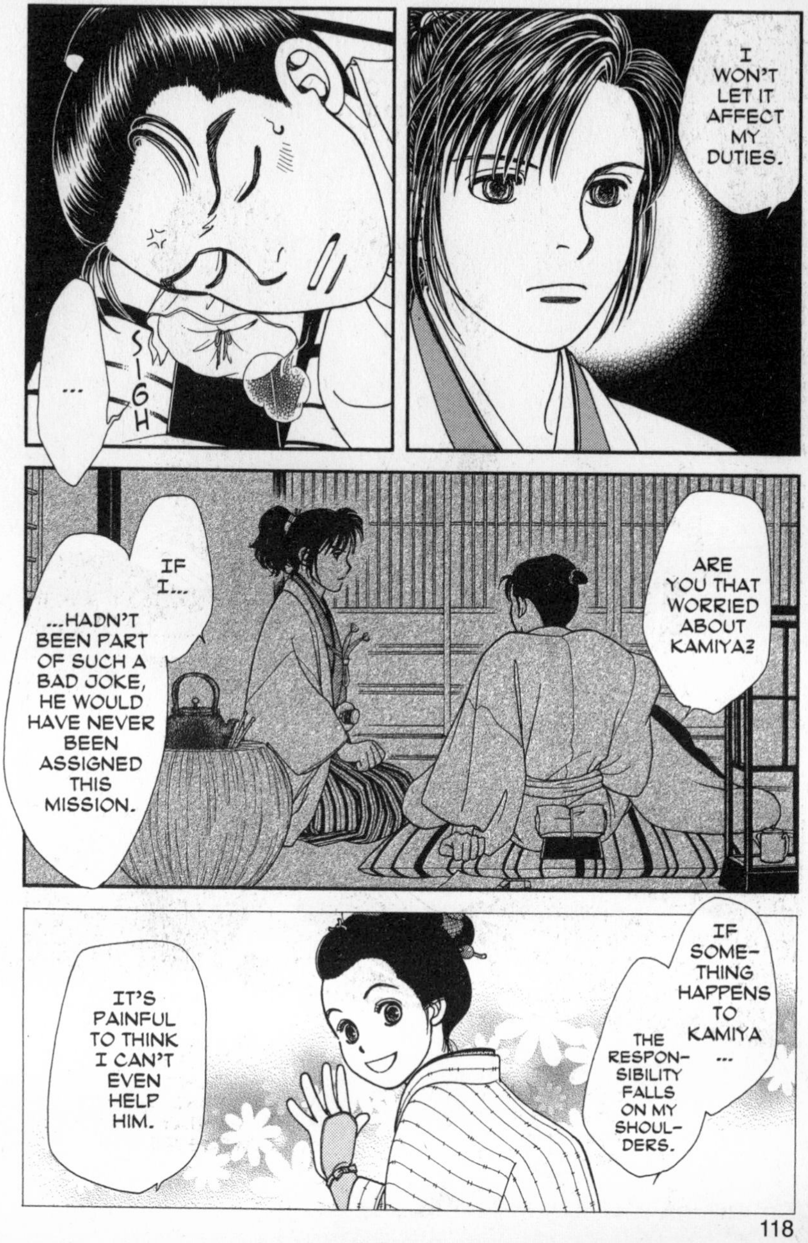

I WON'T LET IT AFFECT MY DUTIES.
SIGH
...
ARE YOU THAT WORRIED ABOUT KAMIYA?
IF I...
...HADN'T BEEN PART OF SUCH A BAD JOKE, HE WOULD HAVE NEVER BEEN ASSIGNED THIS MISSION.
IF SOMETHING HAPPENS TO KAMIYA...
THE RESPONSIBILITY FALLS ON MY SHOULDERS.
IT'S PAINFUL TO THINK I CAN'T EVEN HELP HIM.

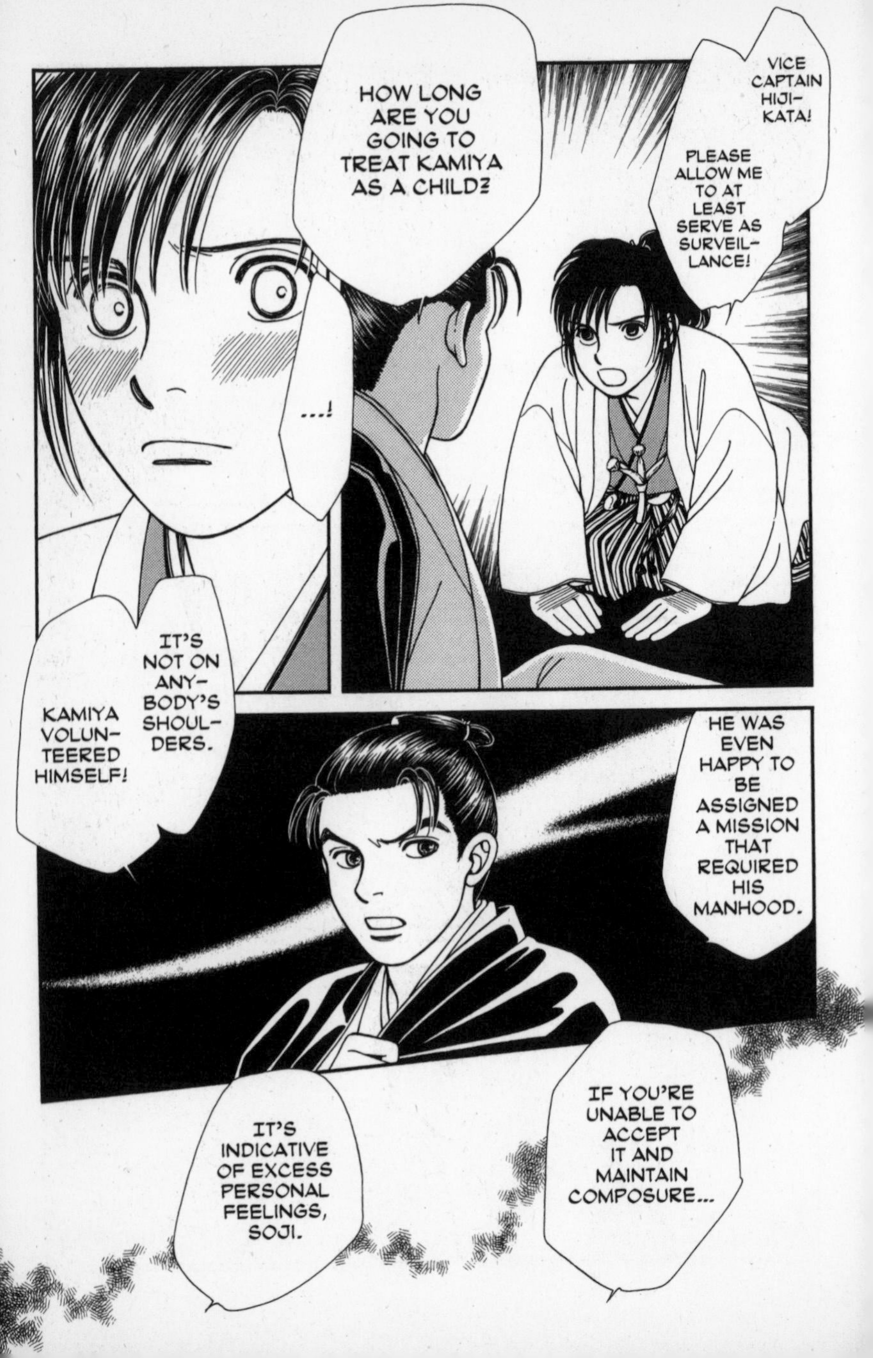
VICE CAPTAIN HIJI-KATA!
PLEASE ALLOW ME TO AT LEAST SERVE AS SURVEIL-LANCE!
HOW LONG ARE YOU GOING TO TREAT KAMIYA AS A CHILD?
...!
IT'S NOT ON ANY-BODY'S SHOUL-DERS.
KAMIYA VOLUN-TEERED HIMSELF!
HE WAS EVEN HAPPY TO BE ASSIGNED A MISSION THAT REQUIRED HIS MANHOOD.
IF YOU'RE UNABLE TO ACCEPT IT AND MAINTAIN COMPOSURE...
IT'S INDICATIVE OF EXCESS PERSONAL FEELINGS, SOJI.

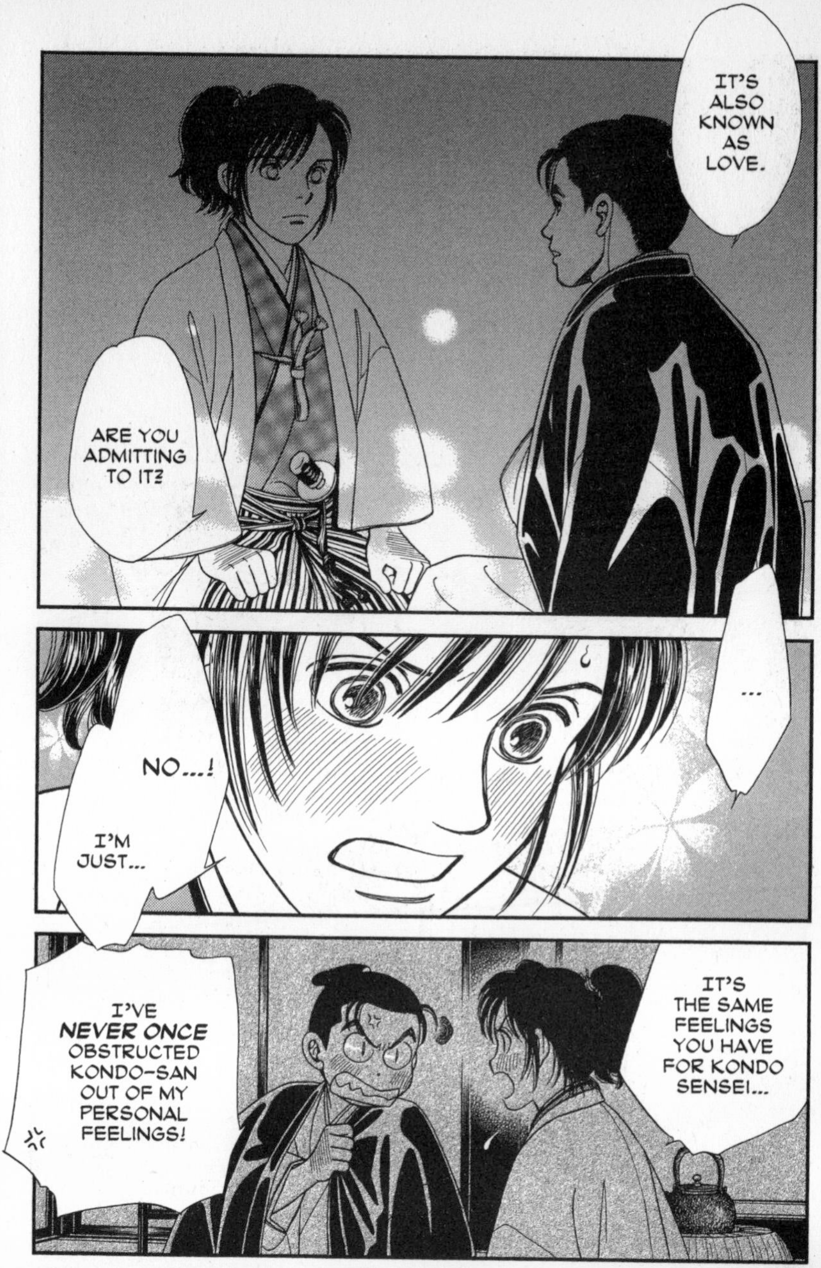
IT'S ALSO KNOWN AS LOVE.
ARE YOU ADMITTING TO IT?
...
NO...!
I'M JUST...
IT'S THE SAME FEELINGS YOU HAVE FOR KONDO SENSEI...
I'VE NEVER ONCE OBSTRUCTED KONDO-SAN OUT OF MY PERSONAL FEELINGS!

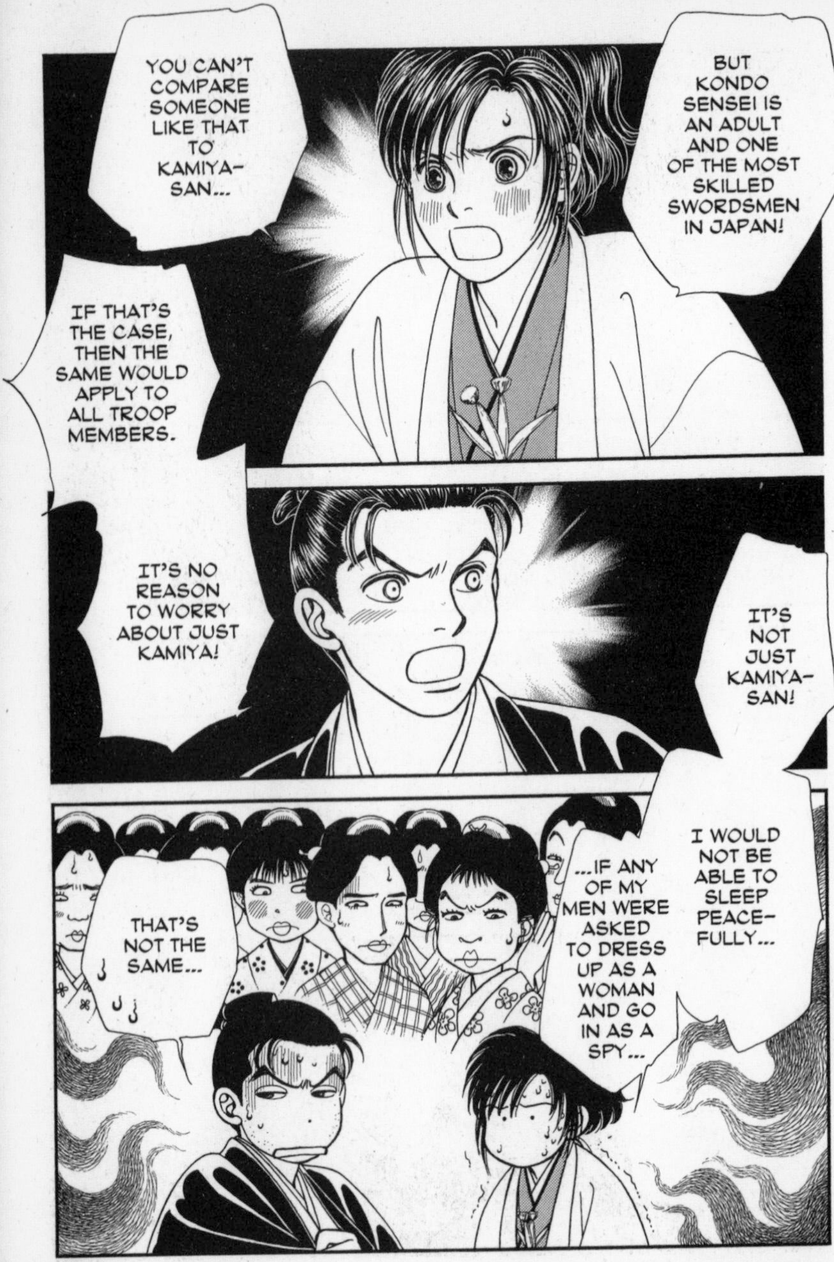
BUT KONDO SENSEI IS AN ADULT AND ONE OF THE MOST SKILLED SWORDSMEN IN JAPAN!
YOU CAN'T COMPARE SOMEONE LIKE THAT TO KAMIYA-SAN...
IF THAT'S THE CASE, THEN THE SAME WOULD APPLY TO ALL TROOP MEMBERS.
IT'S NOT JUST KAMIYA-SAN!
IT'S NO REASON TO WORRY ABOUT JUST KAMIYA!
I WOULD NOT BE ABLE TO SLEEP PEACE-FULLY...
...IF ANY OF MY MEN WERE ASKED TO DRESS UP AS A WOMAN AND GO IN AS A SPY...
THAT'S NOT THE SAME...

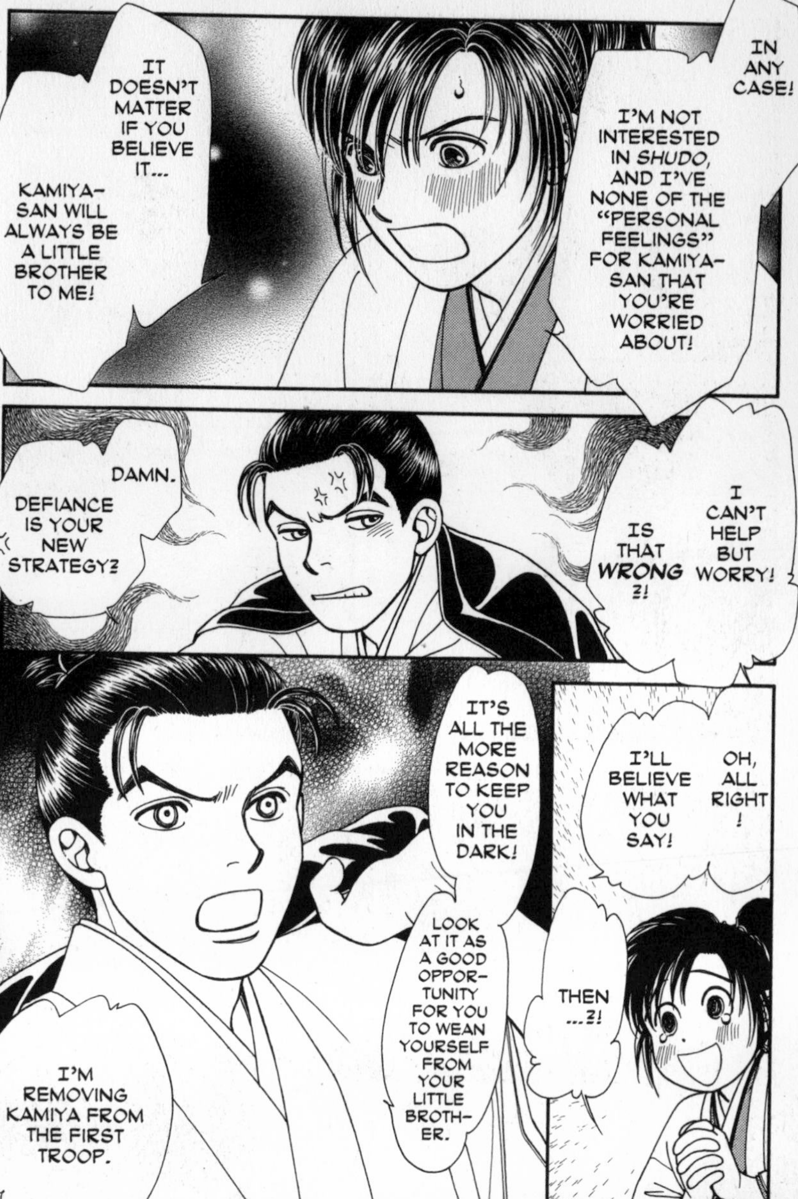
IN ANY CASE!
I'M NOT INTERESTED IN *SHUDO*, AND I'VE NONE OF THE "PERSONAL FEELINGS" FOR KAMIYA-SAN THAT YOU'RE WORRIED ABOUT!
IT DOESN'T MATTER IF YOU BELIEVE IT...
KAMIYA-SAN WILL ALWAYS BE A LITTLE BROTHER TO ME!
I CAN'T HELP BUT WORRY!
IS THAT **WRONG** ?!
DAMN.
DEFIANCE IS YOUR NEW STRATEGY?!
OH, ALL RIGHT!
I'LL BELIEVE WHAT YOU SAY!
THEN ...?!
IT'S ALL THE MORE REASON TO KEEP YOU IN THE DARK!
LOOK AT IT AS A GOOD OPPORTUNITY FOR YOU TO WEAN YOURSELF FROM YOUR LITTLE BROTHER.
I'M REMOVING KAMIYA FROM THE FIRST TROOP.

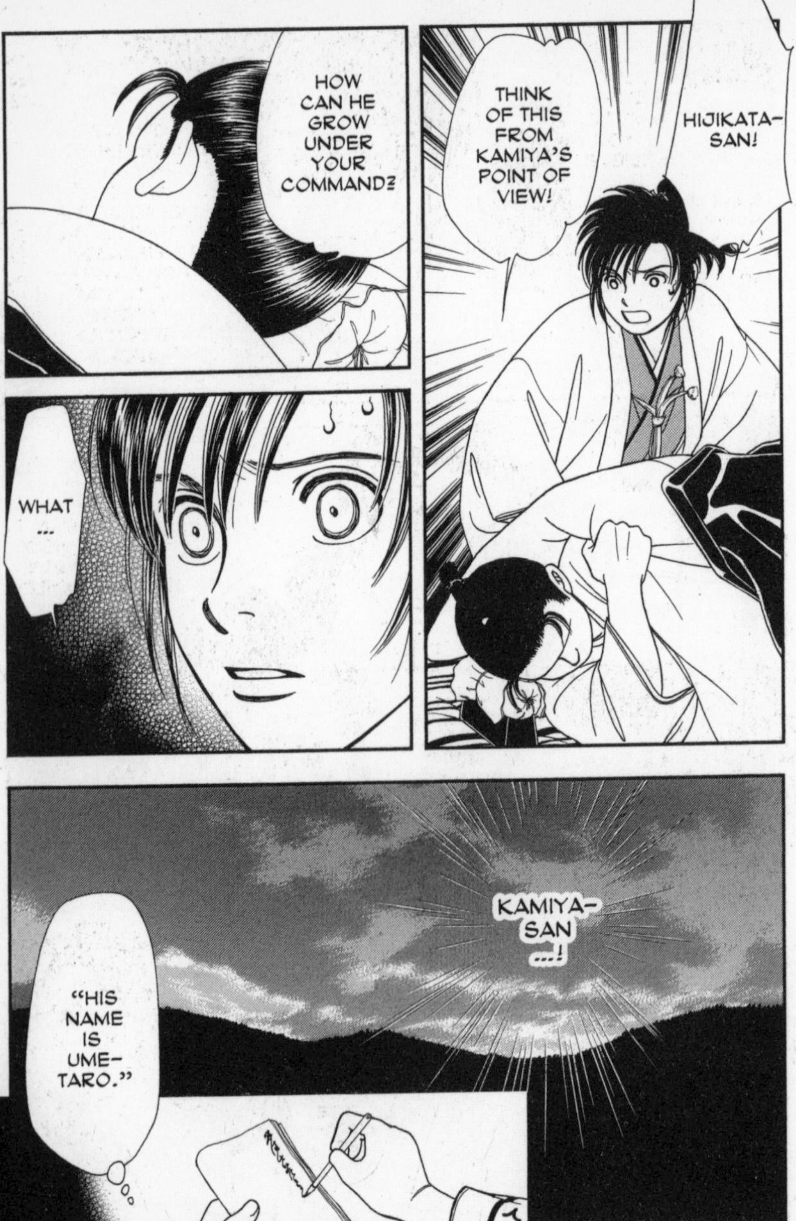
HIJIKATA-SAN!
THINK OF THIS FROM KAMIYA'S POINT OF VIEW!
HOW CAN HE GROW UNDER YOUR COMMAND?
WHAT ...
KAMIYA-SAN ...!
"HIS NAME IS UME-TARO."

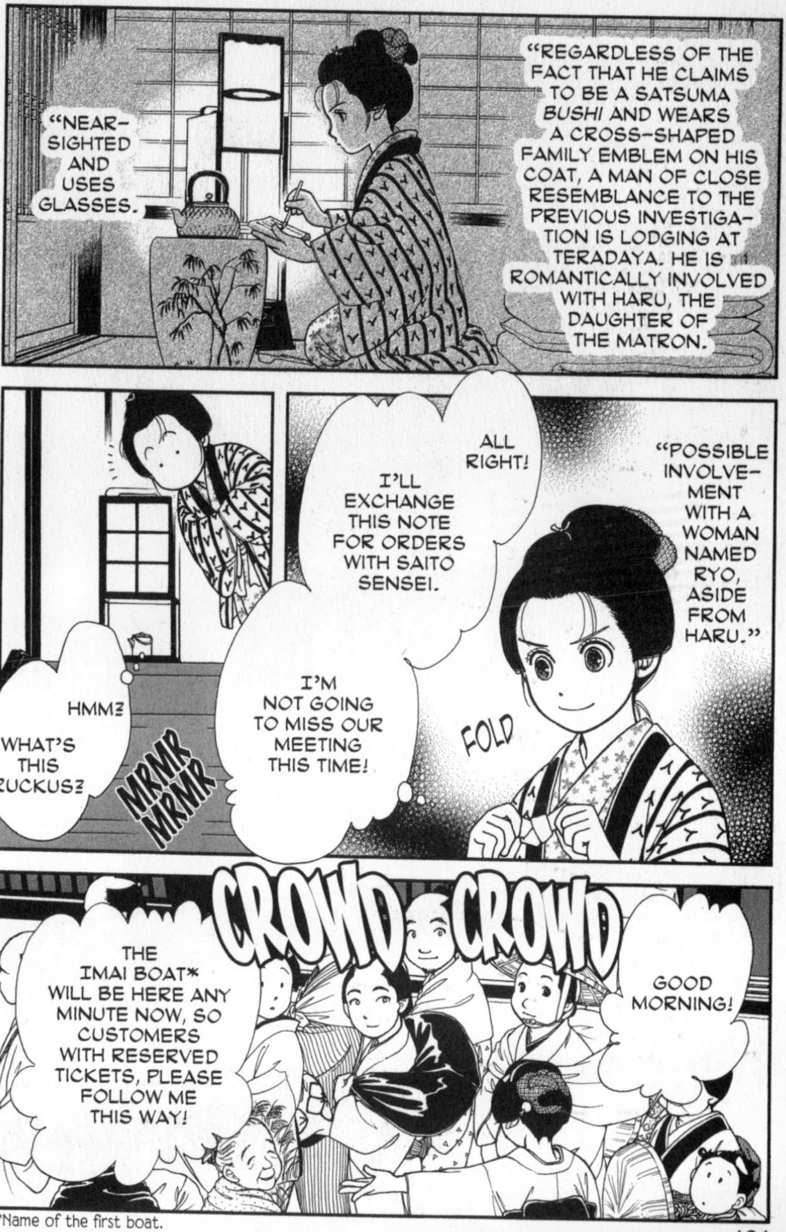
"REGARDLESS OF THE FACT THAT HE CLAIMS TO BE A SATSUMA *BUSHI* AND WEARS A CROSS-SHAPED FAMILY EMBLEM ON HIS COAT, A MAN OF CLOSE RESEMBLANCE TO THE PREVIOUS INVESTIGATION IS LODGING AT TERADAYA. HE IS ROMANTICALLY INVOLVED WITH HARU, THE DAUGHTER OF THE MATRON.
"NEAR-SIGHTED AND USES GLASSES.
"POSSIBLE INVOLVEMENT WITH A WOMAN NAMED RYO, ASIDE FROM HARU."
ALL RIGHT!
I'LL EXCHANGE THIS NOTE FOR ORDERS WITH SAITO SENSEI.
I'M NOT GOING TO MISS OUR MEETING THIS TIME!
FOLD
HMM?
WHAT'S THIS RUCKUS?
MRMR MRMR
CROWD CROWD
GOOD MORNING!
THE IMAI BOAT* WILL BE HERE ANY MINUTE NOW, SO CUSTOMERS WITH RESERVED TICKETS, PLEASE FOLLOW ME THIS WAY!

*Name of the first boat.

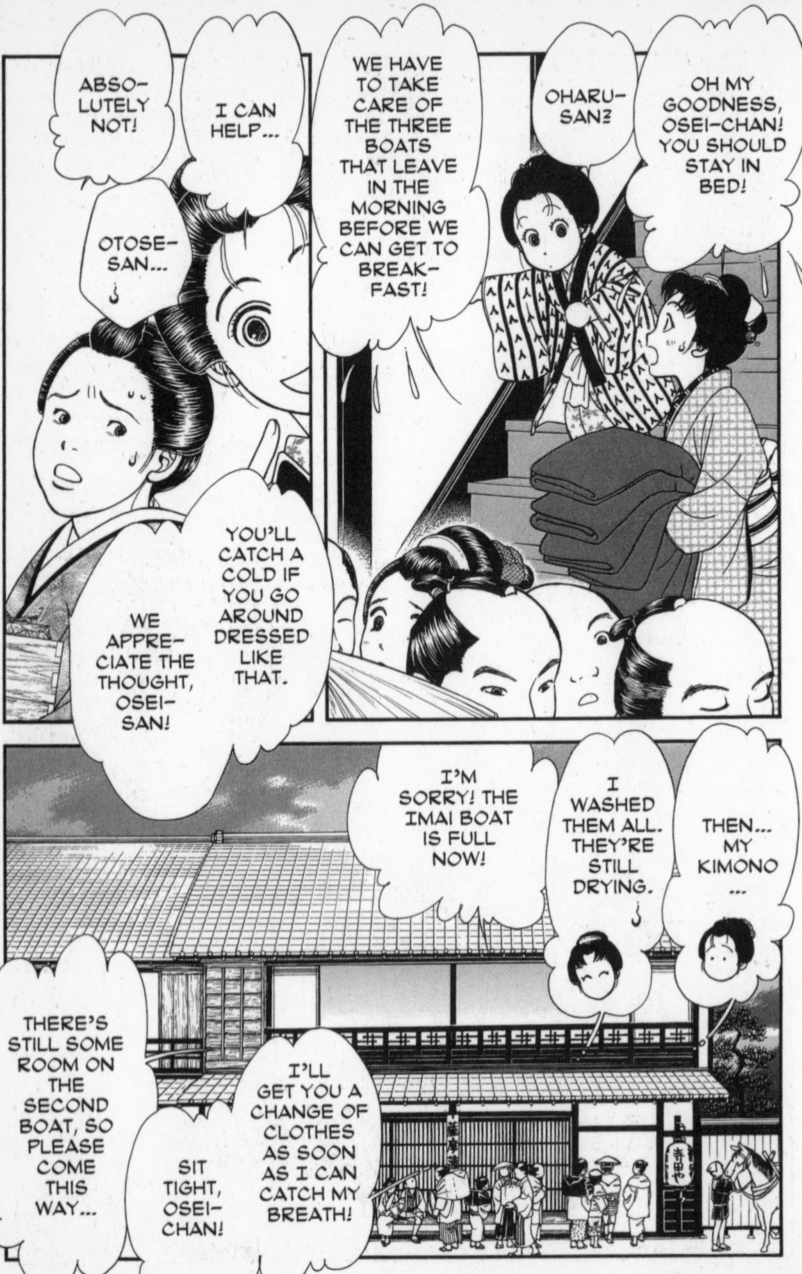
OH MY GOODNESS, OSEI-CHAN! YOU SHOULD STAY IN BED!
OHARU-SAN?
WE HAVE TO TAKE CARE OF THE THREE BOATS THAT LEAVE IN THE MORNING BEFORE WE CAN GET TO BREAKFAST!
YOU'LL CATCH A COLD IF YOU GO AROUND DRESSED LIKE THAT.
WE APPRECIATE THE THOUGHT, OSEI-SAN!
I CAN HELP...
ABSOLUTELY NOT!
OTOSE-SAN...
THEN... MY KIMONO ...
I WASHED THEM ALL. THEY'RE STILL DRYING.
I'M SORRY! THE IMAI BOAT IS FULL NOW!
寺田や
I'LL GET YOU A CHANGE OF CLOTHES AS SOON AS I CAN CATCH MY BREATH!
SIT TIGHT, OSEI-CHAN!
THERE'S STILL SOME ROOM ON THE SECOND BOAT, SO PLEASE COME THIS WAY...

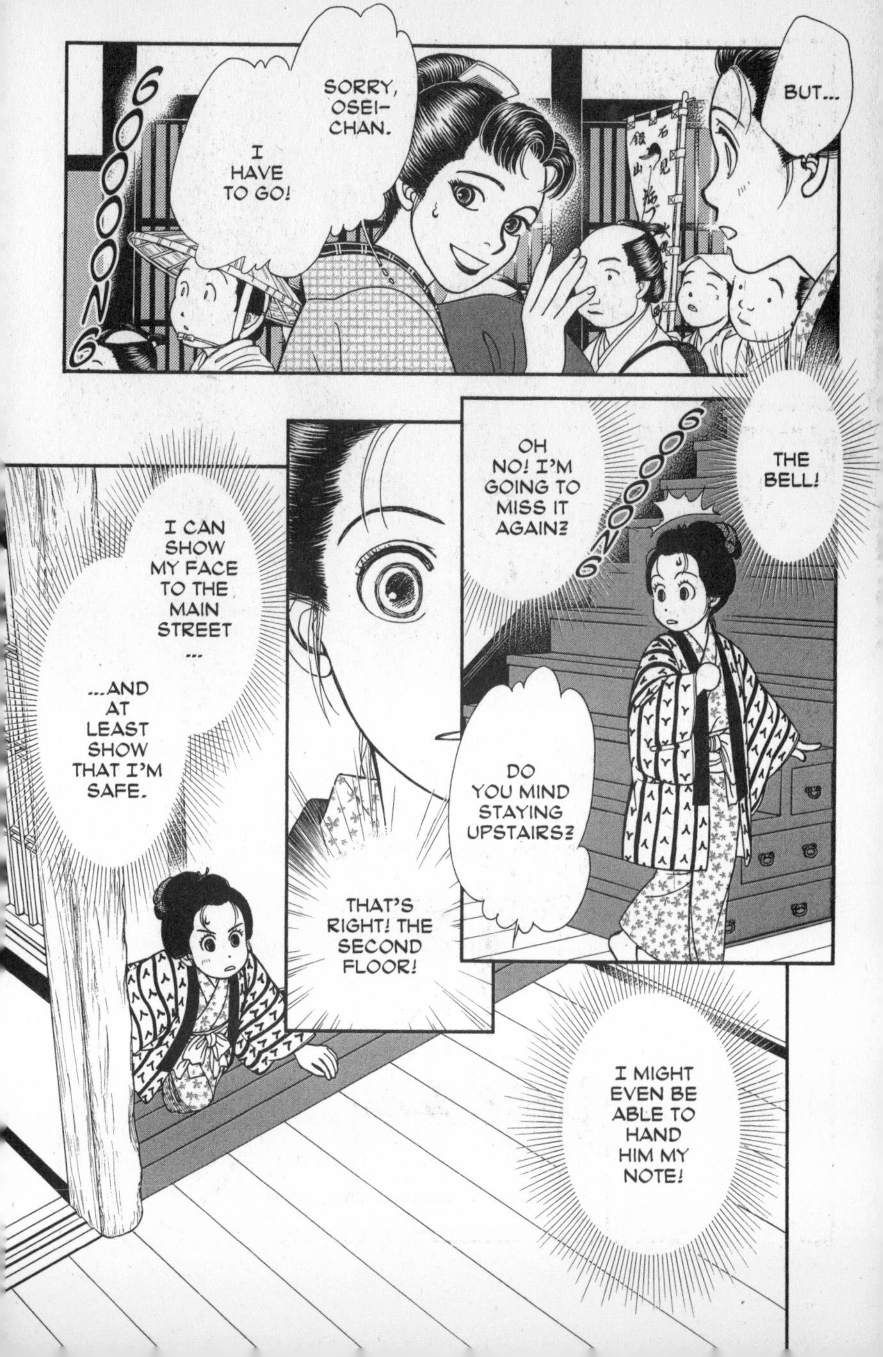
BUT...
SORRY, OSEI-CHAN.
I HAVE TO GO!
GOOOOOONG
THE BELL!
GOOOOOONG
OH NO! I'M GOING TO MISS IT AGAIN?
DO YOU MIND STAYING UPSTAIRS?
THAT'S RIGHT! THE SECOND FLOOR!
I CAN SHOW MY FACE TO THE MAIN STREET...
...AND AT LEAST SHOW THAT I'M SAFE.
I MIGHT EVEN BE ABLE TO HAND HIM MY NOTE!

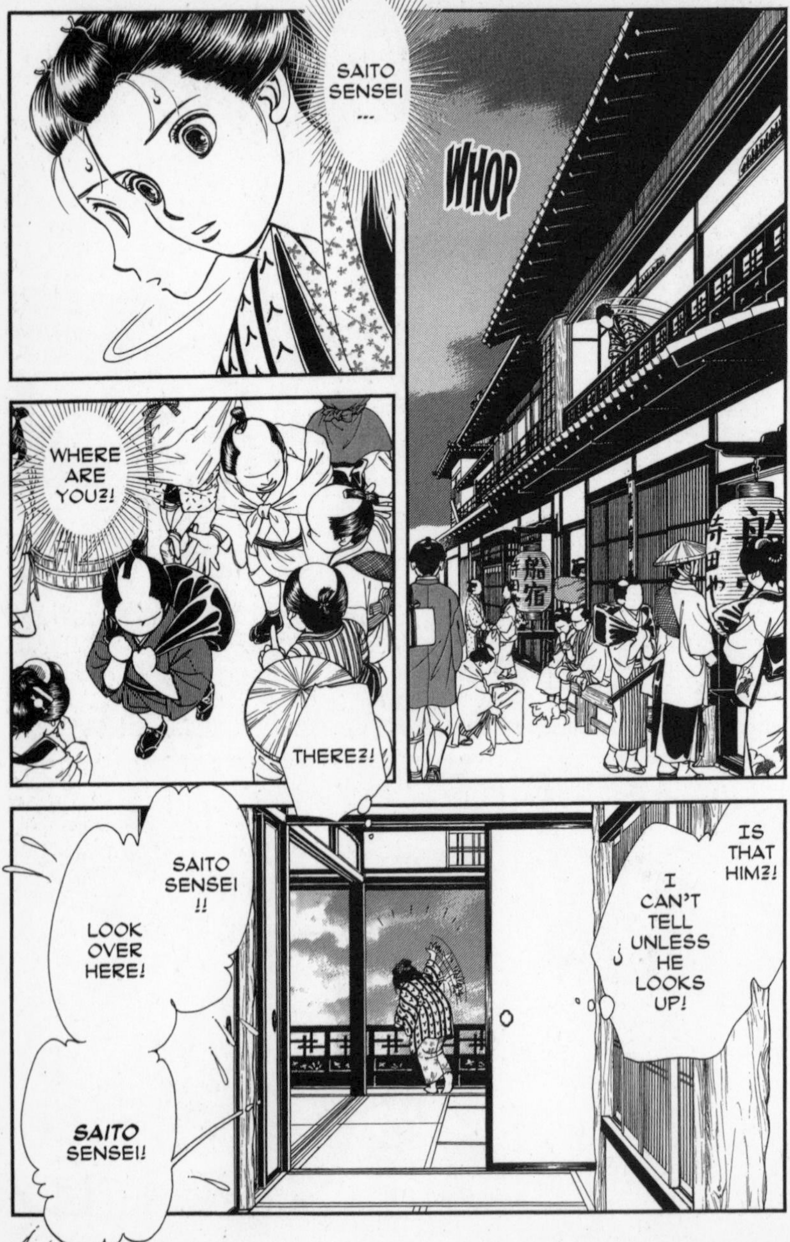
WHOP
船宿
寺田や
SAITO SENSEI ...
WHERE ARE YOU?!
THERE?!
IS THAT HIM?!
I CAN'T TELL UNLESS HE LOOKS UP!
SAITO SENSEI!!
LOOK OVER HERE!
SAITO SENSEI!

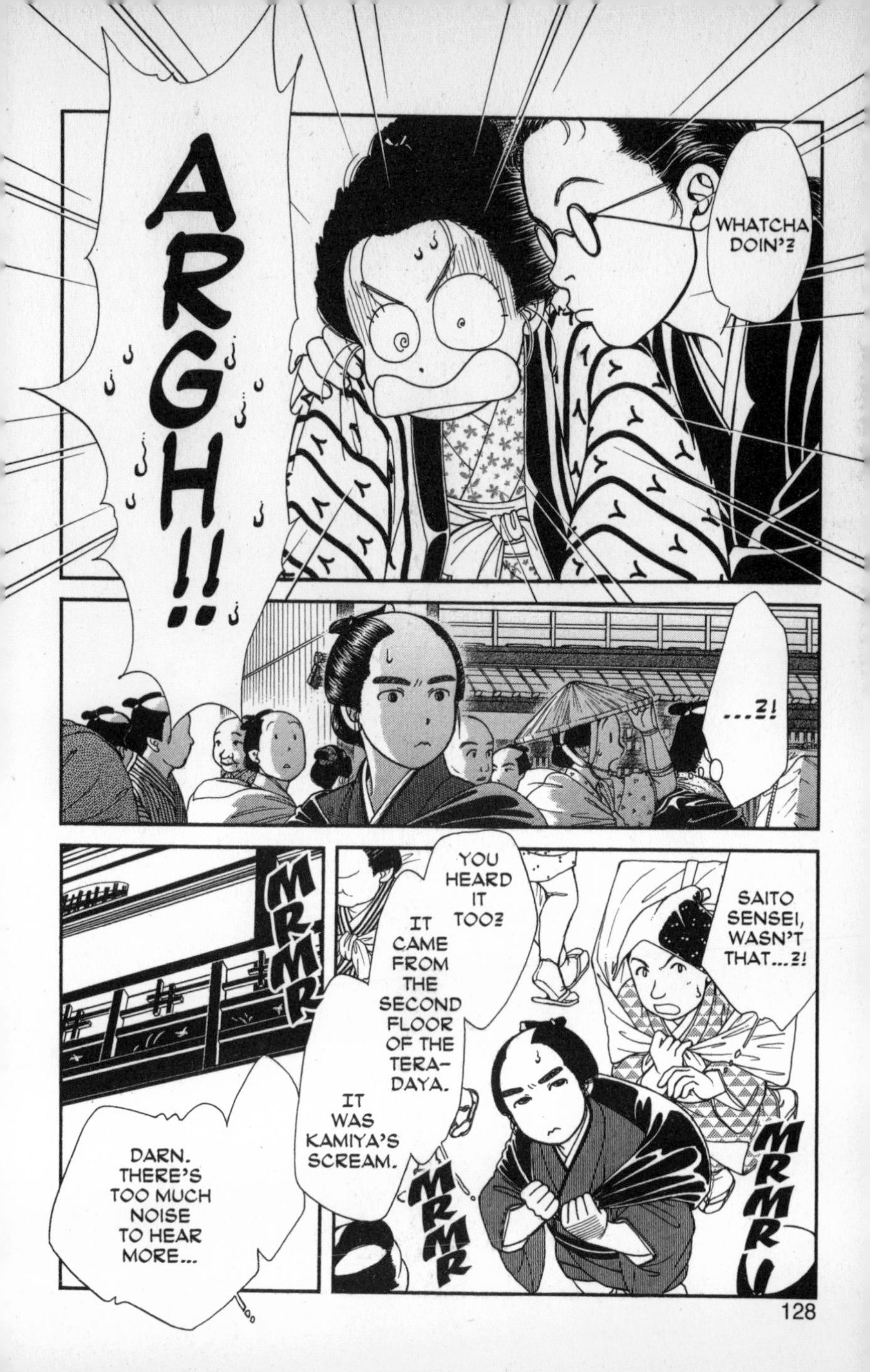
WHATCHA DOIN'?
ARGH!!
...?!
SAITO SENSEI, WASN'T THAT...?!
MRMR
YOU HEARD IT TOO?
IT CAME FROM THE SECOND FLOOR OF THE TERA-DAYA.
IT WAS KAMIYA'S SCREAM.
MRMR
MRMR
DARN. THERE'S TOO MUCH NOISE TO HEAR MORE...

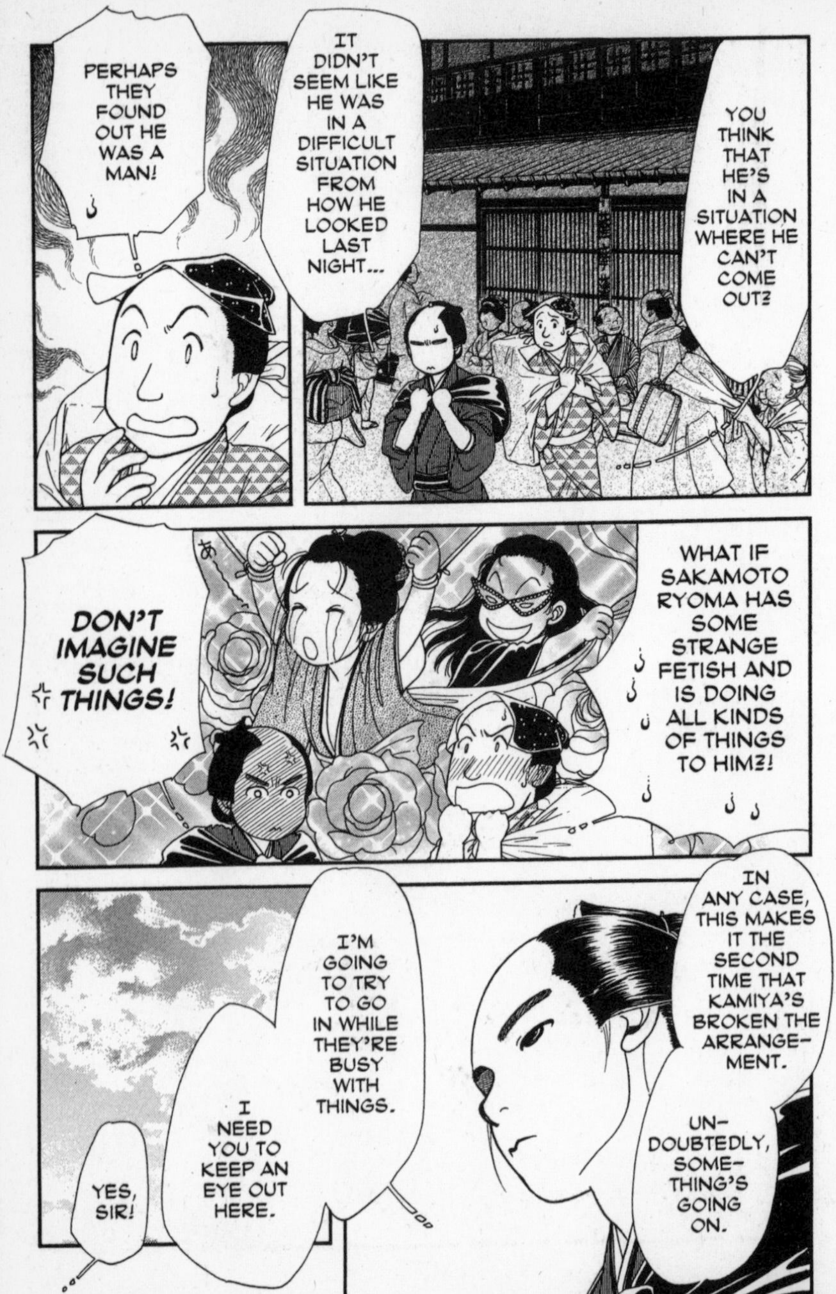
YOU THINK THAT HE'S IN A SITUATION WHERE HE CAN'T COME OUT?
IT DIDN'T SEEM LIKE HE WAS IN A DIFFICULT SITUATION FROM HOW HE LOOKED LAST NIGHT...
PERHAPS THEY FOUND OUT HE WAS A MAN!
WHAT IF SAKAMOTO RYOMA HAS SOME STRANGE FETISH AND IS DOING ALL KINDS OF THINGS TO HIM?!
DON'T IMAGINE SUCH THINGS!
IN ANY CASE, THIS MAKES IT THE SECOND TIME THAT KAMIYA'S BROKEN THE ARRANGEMENT.
UNDOUBTEDLY, SOMETHING'S GOING ON.
I'M GOING TO TRY TO GO IN WHILE THEY'RE BUSY WITH THINGS.
I NEED YOU TO KEEP AN EYE OUT HERE.
YES, SIR!

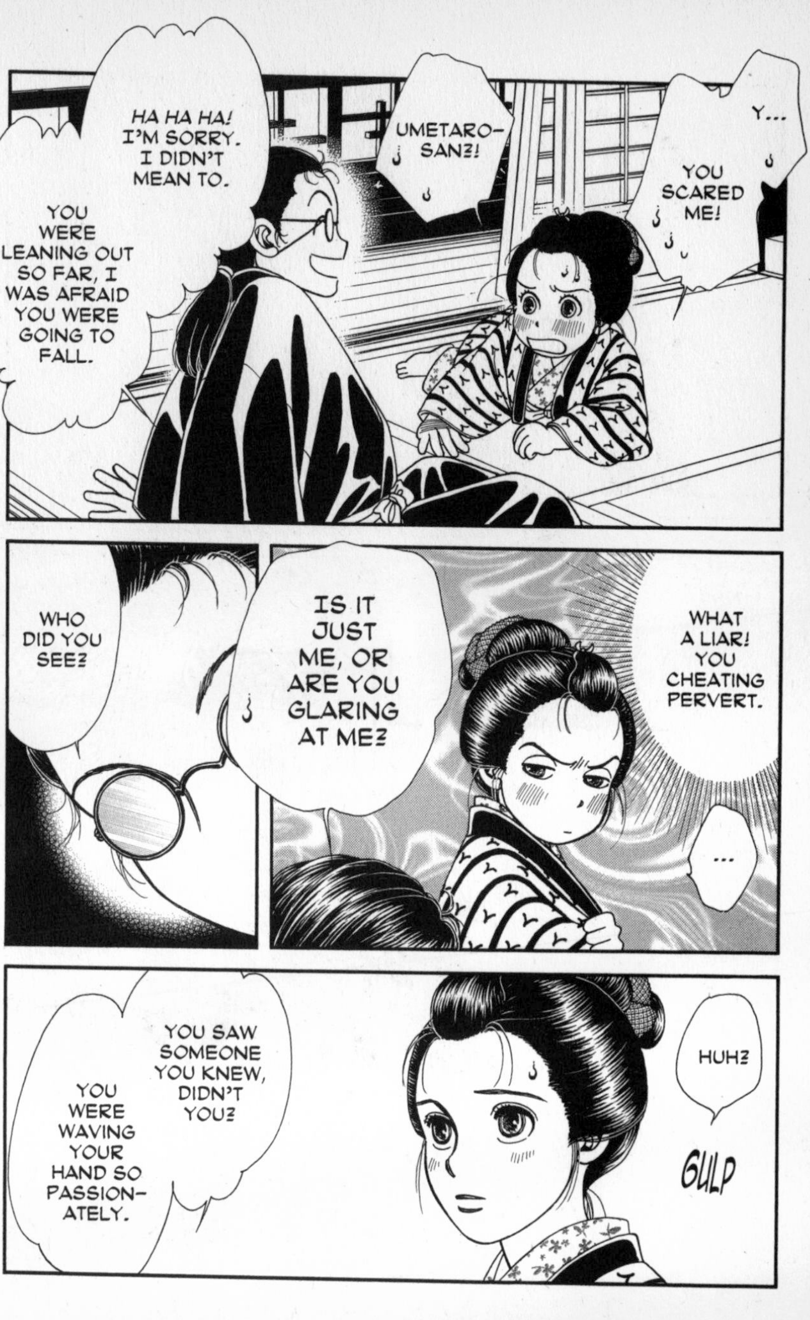
Y...
YOU SCARED ME!
UMETARO-SAN?!
HA HA HA! I'M SORRY. I DIDN'T MEAN TO.
YOU WERE LEANING OUT SO FAR, I WAS AFRAID YOU WERE GOING TO FALL.
WHAT A LIAR! YOU CHEATING PERVERT.
...
IS IT JUST ME, OR ARE YOU GLARING AT ME?
WHO DID YOU SEE?
HUH?
GULP
YOU SAW SOMEONE YOU KNEW, DIDN'T YOU?
YOU WERE WAVING YOUR HAND SO PASSION-ATELY.

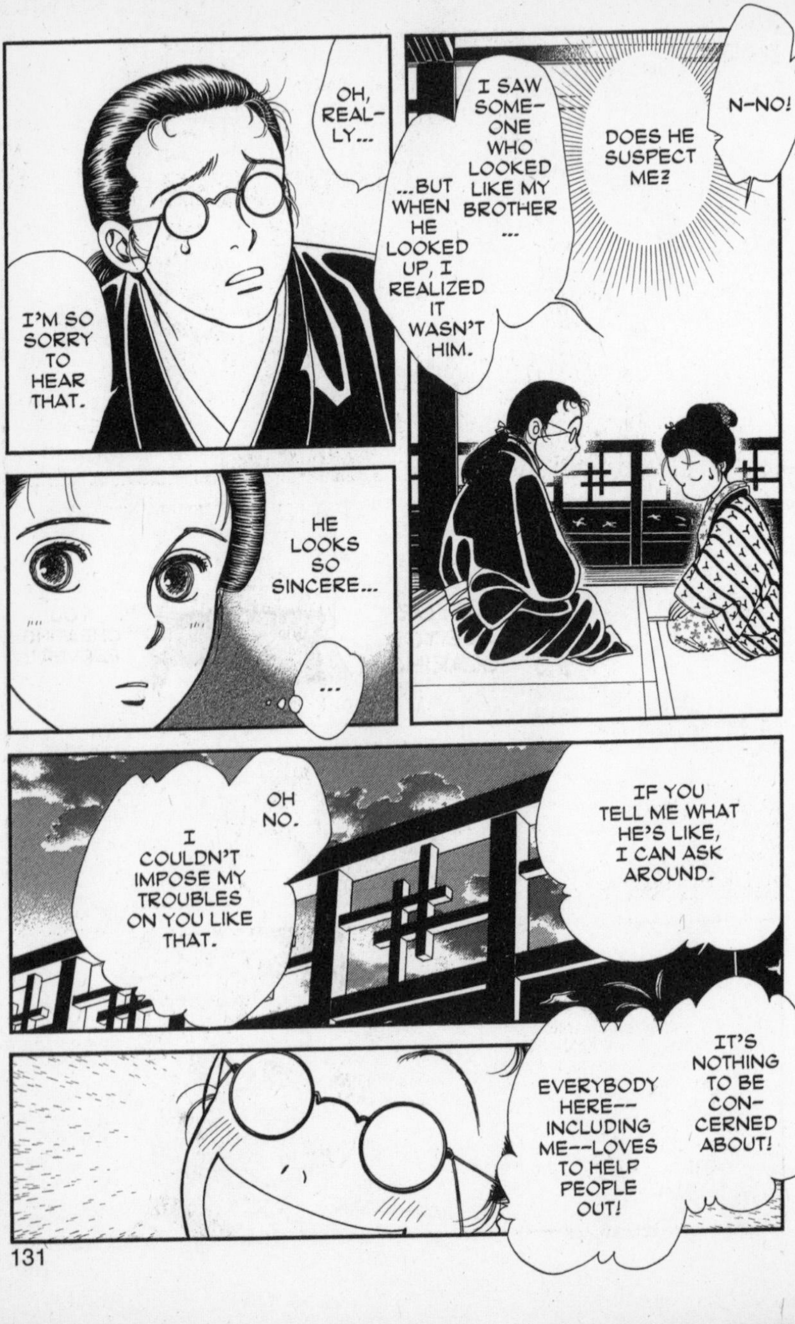
N-NO!
DOES HE SUSPECT ME?
I SAW SOMEONE WHO LOOKED LIKE MY BROTHER...
...BUT WHEN HE LOOKED UP, I REALIZED IT WASN'T HIM.
OH, REALLY...
I'M SO SORRY TO HEAR THAT.
HE LOOKS SO SINCERE...
...
IF YOU TELL ME WHAT HE'S LIKE, I CAN ASK AROUND.
OH NO.
I COULDN'T IMPOSE MY TROUBLES ON YOU LIKE THAT.
IT'S NOTHING TO BE CONCERNED ABOUT!
EVERYBODY HERE--INCLUDING ME--LOVES TO HELP PEOPLE OUT!

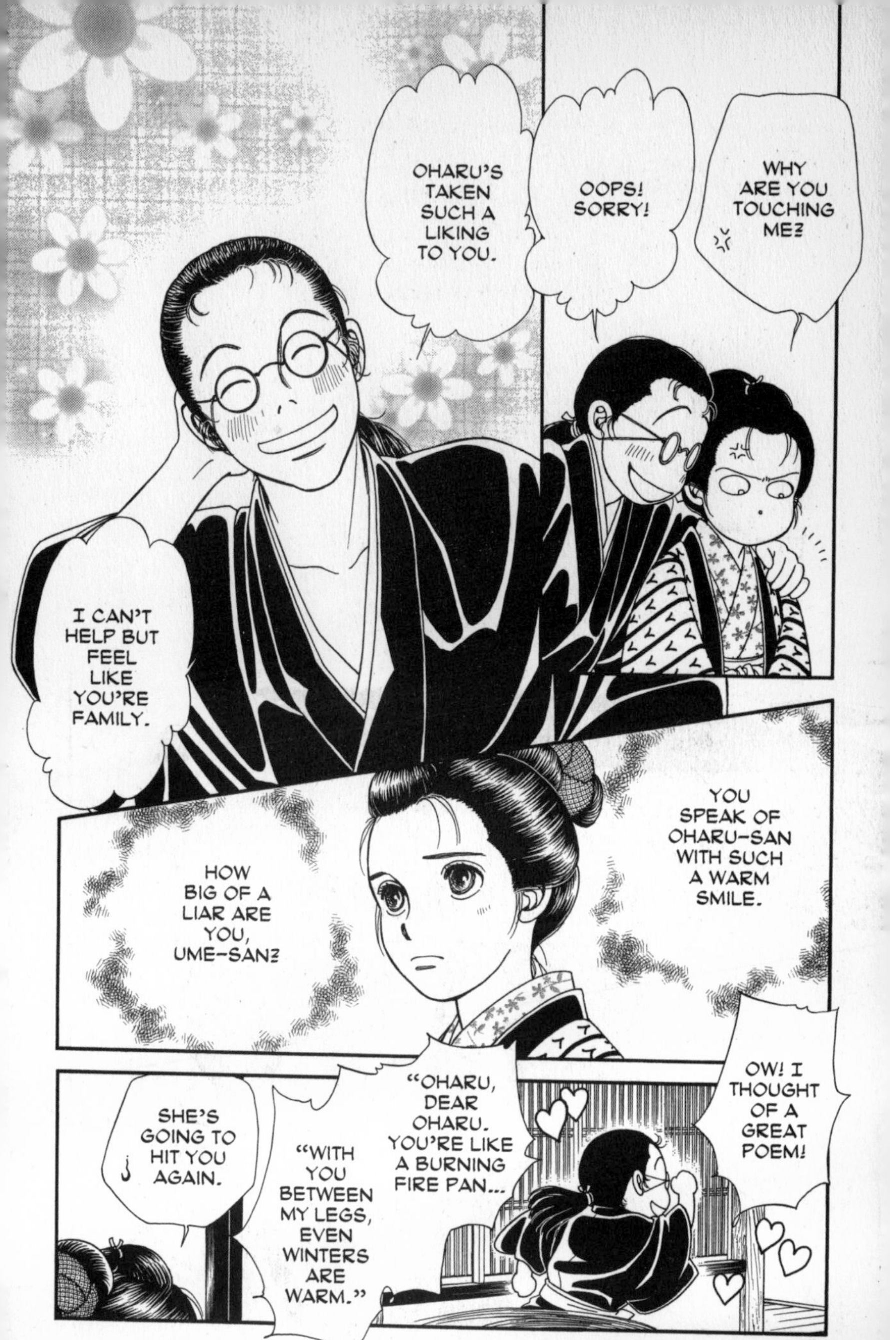
WHY ARE YOU TOUCHING ME?
OOPS! SORRY!
OHARU'S TAKEN SUCH A LIKING TO YOU.
I CAN'T HELP BUT FEEL LIKE YOU'RE FAMILY.
YOU SPEAK OF OHARU-SAN WITH SUCH A WARM SMILE.
HOW BIG OF A LIAR ARE YOU, UME-SAN?
OW! I THOUGHT OF A GREAT POEM!
"OHARU, DEAR OHARU. YOU'RE LIKE A BURNING FIRE PAN...
"WITH YOU BETWEEN MY LEGS, EVEN WINTERS ARE WARM."
SHE'S GOING TO HIT YOU AGAIN.

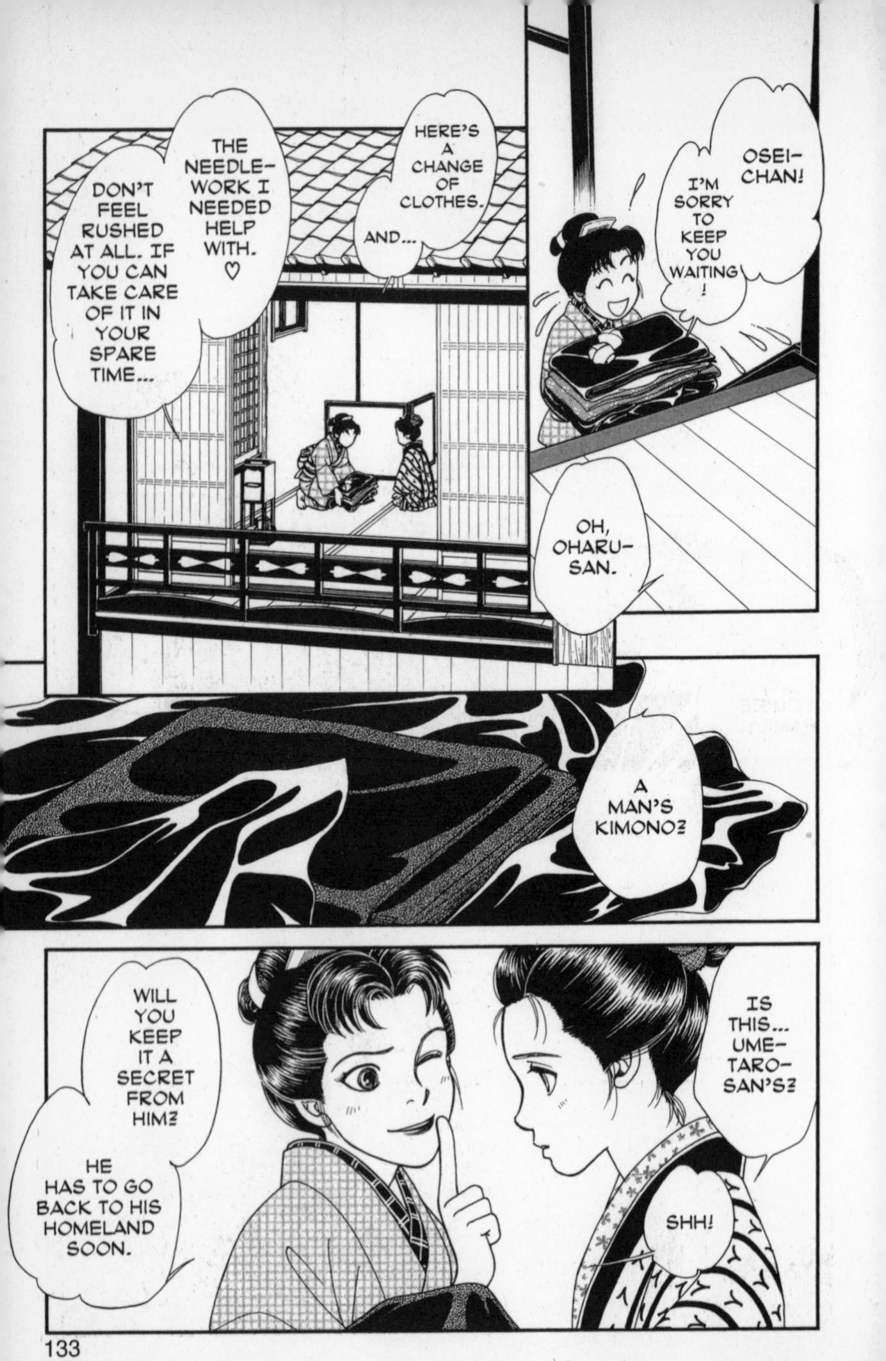
OSEI-CHAN!
I'M SORRY TO KEEP YOU WAITING!
OH, OHARU-SAN.
HERE'S A CHANGE OF CLOTHES.
AND...
THE NEEDLE-WORK I NEEDED HELP WITH. ♡
DON'T FEEL RUSHED AT ALL. IF YOU CAN TAKE CARE OF IT IN YOUR SPARE TIME...
A MAN'S KIMONO?
IS THIS... UME-TARO-SAN'S?
SHH!
WILL YOU KEEP IT A SECRET FROM HIM?
HE HAS TO GO BACK TO HIS HOMELAND SOON.

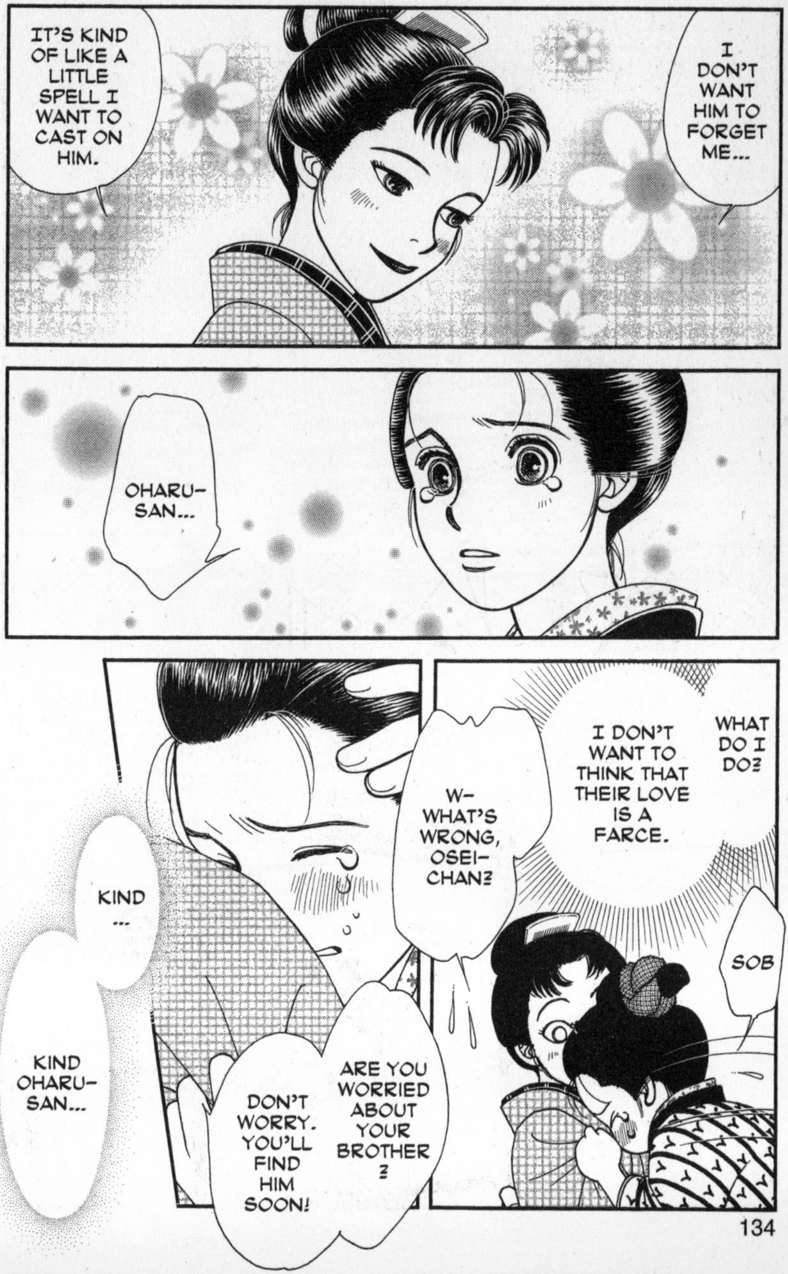
I DON'T WANT HIM TO FORGET ME...
IT'S KIND OF LIKE A LITTLE SPELL I WANT TO CAST ON HIM.
OHARU-SAN...
WHAT DO I DO?
I DON'T WANT TO THINK THAT THEIR LOVE IS A FARCE.
SOB
W-WHAT'S WRONG, OSEI-CHAN?
ARE YOU WORRIED ABOUT YOUR BROTHER?
DON'T WORRY. YOU'LL FIND HIM SOON!
KIND...
KIND OHARU-SAN...

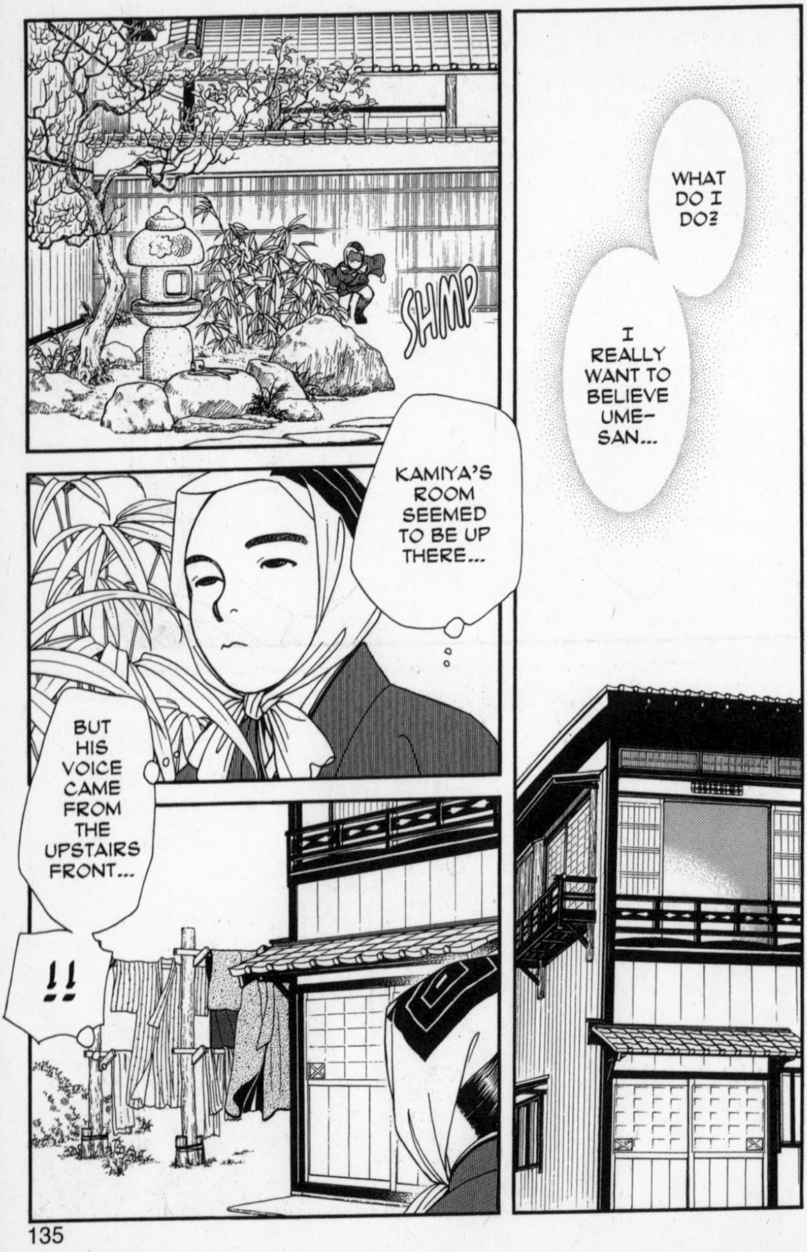
WHAT DO I DO?
I REALLY WANT TO BELIEVE UME-SAN...
SHMP
KAMIYA'S ROOM SEEMED TO BE UP THERE...
BUT HIS VOICE CAME FROM THE UPSTAIRS FRONT...
!!

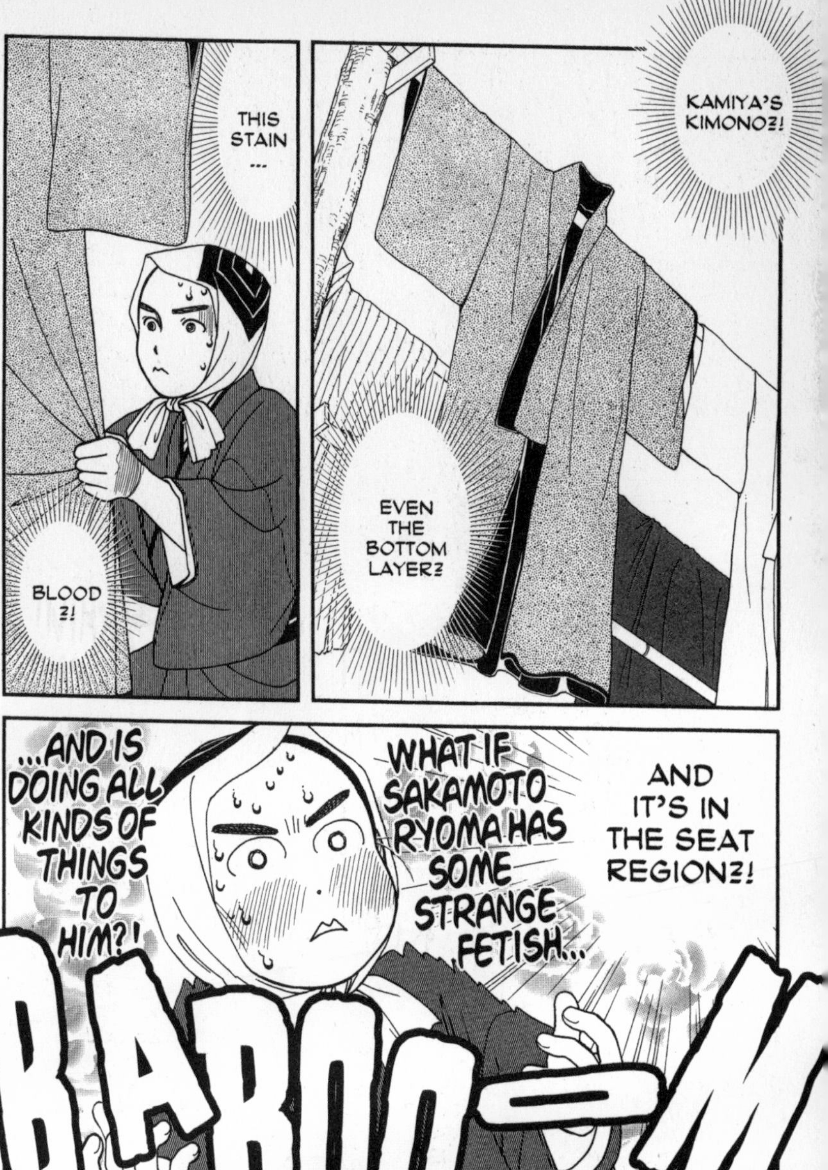
KAMIYA'S KIMONO?!
EVEN THE BOTTOM LAYER?
THIS STAIN ...
BLOOD ?!
AND IT'S IN THE SEAT REGION?!
WHAT IF SAKAMOTO RYOMA HAS SOME STRANGE FETISH...
...AND IS DOING ALL KINDS OF THINGS TO HIM?!
BABOO-M

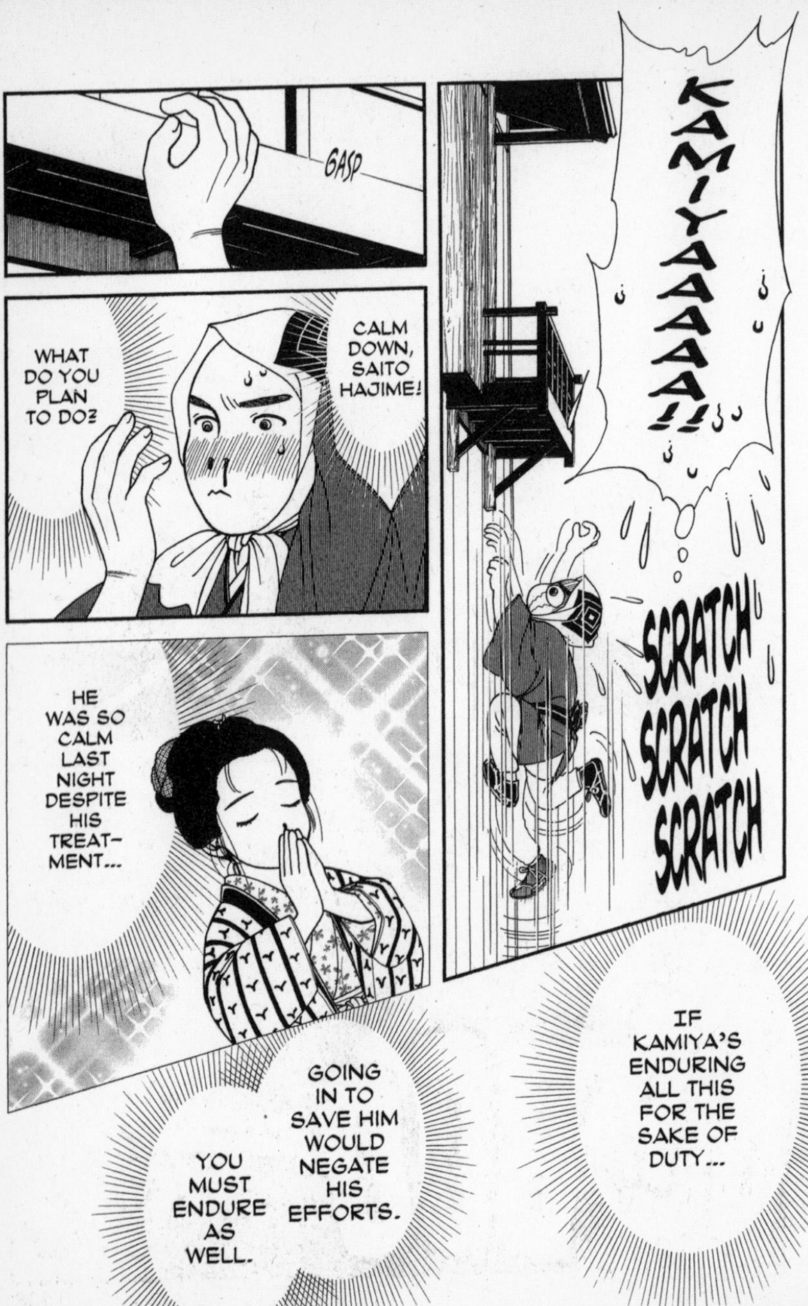
KAMIYAAAAAA!!
SCRATCH SCRATCH SCRATCH
GASP
CALM DOWN, SAITO HAJIME!
WHAT DO YOU PLAN TO DO?
HE WAS SO CALM LAST NIGHT DESPITE HIS TREATMENT...
IF KAMIYA'S ENDURING ALL THIS FOR THE SAKE OF DUTY...
GOING IN TO SAVE HIM WOULD NEGATE HIS EFFORTS.
YOU MUST ENDURE AS WELL.

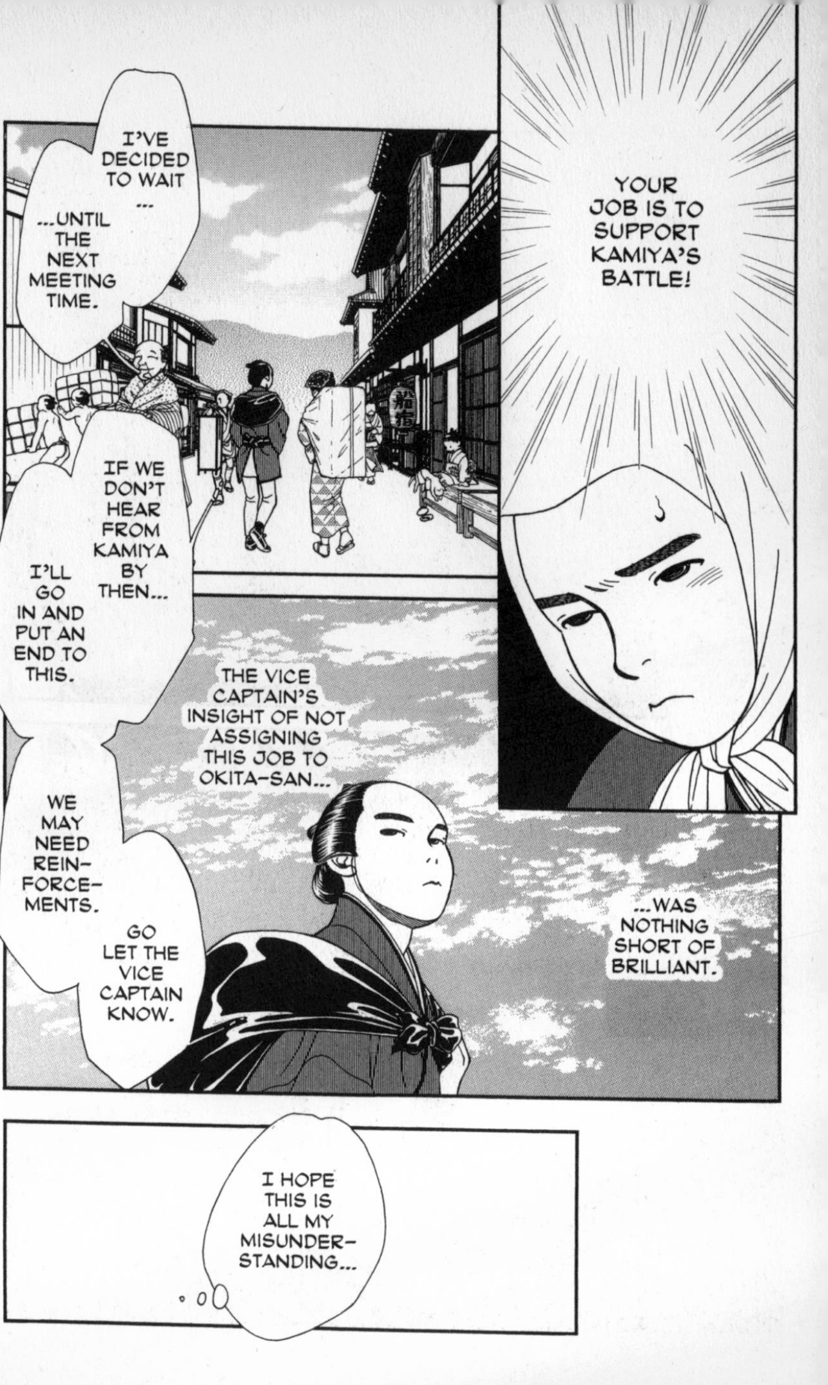
YOUR JOB IS TO SUPPORT KAMIYA'S BATTLE!
I'VE DECIDED TO WAIT ...
...UNTIL THE NEXT MEETING TIME.
IF WE DON'T HEAR FROM KAMIYA BY THEN...
I'LL GO IN AND PUT AN END TO THIS.
WE MAY NEED REIN-FORCE-MENTS.
GO LET THE VICE CAPTAIN KNOW.
THE VICE CAPTAIN'S INSIGHT OF NOT ASSIGNING THIS JOB TO OKITA-SAN...
...WAS NOTHING SHORT OF BRILLIANT.
I HOPE THIS IS ALL MY MISUNDER-STANDING...

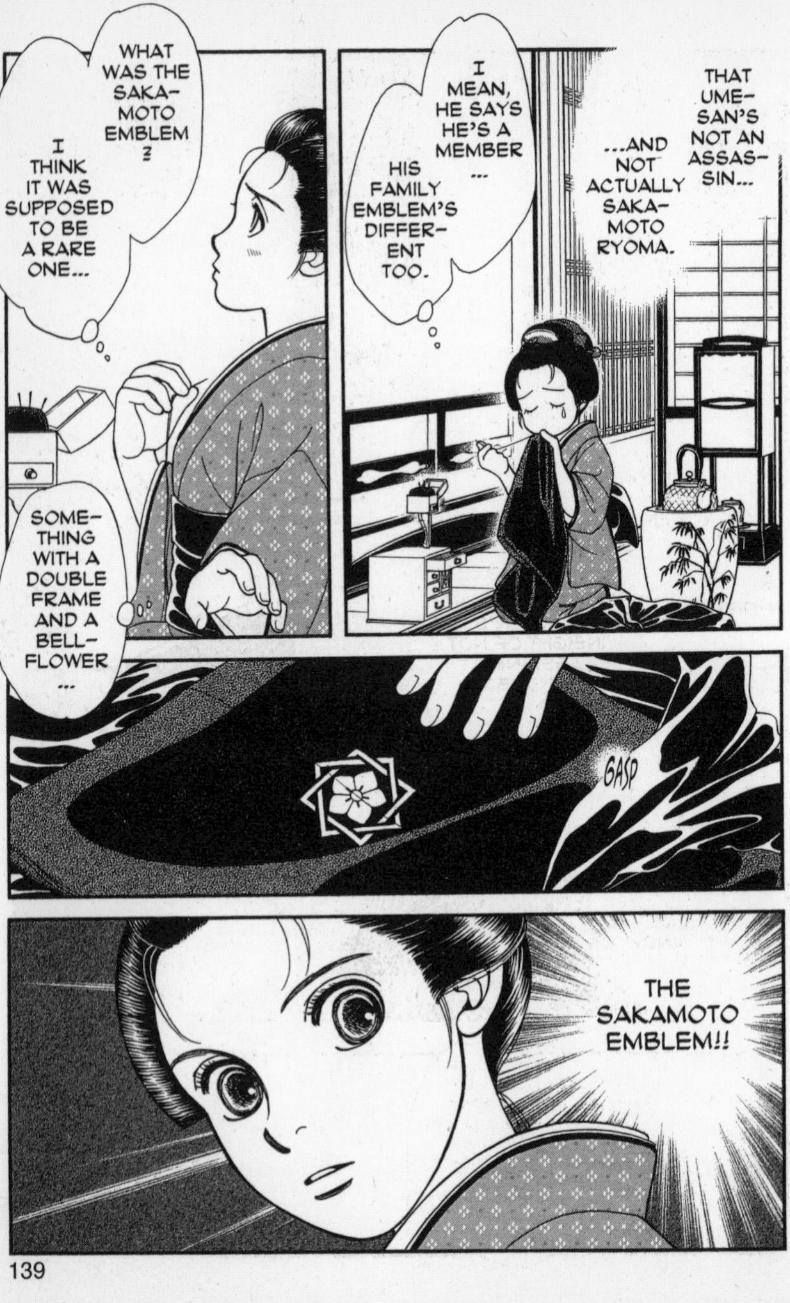
THAT UME-SAN'S NOT AN ASSASSIN...
...AND NOT ACTUALLY SAKAMOTO RYOMA.
I MEAN, HE SAYS HE'S A MEMBER...
HIS FAMILY EMBLEM'S DIFFERENT TOO.
WHAT WAS THE SAKAMOTO EMBLEM?
I THINK IT WAS SUPPOSED TO BE A RARE ONE...
SOMETHING WITH A DOUBLE FRAME AND A BELLFLOWER...
GASP
THE SAKAMOTO EMBLEM!!

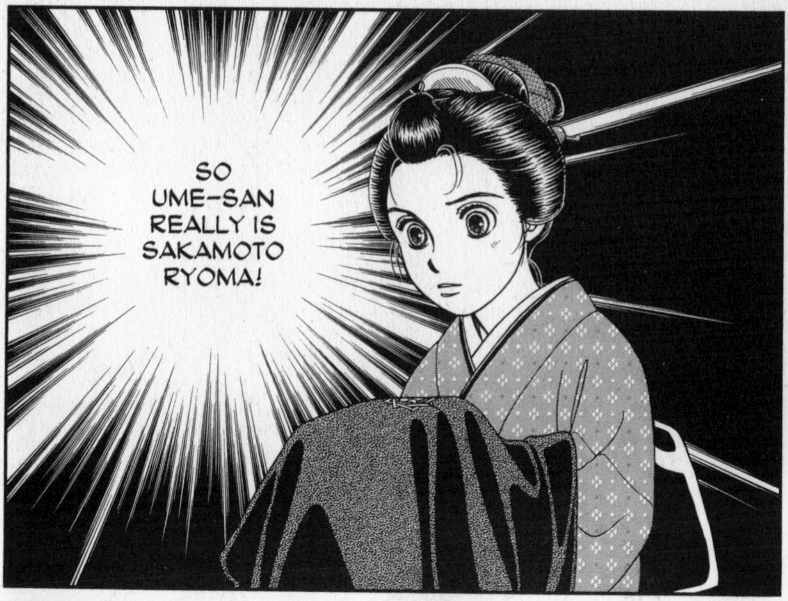
SO UME-SAN REALLY IS SAKAMOTO RYOMA!

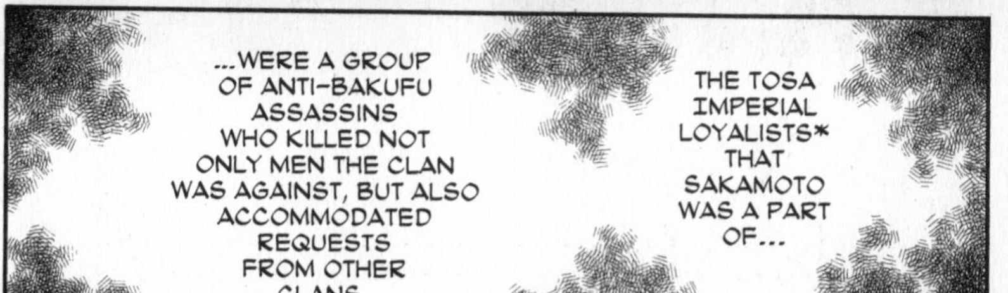
THE TOSA IMPERIAL LOYALISTS* THAT SAKAMOTO WAS A PART OF...
...WERE A GROUP OF ANTI-BAKUFU ASSASSINS WHO KILLED NOT ONLY MEN THE CLAN WAS AGAINST, BUT ALSO ACCOMMODATED REQUESTS FROM OTHER CLANS.

*At this point, they were already dismantled. The head, Takechi Suizan, was imprisoned in the third year of Bunkyu (1863) and ordered to commit seppuku two years later.

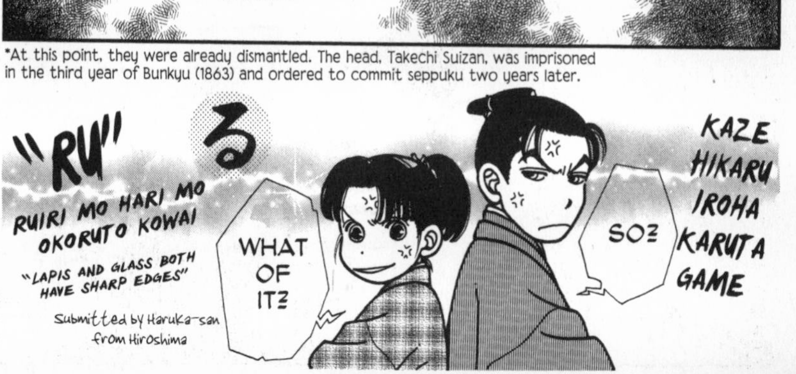
KAZE HIKARU IROHA KARUTA GAME
SO?
WHAT OF IT?
"RU" る
RUIRI MO HARI MO OKORUTO KOWAI
"LAPIS AND GLASS BOTH HAVE SHARP EDGES"
Submitted by Haruka-san from Hiroshima

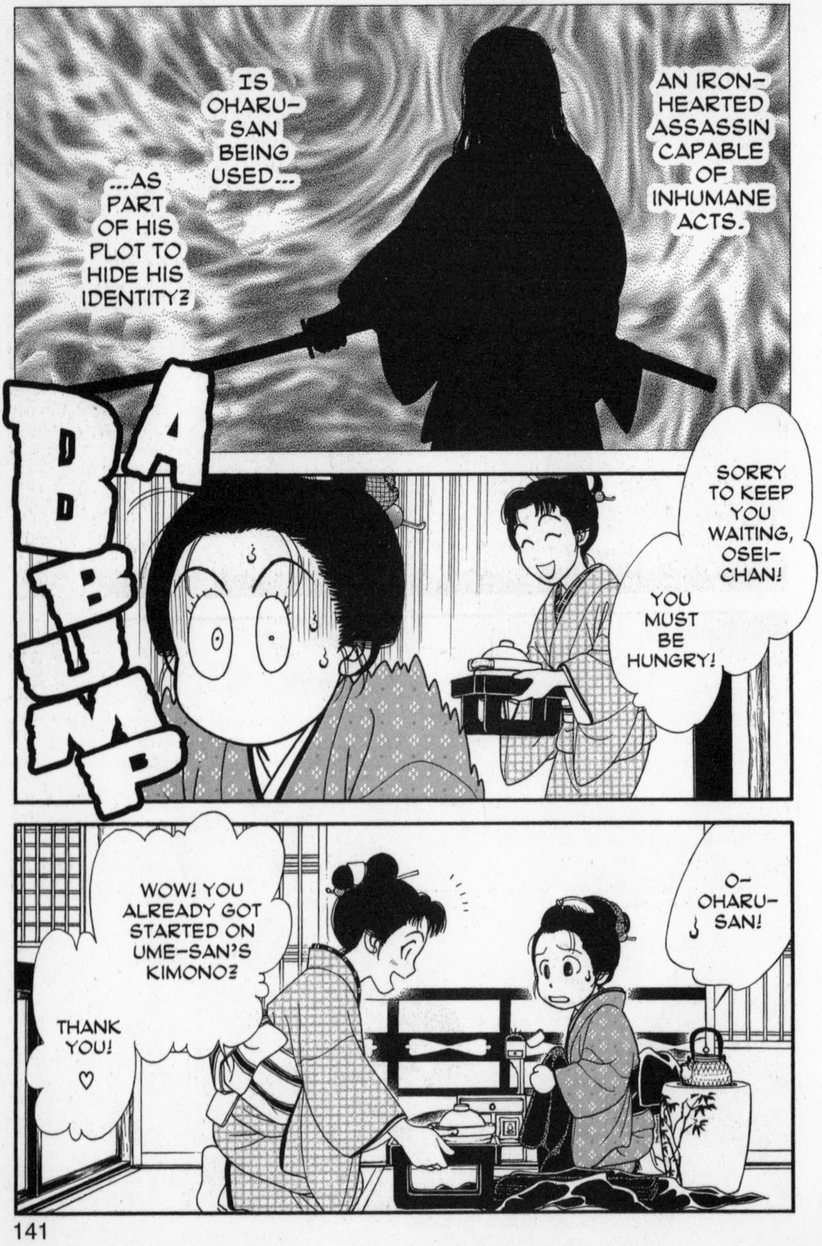
AN IRON-HEARTED ASSASSIN CAPABLE OF INHUMANE ACTS.
IS OHARU-SAN BEING USED...
...AS PART OF HIS PLOT TO HIDE HIS IDENTITY!?
SORRY TO KEEP YOU WAITING, OSEI-CHAN!
YOU MUST BE HUNGRY!
DA BUMP
O-OHARU-SAN!
WOW! YOU ALREADY GOT STARTED ON UME-SAN'S KIMONO!?
THANK YOU! ♡

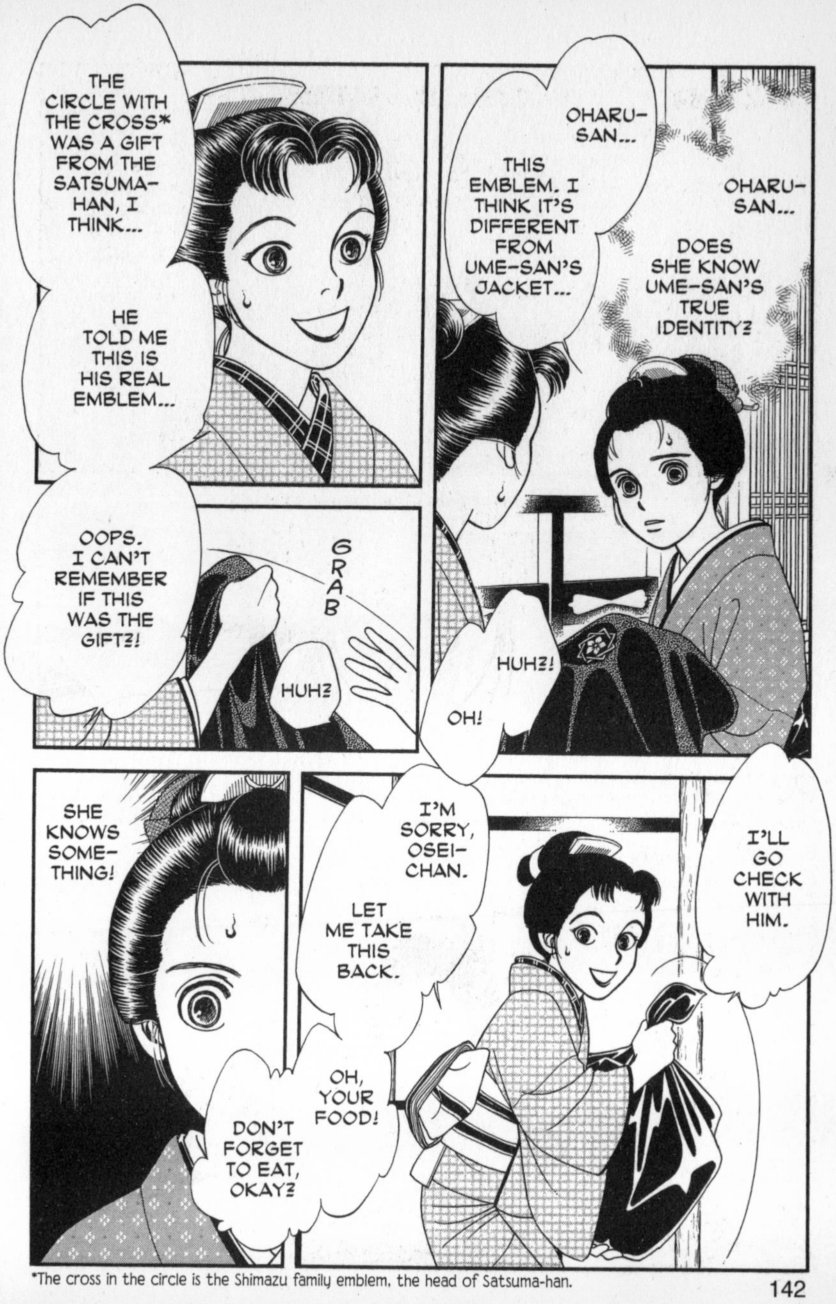

OHARU-SAN...
THIS EMBLEM. I THINK IT'S DIFFERENT FROM UME-SAN'S JACKET...
OHARU-SAN...
DOES SHE KNOW UME-SAN'S TRUE IDENTITY?
THE CIRCLE WITH THE CROSS* WAS A GIFT FROM THE SATSUMA-HAN, I THINK...
HE TOLD ME THIS IS HIS REAL EMBLEM...
OOPS. I CAN'T REMEMBER IF THIS WAS THE GIFT?!
GRAB
HUH?
HUH?!
OH!
I'LL GO CHECK WITH HIM.
I'M SORRY, OSEI-CHAN.
LET ME TAKE THIS BACK.
OH, YOUR FOOD!
DON'T FORGET TO EAT, OKAY?
SHE KNOWS SOMETHING!

*The cross in the circle is the Shimazu family emblem, the head of Satsuma-han.

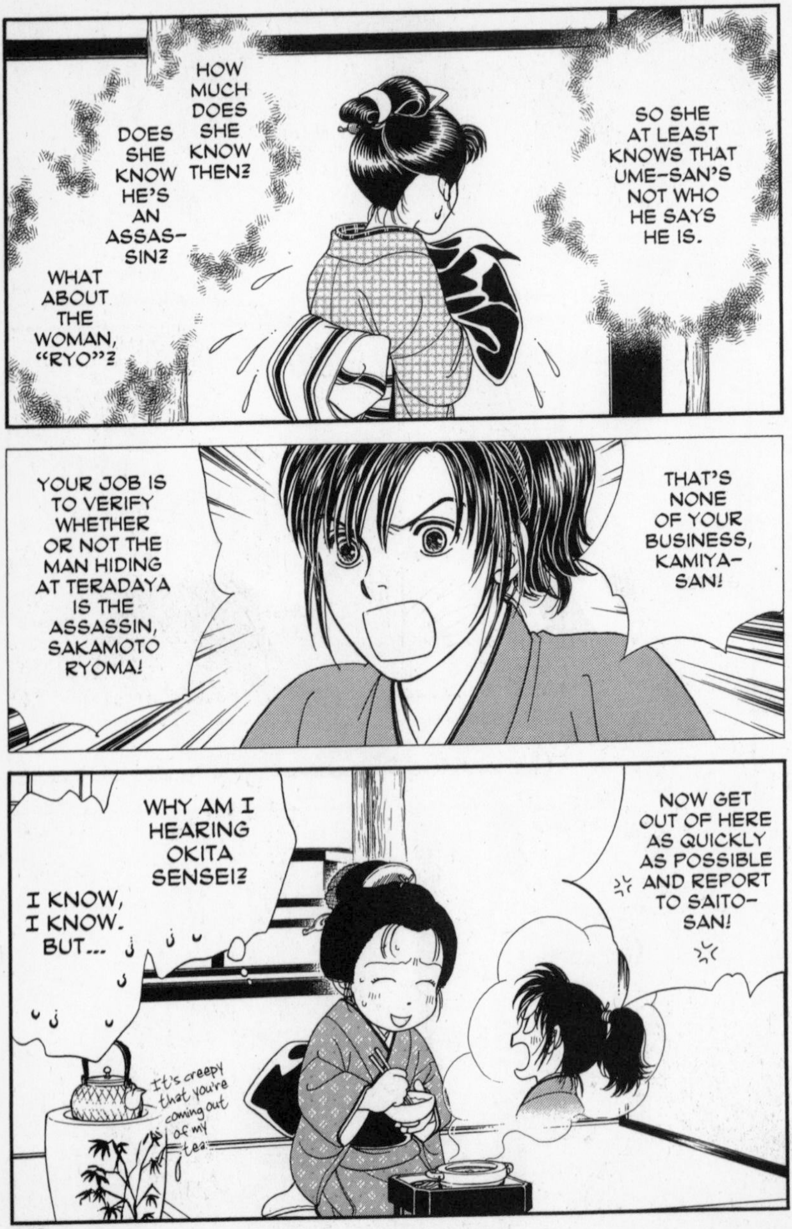
SO SHE AT LEAST KNOWS THAT UME-SAN'S NOT WHO HE SAYS HE IS.
HOW MUCH DOES SHE KNOW THEN?
DOES SHE KNOW HE'S AN ASSAS-SIN?
WHAT ABOUT THE WOMAN, "RYO"?
THAT'S NONE OF YOUR BUSINESS, KAMIYA-SAN!
YOUR JOB IS TO VERIFY WHETHER OR NOT THE MAN HIDING AT TERADAYA IS THE ASSASSIN, SAKAMOTO RYOMA!
NOW GET OUT OF HERE AS QUICKLY AS POSSIBLE AND REPORT TO SAITO-SAN!
WHY AM I HEARING OKITA SENSEI?
I KNOW, I KNOW. BUT...
It's creepy that you're coming out of my tea.

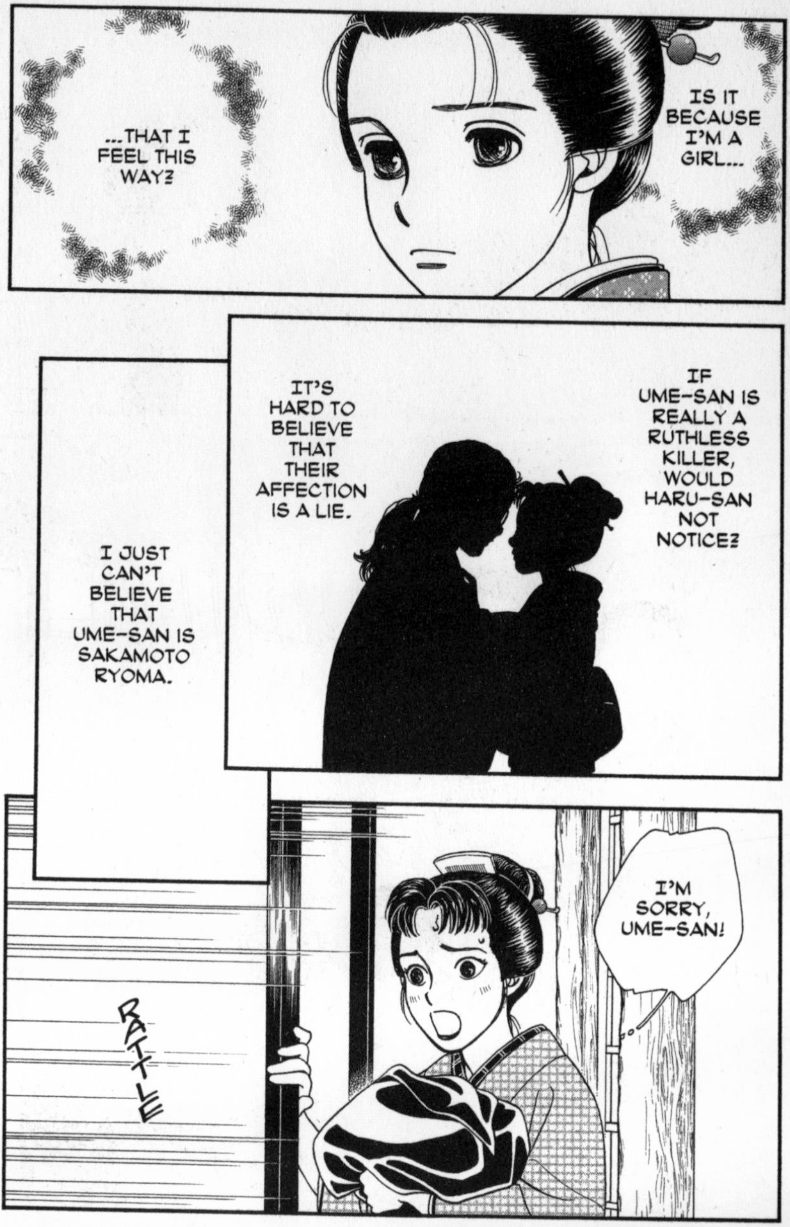

IS IT BECAUSE I'M A GIRL...
...THAT I FEEL THIS WAY?
IF UME-SAN IS REALLY A RUTHLESS KILLER, WOULD HARU-SAN NOT NOTICE?
IT'S HARD TO BELIEVE THAT THEIR AFFECTION IS A LIE.
I JUST CAN'T BELIEVE THAT UME-SAN IS SAKAMOTO RYOMA.
I'M SORRY, UME-SAN!
RATTLE

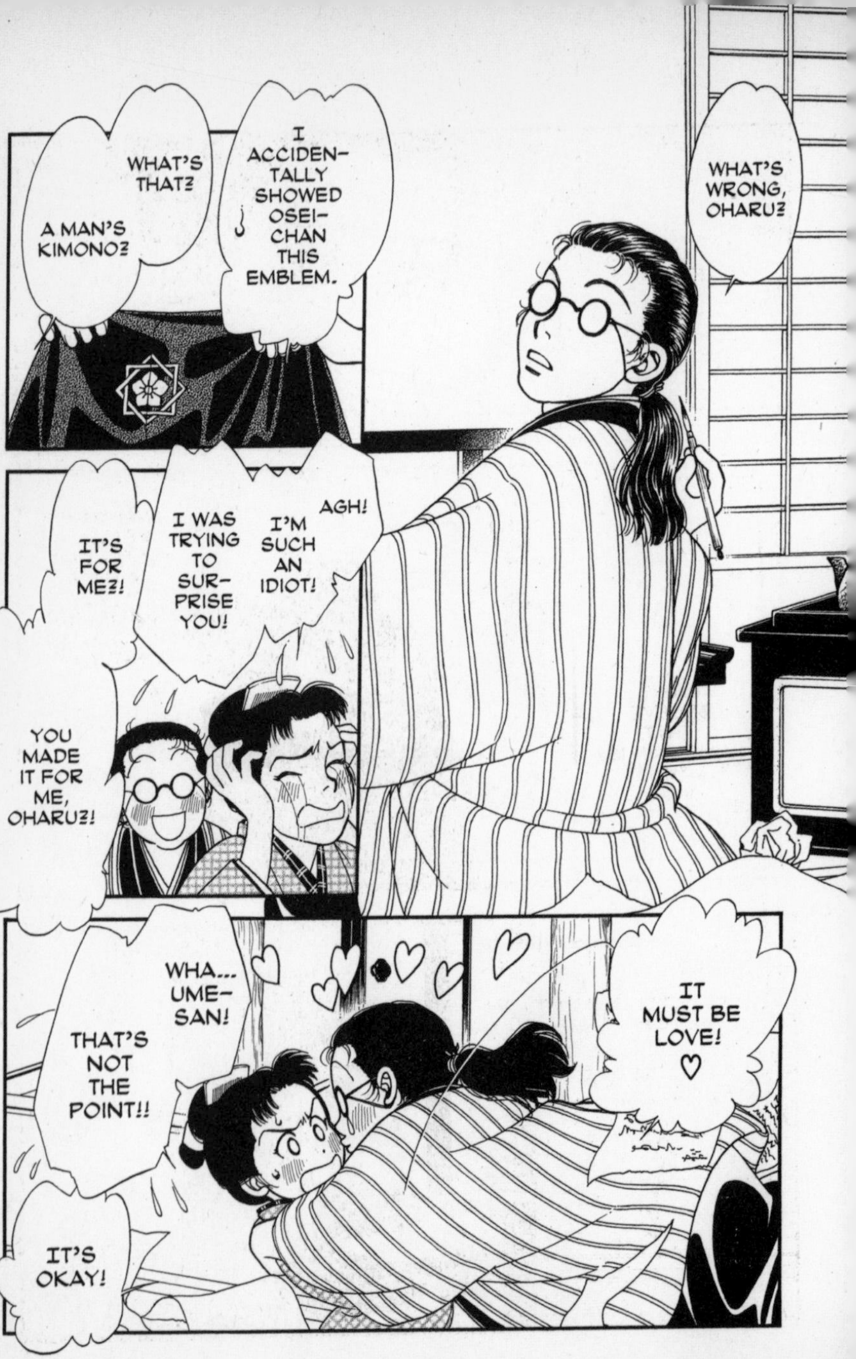
WHAT'S WRONG, OHARU?
I ACCIDENTALLY SHOWED OSEI-CHAN THIS EMBLEM.
WHAT'S THAT?
A MAN'S KIMONO?
AGH!
I'M SUCH AN IDIOT!
I WAS TRYING TO SURPRISE YOU!
IT'S FOR ME?!
YOU MADE IT FOR ME, OHARU?!
IT MUST BE LOVE! ♡
WHA... UME-SAN!
THAT'S NOT THE POINT!!
IT'S OKAY!

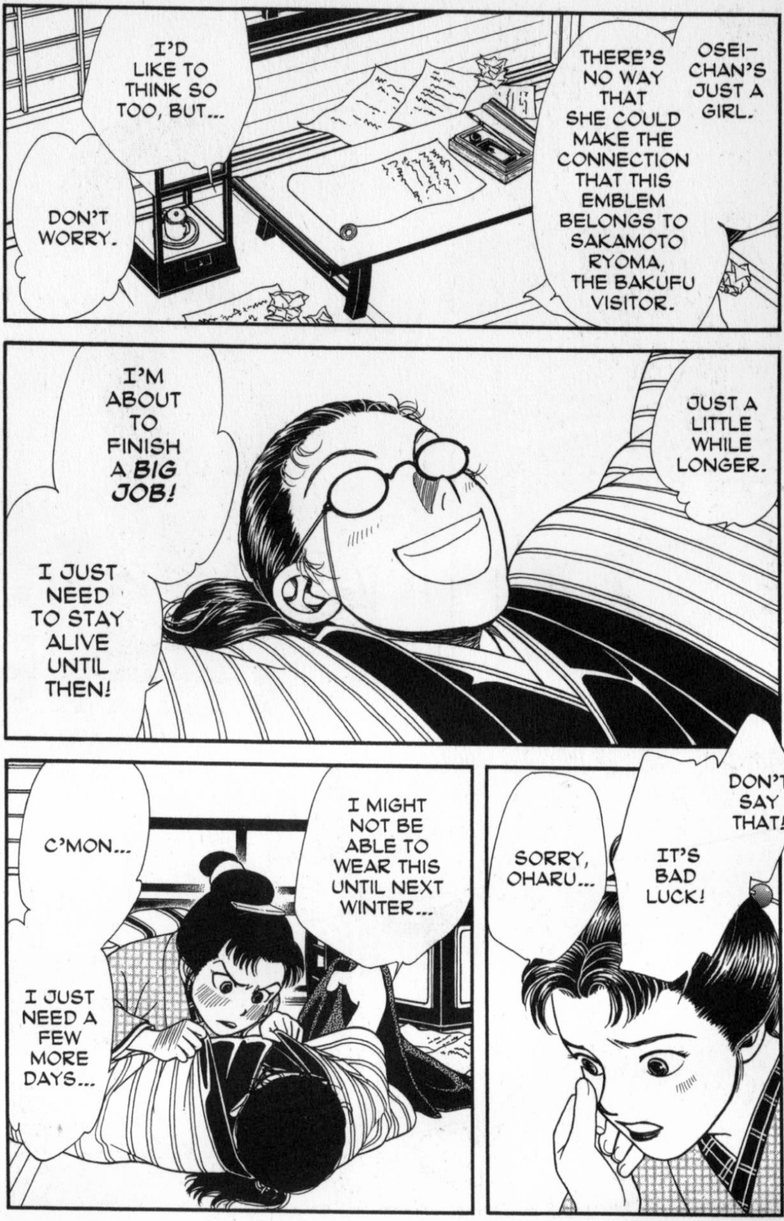
OSEI-CHAN'S JUST A GIRL.
THERE'S NO WAY THAT SHE COULD MAKE THE CONNECTION THAT THIS EMBLEM BELONGS TO SAKAMOTO RYOMA, THE BAKUFU VISITOR.
I'D LIKE TO THINK SO TOO, BUT...
DON'T WORRY.
JUST A LITTLE WHILE LONGER.
I'M ABOUT TO FINISH A ***BIG JOB!***
I JUST NEED TO STAY ALIVE UNTIL THEN!
DON'T SAY THAT!
IT'S BAD LUCK!
SORRY, OHARU...
I MIGHT NOT BE ABLE TO WEAR THIS UNTIL NEXT WINTER...
C'MON...
I JUST NEED A FEW MORE DAYS...

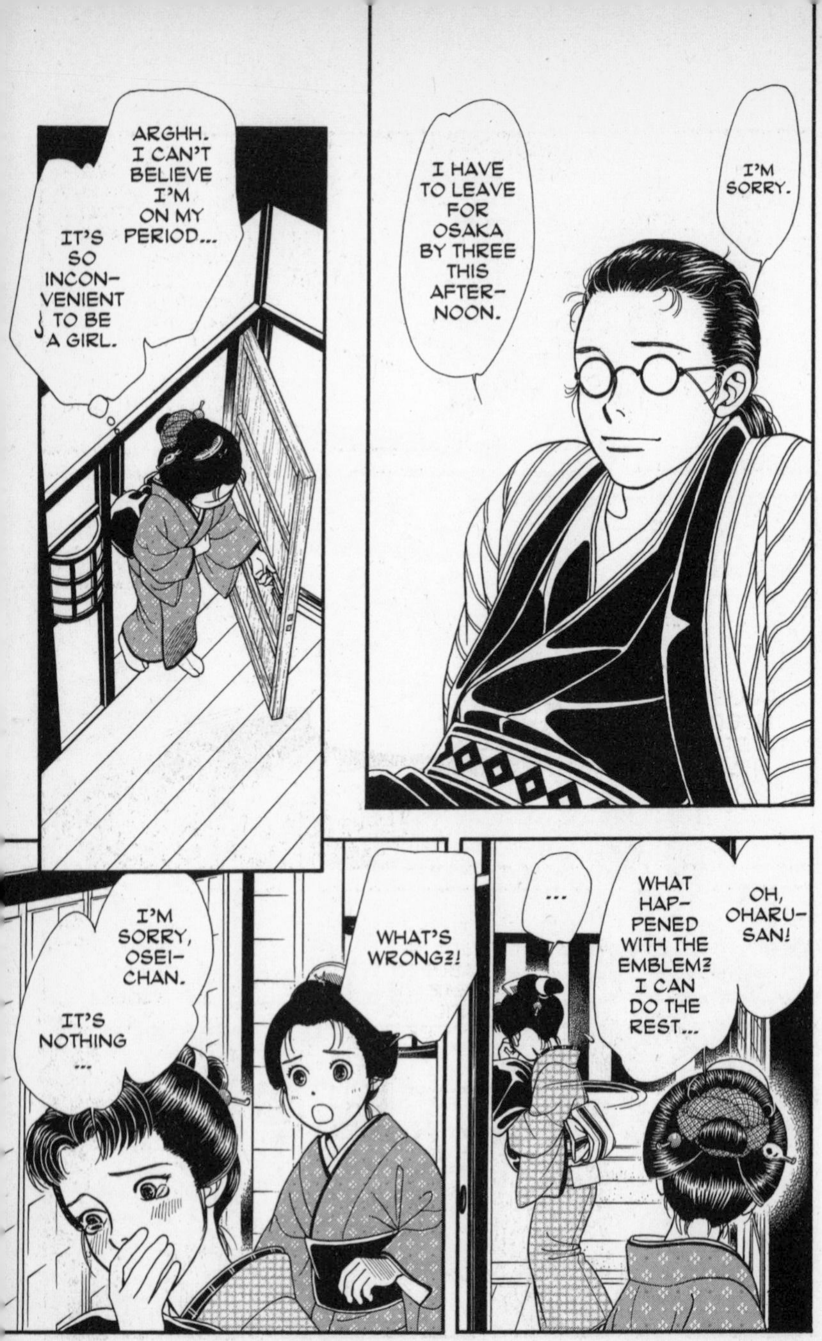
I'M SORRY.
I HAVE TO LEAVE FOR OSAKA BY THREE THIS AFTERNOON.
ARGHH. I CAN'T BELIEVE I'M ON MY PERIOD...
IT'S SO INCONVENIENT TO BE A GIRL.
OH, OHARU-SAN!
WHAT HAPPENED WITH THE EMBLEM? I CAN DO THE REST...
...
WHAT'S WRONG?!
I'M SORRY, OSEI-CHAN.
IT'S NOTHING...

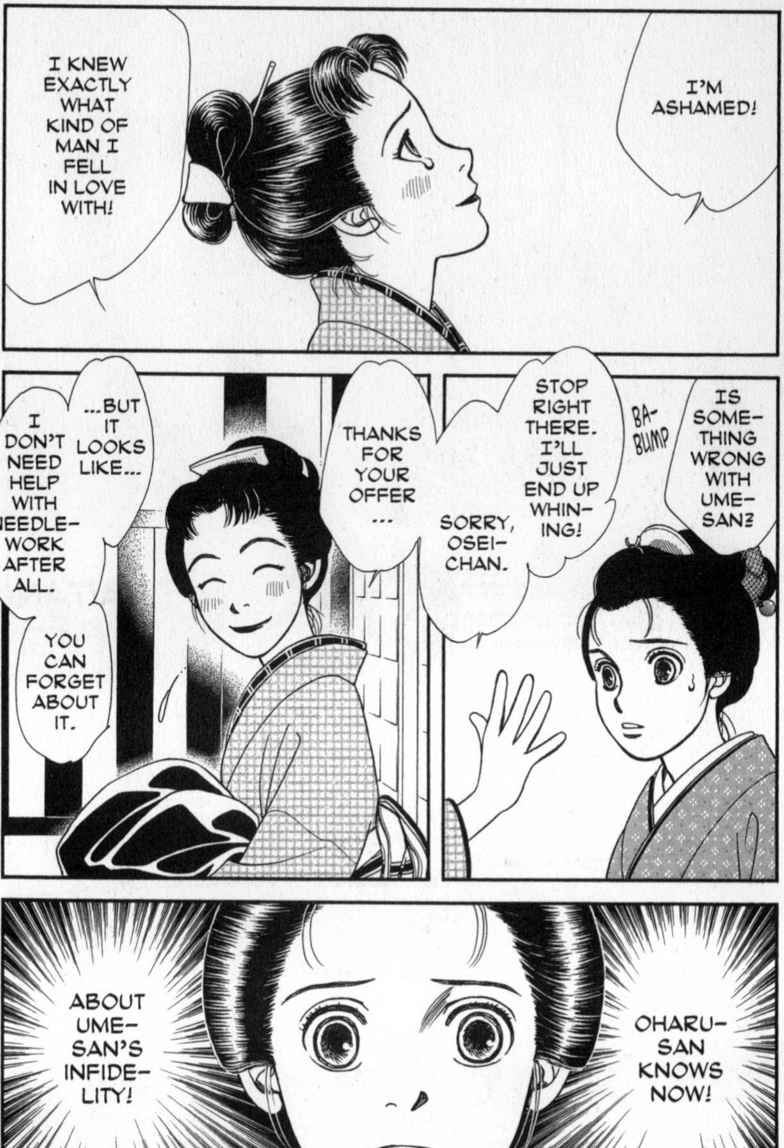
I'M ASHAMED!
I KNEW EXACTLY WHAT KIND OF MAN I FELL IN LOVE WITH!
IS SOMETHING WRONG WITH UME-SAN?
BA-BUMP
STOP RIGHT THERE. I'LL JUST END UP WHINING!
SORRY, OSEI-CHAN.
THANKS FOR YOUR OFFER...
...BUT IT LOOKS LIKE...
I DON'T NEED HELP WITH NEEDLEWORK AFTER ALL.
YOU CAN FORGET ABOUT IT.
OHARU-SAN KNOWS NOW!
ABOUT UME-SAN'S INFIDELITY!

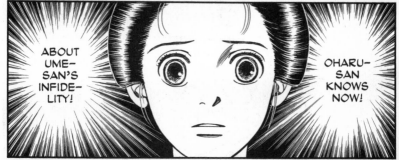

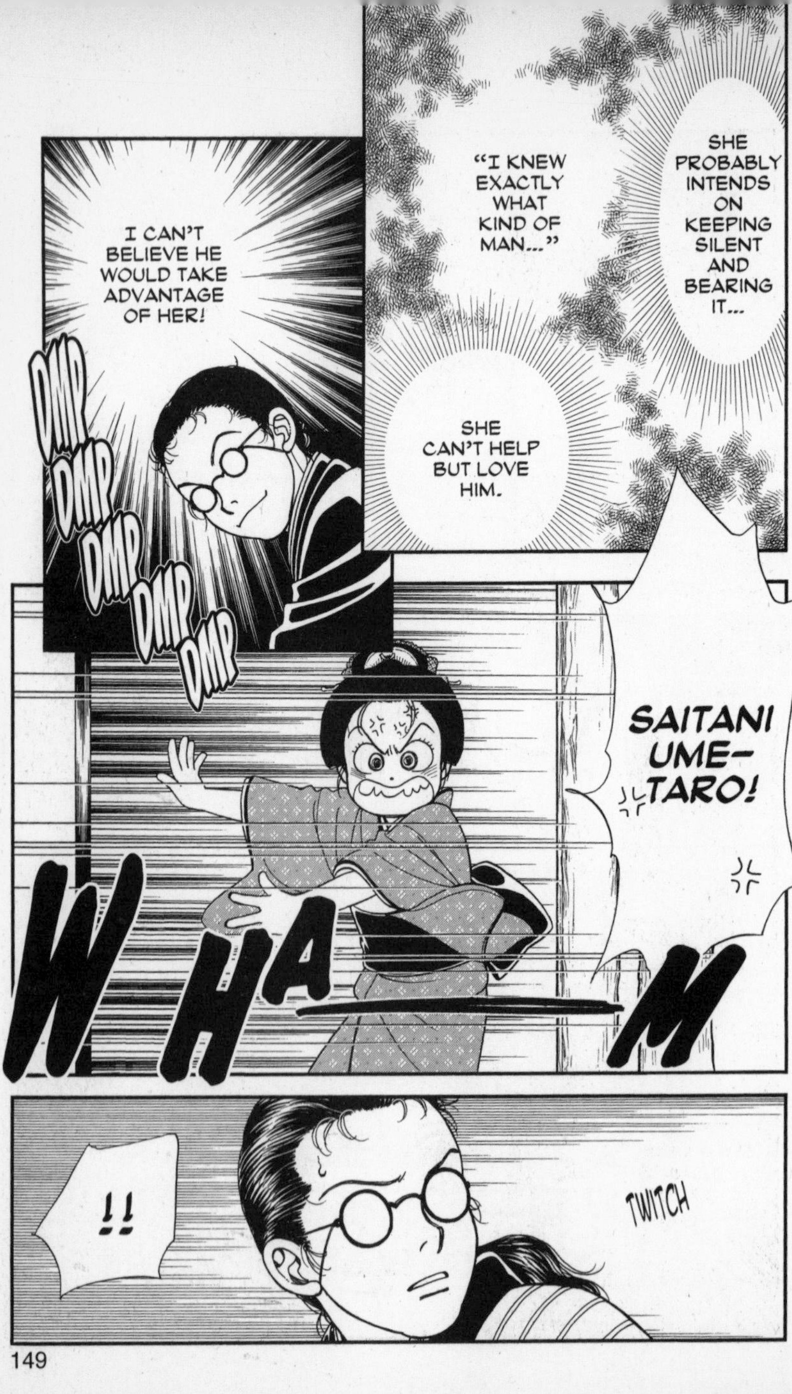
SHE PROBABLY INTENDS ON KEEPING SILENT AND BEARING IT...
"I KNEW EXACTLY WHAT KIND OF MAN..."
SHE CAN'T HELP BUT LOVE HIM.
I CAN'T BELIEVE HE WOULD TAKE ADVANTAGE OF HER!
DMP DMP DMP DMP DMP DMP
SAITANI UME-TARO!
WHA—M
TWITCH
!!

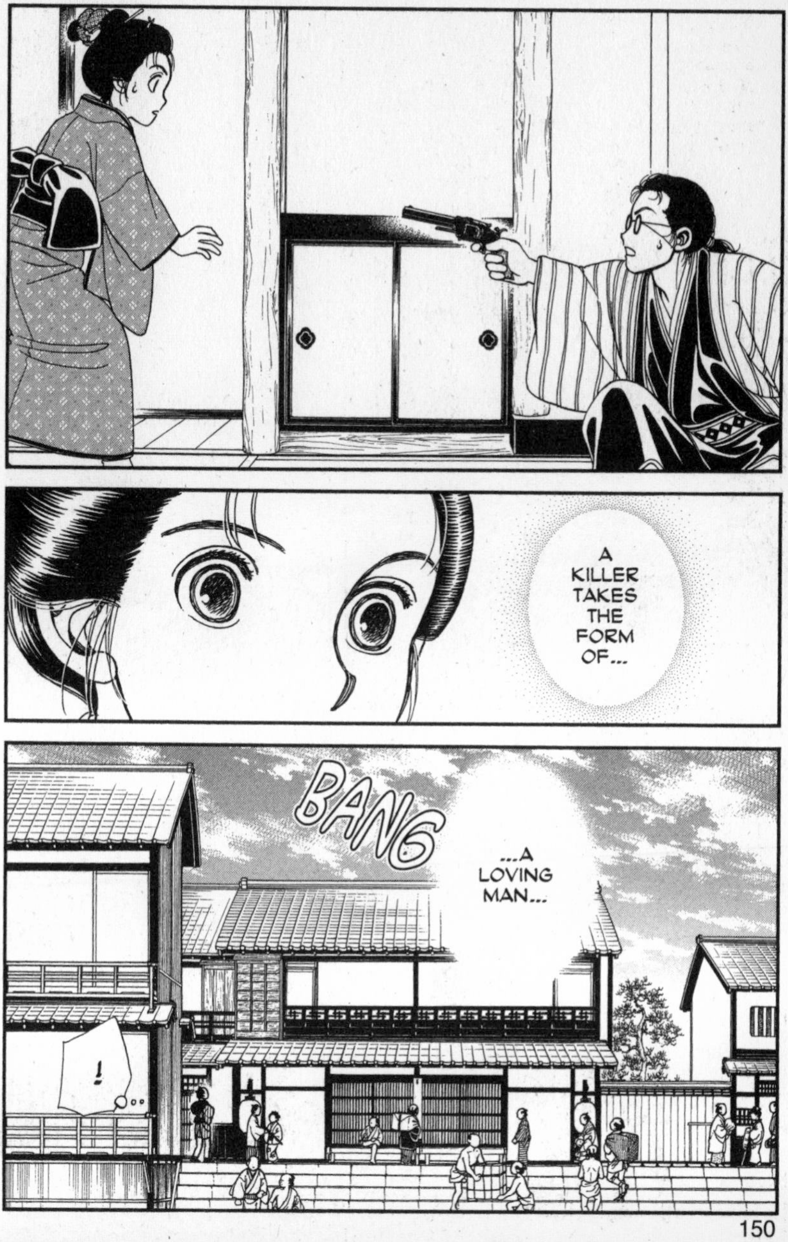
A KILLER TAKES THE FORM OF...
BANG
...A LOVING MAN...
!

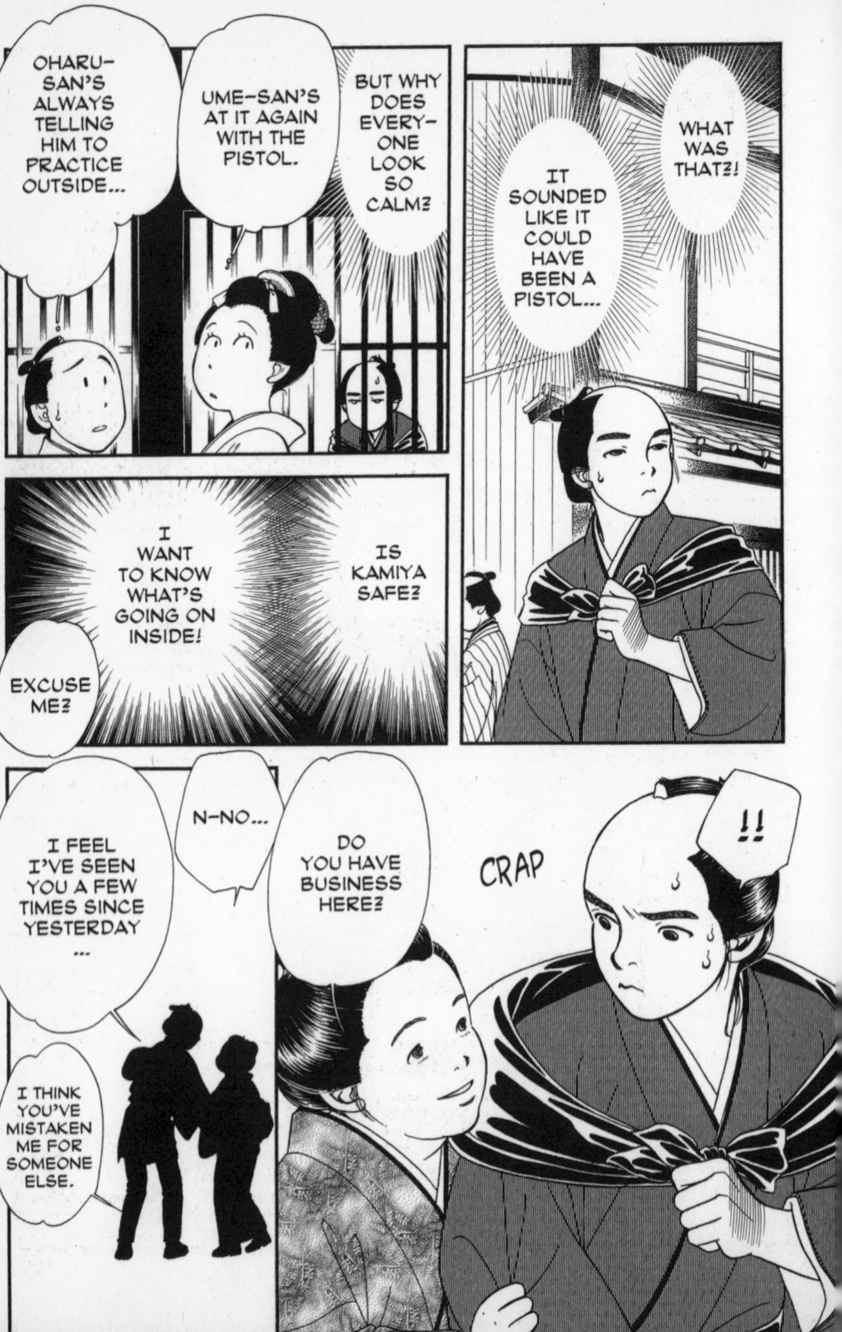
WHAT WAS THAT?!
IT SOUNDED LIKE IT COULD HAVE BEEN A PISTOL...
BUT WHY DOES EVERYONE LOOK SO CALM?
UME-SAN'S AT IT AGAIN WITH THE PISTOL.
OHARU-SAN'S ALWAYS TELLING HIM TO PRACTICE OUTSIDE...
IS KAMIYA SAFE?
I WANT TO KNOW WHAT'S GOING ON INSIDE!
EXCUSE ME?
!!
CRAP
DO YOU HAVE BUSINESS HERE?
N-NO...
I FEEL I'VE SEEN YOU A FEW TIMES SINCE YESTERDAY ...
I THINK YOU'VE MISTAKEN ME FOR SOMEONE ELSE.

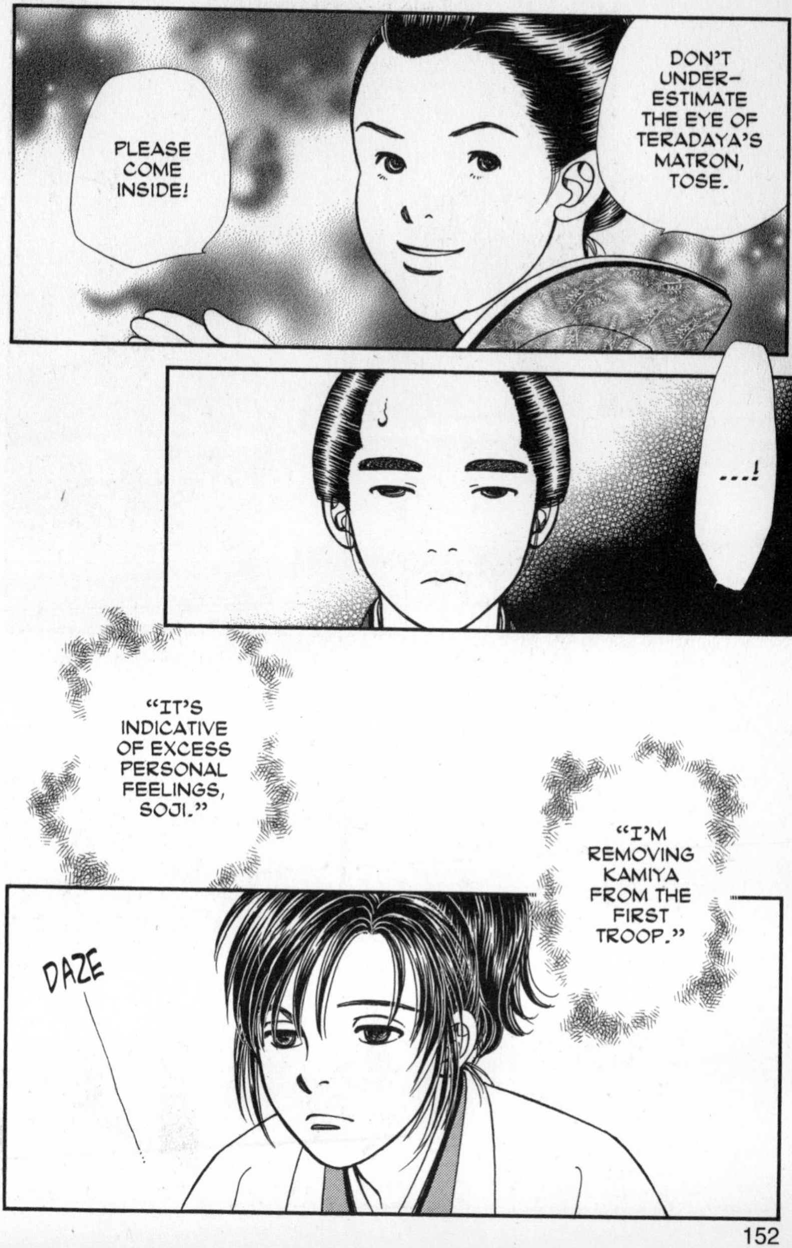
DON'T UNDER-ESTIMATE THE EYE OF TERADAYA'S MATRON, TOSE.
PLEASE COME INSIDE!
...!
"I'M REMOVING KAMIYA FROM THE FIRST TROOP."
"IT'S INDICATIVE OF EXCESS PERSONAL FEELINGS, SOJI."
DAZE

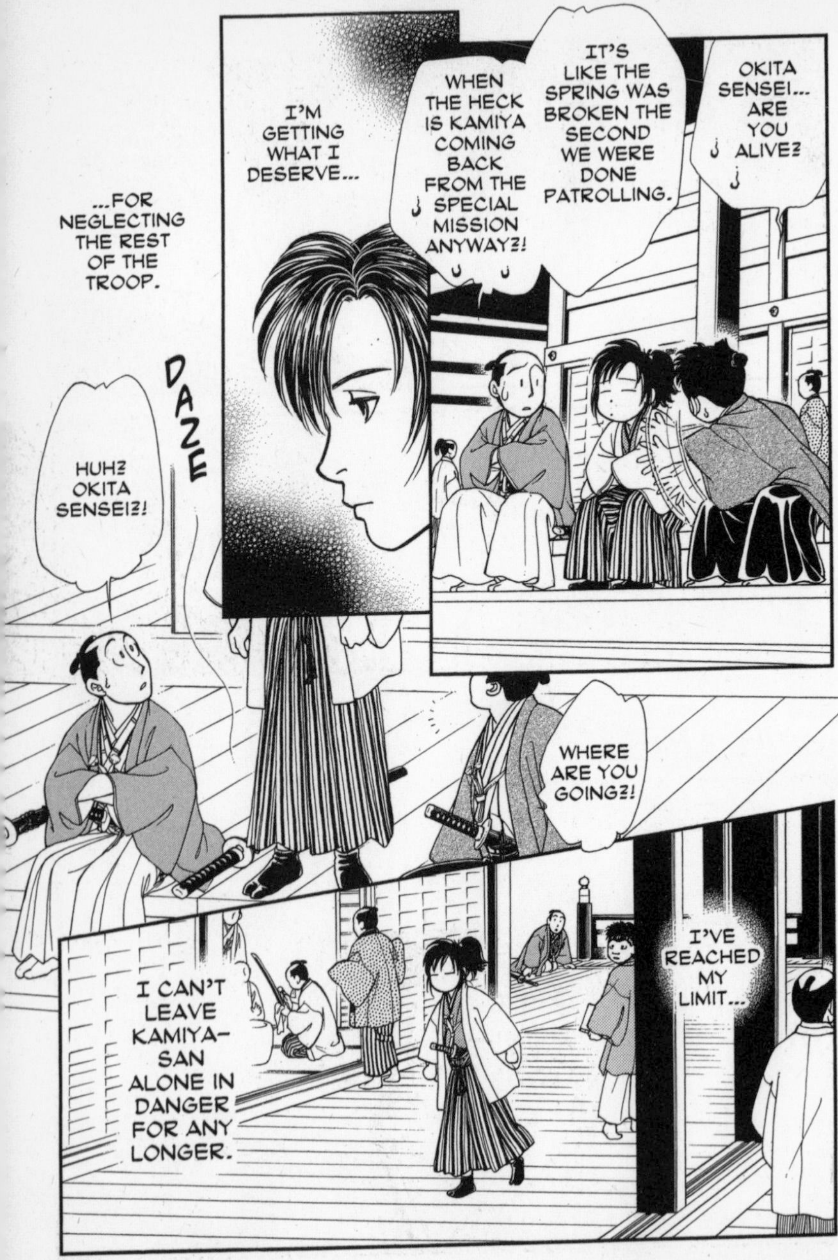
OKITA SENSEI... ARE YOU ALIVE?
IT'S LIKE THE SPRING WAS BROKEN THE SECOND WE WERE DONE PATROLLING.
WHEN THE HECK IS KAMIYA COMING BACK FROM THE SPECIAL MISSION ANYWAY?!
I'M GETTING WHAT I DESERVE...
...FOR NEGLECTING THE REST OF THE TROOP.
DAZE
HUH? OKITA SENSEI?!
WHERE ARE YOU GOING?!
I'VE REACHED MY LIMIT...
I CAN'T LEAVE KAMIYA-SAN ALONE IN DANGER FOR ANY LONGER.

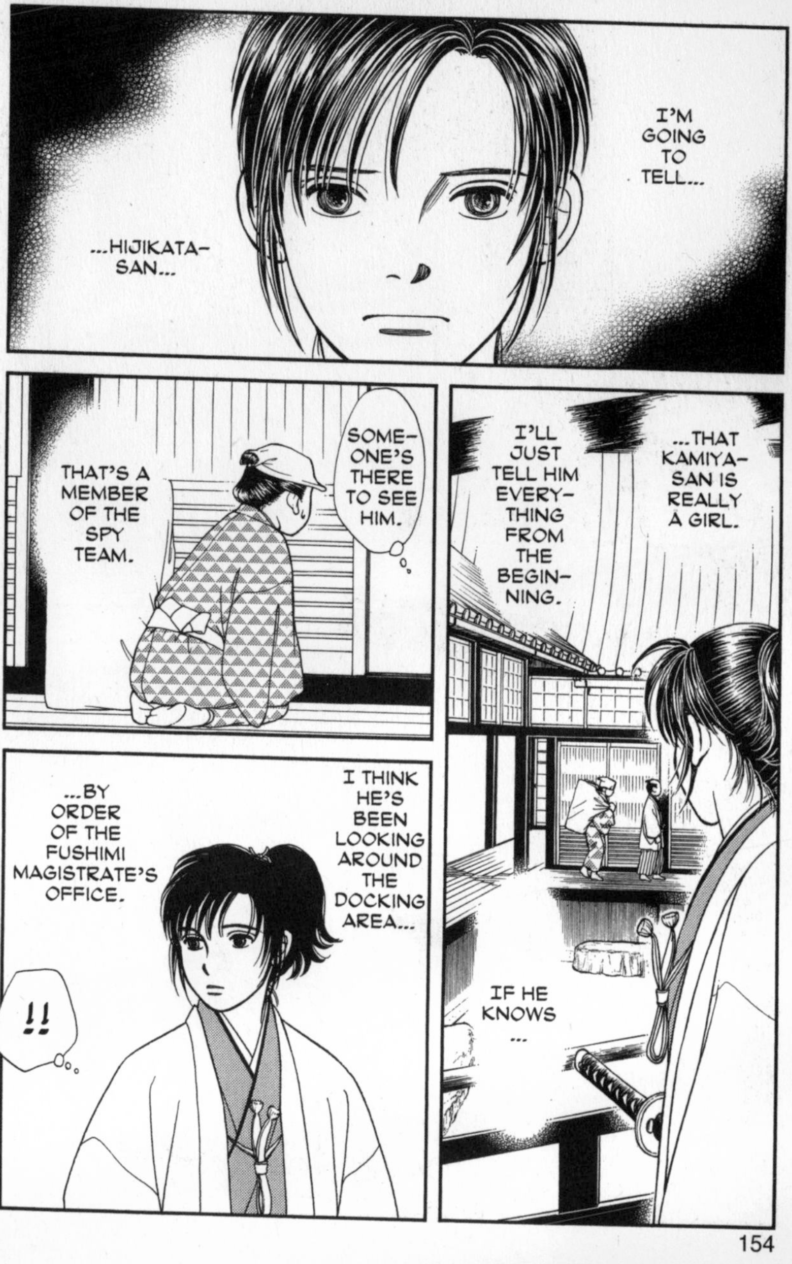
I'M GOING TO TELL...
...HIJIKATA-SAN...
...THAT KAMIYA-SAN IS REALLY A GIRL.
I'LL JUST TELL HIM EVERYTHING FROM THE BEGINNING.
IF HE KNOWS...
SOMEONE'S THERE TO SEE HIM.
THAT'S A MEMBER OF THE SPY TEAM.
I THINK HE'S BEEN LOOKING AROUND THE DOCKING AREA...
...BY ORDER OF THE FUSHIMI MAGISTRATE'S OFFICE.
!!

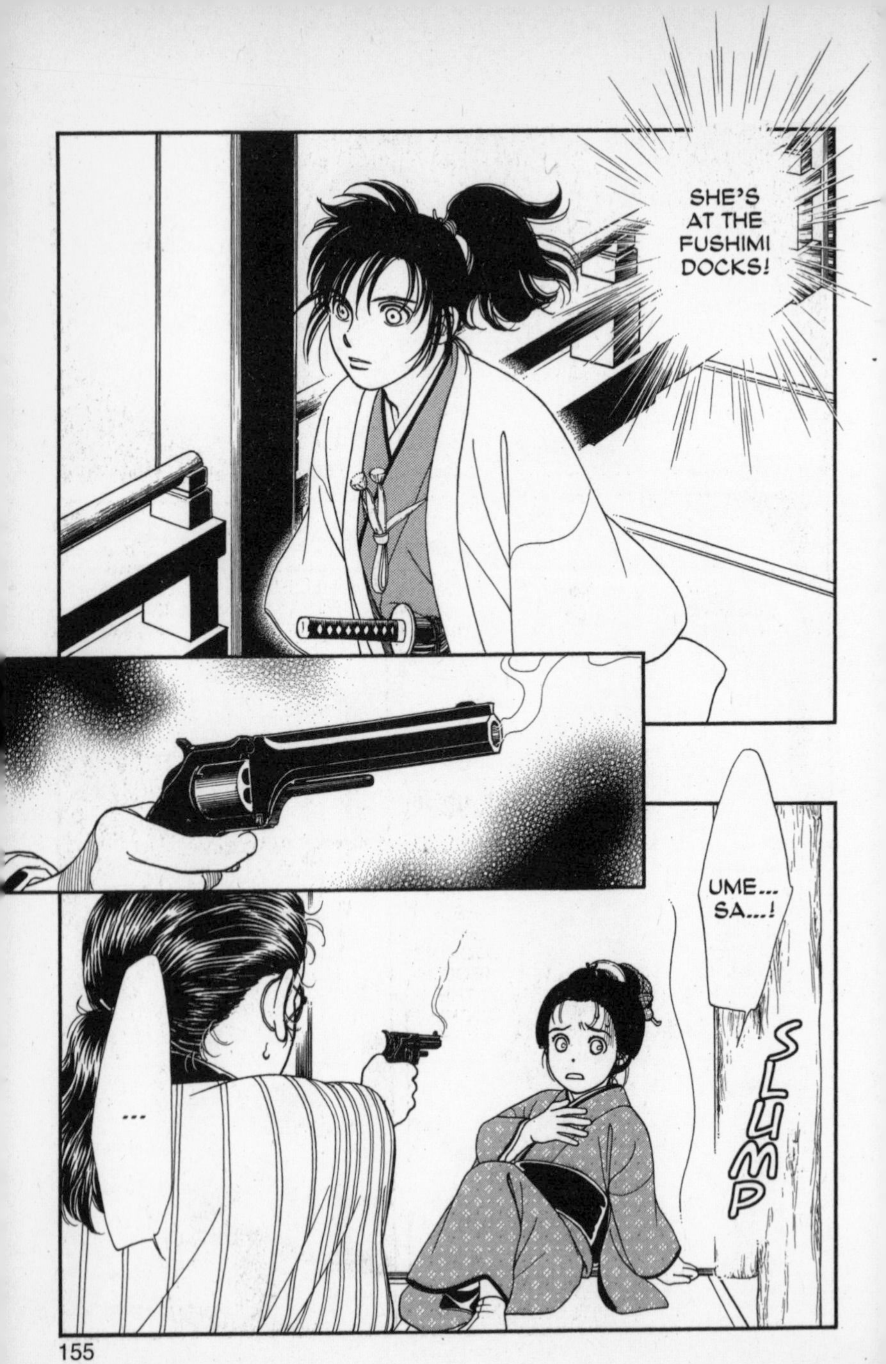
SHE'S AT THE FUSHIMI DOCKS!
UME... SA...!
SLUMP
...

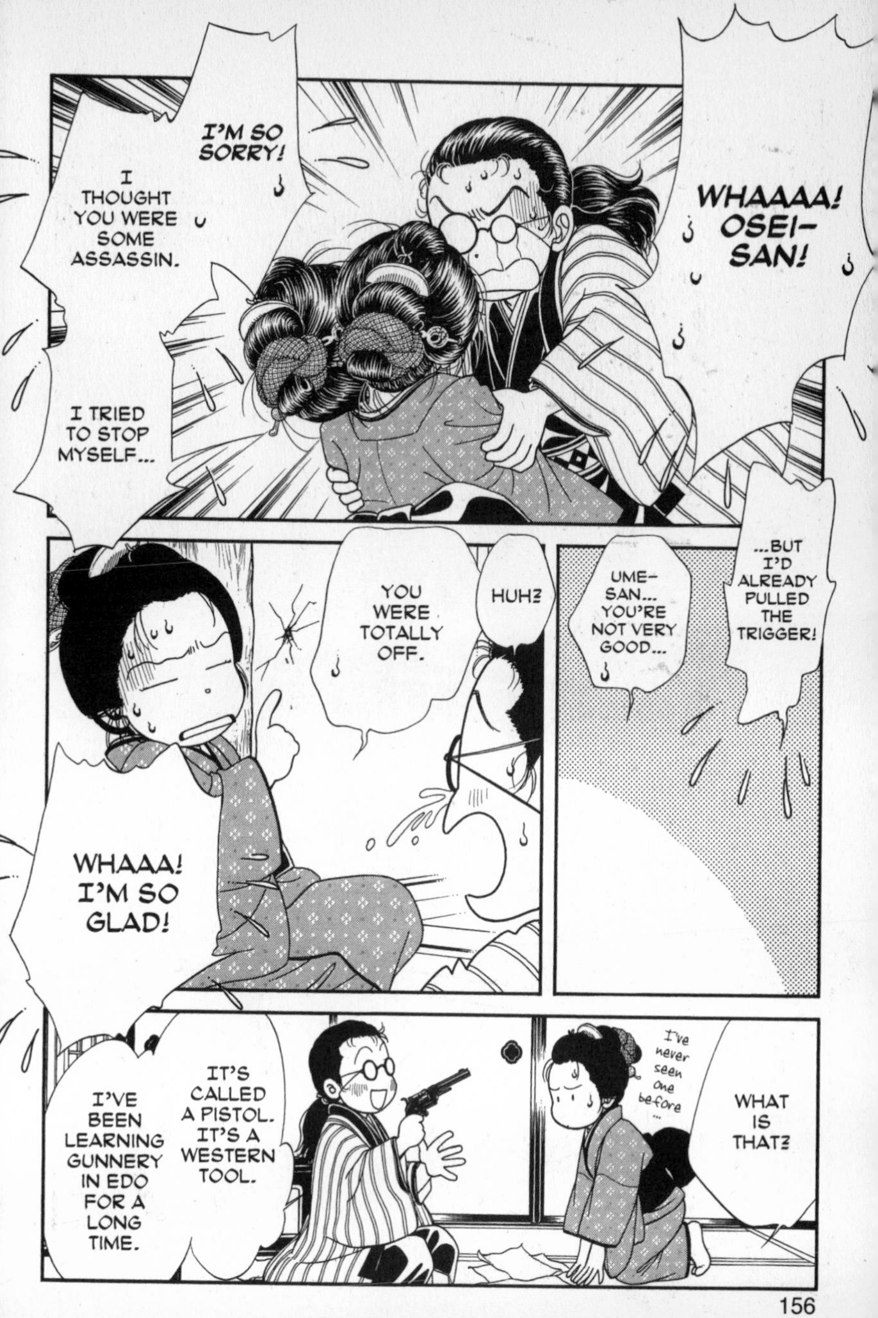
WHAAAA! OSEI-SAN!
I'M SO SORRY!
I THOUGHT YOU WERE SOME ASSASSIN.
I TRIED TO STOP MYSELF...
...BUT I'D ALREADY PULLED THE TRIGGER!
UME-SAN... YOU'RE NOT VERY GOOD...
HUH?
YOU WERE TOTALLY OFF.
WHAAA! I'M SO GLAD!
WHAT IS THAT?
I've never seen one before ...
IT'S CALLED A PISTOL. IT'S A WESTERN TOOL.
I'VE BEEN LEARNING GUNNERY IN EDO FOR A LONG TIME.

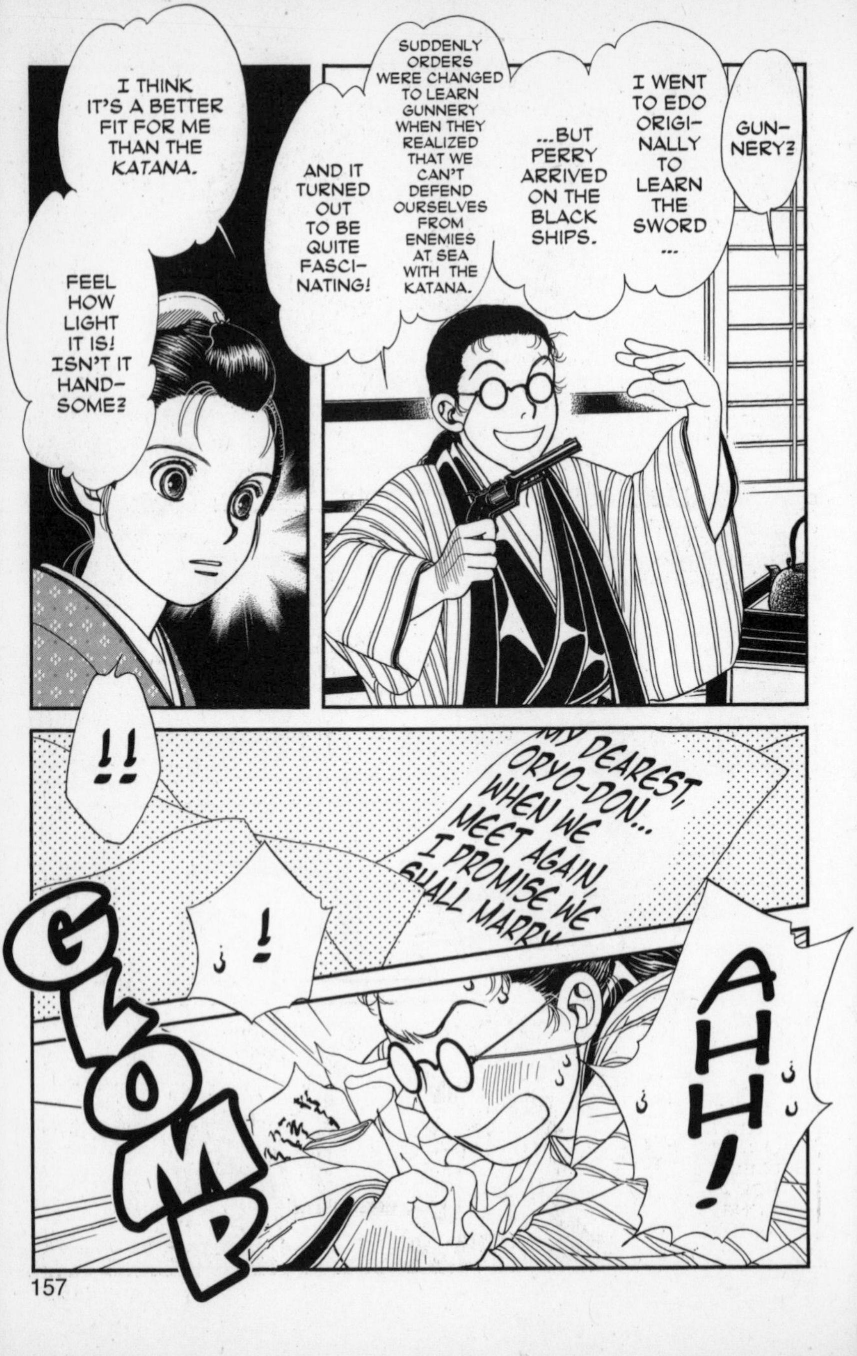
GUNNERY?
I WENT TO EDO ORIGINALLY TO LEARN THE SWORD...
...BUT PERRY ARRIVED ON THE BLACK SHIPS.
SUDDENLY ORDERS WERE CHANGED TO LEARN GUNNERY WHEN THEY REALIZED THAT WE CAN'T DEFEND OURSELVES FROM ENEMIES AT SEA WITH THE KATANA.
AND IT TURNED OUT TO BE QUITE FASCINATING!
I THINK IT'S A BETTER FIT FOR ME THAN THE KATANA.
FEEL HOW LIGHT IT IS! ISN'T IT HANDSOME?
MY DEAREST, ORYO-DON... WHEN WE MEET AGAIN, I PROMISE WE SHALL MARRY
!!
AHH!
!
GLOMP

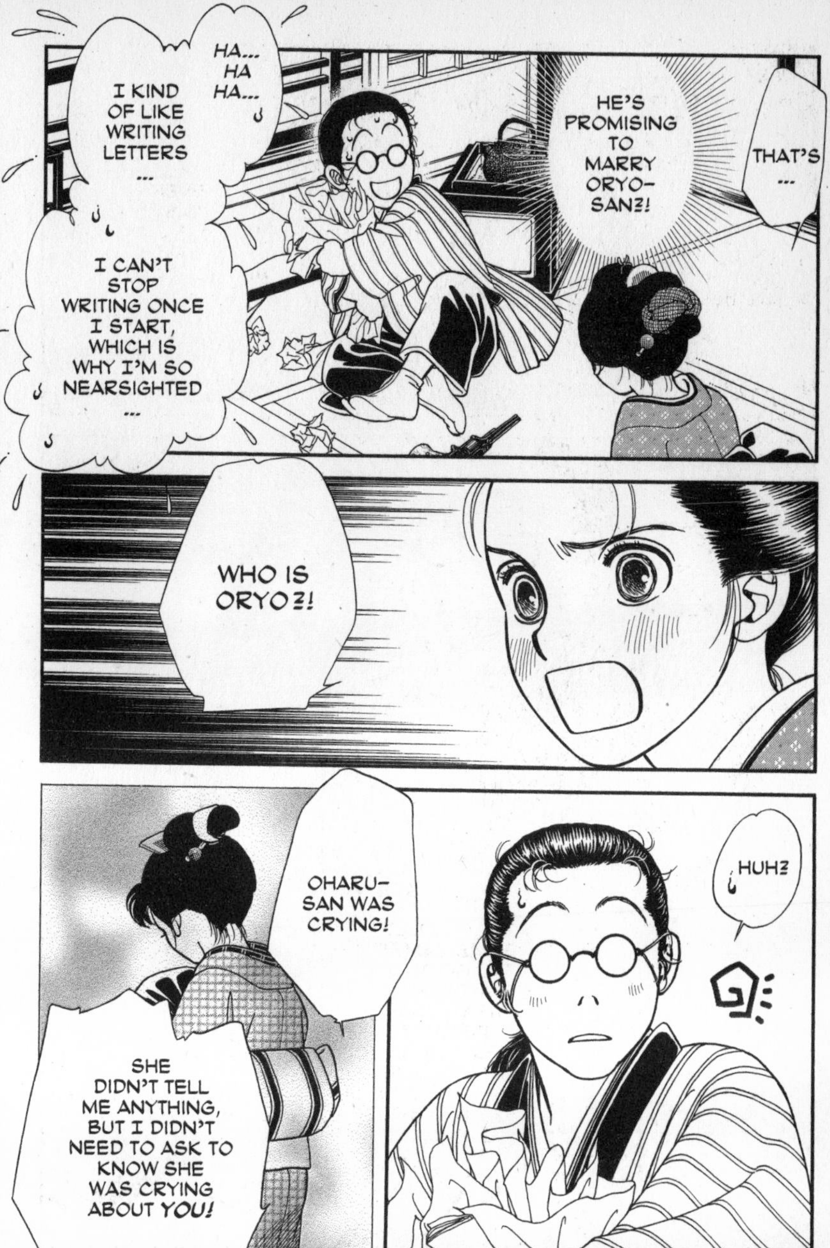
THAT'S ...
HE'S PROMISING TO MARRY ORYO-SAN?!
HA... HA HA...
I KIND OF LIKE WRITING LETTERS ...
I CAN'T STOP WRITING ONCE I START, WHICH IS WHY I'M SO NEARSIGHTED ...
WHO IS ORYO?!
HUH?
OHARU-SAN WAS CRYING!
SHE DIDN'T TELL ME ANYTHING, BUT I DIDN'T NEED TO ASK TO KNOW SHE WAS CRYING ABOUT *YOU!*

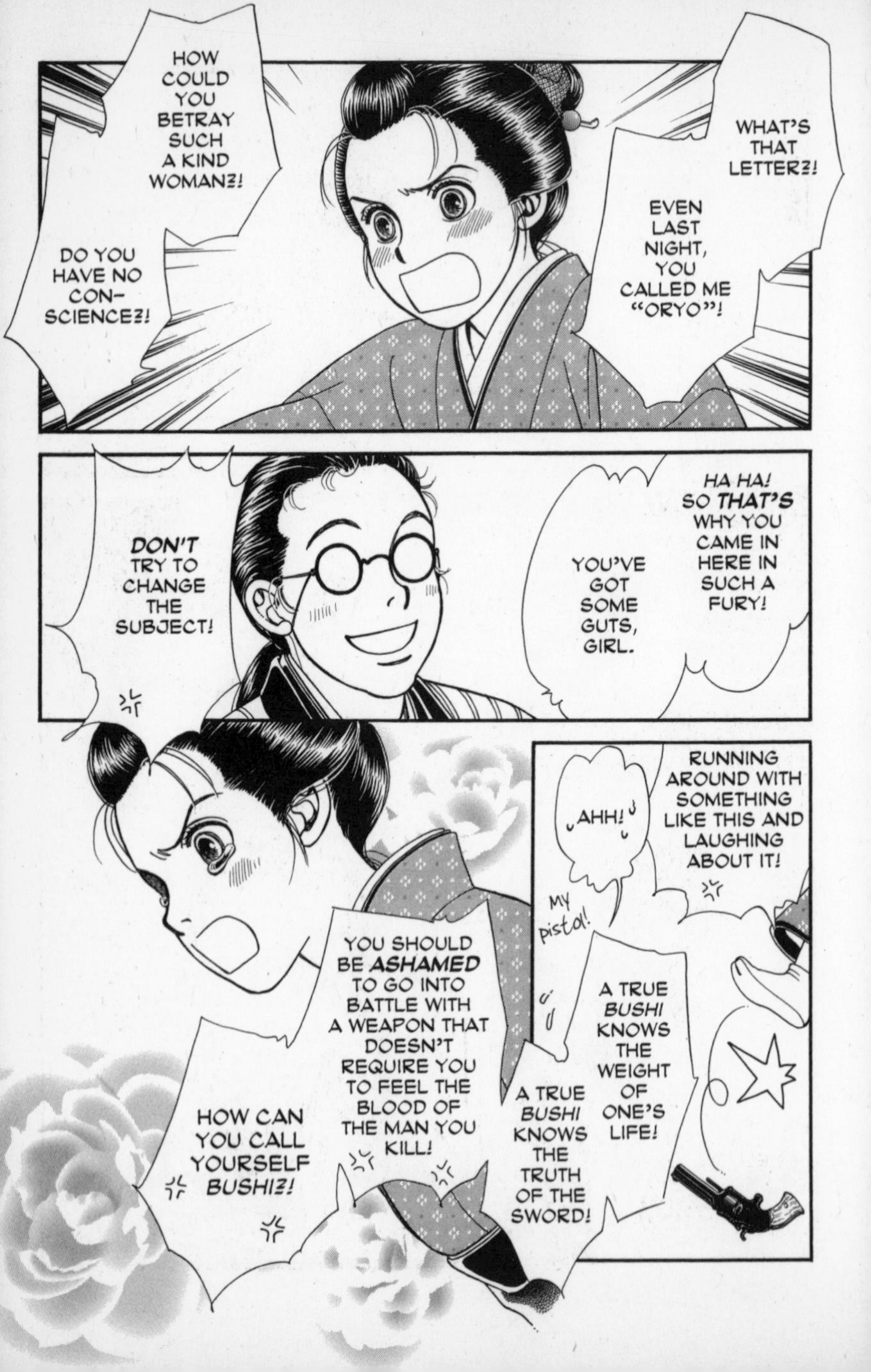
WHAT'S THAT LETTER?!
EVEN LAST NIGHT, YOU CALLED ME "ORYO"!
HOW COULD YOU BETRAY SUCH A KIND WOMAN?!
DO YOU HAVE NO CON-SCIENCE?!
HA HA! SO THAT'S WHY YOU CAME IN HERE IN SUCH A FURY!
YOU'VE GOT SOME GUTS, GIRL.
DON'T TRY TO CHANGE THE SUBJECT!
RUNNING AROUND WITH SOMETHING LIKE THIS AND LAUGHING ABOUT IT!
AHH!
My pistol!
A TRUE BUSHI KNOWS THE WEIGHT OF ONE'S LIFE!
A TRUE BUSHI KNOWS THE TRUTH OF THE SWORD!
YOU SHOULD BE ASHAMED TO GO INTO BATTLE WITH A WEAPON THAT DOESN'T REQUIRE YOU TO FEEL THE BLOOD OF THE MAN YOU KILL!
HOW CAN YOU CALL YOURSELF BUSHI?!

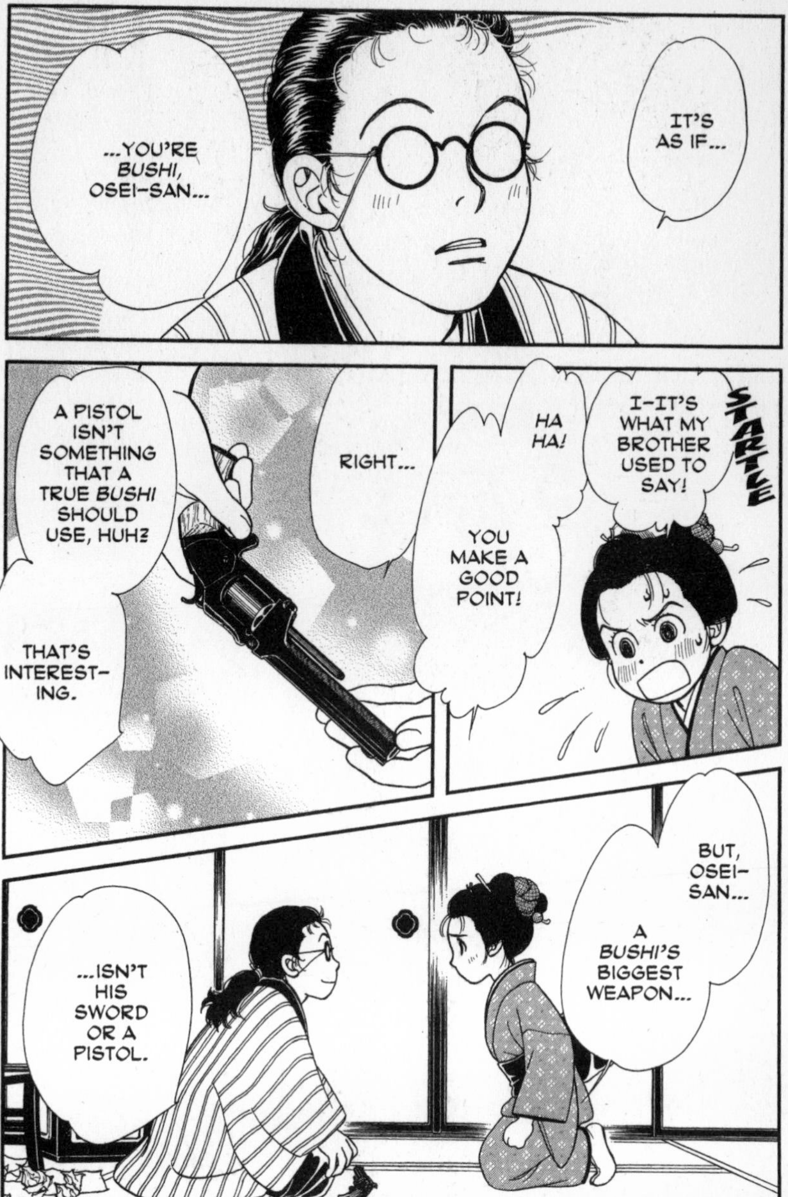
IT'S AS IF...
...YOU'RE *BUSHI*, OSEI-SAN...
STARTLE
I-IT'S WHAT MY BROTHER USED TO SAY!
HA HA!
YOU MAKE A GOOD POINT!
RIGHT...
A PISTOL ISN'T SOMETHING THAT A TRUE *BUSHI* SHOULD USE, HUH?
THAT'S INTERESTING.
BUT, OSEI-SAN...
A *BUSHI'S* BIGGEST WEAPON...
...ISN'T HIS SWORD OR A PISTOL.

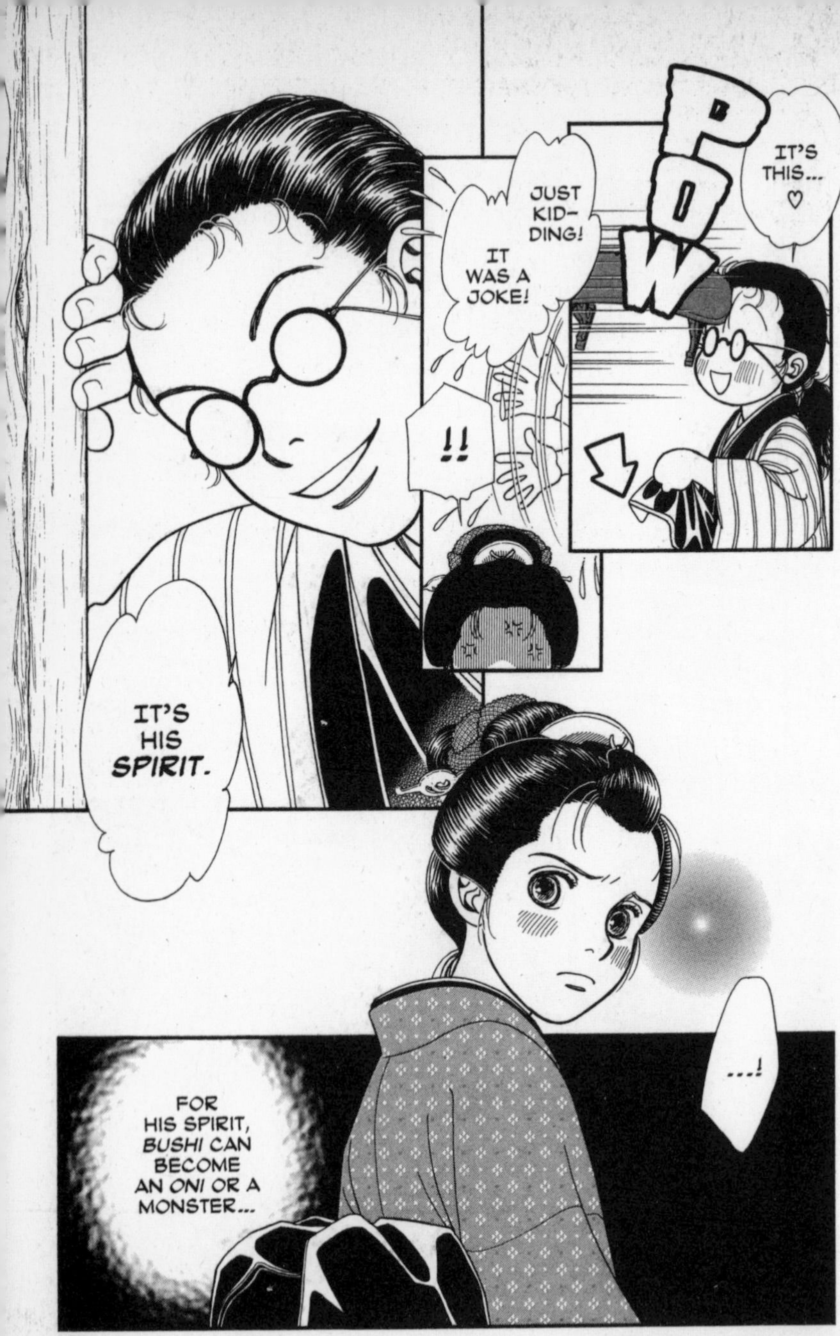
POW
IT'S THIS... ♡
JUST KID-DING!
IT WAS A JOKE!
!!
IT'S HIS *SPIRIT*.
...!
FOR HIS SPIRIT, *BUSHI* CAN BECOME AN *ONI* OR A MONSTER...

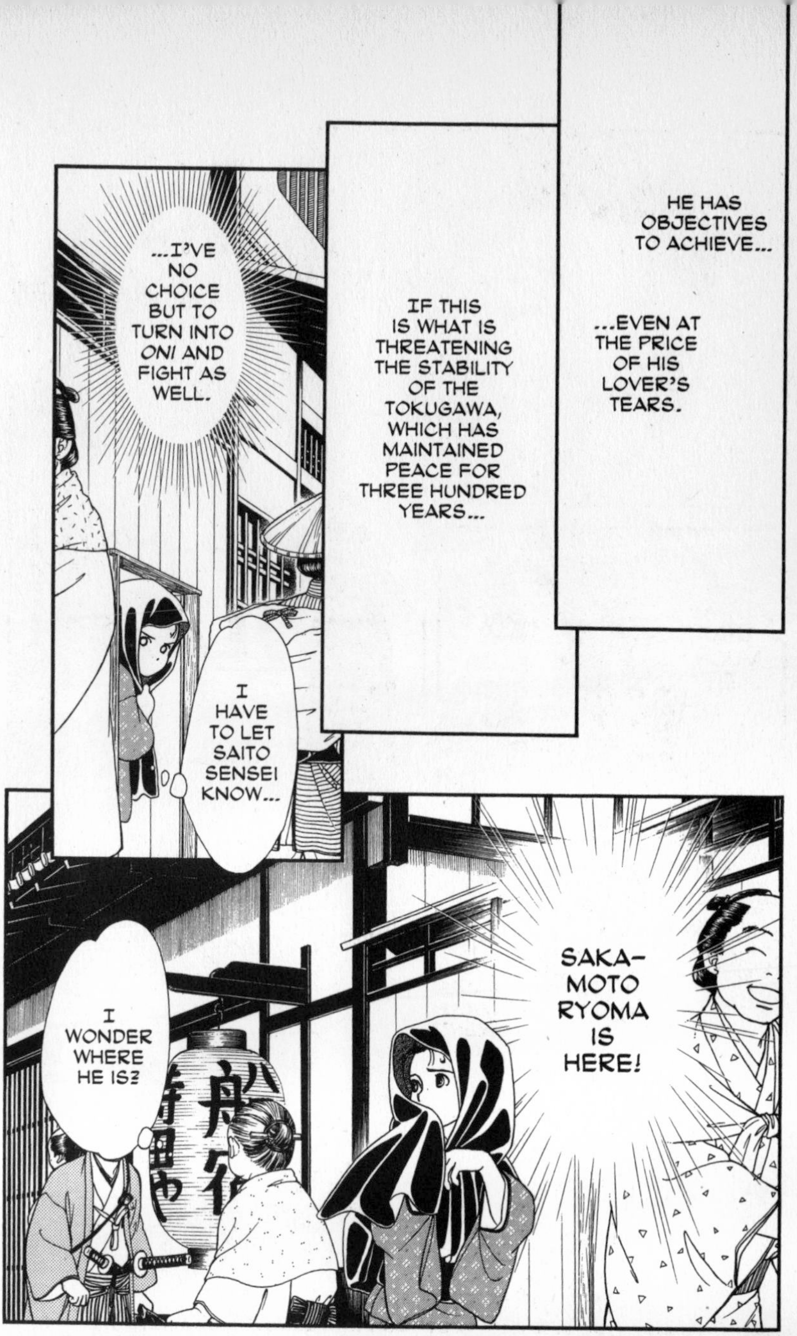
HE HAS OBJECTIVES TO ACHIEVE...
...EVEN AT THE PRICE OF HIS LOVER'S TEARS.
IF THIS IS WHAT IS THREATENING THE STABILITY OF THE TOKUGAWA, WHICH HAS MAINTAINED PEACE FOR THREE HUNDRED YEARS...
...I'VE NO CHOICE BUT TO TURN INTO *ONI* AND FIGHT AS WELL.
I HAVE TO LET SAITO SENSEI KNOW...
SAKA-MOTO RYOMA IS HERE!
I WONDER WHERE HE IS?

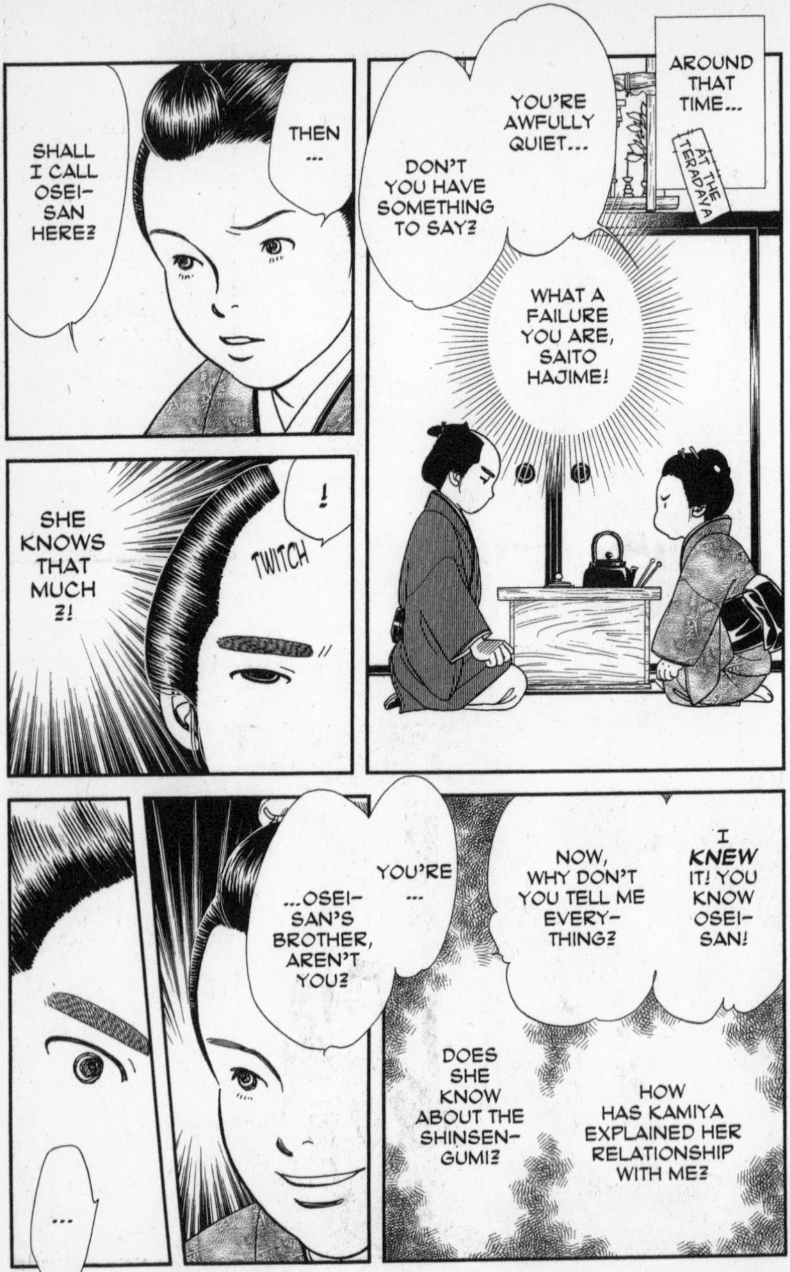
AROUND THAT TIME...
AT THE TERADAYA
YOU'RE AWFULLY QUIET... DON'T YOU HAVE SOMETHING TO SAY?
WHAT A FAILURE YOU ARE, SAITO HAJIME!
THEN ...
SHALL I CALL OSEI-SAN HERE?
!
TWITCH
SHE KNOWS THAT MUCH?!
I *KNEW* IT! YOU KNOW OSEI-SAN!
NOW, WHY DON'T YOU TELL ME EVERYTHING?
HOW HAS KAMIYA EXPLAINED HER RELATIONSHIP WITH ME?
DOES SHE KNOW ABOUT THE SHINSEN-GUMI?
YOU'RE ...
...OSEI-SAN'S BROTHER, AREN'T YOU?
...

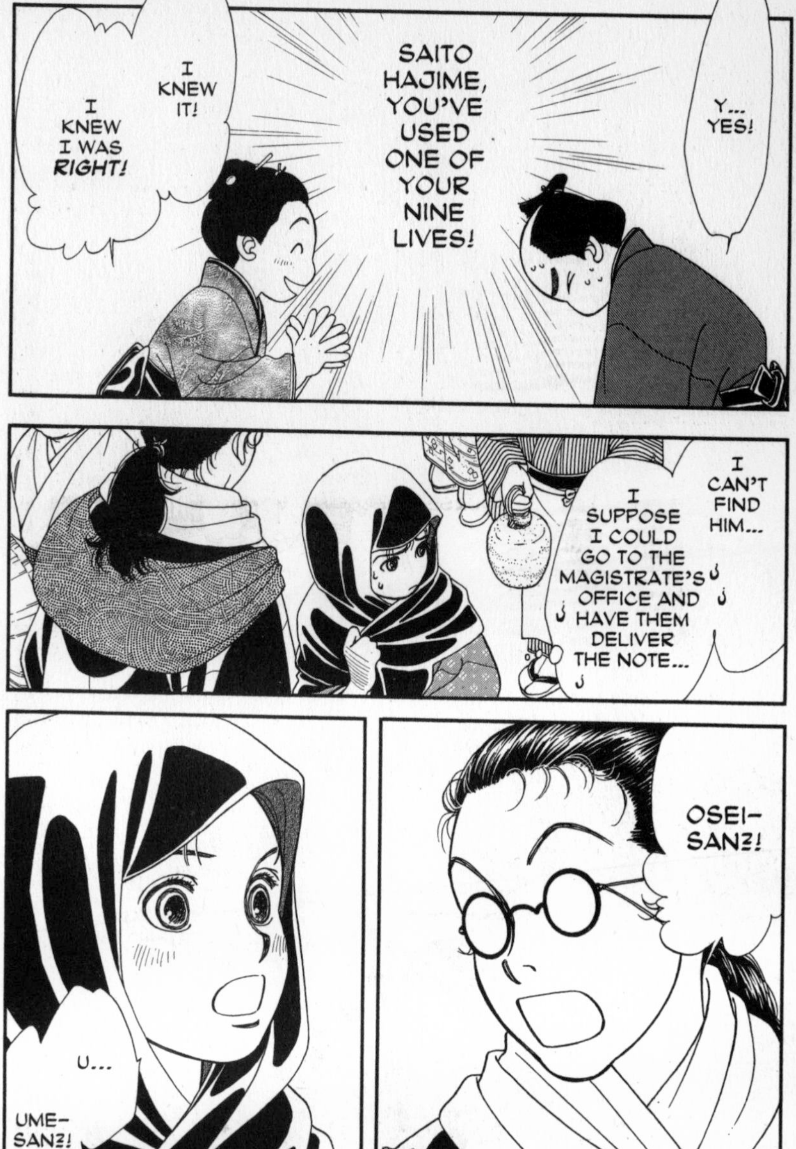
Y... YES!
SAITO HAJIME, YOU'VE USED ONE OF YOUR NINE LIVES!
I KNEW IT!
I KNEW I WAS *RIGHT!*
I CAN'T FIND HIM...
I SUPPOSE I COULD GO TO THE MAGISTRATE'S OFFICE AND HAVE THEM DELIVER THE NOTE...
OSEI-SAN?!
U...
UME-SAN?!

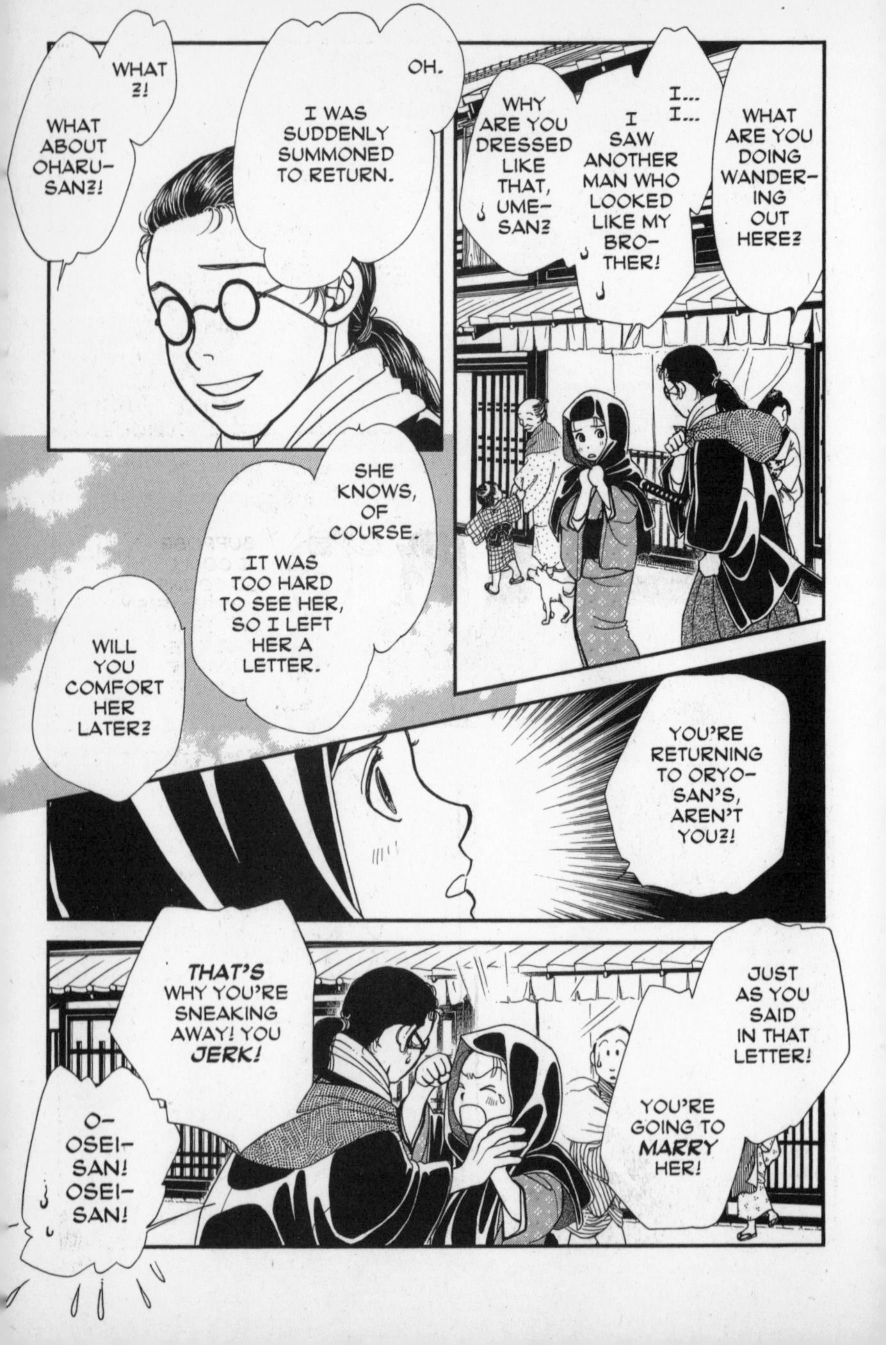
WHAT ARE YOU DOING WANDERING OUT HERE?
I... I... I SAW ANOTHER MAN WHO LOOKED LIKE MY BROTHER!
WHY ARE YOU DRESSED LIKE THAT, UME-SAN?
OH.
I WAS SUDDENLY SUMMONED TO RETURN.
WHAT?! WHAT ABOUT OHARU-SAN?!
SHE KNOWS, OF COURSE.
IT WAS TOO HARD TO SEE HER, SO I LEFT HER A LETTER.
WILL YOU COMFORT HER LATER?
YOU'RE RETURNING TO ORYO-SAN'S, AREN'T YOU?!
JUST AS YOU SAID IN THAT LETTER!
YOU'RE GOING TO MARRY HER!
THAT'S WHY YOU'RE SNEAKING AWAY! YOU JERK!
O-OSEI-SAN! OSEI-SAN!

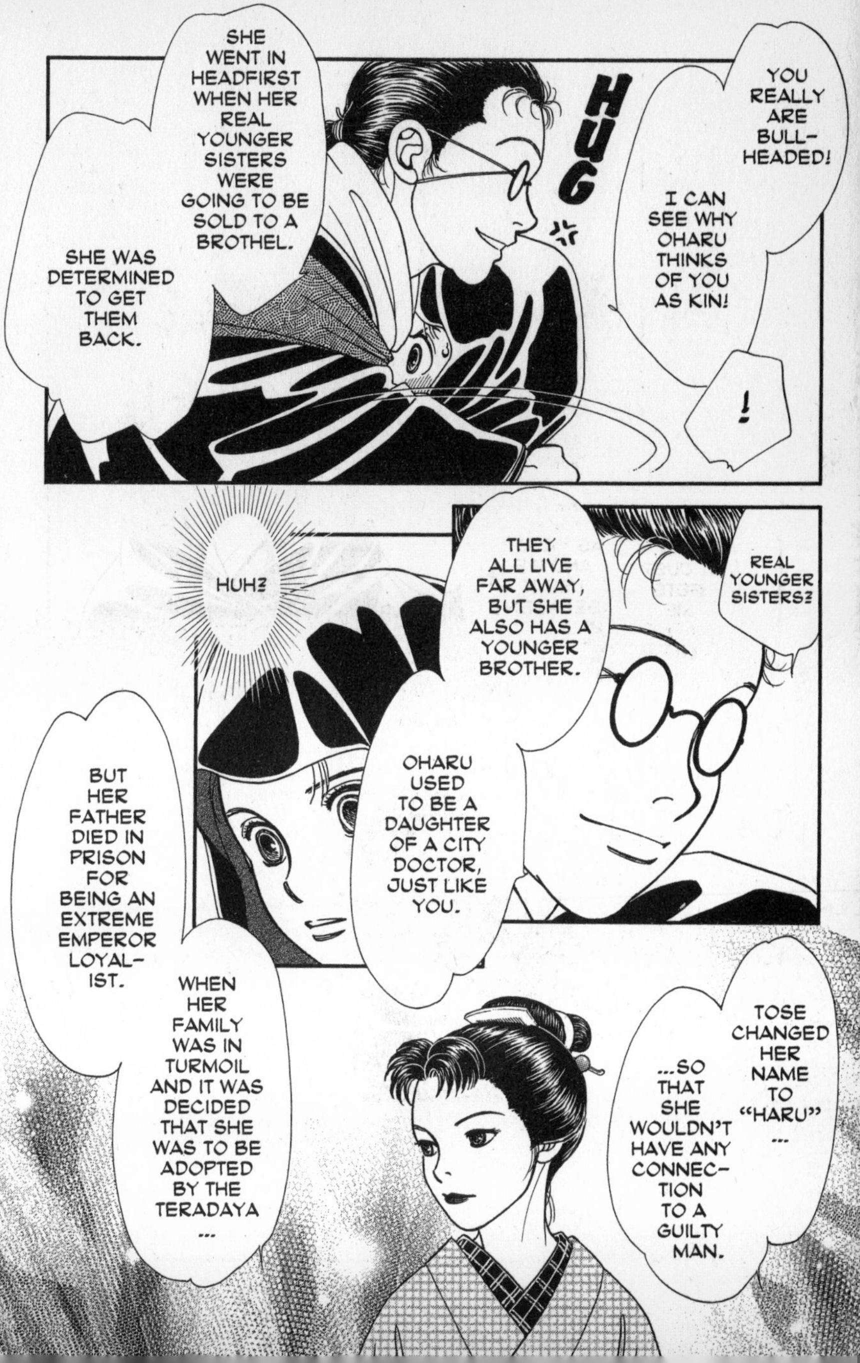
YOU REALLY ARE BULL-HEADED!
I CAN SEE WHY OHARU THINKS OF YOU AS KIN!
HUG
!
SHE WENT IN HEADFIRST WHEN HER REAL YOUNGER SISTERS WERE GOING TO BE SOLD TO A BROTHEL.
SHE WAS DETERMINED TO GET THEM BACK.
REAL YOUNGER SISTERS?
THEY ALL LIVE FAR AWAY, BUT SHE ALSO HAS A YOUNGER BROTHER.
HUH?
OHARU USED TO BE A DAUGHTER OF A CITY DOCTOR, JUST LIKE YOU.
BUT HER FATHER DIED IN PRISON FOR BEING AN EXTREME EMPEROR LOYAL-IST.
TOSE CHANGED HER NAME TO "HARU"...
...SO THAT SHE WOULDN'T HAVE ANY CONNEC-TION TO A GUILTY MAN.
WHEN HER FAMILY WAS IN TURMOIL AND IT WAS DECIDED THAT SHE WAS TO BE ADOPTED BY THE TERADAYA...

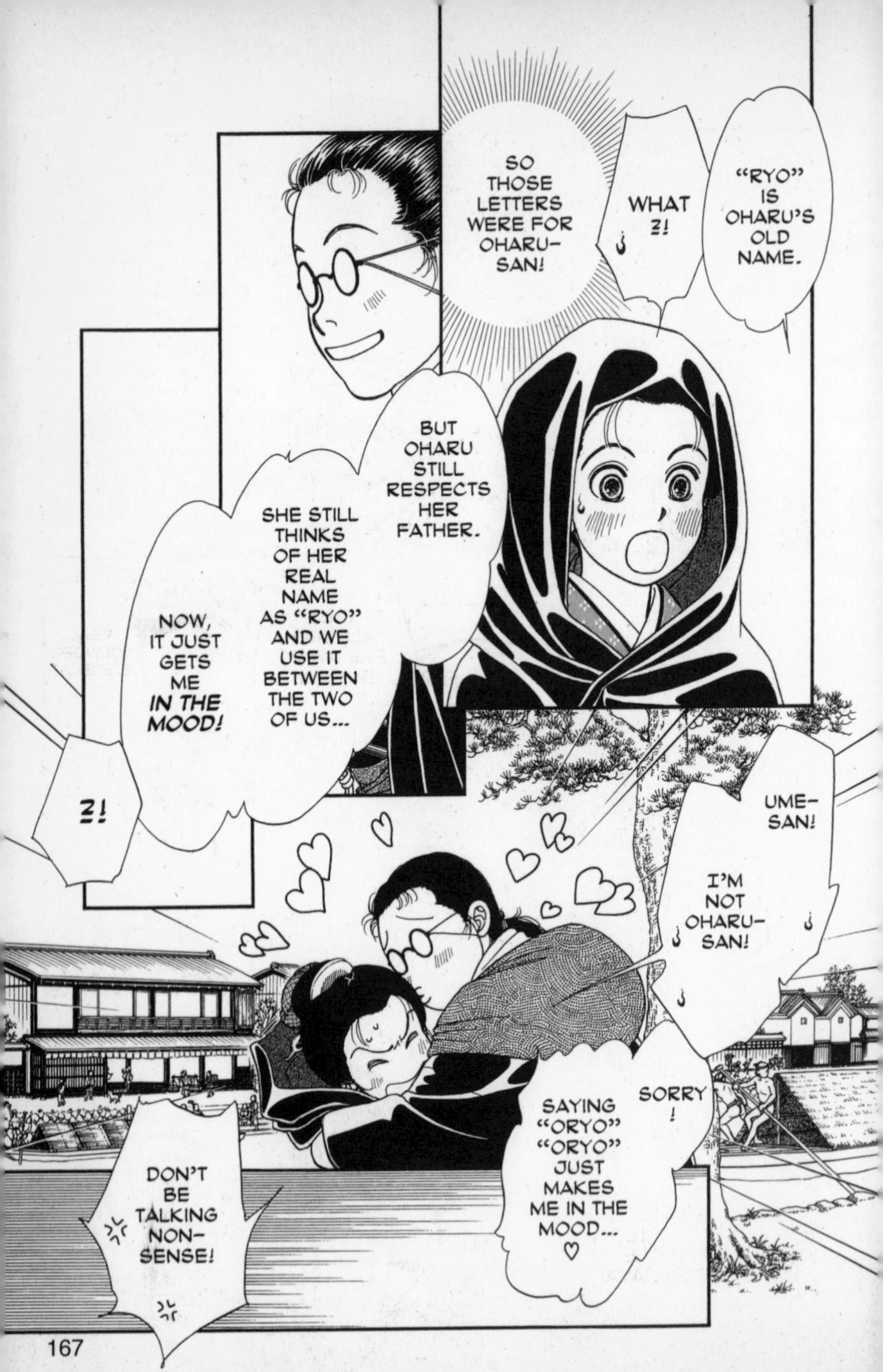
"RYO" IS OHARU'S OLD NAME.
WHAT ?!
SO THOSE LETTERS WERE FOR OHARU-SAN!
BUT OHARU STILL RESPECTS HER FATHER.
SHE STILL THINKS OF HER REAL NAME AS "RYO" AND WE USE IT BETWEEN THE TWO OF US...
NOW, IT JUST GETS ME *IN THE MOOD!*
?!
UME-SAN!
I'M NOT OHARU-SAN!
SORRY!
SAYING "ORYO" "ORYO" JUST MAKES ME IN THE MOOD... ♡
DON'T BE TALKING NON-SENSE!

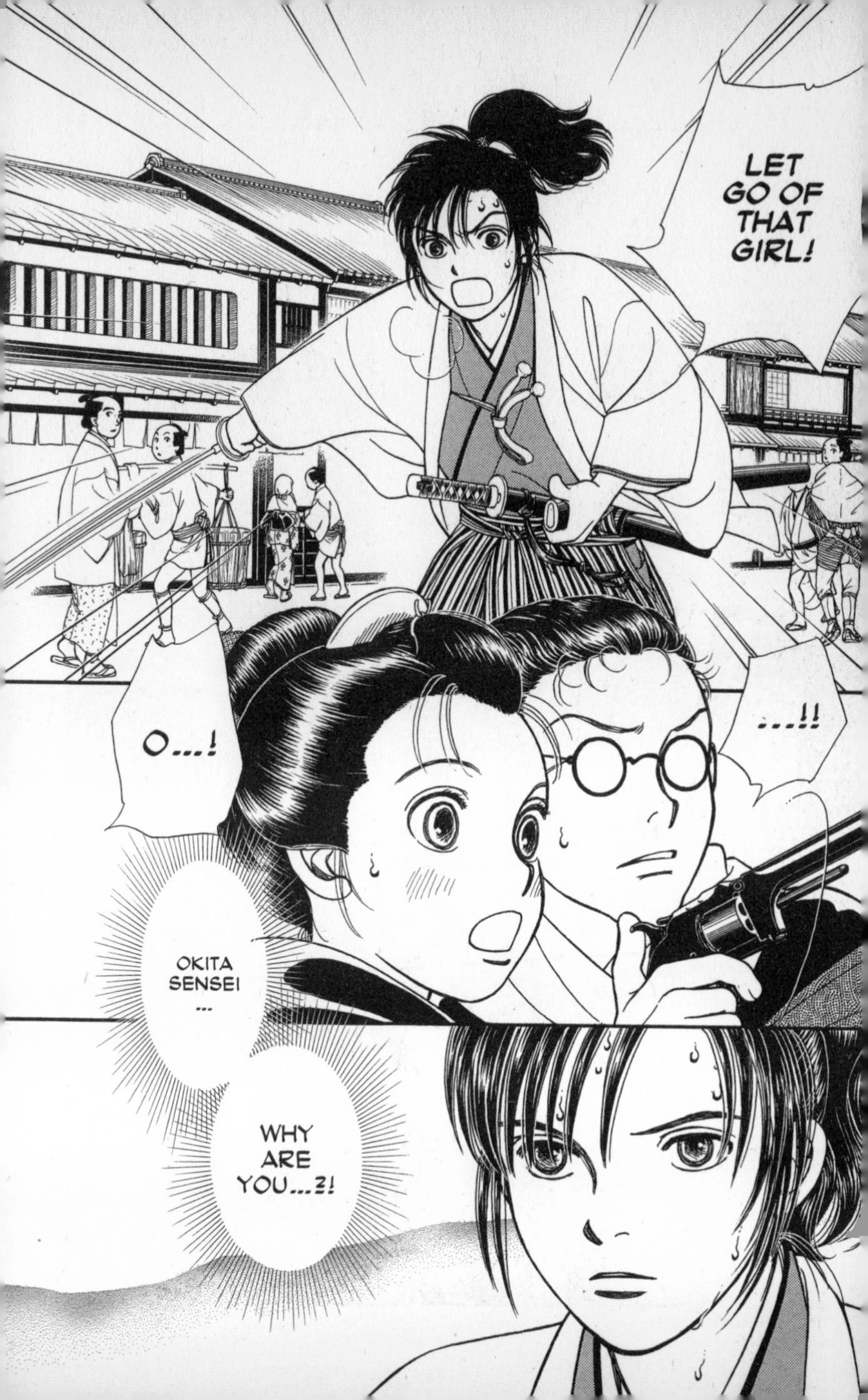
LET GO OF THAT GIRL!
...!!
O...!
OKITA SENSEI ...
WHY ARE YOU...?!

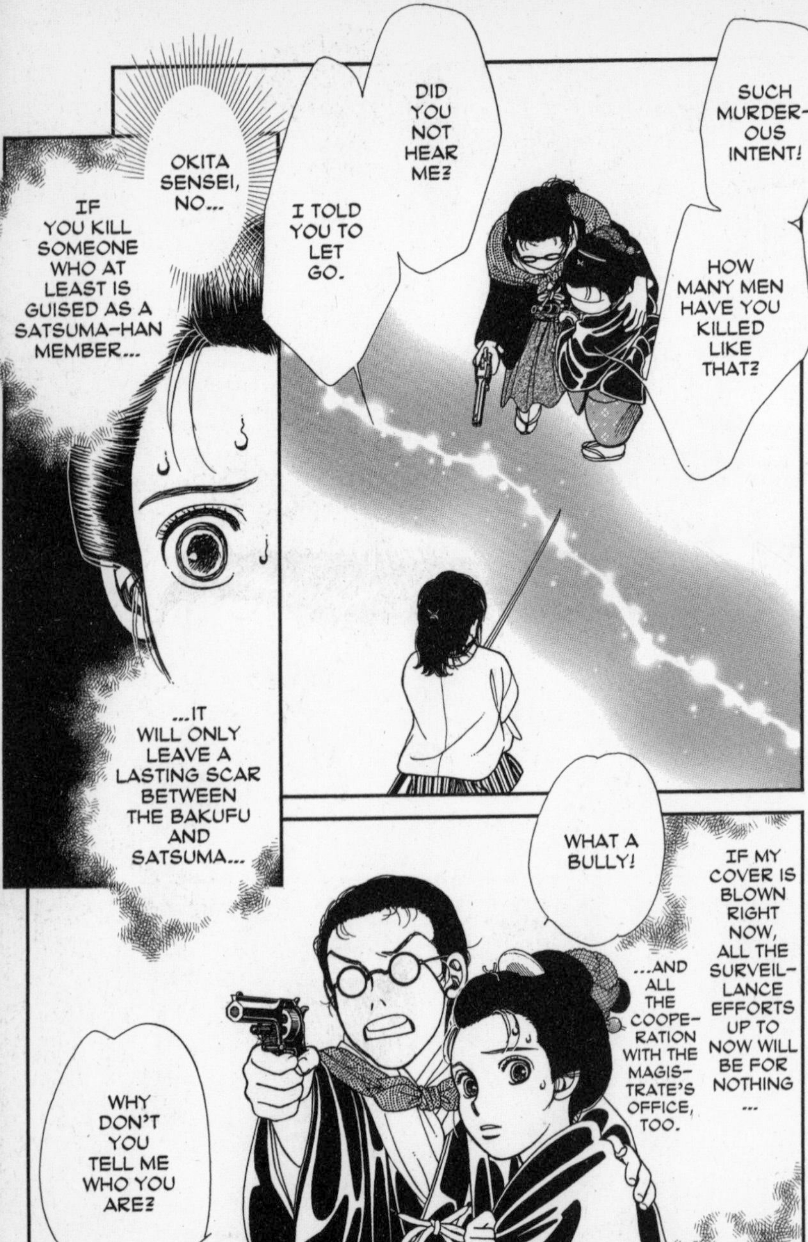
SUCH MURDEROUS INTENT!
HOW MANY MEN HAVE YOU KILLED LIKE THAT?
DID YOU NOT HEAR ME?
I TOLD YOU TO LET GO.
OKITA SENSEI, NO...
IF YOU KILL SOMEONE WHO AT LEAST IS GUISED AS A SATSUMA-HAN MEMBER...
...IT WILL ONLY LEAVE A LASTING SCAR BETWEEN THE BAKUFU AND SATSUMA...
WHAT A BULLY!
IF MY COVER IS BLOWN RIGHT NOW, ALL THE SURVEILLANCE EFFORTS UP TO NOW WILL BE FOR NOTHING...
...AND ALL THE COOPERATION WITH THE MAGISTRATE'S OFFICE, TOO.
WHY DON'T YOU TELL ME WHO YOU ARE?

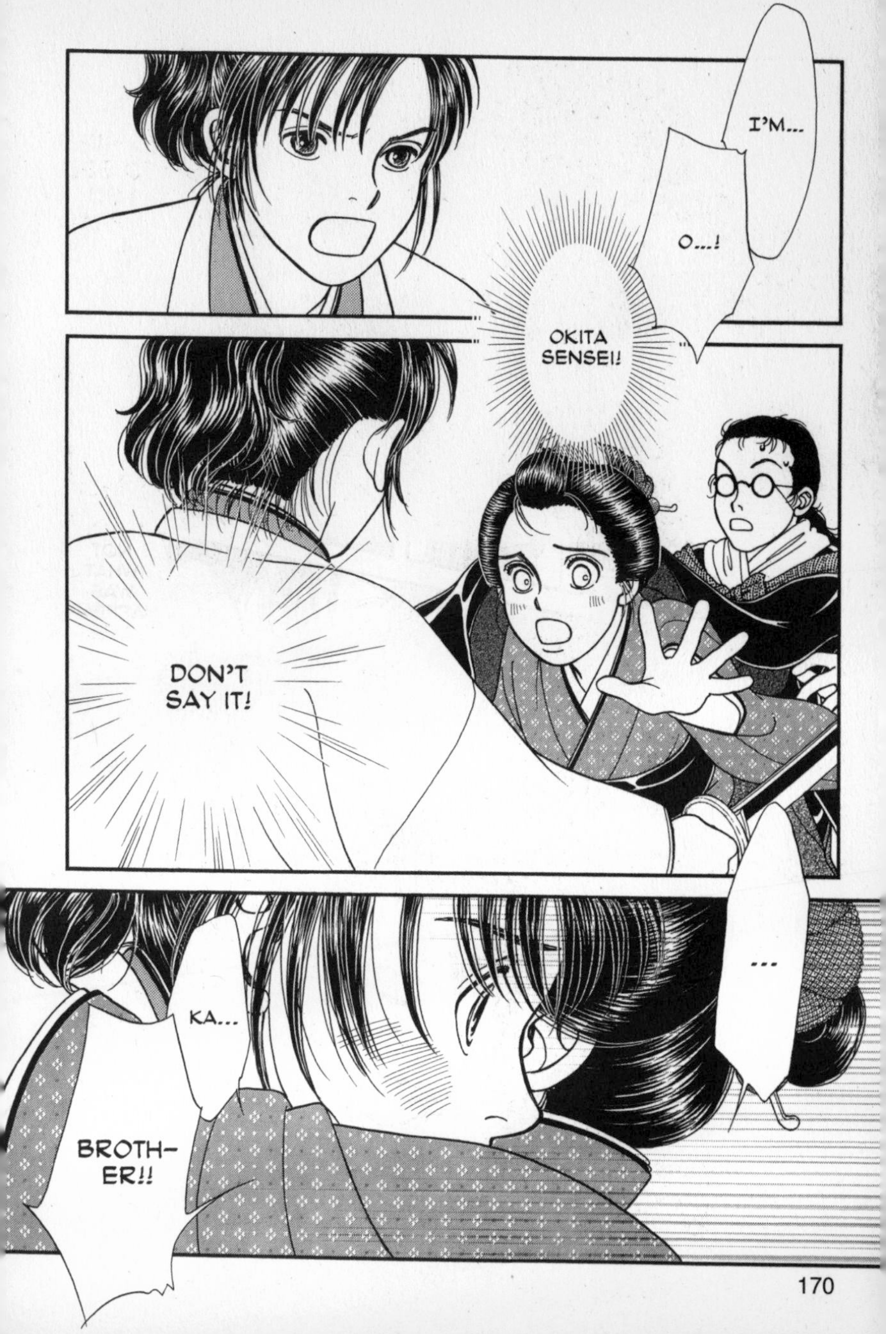
I'M...
O...!
OKITA SENSEI!
DON'T SAY IT!
...
KA...
BROTH-
ER!!

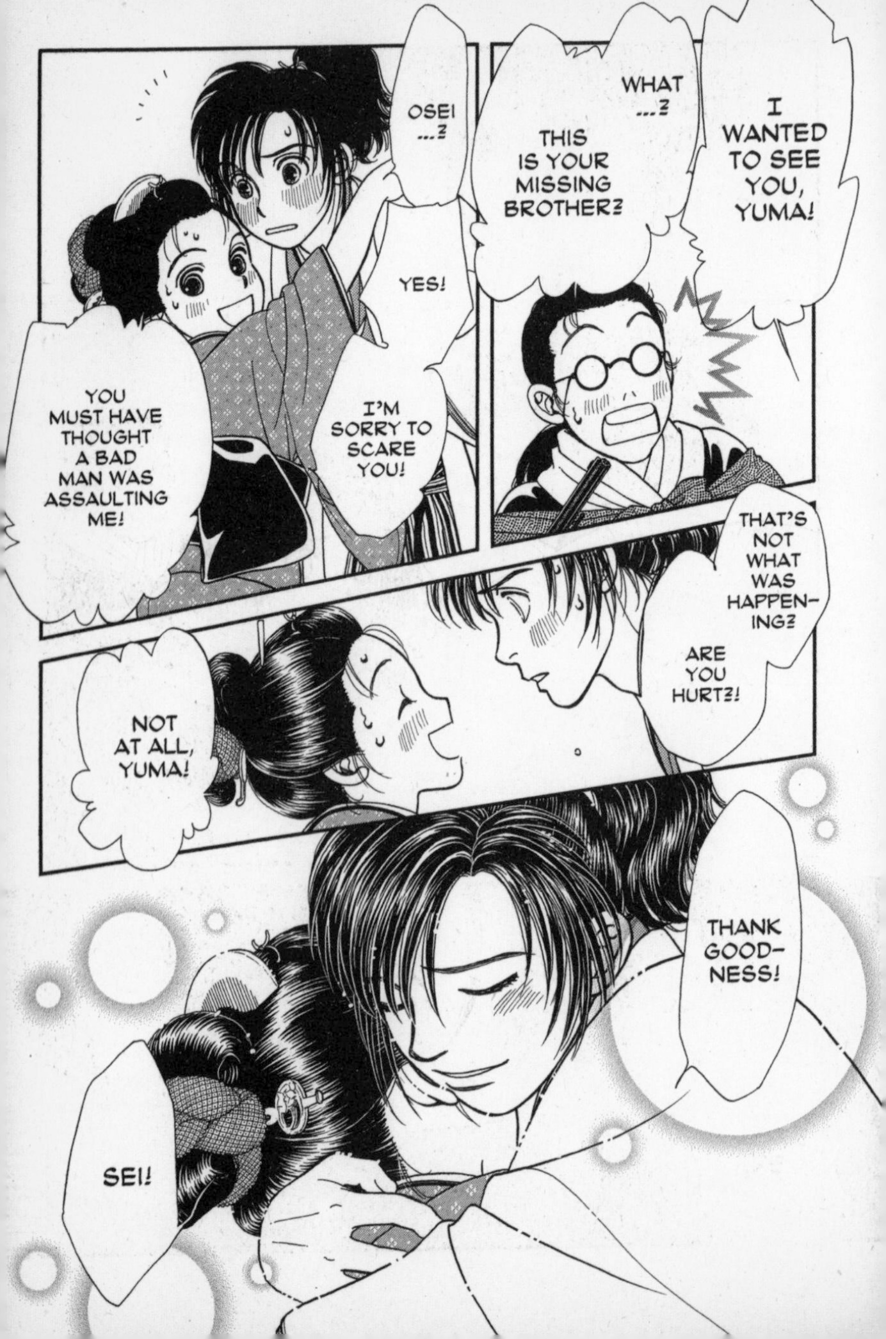
I WANTED TO SEE YOU, YUMA!
WHAT ...?
THIS IS YOUR MISSING BROTHER?
OSEI ...?
YES!
I'M SORRY TO SCARE YOU!
YOU MUST HAVE THOUGHT A BAD MAN WAS ASSAULTING ME!
THAT'S NOT WHAT WAS HAPPENING?
ARE YOU HURT?!
NOT AT ALL, YUMA!
THANK GOODNESS!
SEI!

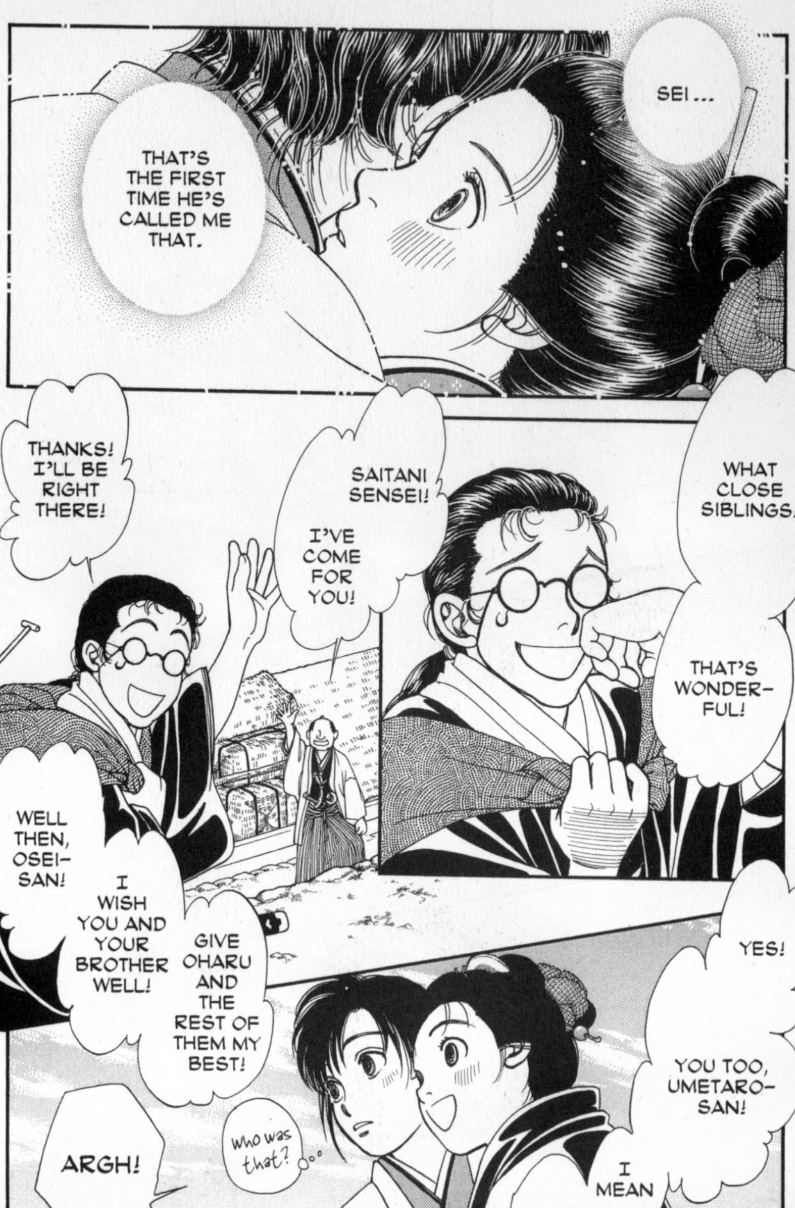
SEI ...
THAT'S THE FIRST TIME HE'S CALLED ME THAT.
WHAT CLOSE SIBLINGS!
THAT'S WONDERFUL!
SAITANI SENSEI!
I'VE COME FOR YOU!
THANKS! I'LL BE RIGHT THERE!
WELL THEN, OSEI-SAN!
I WISH YOU AND YOUR BROTHER WELL!
GIVE OHARU AND THE REST OF THEM MY BEST!
YES!
YOU TOO, UMETARO-SAN!
I MEAN ...
HUH?
who was that?
ARGH!

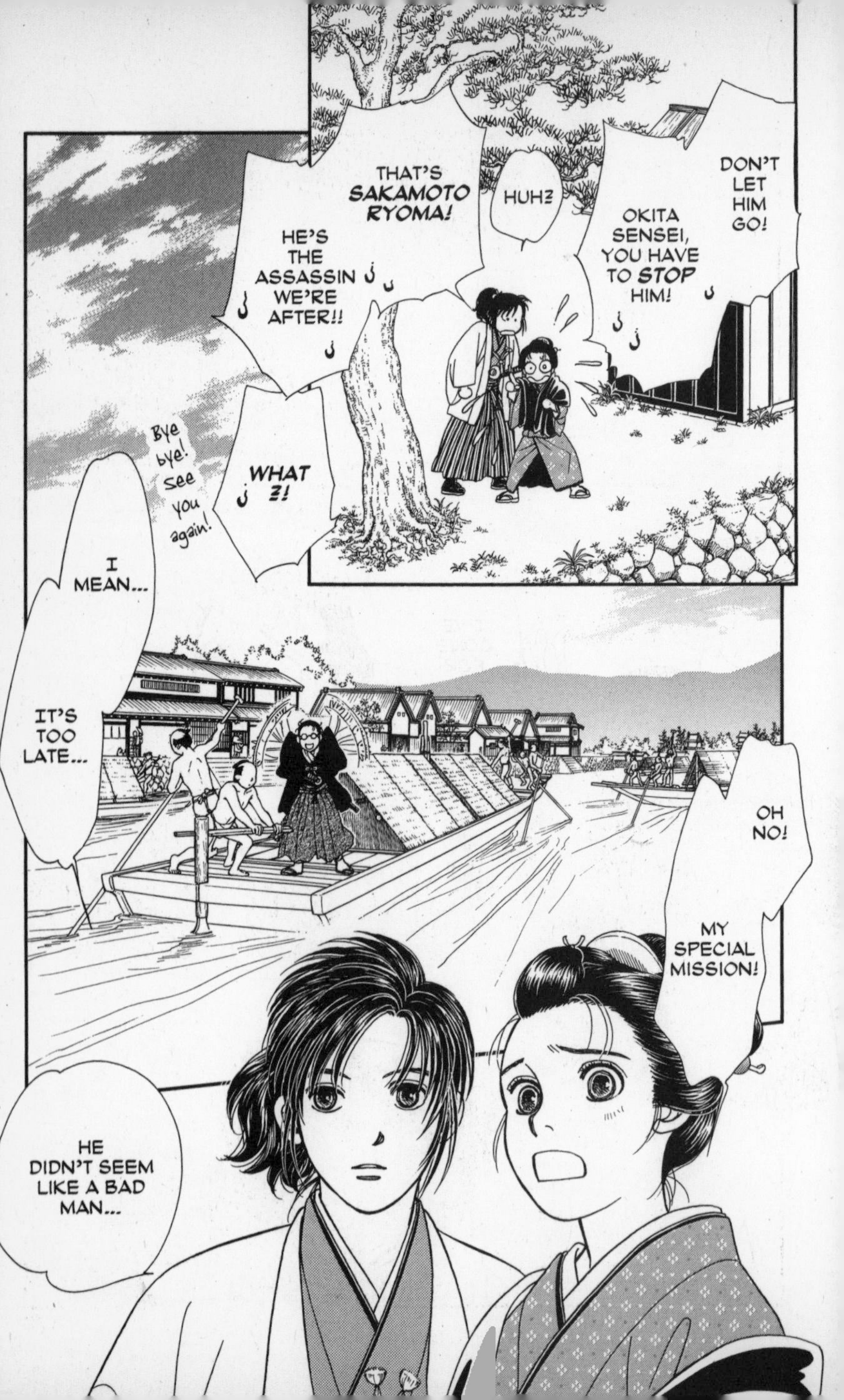

DON'T LET HIM GO!
OKITA SENSEI, YOU HAVE TO STOP HIM!
HUH?
THAT'S SAKAMOTO RYOMA!
HE'S THE ASSASSIN WE'RE AFTER!!
WHAT?!
Bye bye! See you again!
OH NO!
MY SPECIAL MISSION!
I MEAN...
IT'S TOO LATE...
HE DIDN'T SEEM LIKE A BAD MAN...

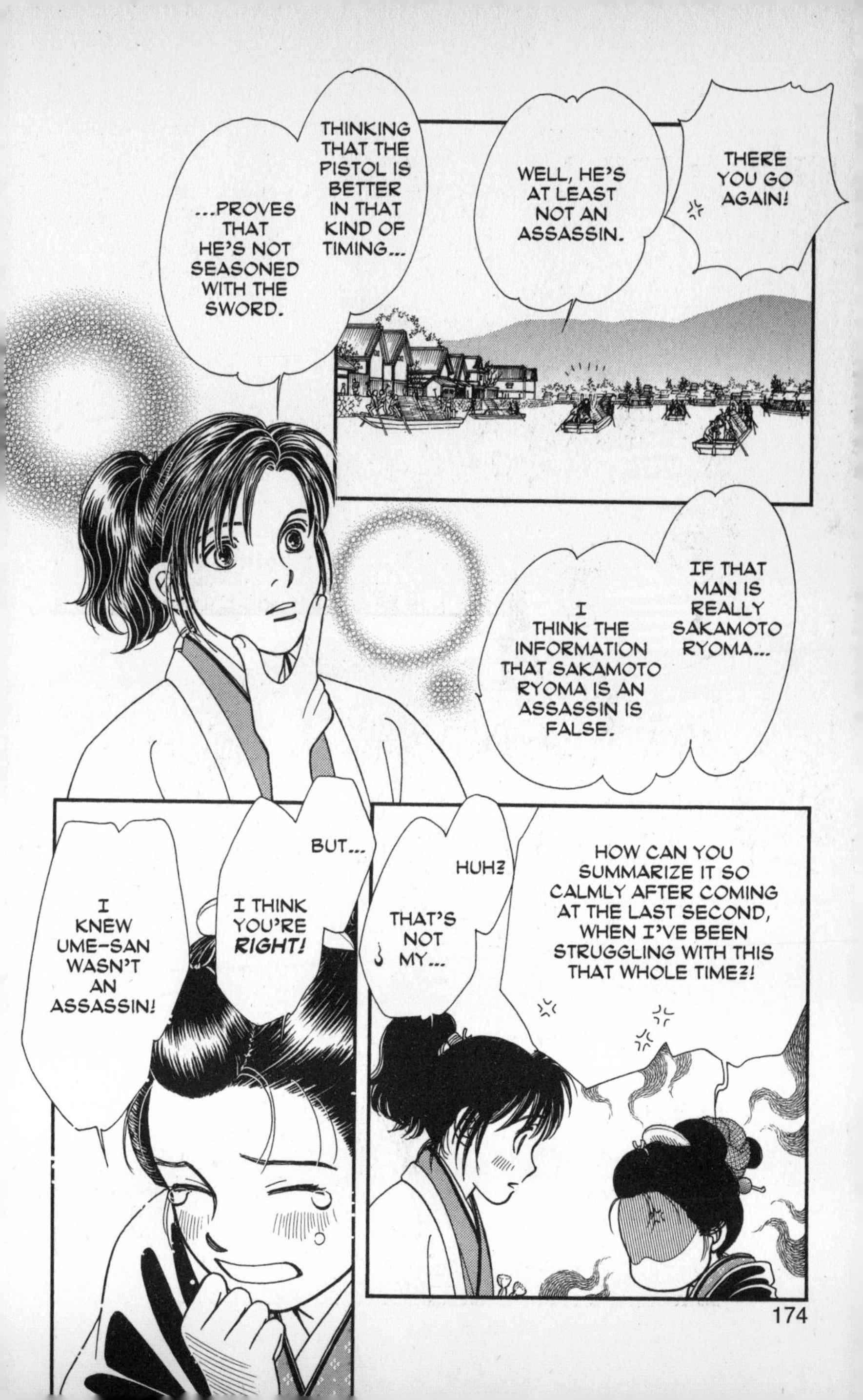
THERE YOU GO AGAIN!
WELL, HE'S AT LEAST NOT AN ASSASSIN.
THINKING THAT THE PISTOL IS BETTER IN THAT KIND OF TIMING...
...PROVES THAT HE'S NOT SEASONED WITH THE SWORD.
IF THAT MAN IS REALLY SAKAMOTO RYOMA...
I THINK THE INFORMATION THAT SAKAMOTO RYOMA IS AN ASSASSIN IS FALSE.
HOW CAN YOU SUMMARIZE IT SO CALMLY AFTER COMING AT THE LAST SECOND, WHEN I'VE BEEN STRUGGLING WITH THIS THAT WHOLE TIME?!
HUH?
THAT'S NOT MY...
BUT...
I THINK YOU'RE ***RIGHT!***
I KNEW UME-SAN WASN'T AN ASSASSIN!

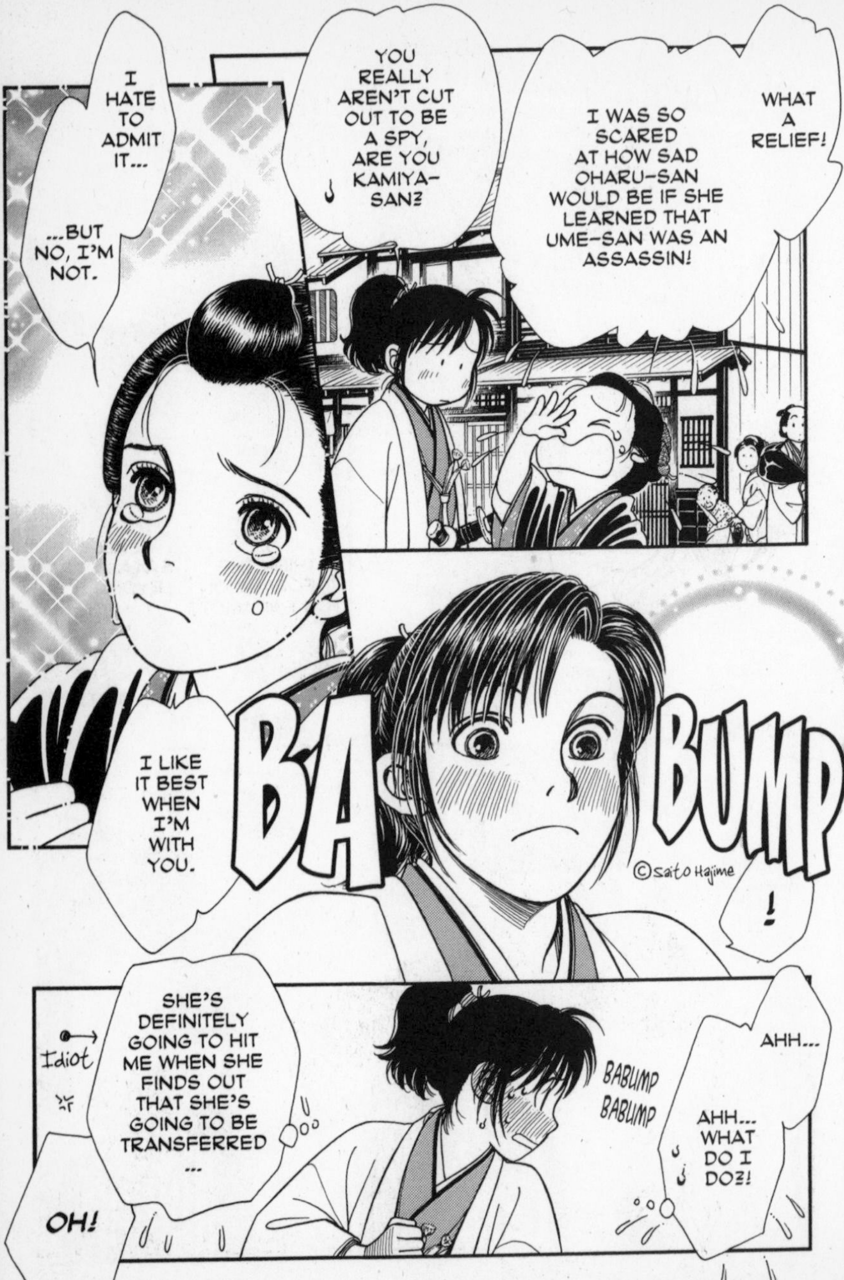

WHAT A RELIEF!
I WAS SO SCARED AT HOW SAD OHARU-SAN WOULD BE IF SHE LEARNED THAT UME-SAN WAS AN ASSASSIN!
YOU REALLY AREN'T CUT OUT TO BE A SPY, ARE YOU KAMIYA-SAN?
!
BUMP
BA
©saito Hajime
I HATE TO ADMIT IT...
...BUT NO, I'M NOT.
I LIKE IT BEST WHEN I'M WITH YOU.
AHH...
AHH... WHAT DO I DO?!
BABUMP BABUMP
SHE'S DEFINITELY GOING TO HIT ME WHEN SHE FINDS OUT THAT SHE'S GOING TO BE TRANSFERRED ...
Idiot
OH!

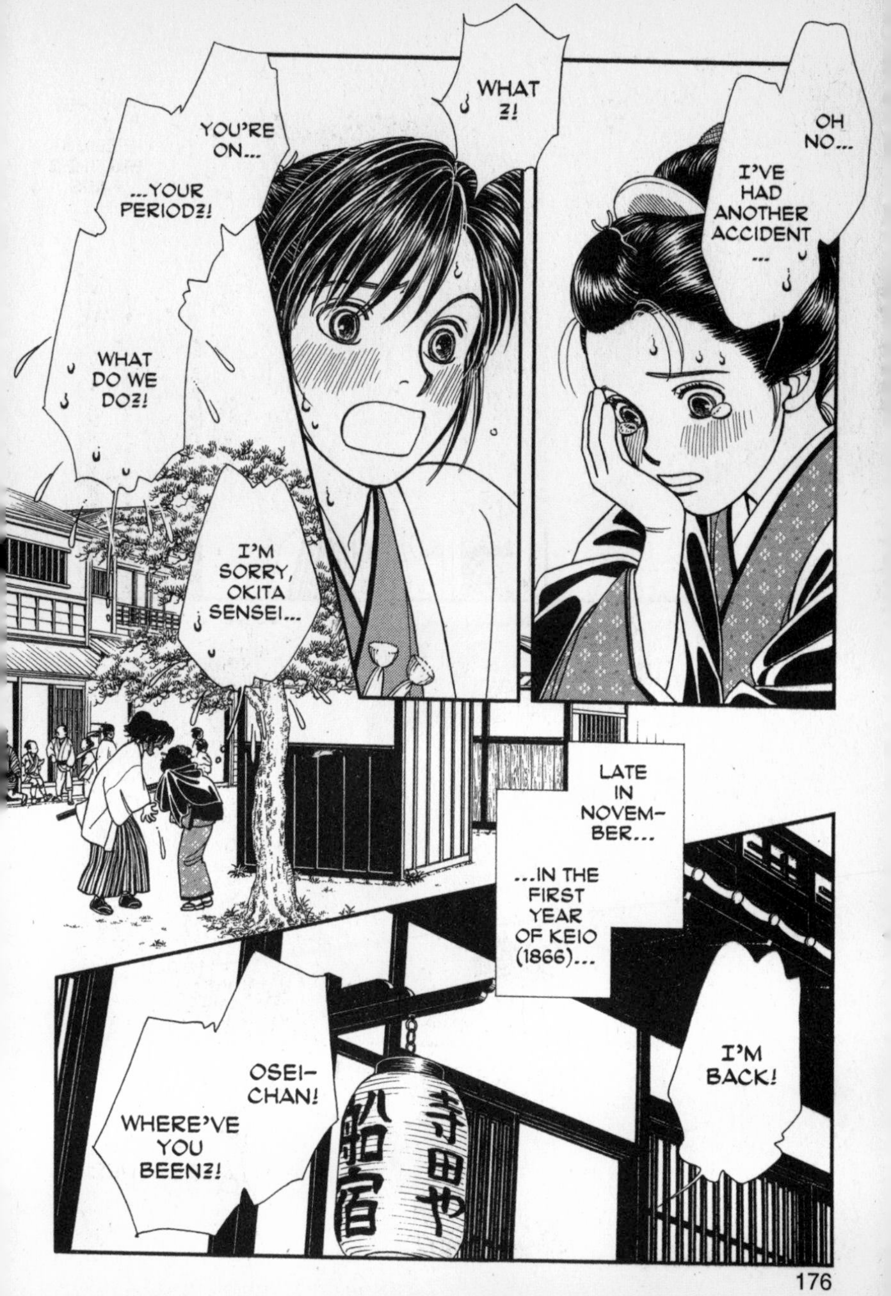
OH NO...
I'VE HAD ANOTHER ACCIDENT ...
WHAT ?!
YOU'RE ON...
...YOUR PERIOD?!
WHAT DO WE DO?!
I'M SORRY, OKITA SENSEI...
LATE IN NOVEMBER...
...IN THE FIRST YEAR OF KEIO (1866)...
I'M BACK!
OSEI-CHAN!
WHERE'VE YOU BEEN?!
寺田や
船宿

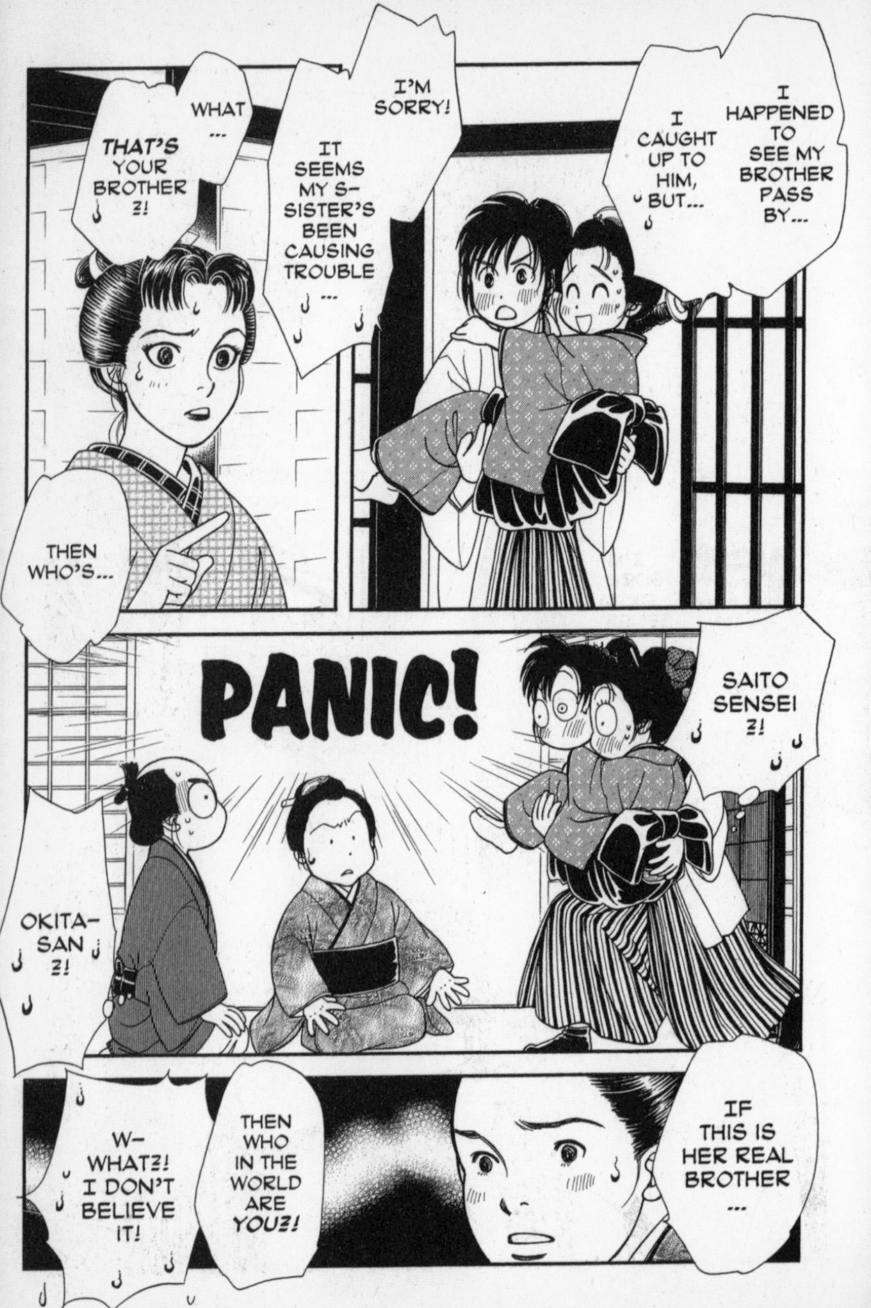
I HAPPENED TO SEE MY BROTHER PASS BY...
I CAUGHT UP TO HIM, BUT...
I'M SORRY!
IT SEEMS MY S-SISTER'S BEEN CAUSING TROUBLE...
WHAT... *THAT'S* YOUR BROTHER?!
THEN WHO'S...
SAITO SENSEI?!
PANIC!
OKITA-SAN?!
IF THIS IS HER REAL BROTHER...
THEN WHO IN THE WORLD ARE *YOU*?!
W-WHAT?! I DON'T BELIEVE IT!

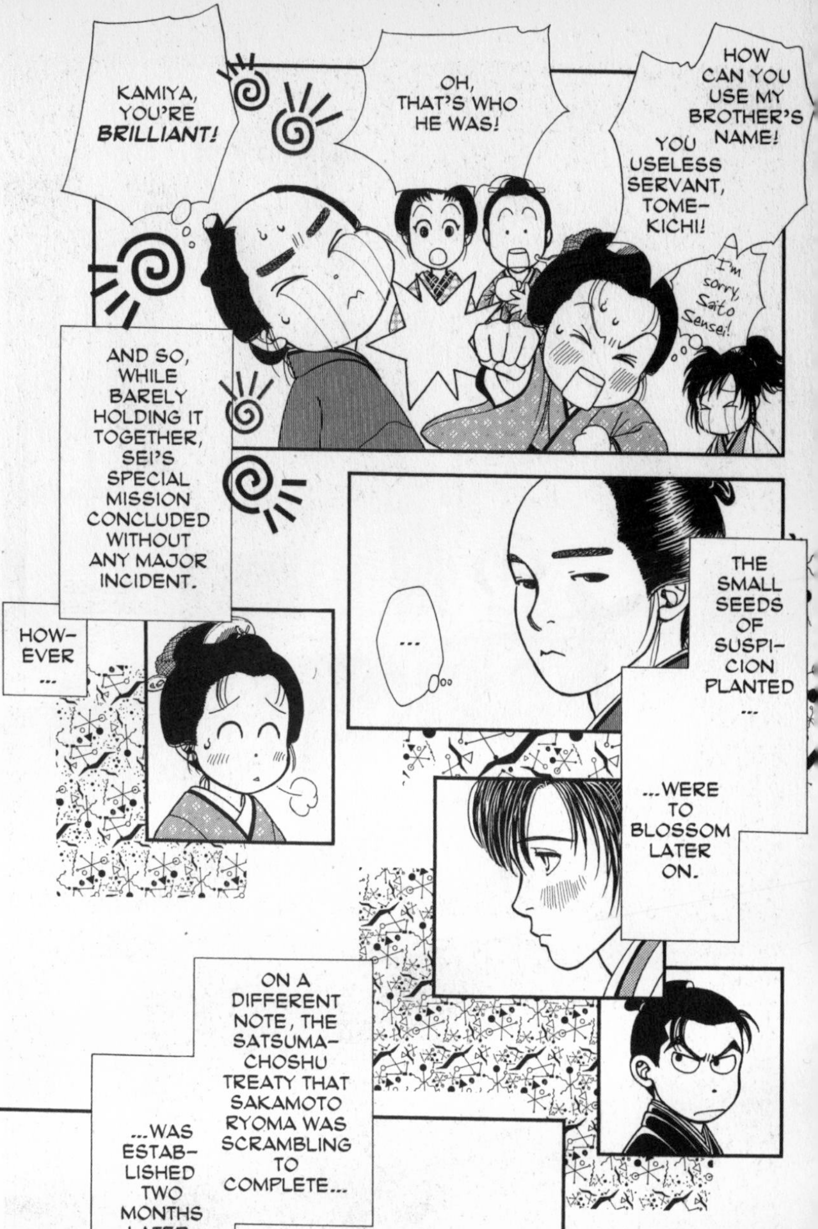
HOW CAN YOU USE MY BROTHER'S NAME!
YOU USELESS SERVANT, TOME-KICHI!
I'm sorry, Saito Sensei!
OH, THAT'S WHO HE WAS!
KAMIYA, YOU'RE **BRILLIANT!**
AND SO, WHILE BARELY HOLDING IT TOGETHER, SEI'S SPECIAL MISSION CONCLUDED WITHOUT ANY MAJOR INCIDENT.
HOW-EVER...
...
THE SMALL SEEDS OF SUSPI-CION PLANTED...
...WERE TO BLOSSOM LATER ON.
ON A DIFFERENT NOTE, THE SATSUMA-CHOSHU TREATY THAT SAKAMOTO RYOMA WAS SCRAMBLING TO COMPLETE...
...WAS ESTAB-LISHED TWO MONTHS LATER.
TO BE CONTINUED!

TAEKO WATANABE PRESENTS

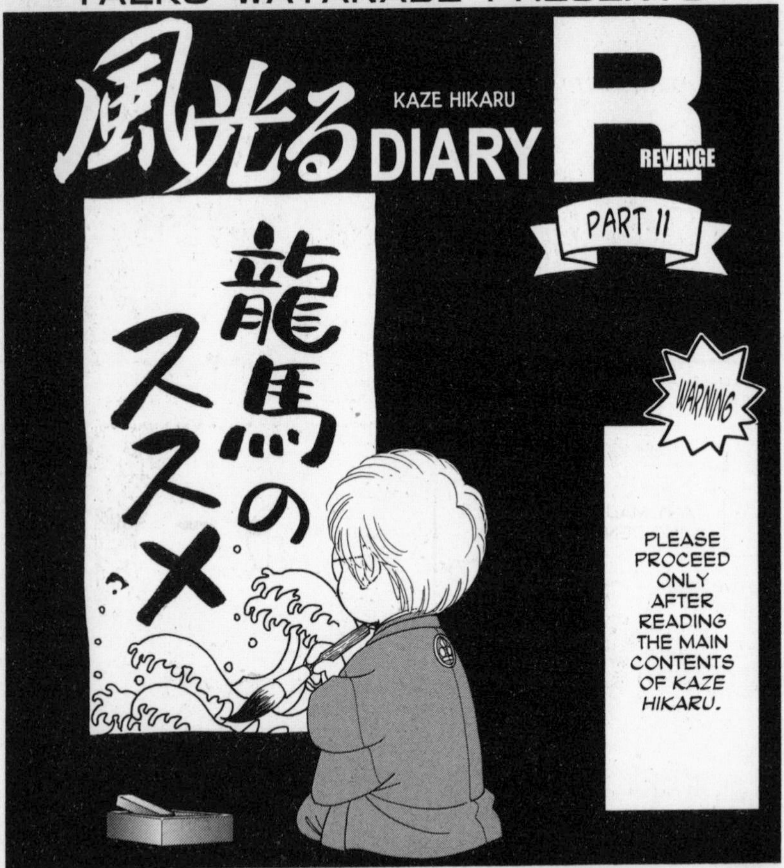
風光る
KAZE HIKARU
DIARY
R
REVENGE
PART 11
龍馬のススメ
WARNING
PLEASE PROCEED ONLY AFTER READING THE MAIN CONTENTS OF KAZE HIKARU.

*Sign: Recommending Ryoma

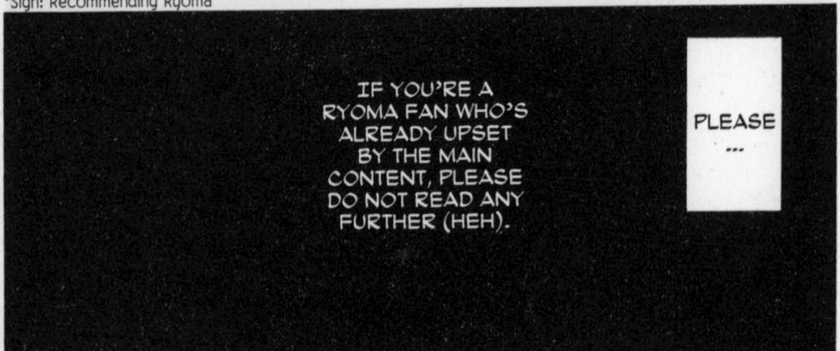
PLEASE ...
IF YOU'RE A RYOMA FAN WHO'S ALREADY UPSET BY THE MAIN CONTENT, PLEASE DO NOT READ ANY FURTHER (HEH).

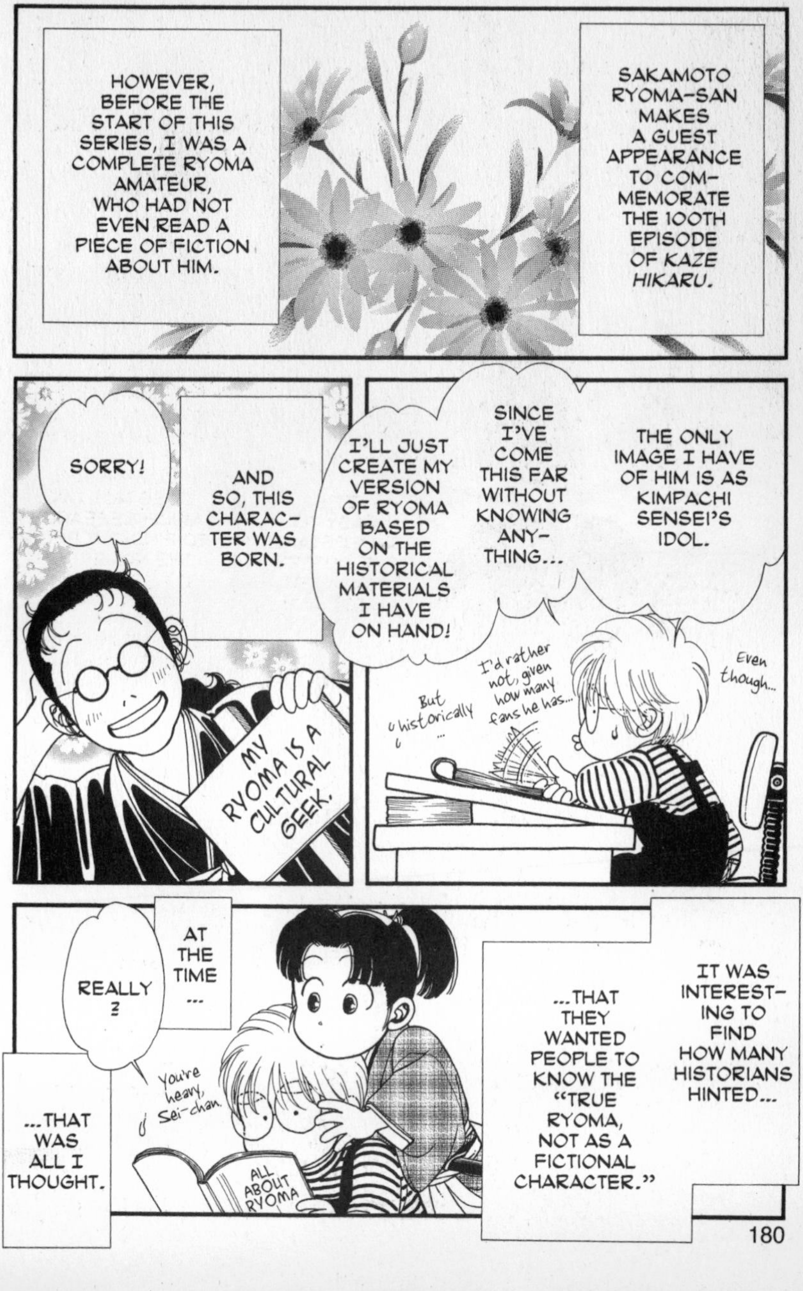
SAKAMOTO RYOMA-SAN MAKES A GUEST APPEARANCE TO COMMEMORATE THE 100TH EPISODE OF *KAZE HIKARU*.
HOWEVER, BEFORE THE START OF THIS SERIES, I WAS A COMPLETE RYOMA AMATEUR, WHO HAD NOT EVEN READ A PIECE OF FICTION ABOUT HIM.
THE ONLY IMAGE I HAVE OF HIM IS AS KIMPACHI SENSEI'S IDOL.
SINCE I'VE COME THIS FAR WITHOUT KNOWING ANYTHING...
I'LL JUST CREATE MY VERSION OF RYOMA BASED ON THE HISTORICAL MATERIALS I HAVE ON HAND!
Even though...
I'd rather not, given how many fans he has...
But historically...
AND SO, THIS CHARACTER WAS BORN.
SORRY!
MY RYOMA IS A CULTURAL GEEK.
IT WAS INTERESTING TO FIND HOW MANY HISTORIANS HINTED...
...THAT THEY WANTED PEOPLE TO KNOW THE "TRUE RYOMA, NOT AS A FICTIONAL CHARACTER."
AT THE TIME...
REALLY?
You're heavy, Sei-chan.
...THAT WAS ALL I THOUGHT.
ALL ABOUT RYOMA

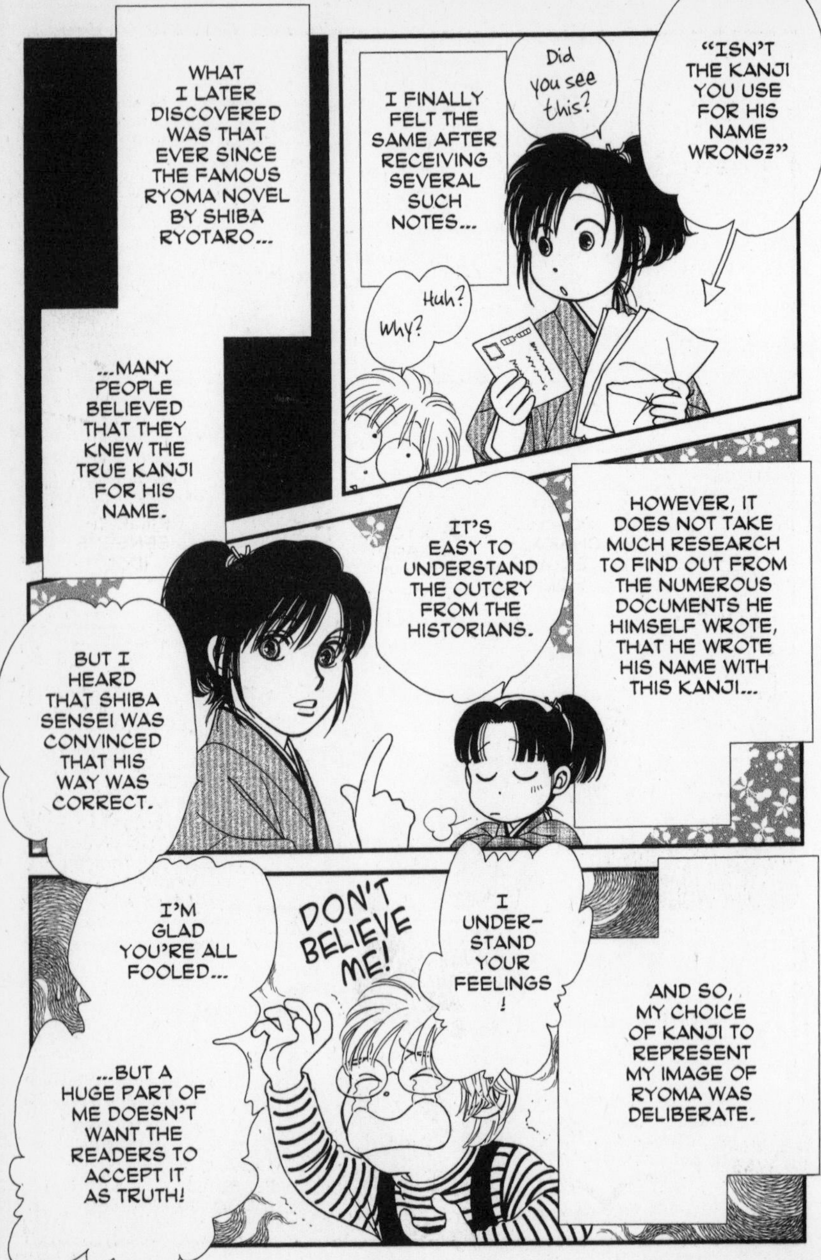

"ISN'T THE KANJI YOU USE FOR HIS NAME WRONG?"
Did you see this?
I FINALLY FELT THE SAME AFTER RECEIVING SEVERAL SUCH NOTES...
Huh?
Why?
WHAT I LATER DISCOVERED WAS THAT EVER SINCE THE FAMOUS RYOMA NOVEL BY SHIBA RYOTARO...
...MANY PEOPLE BELIEVED THAT THEY KNEW THE TRUE KANJI FOR HIS NAME.
HOWEVER, IT DOES NOT TAKE MUCH RESEARCH TO FIND OUT FROM THE NUMEROUS DOCUMENTS HE HIMSELF WROTE, THAT HE WROTE HIS NAME WITH THIS KANJI...
IT'S EASY TO UNDERSTAND THE OUTCRY FROM THE HISTORIANS.
BUT I HEARD THAT SHIBA SENSEI WAS CONVINCED THAT HIS WAY WAS CORRECT.
AND SO, MY CHOICE OF KANJI TO REPRESENT MY IMAGE OF RYOMA WAS DELIBERATE.
I UNDER-STAND YOUR FEELINGS!
DON'T BELIEVE ME!
I'M GLAD YOU'RE ALL FOOLED...
...BUT A HUGE PART OF ME DOESN'T WANT THE READERS TO ACCEPT IT AS TRUTH!

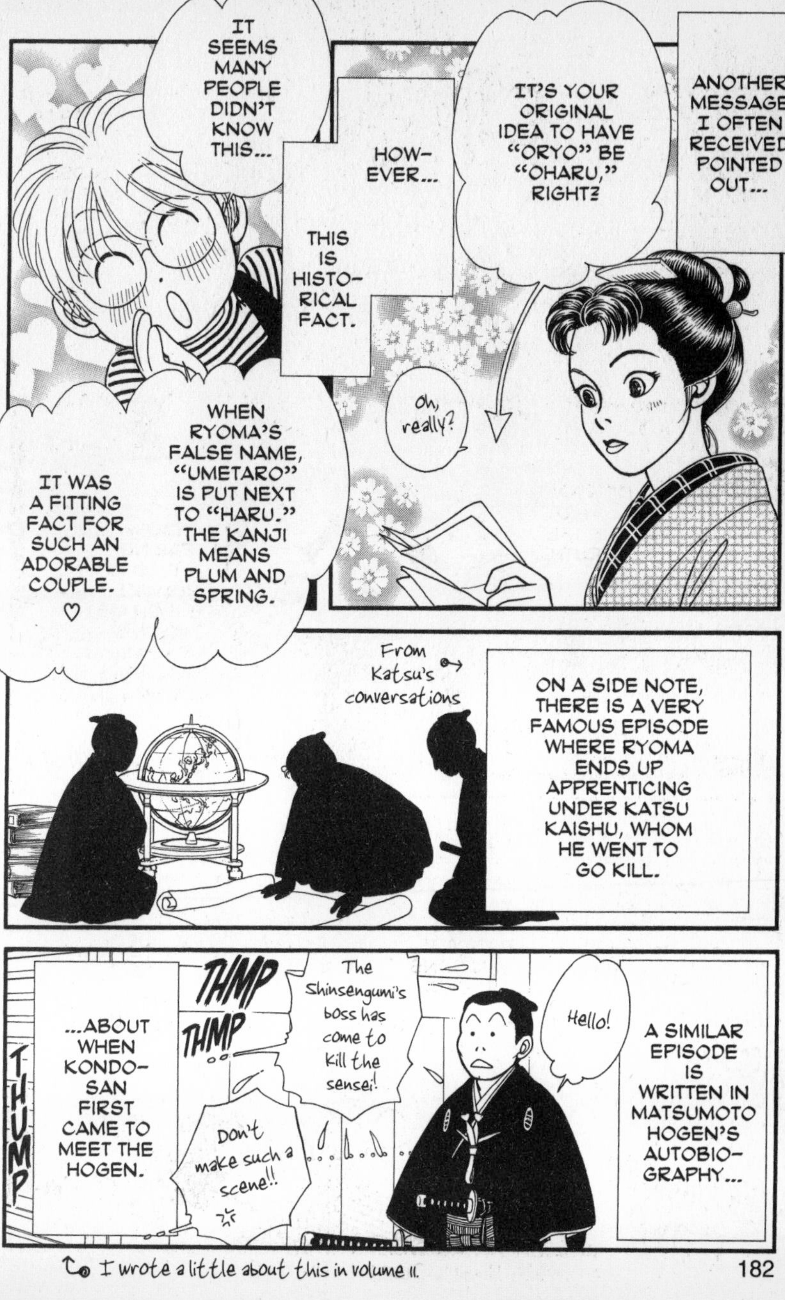
ANOTHER MESSAGE I OFTEN RECEIVED POINTED OUT...
IT'S YOUR ORIGINAL IDEA TO HAVE "ORYO" BE "OHARU," RIGHT?
Oh, really?
HOW-EVER...
THIS IS HISTORICAL FACT.
IT SEEMS MANY PEOPLE DIDN'T KNOW THIS...
WHEN RYOMA'S FALSE NAME, "UMETARO" IS PUT NEXT TO "HARU." THE KANJI MEANS PLUM AND SPRING.
IT WAS A FITTING FACT FOR SUCH AN ADORABLE COUPLE. ♡
From Katsu's conversations
ON A SIDE NOTE, THERE IS A VERY FAMOUS EPISODE WHERE RYOMA ENDS UP APPRENTICING UNDER KATSU KAISHU, WHOM HE WENT TO GO KILL.
A SIMILAR EPISODE IS WRITTEN IN MATSUMOTO HOGEN'S AUTOBIO-GRAPHY...
Hello!
The Shinsengumi's boss has come to kill the sensei!
THMP
THMP
Don't make such a scene!!
...ABOUT WHEN KONDO-SAN FIRST CAME TO MEET THE HOGEN.
THUMP

I wrote a little about this in volume 11.

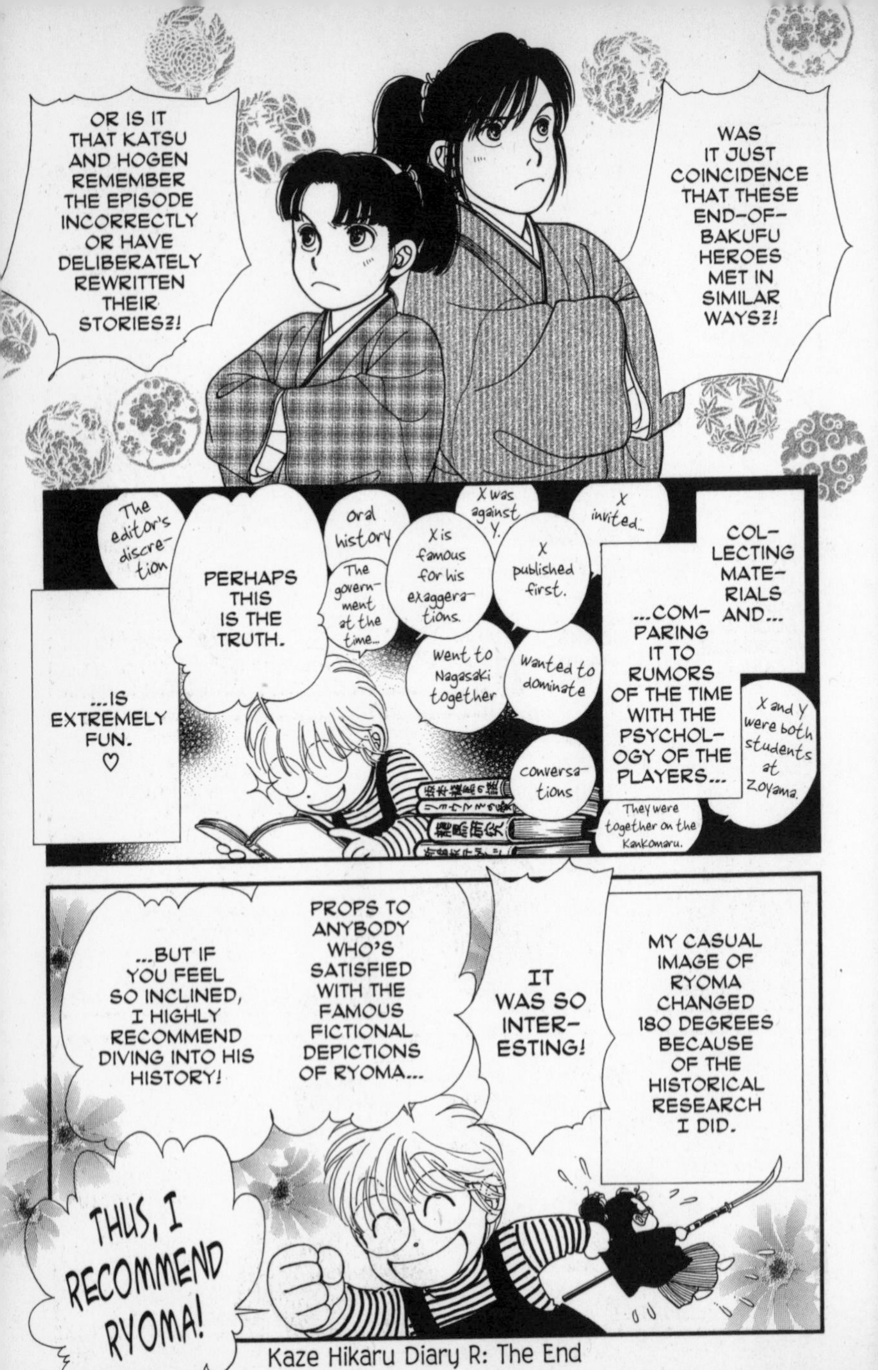
WAS IT JUST COINCIDENCE THAT THESE END-OF-BAKUFU HEROES MET IN SIMILAR WAYS?!
OR IS IT THAT KATSU AND HOGEN REMEMBER THE EPISODE INCORRECTLY OR HAVE DELIBERATELY REWRITTEN THEIR STORIES?!
COLLECTING MATERIALS AND...
...COMPARING IT TO RUMORS OF THE TIME WITH THE PSYCHOLOGY OF THE PLAYERS...
X and Y were both students at Zoyama.
They were together on the Kankomaru.
X invited...
X was against Y.
X published first.
Wanted to dominate
conversations
X is famous for his exaggerations.
went to Nagasaki together
Oral history
The government at the time...
The editor's discretion
PERHAPS THIS IS THE TRUTH.
...IS EXTREMELY FUN. ♡
MY CASUAL IMAGE OF RYOMA CHANGED 180 DEGREES BECAUSE OF THE HISTORICAL RESEARCH I DID.
IT WAS SO INTERESTING!
PROPS TO ANYBODY WHO'S SATISFIED WITH THE FAMOUS FICTIONAL DEPICTIONS OF RYOMA...
...BUT IF YOU FEEL SO INCLINED, I HIGHLY RECOMMEND DIVING INTO HIS HISTORY!
THUS, I RECOMMEND RYOMA!

Kaze Hikaru Diary R: The End

Decoding Kaze Hikaru

Kaze Hikaru is a historical drama based in 19th century Japan and thus contains some fairly mystifying terminology. In this glossary we'll break down archaic phrases, terms and other linguistic curiosities for you so that you can move through life with the smug assurance that you are indeed a know-it-all.

First and foremost, because *Kaze Hikaru* is a period story, we kept all character names in their traditional Japanese form—that is, family name followed by first name. For example, the character Okita Soji's family name is Okita and his personal name is Soji.

AKO-ROSHI:

The *ronin* (samurai) of Ako; featured in the immortal Kabuki play *Chushingura* (Loyalty), aka *47 Samurai*.

ANI-UE:

Literally, "brother above"; an honorific for an elder male sibling.

BAKUFU:

Literally, "tent government." Shogunate; the feudal, military government that dominated Japan for more than 200 years.

BUSHI:

A samurai or warrior (part of the compound word *bushido*, which means "way of the warrior").

CHICHI-UE:

An honorific suffix meaning "father above."

DO:

In kendo (a Japanese fencing sport that uses bamboo swords), a short way of describing the offensive single-hit strike *shikake waza ippon uchi*.

-HAN:

The same as the honorific *-san*, pronounced in the dialect of southern Japan.

-KUN:

An honorific suffix that indicates a difference in rank and title. The use of *-kun* is also a way of indicating familiarity and friendliness between students or compatriots.

MEN:

In the context of *Kaze Hikaru*, *men* refers to one of the "points" in kendo. It is a strike to the forehead and is considered a basic move.

MIBU-ROSHI:

A group of warriors that supports the Bakufu.

NE'E-SAN:

Can mean "older sister," "ma'am" or "miss."

NI'I-CHAN:

Short for *oni'i-san* or *oni'i-chan*, meaning older brother.

OKU-SAMA:

This is a polite way to refer to someone's wife. *Oku* means "deep" or "further back" and comes from the fact that wives (in affluent families) stayed hidden away in the back rooms of the house.

ONI:

Literally "ogre," this is Sei's nickname for Vice Captain Hijikata.

RANPO:

Medical science derived from the Dutch.

RONIN:

Masterless samurai.

RYO:

At the time, one *ryo* and two *bu* (four *bu* equaled roughly one *ryo*) were enough currency to support a family of five for an entire month.

-SAN:

An honorific suffix that carries the meaning of "Mr." or "Ms."

SENSEI:

A teacher, master or instructor.

SEPPUKU:

A ritualistic suicide that was considered a privilege of the nobility and samurai elite.

SONJO-HA:

Those loyal to the emperor and dedicated to the expulsion of foreigners from the country.

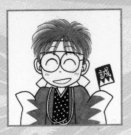

Can you believe that we've reached the 20th volume mark?! I'm impressed with myself for being able to continue without getting bored. But even more props to you, the reader! I'm incredibly grateful! I hope you continue to support the series.

So, the last seasonal work of the "touch" series is *kazabana* (wind flower). It's the flakes of snow that ride the high layers of the strong wind on a clear day and glisten as they fall. Isn't that a beautiful name for it? I'm constantly amazed by the beauty of the Japanese language. I'm confident of my ability to speak the gutter language of daily life (?), but I've recently begun to aspire to being the kind of adult who's capable of speaking properly... I know it's a lot to shoot for.

Taeko Watanabe debuted as a manga artist in 1979 with her story *Waka-chan no Netsuai Jidai* (Love Struck Days of Waka). *Kaze Hikaru* is her longest-running series, but she has created a number of other popular series. Watanabe is a two-time winner of the prestigious Shogakukan Manga Award in the girls' category—her manga *Hajime-chan ga Ichiban!* (Hajime-chan Is Number One!) claimed the award in 1991, and *Kaze Hikaru* took it in 2003.

Watanabe read hundreds of historical sources to create *Kaze Hikaru*. She is from Tokyo.

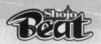

KAZE HIKARU
VOL. 20
Shojo Beat Edition

STORY AND ART BY
TAEKO WATANABE

© 1997 Taeko WATANABE/Shogakukan
All rights reserved.
Original Japanese edition "KAZE HIKARU" published by SHOGAKUKAN Inc.

Translation & English Adaptation/Mai Ihara
Touch-up Art & Lettering/Rina Mapa
Design/Veronica Casson
Editor/Jonathan Tarbox

The stories, characters and incidents mentioned in this publication are entirely fictional.

Printed in Canada

Published by VIZ Media, LLC
P.O. Box 77010
San Francisco, CA 94107

10 9 8 7 6 5 4 3 2 1
First printing, August 2012

www.viz.com

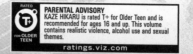
PARENTAL ADVISORY
KAZE HIKARU is rated T+ for Older Teen and is recommended for ages 16 and up. This volume contains realistic violence, alcohol use and sexual themes.
ratings.viz.com

www.shojobeat.com

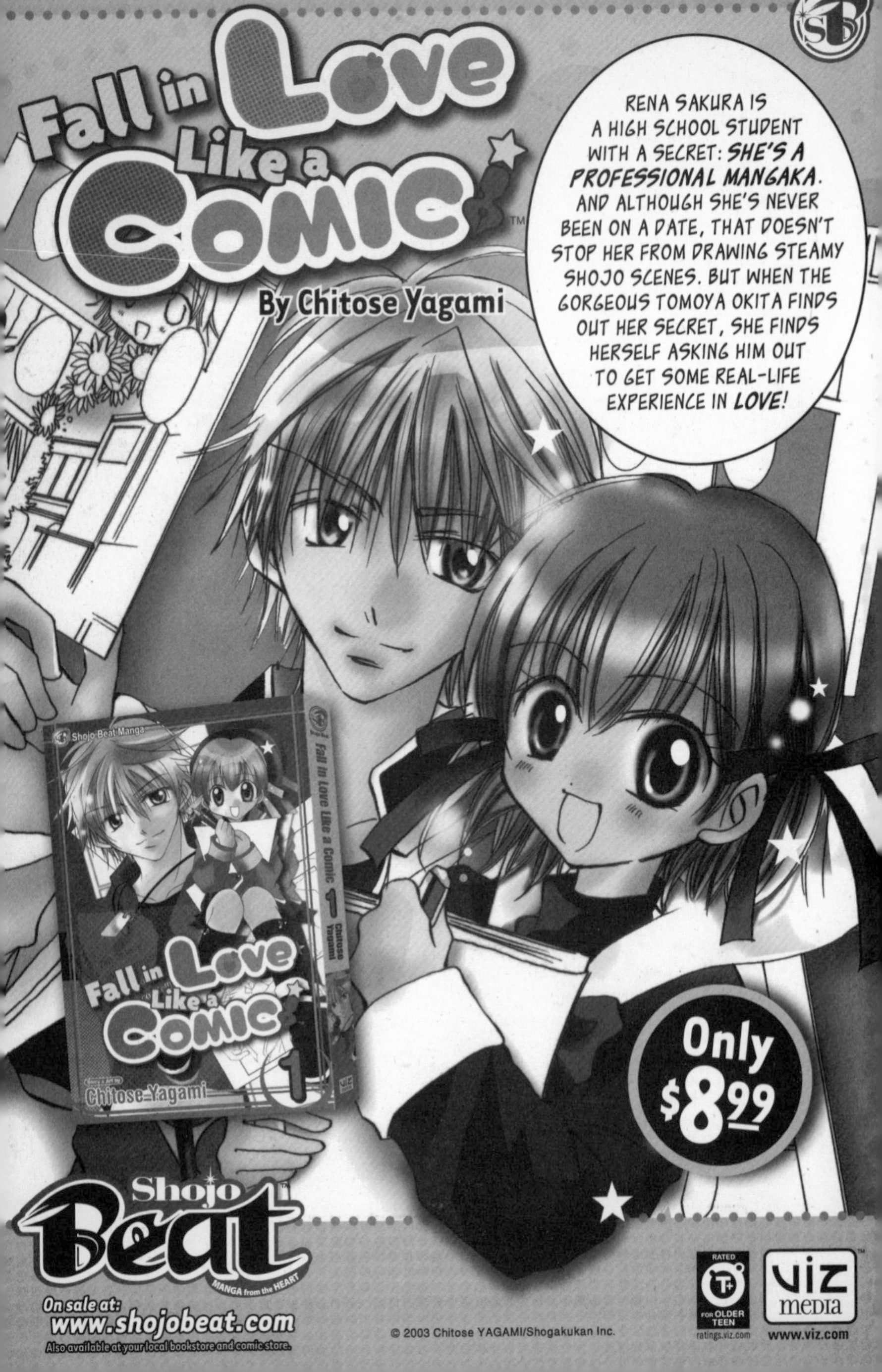
Fall in Love Like a Comic™
By Chitose Yagami
RENA SAKURA IS A HIGH SCHOOL STUDENT WITH A SECRET: SHE'S A PROFESSIONAL MANGAKA. AND ALTHOUGH SHE'S NEVER BEEN ON A DATE, THAT DOESN'T STOP HER FROM DRAWING STEAMY SHOJO SCENES. BUT WHEN THE GORGEOUS TOMOYA OKITA FINDS OUT HER SECRET, SHE FINDS HERSELF ASKING HIM OUT TO GET SOME REAL-LIFE EXPERIENCE IN LOVE!
Only $8.99
Shojo Beat
MANGA from the HEART
On sale at:
www.shojobeat.com
Also available at your local bookstore and comic store.
© 2003 Chitose YAGAMI/Shogakukan Inc.
RATED T+ FOR OLDER TEEN
ratings.viz.com
VIZ media
www.viz.com

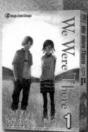

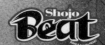

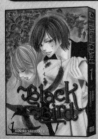

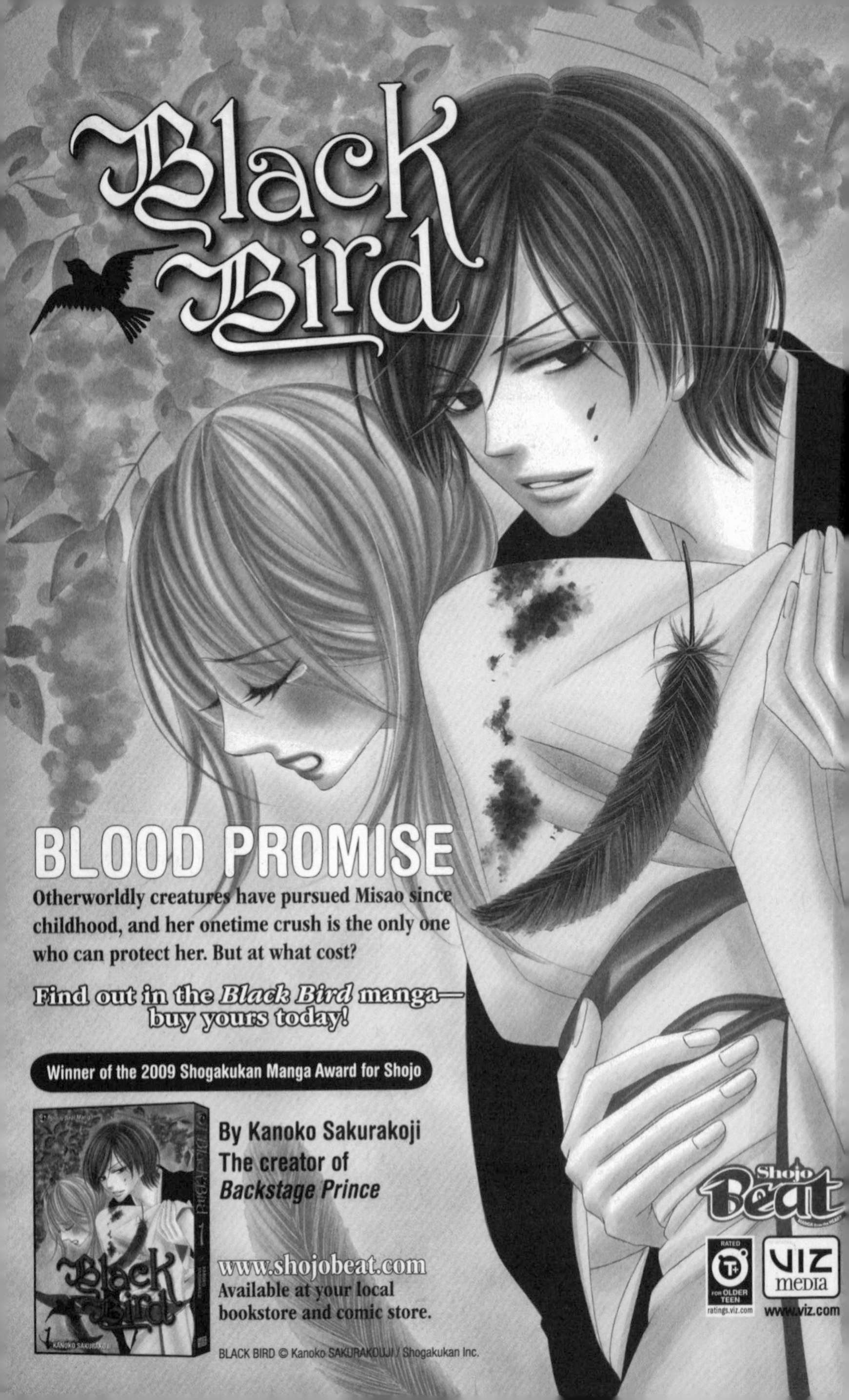

SURPRISE!

You may be reading the wrong way!

It's true: In keeping with the original Japanese comic format, this book reads from right to left—so action, sound effects, and word balloons are completely reversed. This preserves the orientation of the original artwork—plus, it's fun! Check out the diagram shown here to get the hang of things, and then turn to the other side of the book to get started!

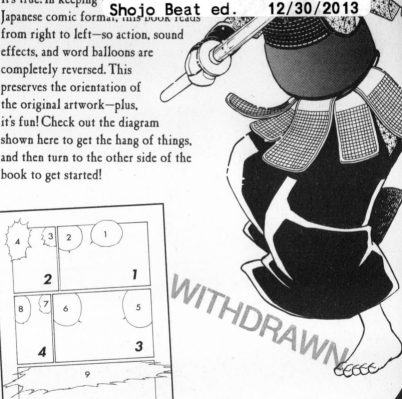

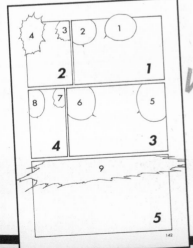

142